SACRED RIVALS

Sacred Rivals

*Catholic Missions and the Making of Islam in
Nineteenth-Century France and Algeria*

Joseph W. Peterson

OXFORD
UNIVERSITY PRESS

Oxford University Press is a department of the University of Oxford. It furthers the University's objective of excellence in research, scholarship, and education by publishing worldwide. Oxford is a registered trade mark of Oxford University Press in the UK and certain other countries.

Published in the United States of America by Oxford University Press
198 Madison Avenue, New York, NY 10016, United States of America.

Portions of Chapter 1 are adapted from Joseph W. Peterson, "'Admiration . . . for All That Is Sincerely Religious': Louis Veuillot and Catholic Representations of Islam and Empire in July Monarchy France" in *French Historical Studies* Vol. 40, No. 3, pp. 475–507. Copyright, 2017, Society for French Historical Studies. All rights reserved. Republished by permission of the publisher. www.dukeupress.edu

Portions of Chapter 2 are adapted from Joseph W. Peterson, "Honor, Excrement, Ethnography: Colonial Knowledge Between Missionary and *Militaire* in French Algeria," *Journal of Modern History*, Volume 93, Number 1, March 2021, pp. 34–67. © 2021 by The University of Chicago.

Library of Congress Cataloging-in-Publication Data

Names: Peterson, Joseph W., author.
Title: Sacred rivals: Catholic missions and the making of Islam in
nineteenth-century France and Algeria / Joseph W. Peterson.
Description: New York, NY: Oxford University Press, [2022] |
Includes bibliographical references and index. |
Identifiers: LCCN 2022000787 (print) | LCCN 2022000788 (ebook) | ISBN 9780197605271
(hardback) | ISBN 9780197605295 (epub) | ISBN 9780197605301
Subjects: LCSH: Catholic Church--Missions--Algeria--History. | Catholic
Church--Relations--Islam. | Missions, French--Algeria--History. |
Islam--Relations--Catholic Church. | Islam--Public opinion--History. |
Algeria--Religion--19th century. | Algeria--Foreign public opinion,
French. | Algeria--Relations--France. | France--Relations--Algeria.
Classification: LCC BV3585 .P48 2022 (print) | LCC BV3585 (ebook) | DDC
266/.20965--dc23/eng/20220315
LC record available at https://lccn.loc.gov/2022000787
LC ebook record available at https://lccn.loc.gov/2022000788

1 3 5 7 9 8 6 4 2

Printed by Integrated Books International, United States of America

CONTENTS

Contents

ACKNOWLEDGMENTS

It is a pleasure to recognize some of the people who helped make this book a reality. I am thankful to John Merriman at Yale University, not only for his scholarly guidance but also for his friendship. John passed away as this book was making its way through production. He was a deeply generous person—generous with his time; generous in facilitating contact with his innumerable friends in the field of French history; generous in offering his understanding and support. He was well-known across the historical profession and beyond for being a captivating lecturer and a clear and prolific writer. He was also known for his devotion to family, kindness, and lack of pretension. In me, he took a chance on a relatively inexperienced historian of France and faithfully supported me throughout my studies and afterward. I owe him more than I can express. Likewise, Maurice Samuels and Jay Winter at Yale University, and Thomas Kselman at Notre Dame University offered encouragement and constructive suggestions at crucial moments throughout the process of writing this book. I owe them each a debt of gratitude. Adam Tooze and Charles Walton were both also a source of encouragement and support. Miranda Sachs and Grey Anderson both carefully slogged through portions of what became this book and gave valuable feedback.

Many other scholars have offered perceptive comments on individual chapter drafts, at various conferences and workshops—too many thoughtful interventions to recount. An interdisciplinary workshop with other Social Science Research Council dissertation research fellows introduced me to concepts and scholars that became useful in my work. Chapter 1, in particular, benefited from the help of Chantal Verdeil, Carol Harrison, and the reviewers of *French Historical Studies*, where an earlier version of this chapter (as well as portions of the introduction and epilogue) appeared. Parts of the introduction, chapter 2, and chapter 3 have previously appeared in the *Journal of Modern History*, where Jan Goldstein and the outside readers made many suggestions for improvement. Some lines and research from chapter 2 also appeared in the *Los Angeles Review of Books*. Todd Shepard graciously invited me to workshop a section with the history department at Johns Hopkins University, where comments by Faisal Abualhassan and others were thought-provoking and led to some last-minute but substantive additions. And Julia Clancy-Smith, whose work I have long admired, has responded kindly to my emails, read my work, and encouraged me. A line in the book *True France* by Herman Lebovics inspired the title of chapter 7. The outside readers both for Oxford University Press and for another academic publisher brought important references to my attention and helped me clarify and strengthen the book's arguments. Susan Ferber has been a wonderful editor, tightening my prose wherever possible and steadily guiding me and my manuscript through the publication process.

Stephanie Barczewski, Alan Grubb, and Steven Marks at Clemson University were some of my earliest mentors in the historical discipline, and I acknowledge them with deep appreciation. At the University of Mississippi, faculty welcomed and supported me both personally and professionally. For their hospitality and advice, my thanks to Joshua First, Susan Gaunt Stearns, Darren Grem, Frances Kneupper, Theresa Levitt, Alexandra Lindgren-Gibson, Rebecca Marchiel, Peter Thilly, Jeffrey Watt, and Noell Howell Wilson. Paul Polgar kept his door open to answer my many questions. And Marc Lerner, above all, took the time to mentor and include me. Since arriving at the University of Southern Mississippi, I am grateful for the friendship and guidance of Allison Abra and Courtney Luckhardt, the friendship and hospitality of Craig and Amy Carey, and many others. Matthew Casey and Heather Stur even performed the collegial labor of reading some or all of my manuscript and suggesting some final revisions. And David Holt designed a wonderful map for the book.

This project would have been impossible without the help of many archivists. Among them, Père Robert Bonfils of the Society of Jesus, Père François Richard of the Missionaries of Africa (White Fathers), Lâm Phan-Thanh at the Archives of the Congregation of the Mission, Odile Lolom at the Œuvres pontificales missionnaires, Julien-Antoine Desforges at the offices of the Œuvre d'Orient, and Lionel Chénedé at the Bibliothèque du Ministère des Affaires étrangères all distinguished themselves by their kindness and patience. I am also thankful for the numerous digital resources and databases that enabled me to access articles and verify bibliographic information, from Gallica to HathiTrust, Worldcat, Google Books, Persée, JSTOR, and more. Many of the resources used in this project were accessed using these sites. The research for this book was made possible by a number of grants: the Clara Levillain Prize at Yale, an International Dissertation Research Fellowship from the Social Science Research Council, a Smith-Richardson Research and Travel Award in International Security Studies, and a MacMillan Center International Dissertation Research Grant. Charley Ellis and Linda Lorimer gave me and my family the extraordinary gift of housing in our first years in New Haven, allowing us into their home and significantly reducing the financial pressures of graduate school.

I have never struggled with the feelings of isolation described by some who undertake graduate study and the research and writing of an academic work. Many friends and family members have kept me company along the way, have feigned interest in my research, and have distracted me whenever possible. At Yale, the friendship of Aner Barzilay, Miranda Sachs, Kate Brackney, Rachel Johnston-White, Sara Silverstein, Grey Anderson, and Ryan and Andrea Patrico meant a great deal to me. Thanks to Audrey Bourriaud for French conversation and help with the finer points of some translations over the years. To Dan and Rebecca, Sam and Sanjana, and our other Whitehall friends: thank you for your companionship and conversation. And friends in our faith community—Nick and Beth, Greg and Linda, James and Kim, Kelly, Rick and Soozie and many others—kept me and my family centered and supported with meals, parenting advice, spiritual guidance, and much more than we can recount or repay.

My late dad, Robert Peterson, was a high school history teacher, administrator, and local historian who wore his learning lightly and enjoyed conversing with anyone. I am thankful for his influence and for the past that still connects us. Special thanks to my mom, Susanna Peterson, my first and most influential teacher, whose spirit of sacrifice, intellectual curiosity, and many other gifts I hope to live up to. Above all, my wife, Jenny, and our daughters, Helen and Harriet, have filled my days with joy, both motivating me to do my work well and helping me not to take my work too seriously. Helen was only an infant one summer years ago when we flew to Paris to begin researching this project. She spent many a tearful night adjusting to the new environment and time zone. Harriet was born in time to endure a similar trial one summer in Rome. One of the first books I cracked open at the Bibliothèque nationale contained this dedication: "My dear children, It is close to your cradles that these *Études* were written, and more than once you interrupted their composition with your cries. I hope that one day you will read them and think of me."[1] In that same hope, I dedicate this book to my daughters; and to Jenny, a better thinker and writer than I will ever be, with whom I shared those days and nights, and whose love and support has gotten us all through.

Unless otherwise noted, all translations are my own.

SACRED RIVALS

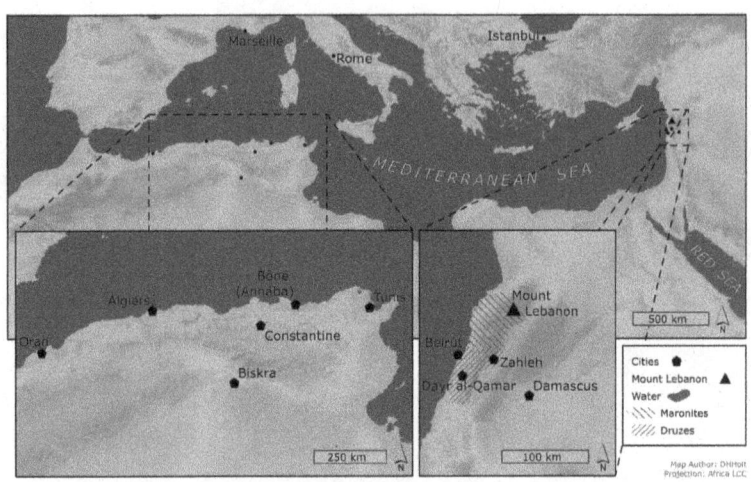

A French Catholic Mediterranean, c. 1860. The Maronite and Druze
districts are based on F. A. Garnier, *Turquie, Syria, Liban, Caucase* (Paris:
Veuve Jules Renouard, 1862). Cartography by David H. Holt.

Introduction

In 1839, Abbé Jacques Suchet arrived in the Algerian city of Constantine, an important North African crossroads and citadel dating back to the days of the Roman Empire. The city, perched on a rock and surrounded by cliffs on three sides, had been conquered with much bloodshed only two years before, in colonial France's first successful foray into the Algerian interior.[1] Suchet had been sent to Constantine by the bishop of Algiers to minister to the new French population there, which comprised mainly soldiers. But the *abbé* could not help but turn his thoughts to the indigenous Arabs. Suchet was pleased with their Muslim religiosity, perhaps seeing them as fertile ground for missionary work. "Truly the dispositions of these good Arabs, the respect, the affection that they bear for priests and nuns astonishes us and fills us with admiration," he wrote in letters that were published back in France. These Arabs were "true descendants of Ishmael; they have pure and completely patriarchal values."[2] Nearly forty years later, another priest—Abbé Edmond Lambert—toured the Algerian city of Oran to record ethnographic observations about the nature of "the Arab" and other Algerian races. Like Suchet, he paid lip service to the Arabs' "respectful curiosity" and "decorum" as they stopped to observe a passing Catholic religious procession.[3] Unlike Suchet, though, he believed that, at their core, Arabs were "liars, thieves, lazy in body and spirit," and that even their seeming piety was not sincere but rather for external show alone.[4]

Suchet's admiration was not unique among French Catholic observers of Algerian Islam around 1840. But neither was Lambert's disdain for Algeria's Arabs uncommon for Catholics by the 1870s. In the first decades of the Algerian conquest after 1830, some mission-minded Catholics both at home in France and on the ground in Algeria viewed Muslim Algerians sympathetically, as potential converts and allies against the forces of French secularism. In the space of less than forty years, however, French Catholics would come to abandon this philo-Islamic view. Far from admiring Muslims as fellow religious devotees, fin-de-siècle French Catholics would participate enthusiastically in the ideological invention of the "Muslim" as the enemy of civilization and in the ethnographic invention of "the Arab" as inconstant, crafty, nomadic, and sexually deviant. This book traces that process.

The chapters that follow focus on French Catholic ideas about Islam and Arab-ness—"Catholic orientalism"—in the context of religious culture wars in France and missionary work in colonial Algeria. Bringing domestic French representations together with colonial realities of Islamo-Christian contact, this book uncovers how prevailing Catholic ideas about Islam influenced and were influenced by missionary experiences. Counterintuitively, it was sometimes the most conservative (ultramontane) Catholics who spoke most sympathetically of Muslim religiosity because they felt embattled by the rise of secularization in France, optimistic about the sudden opportunity for Catholic missions in Algeria, and envious of the apparent piety and unity of Muslim society. By contrast, "liberal," mainstream Catholics—who loudly professed their respect for the liberty of Muslim consciences and hence their opposition to Catholic missions in French Algeria—were often quicker to denigrate Islam as backward, fanatical, and dangerously theocratic. Ultramontane Catholics admired the pre-secular character of Islam, what they perceived as Islam's all-pervasive religiosity and unity of mosque and state. For liberal Catholics, this allegedly "theocratic" fanaticism was precisely what they claimed to detest most about Islam. As the century wore on, and as Catholics increasingly came to identify with France's more secular "civilizing mission," the conservatives' erstwhile admiration for Islam would be eclipsed by a more racialized, colonialist orientalism. Disillusioned with the possibility of Muslim conversion and seeking an explanation for their failure, even missionaries in Algeria joined in with racially coded attacks on "Arab" Islam.

The past decade or so has witnessed an explosion of interest in missionaries and their role in France's empire. Historians have begun to uncover the exceptional richness of missionary archives, the extent and intimacy of missionaries' encounters with indigenous peoples throughout and beyond France's imperial borders, and the "global impact of French Christian evangelization"—still visible from rugby associations in New Zealand and the cathedral in Dakar, to innumerable schools, hospitals, chapels, and cemeteries from Lebanon to Laos. Above all, historians have sought to capture the complexity of missionaries' relationships with secular colonial authorities.[5] What guides much of this new generation of scholarship is the uneasy collaboration between missionaries and colonial modernity—between the traditional desire to save souls and the ostensibly secular ideology of modern imperialism's "civilizing mission."[6] At the heart of France's global missionary movement is a paradox: the movement was an attempt to reconstruct the Catholic France lost by the Revolution, but missionaries relied on the power, personnel, and industrial technologies of those same, postrevolutionary regimes.[7]

From studies across France's colonies, the picture that has emerged is one of routine friction between missionaries and colonial administrators, but also of increasing cooperation by the end of the nineteenth century, as missionaries sought to shore up state funding and support, to prove their patriotism, or simply because the power structure of colonial environments encouraged white colonizers to stick together.[8] In French Indochina, for example, the presence of large populations of Vietnamese Christians sometimes made the relationship between missionaries and administrators more conflictual. But missionaries and colonial officials found "common ground" when it came to opposing the rise of Vietnamese nationalism in the years surrounding the Great War.[9] And in Senegal in the 1890s, missionaries even portrayed themselves as more committed to the Republican civilizing mission than colonial administrators were. In the West African context, where colonial officials pragmatically relied on Muslim (Wolof) leaders as their middlemen in the region, missionaries weaponized the Republican rhetoric of assimilation to defend their own "civilized" Christian converts from alleged Muslim abuses.[10] Especially in the acrimonious years of the Dreyfus affair (which exposed the anti-Semitism of right-wing French Catholics and culminated with the separation of church and state in 1905), missionaries and their publicists back in France protected themselves from Republican political retribution by downplaying traditional conversion narratives and decisively aligning their rhetoric with the civilizing project.[11]

Yet French Algeria—the "jewel of the French empire and its only colony of large-scale European settlement"[12]—has by and large escaped this wave of interest in missions and Christian globalization. The reasons for this relative neglect are varied. Some historians have emphasized that Algeria's colonial administrators effectively blocked missionary efforts out of fear that the blundering missionaries would provoke Muslim fanaticism and jihad. Others have highlighted Algeria's unique demographic and juridical status among France's colonial holdings. Populated by more than half a million European settlers by the end of the nineteenth century and politically assimilated to the metropole,[13] Algeria was technically not a mission field—not an apostolic vicariate reporting directly to Rome—but rather a French diocese, its clergymen appointed and paid by the French state and answerable to the Minister of Cults in Paris.[14] These "secular" parish clergymen (not members of a "regular" order or rule) had neither the desire nor the language skills to proselytize among Algerian Muslims and concentrated their ministrations on the European villages they were paid to serve.[15]

Finally, for the generation of historians who came of age during decolonization and for their students, the most pressing concern about French Algeria was understandably not the Catholic Church but rather the violent impact of French conquest and settlement on indigenous Algerians.[16] Scholars have painstakingly cataloged what James McDougall called the "means of domination" in French Algeria:[17] the staggering, near-genocidal loss of Algerian life in France's wars of "pacification";[18] the environmental and social upheaval caused by the French destruction of oases, seizure of common lands and charitable funds, and disruption of trade and migration networks; and the vast and destructive series of decrees and laws that carved up indigenous land for European purchase, imposed onerous taxes, and denied Algerians the rights of citizenship.[19] French mismanagement exacerbated a deadly famine in 1867–68, killing hundreds of thousands and provoking a massive rebellion. But colonial administrators and propagandists blamed the Algerians for their own suffering and used the rebellion as a pretext for further land confiscation.[20] When the Catholic Church does occasionally surface in these studies of physical, environmental, or juridical violence, it is rightly depicted as complicit with the violent project of transplanting "another France" onto Algerian soil.[21] For example, when French troops conquered the Saharan outpost of Laghouat in 1852, indiscriminately massacring thousands of men, women, and children, they crowned their victory with a mass. At a ceremony to celebrate the transformation of Laghouat's principal mosque into a Catholic church, the vicar general of Algiers told the assembled soldiers, "In conquering Algeria . . . [you] do *the work of God*."[22]

With few exceptions, then, previous historians of church and state in French Algeria have assumed that missionaries initially made no significant effort to proselytize among Algeria's Muslims. France's culture wars—political debates about the place of religion in French society—were thus not exported to the Algerian colony.[23] Confronted with the fanatical Muslims, missionaries and imperialists did not fight among themselves or compete for influence over indigenous souls to the same extent as in other colonies; instead, they banded together in a "colonial pact" against the common Muslim foe.[24] According to this narrative, even Catholic priests tended to view Muslims as fanatical and unconvertible, or at least these priests never tried to disobey the pragmatic policies of anti-missions officials. To be sure, scholars such as Sarah Curtis and Julia Clancy-Smith have called attention to the vital role of women's religious orders in the "civilizing mission"—their private attempts to evangelize, or their covert baptisms of infants. But the colonial administration remained deeply committed to safeguarding "Muslim religious sensibilities" and tolerated female missionaries precisely because their work was gendered as domestic, charitable, and "religiously neutral."[25] Most historians assume that public, provocative, and persistent missionary efforts began only with the arrival of Bishop Charles Lavigerie and his "White Father" congregation in the late 1860s, and with Lavigerie's famously aggressive campaign to seize and convert indigenous orphans and his outspokenly racialized preference for missions among the Kabyles (Berbers) rather than the Arabs.[26]

From the start of the conquest, however, some missionaries and their supporters admired Muslim religiosity, sincerely believed they would be able to convert Algeria's Muslims, and regularly tussled with colonial administrators for the right to proselytize among the Muslims. The Lazarists, for example, established a refuge at Algiers for Jewish and Muslim converts to Catholicism fleeing persecution in the Ottoman Empire. But when the Lazarist Père Girard tried to develop this shelter into a wider Muslim mission by recruiting prospective converts among the youthful pickpockets and beggars of Algiers, he narrowly escaped prosecution for "corruption of minors."[27] It was the Jesuits who most insistently and most frequently attempted to establish evangelistic contact with Algeria's Muslims and who attracted the most hostility from the colonial administration.

In addition to their responsibilities among the European colonial population, the Jesuits established a hostel-cum-seminary outside Algiers (modeled on the Sufi lodge or *zawiya*), at which they hoped to offer hospitality, coffee, and "religious advice" to traveling Arabs.[28] Especially at Constantine—the provincial capital of Eastern Algeria, where the Jesuits served as parish priests—the *pères* undertook repeated experiments in Muslim evangelization in the 1850s and 1860s, catechizing and baptizing numerous Arab and Kabyle children. The Jesuits even brought their star converts, two brothers whom the Jesuits baptized "Louis" and "Stanislas," from Constantine to France in the early 1860s to train for the priesthood, in the hope that they would form the beginnings of an indigenous clergy. Jesuits at Constantine preached and sang songs in Arabic, regularly invited Arab notables to their house, shared meals of couscous and coffee, and exchanged gifts. The Jesuits encouraged their Muslim friends and students to think of them as marabouts, local holy men bearing a kind of spiritual power or charisma. These missionaries did not arrive in the colony with a set of readymade, ahistorical prejudices against Islam and Arabs. Such prejudices would be constructed in the course of the century as deeply personal, contingent experiences of failure and disappointment transformed these missionaries' religious admiration for Algeria's Muslims into more racial modes of thinking about difference.

At the same time, back in metropolitan France, more liberal Catholics—eager to prove their liberalism and to keep Catholicism within the patriotic mainstream—participated in the elaboration of the secular rhetoric of the imperial civilizing mission. Especially in response to the "massacres of Syria" perpetrated

against Catholic Maronites in 1860, the liberal Catholics' unifying strategy consisted of a kind of "clash of civilizations," encouraging Catholic and unbelieving
French alike to unite against civilization's common Muslim foe. The parallels
between the liberal Catholics' negative view of Islam, their aversion to controversial missions to Muslims in Algeria, and their disdain for ultramontane Catholics at home in France is striking. Muslims, these liberal Catholics believed,
were inherently theocratic, violent, and fanatical. It was not only because of the
liberals' own self-proclaimed respect for religious liberty, then, but because of
their belief in Muslim fanaticism that they considered Catholic proselytism in
Algeria foolish and unnecessarily provocative. Similarly, they accused their more
conservative Catholic rivals in France of being theocrats, of being fanatical and
illiberal just like the Muslim foe.

   By the end of the nineteenth century liberal Catholicism was crushed by an
ascendant, reactionary ultramontanism.[29] Various "antimodern" papal decrees
punctuated the latter half of the century. Marian apparitions, miracles, and
prophesies—derided as anti-intellectual and saccharine by Catholics of more
liberal sensibility—proliferated and increased in popularity. This ascendancy
of the Catholic right wing culminated with the doctrine of papal infallibility
in 1871, a resounding defeat for liberal Catholicism. But one strain of the liberal
worldview survived and triumphed among French Catholics: the tendency to
condemn Islam for its religiosity or "fanaticism."

Catholic Orientalism(s): between Metropole and Colony

To the extent that this is a study of orientalist discourse—representations of
Islam invented and intended for domestic consumption—the "Catholic Orientalism" described here is firmly in the methodological furrow plowed by Edward Said.[30] Yet Said has been accused of not paying sufficient attention to the
different social, political, and imperial contexts of the various orientalist figures
he analyzes.[31] Said was also primarily interested in a secular and academic discourse about Islam, not in other variants of orientalism that were mobilized for
explicitly religious purposes.[32] Taking account of such critiques, this book aims
to identify and uncover the historical contexts behind two different, historically
situated discourses about Islam: France's "ultramontane Catholic" and its "liberal Catholic" engagements with Algeria and the Mediterranean world. These
discourses about Islam were not secular products of the orientalist academy; on
the contrary, they were apologetics explicitly deployed in order "to corroborate
religion, not undermine it."[33]

But more than just a history of metropolitan discourses and culture wars, this book intentionally connects the social and intellectual history of religious politics in France with more concrete microhistorical narratives of missionary and colonial practice on the ground in Algeria. On the one hand, it presents a portrait of French Catholic ideas about Islam and the metropolitan religious and political debates that forged those complex ideas; on the other hand, it charts how these ideas collided and were transformed in the intercultural "contact zone" of Algeria.[34] By tacking back and forth between metropolitan France— the rhetorical use and abuse of "Islam" in religious culture wars there—and the Algerian colony, where Catholic missionaries insistently tangled with colonial administrators, catechized indigenous Algerians, and produced bundles of missionary letters and ethnographic reportage, this book attempts to bridge metropolitan rhetoric and colonial "reality."[35] Examining French Catholic encounters with Islam along these two parallel tracks yields insights not only into the history of French Catholicism but also into the history of French Algeria and the production of racialized colonial ethnography there.

In the metropolitan context, looking closely at Catholic arguments about Islam and empire suggests that Catholic polemicists were every bit as influential as secular or Republican commentators in forging the imperial ideology of the "civilizing mission" and in inventing a racialized view of the Muslim world. Nineteenth-century France has conventionally been narrated as a place of ever-increasing opposition between religion and modernity, with reactionary ultramontanes on one side, anticlerical secularizers on the other, and moderate voices gradually drowned out.[36] In the last several decades, scholars have done much to nuance this binary narrative. Breton curés, for example, remained relevant well into the twentieth century by organizing sporting events and movie nights, and by supporting left-leaning social concerns,[37] while pilgrims to the Marian shrine at Lourdes adapted technologies of transportation, mass publicity, medical science, and commerce in their quest for physical and spiritual healing.[38] Catholics' ambiguous posture between "progress" and "reaction" in this period led to some contradictory legacies: while anticlerical politics certainly provoked a more embattled, insular, apocalyptically minded Catholicism, the Church also—in an attempt to consolidate the faithful—became more democratic (less skeptical of popular religious practices), provided unprecedented avenues of engagement for women, and shifted in its emphasis "from a God of fear to a God of love."[39]

The Catholic encounters with Islam presented here are modeled closely on these attempts to get at the dialectical nature and ambiguous legacies of French

Catholicism in the nineteenth century. In imperial fields of knowledge as well—orientalism, colonial ethnography, and the ideology of the civilizing mission—the relationship between Catholicism and modernity was similarly dialectical, as Catholics participated in the invention of each of these bodies of knowledge. Indeed, Catholic missionaries and polemicists were leaders in the formation of "modern" stereotypes of Islam. French Catholics were among the first to portray the Muslim world as a monolithic, almost racial, geopolitical unit and were among the first to portray Muslims as inescapably, almost biologically "fanatical."[40]

This book also engages with the growing body of work on Catholic and missionary views of France's empire and civilizing rhetoric more generally. While there are differences over the exact chronology, cause, and extent of the change, many historians agree that not until the last third of the century did Catholic missionaries and their metropolitan publicists began emphasizing their cooperation with a more secular, Republican "civilizing mission."[41] While my work follows the broad strokes of this narrative—of a Third Republic rise in a more racist *mission civilisatrice* that eclipsed more sympathetic portrayals of colonized subjects—it also highlights Catholic invocations of "civilization" earlier in the century. Already in the midcentury, liberal Catholics invoked not only "Christian civilization" but also the more secular-sounding "civilizing mission," precisely in order to signal their allegiance to France's imperial ventures. This appropriation of civilizational rhetoric permitted Catholic polemicists to claim alliance with the French imperial project (and cultural superiority over Islam) while sometimes turning civilizing ideals against the very regimes that might attempt to curtail their activities.[42]

Although largely a social and intellectual history of the ways Catholic culture warriors in France talked about Islam, this research also yields new insights into the history of colonialism in Algeria. By uncovering a series of previously unknown stories of Muslim-Christian encounter—by insisting that missionaries challenged colonial administrators for the right to proselytize—I raise important questions in French colonial history that are overlooked if missions to Muslims are left out. First, conflicts between missionaries and colonial administrators confirm that French civilization was not at all united or monolithic in its vision of Islam or of Muslims' future place in French civilization. Catholic colonial ethnographies had their own motive and logic that overlapped with but were distinct from secular ethnographies. In other words, conflicts about missionary prerogatives in Algeria are a rich site of competing representations of Islam, revealing divisions within French orientalism and ethnography.

A second issue these missionary encounters raise is the process of how religious differences in French Algeria were transformed into racial differences. Recent work has done much to reconstruct France's relationship with North Africa and the Mediterranean world in the period leading up to the Algerian conquest of 1830. The eighteenth century was a time when religion, not race, was still the primary marker of difference, and the Mediterranean was still a site of cultural "mobility," of "interconnected" identities, with no rigid binary between "French" and "Arab."[43] It was the rise of French nationalism, and above all the violence of Algerian colonization, that was the watershed.[44] Algerian colonization began to demarcate "French" from "Arab," transforming religious identities into racial ones through a series of legal and economic discriminatory acts. But this inequality also shaped and was shaped by individual relationships on the ground: in close encounters that often resulted in misunderstanding and resentment. In the case of the Jesuits, it was only once these missionaries met with failure and disappointment that they began turning more systematically to racially coded attacks on "Arab" Islam. Narrating these stories of missionary disappointment demonstrates that racial prejudice—ethnographic "knowledge"—is not universal or ahistorical. It gets constructed in contingent, historical ways. Some missionaries turned their individual, personal disappointments into vast ethnographic generalizations about Arab "fanaticism."

One final reason why it is essential to recognize that France's colonial front was not so unified in its approach to Algeria's Muslims is that it enables exploration of how Algerians themselves interpreted, navigated, and exploited divisions between missionaries and colonialists. There are clues throughout the archives that some Muslim Algerians were well aware of French debates over the place of religion in society and that they spoke the "scripts" necessary to receive help and resources both from missionaries and from secular, Republican administrators.[45] Algerian students' own experiences with competing varieties of French modernity may have "secularized" them in one sense—encouraging them to relativize their faith, to speak the language of Islam, Catholicism, or of secular Republicanism depending on their intended audience.

In its broadest strokes, the narrative told here will be familiar to historians of the nineteenth century. Religious ways of thinking about difference transformed into racial ones. "Cultural racism" was, in the course of the nineteenth century, supplanted by a more inflexible "biological racism." Yet in practice there has never been a clear division between "cultural racism" and "biological racism"—never a moment when a purely "biological" racism triumphed definitively over cultural markers of difference. Certainly, anthropological and biological understandings of racial difference exerted great influence by the end of the nineteenth century. However, climate, hygiene, and cultural habits remained important environmental explanations of racial difference,[46] and many colonial educators and social planners continued to believe that French education could overcome those differences.[47] It is precisely because race could not in practice be reduced to heritable biology alone that colonial officials and reformers were so obsessed with segregating populations, protecting themselves from racial degeneration and contagion. Conversely, some colonial reformers still believed that if they got ahold of "mixed" or indigenous children at an early enough age and insulated them in a state school or orphanage, those children could be made European, regardless of their ethnic antecedents.[48] Clearly, colonial racism was marked by a confused "mixture of biological and cultural factors," not "the predominance of one [factor] or the other."[49]

In French Algeria, this overlap between cultural and biological accounts of racial difference was even more muddled by racialized ideas about Islam. The period witnessed a burgeoning cottage industry of ethnographic speculation about Arabs, Kabyles, and other Algerian populations. But ultimately "Colonial rule [flattened] Algerians into Muslims and Muslims only," regardless of their social or ethnic origins.[50] This racialization culminated in a legal regime that denied rights to Algerians on the basis of their Muslim-ness and then locked them into that religio-racial legal status. Colonial law refused citizenship rights to Algerians on the pretense that their civil law and marriage practices (for example, polygamy and child marriage) were not compatible with French law.[51] Yet Algeria's Jews—many of whom likewise practiced polygamy and showed no great desire to become French—were naturalized en masse in 1871.[52] Meanwhile, settlers from Spain and Italy, for example, were fast-tracked to French citizenship to form a united front of white settlers.[53] This left Muslim Algerians as the only "*indigènes*" [natives], noncitizens in their own land, subject to the repressive legal regime of the 1881 "Indigenous Code" (*Indigénat*): limited movement, fines, and imprisonments, all without due process.[54] In French Algeria, "*indigène*" thus not only "became virtually synonymous with *musulman*," but was also a very real legal category, entailing very real restrictions.[55] One of the Code's many contradictions—characteristic of colonial law's combination of rigid racism and color-blind ambiguity—was that, although it was intended and assumed to control Muslims, it regulated all "*indigènes*" who had not been naturalized French. Thus, even the rare Muslim Algerians who converted to Catholicism still found themselves subject to Muslim civil law and the arbitrary punishments of the *indigénat.*[56]

*

This book spans the decades from the French occupation of Algeria in the 1830s and 1840s to the 1890s: a period corresponding to the careers of colonial Algeria's first three bishops, but also a period that culminated with the consolidation of civilian settler control in Algeria, and with the high point of Republican imperial expansion and civilizing ideology. The story moves between political debates about religion in France and missionary encounters with Muslims in Algeria.

Chapter 1 opens with the political and religious scene in France at the start of Algerian colonization in the 1840s. It explores how culture warriors like Louis Veuillot, the leading Catholic journalist in France, and his allies employed an idealized view of Muslim unity and religiosity to criticize France's divided, anticlerical July Monarchy. Veuillot and other ultramontane Catholics viewed Algeria's Muslims as religious noble savages, whose devoutness condemned the decadent, secular civilization of France. They also believed that an avowedly Catholic, pro-missionary colonial policy would (paradoxically) be more intelligible and palatable to the Muslims than a policy of religious indifference and toleration. Nevertheless, the roots of a more secularized civilizational rhetoric—the use of "civilization" and its fruits to condemn Islam as inferior—already existed even within Veuillot's philo-Islamism.

Chapters 2 and 3 sketch out the realities of missionary and administrator conflict on the ground in Algeria, especially where Jesuit missionaries were concerned. The Jesuits brought with them to Algeria something of the philo-Islamic optimism inspired by Veuillot and the ultramontane milieu. The congregation of the Jesuits was already a flash point in French debates about religion in education and public life: only the most right-wing Catholics would openly defend the Jesuits' prerogatives. So, their attempts to proselytize among Muslims were all the more galling to laic administrators and all the more thrilling to antisecular provocateurs like Veuillot.

Chapter 2 argues that the main difference between the military administration's and the Jesuits' approaches to Algerian Muslims was whether or not to "secularize" them, that is, whether or not to teach them to interiorize their Muslim faith. The military administrators wanted to convince their colonial subjects that religion was an internal matter and that they could thus accept the benefits of French civilization, medicine, and governance without compromising their religious belonging. The Jesuits, on the contrary, wanted to preserve the all-pervasive religiosity of indigenous society, yet to transfer that theocratic religious loyalty to themselves, the Christian marabouts. Chapter 3 homes in on the Jesuit mission to Muslims in Constantine, the provincial capital of Eastern Algeria, and the Jesuits' two star pupils—baptized "Louis" and "Stanislas" Khodja—who were sent to France for religious education in the 1860s. When the boys returned to Algeria, however, they rejoined the Islamic faith of their family, symbolizing the larger rise and fall of the Jesuits' hopes for Muslims in Algeria. The missionaries transformed their personal disappointment into generalized ethnographic reflections about the inconstancy and ingratitude of all Arabs. But Louis, the elder of the brothers, went on to become a lawyer and spokesman for colonial reforms and left some tantalizing glimpses of how he perceived the competing French modernities represented by missionaries and colonial administrators.

Chapters 4 and 5 detail the convergence between France's Catholics and the imperial, "civilizing" project, as Catholics increasingly unified with the French nation against the supposedly uncivilized, Islamic foe and abandoned any pretense of wanting to convert Muslims. These chapters focus on the Catholic charitable organization the Œuvre des écoles d'Orient, which raised funds for the allegedly oppressed Christian minorities of the Ottoman Empire, and the milieu of liberal Catholic notables that animated it. In the wake of the "massacres of Syria" in 1860, in which Maronite Christians in Lebanon were killed by Druze rivals, the liberal Catholics of the Œuvre, led by Abbé Charles Lavigerie and the diplomat and orientalist Melchior de Vogüé, actively fomented anti-Islamic sentiment. Unlike the conservative admirers of Muslim religiosity, these liberal Catholics denigrated Islam precisely for its supposed religious fanaticism and its pre-secular, theocratic inability to distinguish between (private) religion and (public) politics. The Œuvre was also at the forefront of those who stoked fears of pan-Islamic plots and expansion around the world.

Perhaps no event in the nineteenth century provoked as many Catholics to talk and write publicly about Islam as the Syrian events of 1860. Moreover, French Catholic observers made no distinction between Syrian and Algerian Muslims: what Muslims did in Ottoman Syria was a good indication of what they might do in French Algeria. For the French, Lebanon could be "an analogue of sorts to Algeria" and was "bound to [Algeria] by the circulation of personnel and discourses."[57] Indeed, the future archbishop of Algiers, Charles Lavigerie, acquired his training and sense of vocation for the "Muslim world" through his work at the Œuvre in the wake of the 1860 conflict.

The final two chapters, 6 and 7, return to Algerian missions, focusing on Charles Lavigerie and his newly founded "White Fathers" (Pères Blancs) missionary congregation. The White Fathers represented a new, more modern phase in French Catholic thinking about Algerian Islam. Their bulletins and fundraising materials employed sophisticated tactics of humanitarian publicity, such as distributing photographs of starving children and offering the chance for interested Catholics to financially "adopt" an Algerian orphan. The White Fathers were also more "liberal" than the Jesuits had been: they made a show of how impartial and diplomatic their missionary methods were. They believed that using charity exclusively, without proselytization, would prove their goodness and would wear down the resistance of Algeria's Muslims. Only after the Muslims had been civilized, torn away from allegiance to their local marabouts and seduced by the "disinterested" charity of France, could the missionaries begin to think of broaching the topic of religion. Ironically, although this method vaunted itself as more sensitive to Muslim consciences, it was predicated on a more imperialistic, "civilizing," anti-Islamic project than that of previous missionaries. While earlier missionaries had hoped to accommodate the Christian message to indigenous, tribal lifeways, the White Fathers worked to secularize and destroy local social ties and spiritual economies, making Algerians socially dependent on the missionaries. It is no coincidence that the White Fathers' rhetoric about Islam was much harsher and racialized than that of previous missionaries.

At the beginning of the Algerian conquest, some Catholics—especially ultramontane, aggressively pro-missionary Catholics—professed to admire Algeria's Muslims for their devoutness and even to see them as allies against the forces of French decadence and secularization. By the end of the century, Catholics had changed their position to ally with their unbelieving fellow Frenchmen to condemn Muslims as enemies of civilization. This shift reflected the spectacular failure of missionaries on the ground in Algeria, as well as the irresistible political temptation back in France to grasp at the unity offered by the rhetoric of liberalism and civilization. Recounting these failures and temptations helps recover the extent to which Catholics contributed to the production of colonial ethnography and the civilizing mission, concepts often coded as secular. This study also suggests that disaffected, reactionary

Catholics were some of the first critics of secular imperialism (however cynical and self-serving their critiques).

Beyond these historical questions, I offer the following pages to readers interested in the long-term nature of Muslim-Christian encounter. This book contributes to the project of interfaith understanding by showing that much of contemporary Islamophobic rhetoric has roots in Christian and colonialist prejudices that should be abandoned. Nonetheless, the Christian tradition also sometimes yields unexpected resources for toleration, even from within the reactionary currents of nineteenth-century Catholicism.

CHAPTER I

"Sincerely Religious"

Louis Veuillot and Catholic Representations of Islam and Empire

In 1841, the up-and-coming Catholic journalist Louis Veuillot traveled to Algeria as secretary to the newly appointed Governor General Thomas Bugeaud.[1] As they steamed into view of Algiers, its houses and minarets "bathed" in sun and looking from the sea like a "colossal pyramid" of white, Veuillot prayed that God would bless the soldiers shedding their blood to conquer this land. Whether France's foot soldiers of imperialism knew it or not, Veuillot believed, they were avenging centuries of Christian enslavement and persecution and blazing new paths for the preaching of the Gospel. Drums and cannons saluted the arrival of the new governor general, who would soon become notorious for his brutal campaign of scorched earth and collective punishments against those who resisted French domination.[2]

Veuillot's notes and letters from this voyage were gathered into a book published in 1845 entitled *Les français en Algérie*, a book reprinted in at least ten editions by the end of the nineteenth century.[3] As a Catholic journalist, he would go on to write other articles devoted to France's relationship with Algeria and Islam. His writings on Algeria centered on the idea that the colonial administration should not pursue a policy of "toleration" for Algeria's Muslims—should not fear Muslim resistance to Catholic proselytization—but should instead give clerics and missionaries free rein.[4] At the time of his voyage, Veuillot (see figure 1.1) was working at the Ministry of the Interior and accompanied Bugeaud as the civilian eyes-and-ears of Minister François Guizot. But Veuillot had also recently embraced the "militant Catholicism" that would mark his life and had begun dabbling as a Catholic polemicist at *L'Univers*.[5] He would soon abandon the ministerial bureaucracy and go on to lead the assault on the July Monarchy's anticlerical educational policies. In the process, his journal became "the most combative and influential organ of European ultramontanism," and his populist broadsides were "avidly read by most

FIGURE 1.1. "Louis Veuillot, based on a portrait by J. E. Lafon – 1854."
From Eugène Veuillot, *Louis Veuillot (1813–1845)* (Paris: Victor
Retaux, [1899?]). Courtesy Bibliothèque nationale de France.

parish priests" all over France.[6] Veuillot's sway over French Catholics would become so great that by 1860 he was conferring regularly with the papal nuncio in Paris and publishing news favorable to the Pope and his supporters.[7] In his lifelong struggles against "liberalism" in religion and politics, Veuillot saw himself as the spiritual successor of the famed counterrevolutionary thinker Joseph de Maistre, even suggesting that he had been born, providentially, to further the ultramontane crusade inaugurated by Maistre.[8] Indeed, Veuillot would be the most important figure in preparing French Catholics to accept the doctrine of the infallibility of the Pope promulgated at the First Vatican Council in 1869–70.[9] But on the subject of Islam, which he encountered firsthand in Algeria, he differed significantly from his professed master.

According to Maistre, writing in his last published work *Du pape* (1819), "the disciple of Mahomet . . . is thoroughly alien, incapable of associating and of mixing with us. . . . War between us and them is natural, peace the reverse. As soon as the Christian and the Musulman come in contact, the one or the other must yield or perish."[10] Veuillot, writing during France's violent "pacification" of Algeria, was more ambivalent. Certainly, he saw the relationship between Christendom and Islam as fundamentally one of enmity, and his hope for the Algerian conquest was that it would be a new crusade, causing Islam to "perish in the desert from whence it came."[11] Moreover, he repeatedly invoked France's civilizational superiority as proof that French (Catholic) conquest and tutelage over Muslims was justified. Yet, unlike Maistre, he insisted that Muslims were "made in the image of God," were intuitively drawn to the good and the beautiful, and had a natural respect for religion that made them especially suitable for conversion to Christianity.[12] Veuillot even presented the organic unity and spirituality of Islamic civilization as a virtue and compared Islam favorably to the sterility and decadence of secular France. It was the laudable "religious sentiment" of Algerian Muslims, Veuillot wrote in the opening pages of *Les Français en Algérie*, that had made colonial conquest so difficult: "The war against us was not only patriotic, it was holy. . . . Some of these Arabs fought as heroes and died as martyrs."[13]

What factors account for Veuillot's philo-Islamism, even as he affirmed France's civilizing prerogatives in Algeria? What motives led him and other conservative Catholics to depict Muslims as a sort of religious noble savages, their very devoutness a reproach to the metropolitan French? This chapter puts Veuillot's writings on Islam into conversation with two of his contemporaries: the literary historian and Romantic orientalist Edgar Quinet and the devout Catholic orientalist-turned-missionary Eugène Boré. Quinet was no ultramontane Catholic; on the contrary, in the 1840s' rancorous debates about Catholic education, the liberal Protestant and famous critic of the Jesuits was one of Veuillot's principal adversaries.[14] Yet, in the postrevolutionary atmosphere of the 1830s–40s, Catholics, liberals, and socialists alike felt that the relationship between state and society was broken and that a new (or restored) civil religion was needed to resacralize the body politic. In an age of Romantic orientalism and of Algerian conquest, Quinet and Veuillot both looked to Algeria, to Islam's alleged "theocratic" unity of state and religion, as a critique of—and as a model for resolving—postrevolutionary France's divisions.[15]

Beyond these general conditions for his orientalist imaginary, Veuillot's writings were motivated by specifically Catholic, ultramontane concerns—concerns he shared with a friend, the orientalist-turned-missionary Eugène Boré. Boré and Veuillot used Muslim piety to condemn the perceived anticlericalism and religious indifference of the liberal July Monarchy. They also shared an evangelistic optimism that accompanied the explosion of French missions in the 1840s.[16] Consequently, both men represented Muslims as people of great religious faith and as potentially ideal Christians, once they inevitably converted. That Veuillot and Boré—one an amateur "colonial ethnographer" at best, the other an academically trained orientalist[17]—should have represented and used Islam in such rhetorically similar ways in the context of the 1840s only confirms the overriding importance, beyond their social and professional contexts, of their identity as Catholic apologists.

Veuillot's writings on Algerian Islam—in which the trope of superior Muslim unity and piety coexisted with legitimations of empire based on France's superior civilization—are deeply contradictory. Among later Catholic observers of Islam, the sympathetic elements in this unstable compound would be overcome by civilizational denigrations of Muslims or racial denigrations of Arabs. Yet in the early decades of French Algeria, some missionaries in the colony shared Veuillot and Boré's sympathetic view of Algerian Islam and their optimism about imminent Muslim conversion. But in the course of the nineteenth century, Catholic views of Islam hardened as missionary efforts to convert Algerian Muslims met with failure and frustration, and as Catholics increasingly allied themselves by the end of the century in a "colonial pact" with the Third Republic and its "civilizing mission."[18] Nevertheless, however short-lived, Veuillot and other ultramontane Catholics' ambivalent orientalism—caught between admiration for Islamic religiosity and belief in European superiority—provides a new lens onto the history of nineteenth-century French Catholicism and empire.

Enlightenment Antecedents

Maistre, Veuillot, Boré, and other Catholic observers of Islam in the early nineteenth century were part of a long-standing French tradition of discussing Islam in ambivalent ways. From the travel writers and diplomats of the seventeenth century, to the philosophes of the eighteenth century, French writers had constructed a double-edged approach to "Islam," using stereotypes of the Muslim world both as negative and positive comparisons, sometimes even within the same text. French Protestants used representations of the Ottoman Empire in this polyvalent way in the 1600s, accusing French Catholic kings of being just as intolerant as the stereotypically "despotic" Ottomans, while simultaneously holding Islamic states up as more tolerant than absolutist France.[19] Enlightenment philosophes followed suit: Montesquieu's *Persian Letters* sometimes portrays the Persians as despotic and inferior to the French—especially in their treatment of women—but the novel also places Montesquieu's own normative critiques of French society in the mouths of enlightened Persians.[20] The Enlightenment's ambivalence toward Islam is perhaps nowhere more evident than in the career of Voltaire. Voltaire's controversial 1741 play *Fanaticism, or Mahomet the Prophet* depicts the Prophet as a sexually voracious fraud and manipulator of his superstitious followers; but the play was also widely recognized as a veiled critique of Catholic superstition and intolerance, and in France it "was banned after three performances."[21] Ultimately, in his celebrated *Essai sur les mœurs et l'esprit des nations*, Voltaire defended Muhammad as a heroic force for progress and characterized Islam as more rational than Christianity, since it does not preach such seemingly nonsensical doctrines as the Trinity.[22]

In their attacks on religious intolerance and on Christianity, in other words, the philosophes "instrumentalized" Islam in rhetorically contradictory ways.[23] Islam was criticized as an example of superstition and used as a stereotype of intolerance, but it was also defended as more tolerant than Christianity and examined with a more open mind than in any previous period of European history. The Enlightenment's inconsistency toward Islam was not just rhetorical. The philosophes were deeply ambivalent about religion in general, especially about the social role of religion. While Voltaire and other philosophes famously hoped to "crush" institutional religion and intolerance, they were nearly unanimous in their belief that some minimum of "natural" religious faith was still indispensable for a civil society to function.[24] Hence the author of the *Encyclopédie*'s article on "Tolérance" saw no contradiction in expelling atheists from his otherwise tolerant society.[25] Though Enlightenment writers often invoked the language of individual "liberty of conscience," what most were really after was not anything so anarchic and limitless, but rather a state-regulated "tolerance" for recognized, socially useful groups, such as the Huguenots (French Calvinists).[26] Philosophes could not decide between valorizing the rights of individual consciences, on the one hand, and their conviction, on the other hand, that states had a vested interest in encouraging civil religion and prohibiting antisocial religions. Thus Rousseau famously admired Muhammad for having solved the problem of devising a suitable civil religion: "Mahomet, in his wisdom, knit his political system into a strong whole... it was completely unified, and, in so far as unified, good."[27] This Enlightenment uncertainty between state "tolerance" for recognized religious collectives and the more revolutionary concept of "liberty of conscience" for individuals maps directly on to the philosophes' ambivalence toward Islam. On the one hand, Islamic polities such as the Ottoman Empire had long institutionalized collective "tolerance" for religious minorities; on the other hand,

Islamic jurisprudence did not affirm the emerging concept of individual liberty
of conscience.

Especially in the late eighteenth and early nineteenth centuries, French writers became increasingly disillusioned with the Islamic world and began portraying Islam as degraded and uncivilized. Writers of the Enlightenment had long
been unsure where to place Muslims on their scale of civilizational development.
Since Islamic states such as those of the Barbary Coast were capable of urban settlement, trade, and naval warfare, they were clearly not populated by primitive
(and naturally virtuous) men; at the same time, they had not followed in the path
of nor shared the values of European civilization.[28] Eighteenth-century visitors
to Algiers, in search of noble savages, expressed disappointment with the alleged
immorality and unscrupulousness of Algerian Arabs and came to view North
Africans as being in a state of decline or, worse, as congenitally deformed by Islamic and "Oriental" despotism. Even Abbé Raynal's famously anti-imperialist
Philosophical History advocated the conquest of the "Barbary States" as the only
means of civilizing them.[29] Not only did the early nineteenth century abandon
earlier appreciations of Islamic civilization but Enlightenment anti-imperialism
in general went into decline, as race became a more "hegemonic explanation of
cultural difference" and as the political breakthroughs of the French Revolution
gave Europeans increased confidence in their civilizational superiority.[30]

Thus, despite his counter-Enlightenment bona fides, Joseph de Maistre's criticisms of Islam were perfectly in keeping with the late Enlightenment mainstream.[31] While Maistre was certainly out of step with many of his contemporaries in his valorization of the Pope, Crusades, and Christendom, his comments
on Islam were typical of the late Enlightenment's growing disillusionment with
Islam and with the related category of the "noble savage." In short, Maistre was
drawing from traditional religious as well as from contemporary mentalities
in his characterization of Muslims as irredeemable enemies of Christendom
and—by extension—of humanity. "Seeking . . . my arms in the camp of the
enemy"[32] both wittingly and unwittingly, Maistre at once subverted and confirmed Enlightenment values and civilizational classifications. In a well-known
passage from the posthumously published *Soirées de Saint-Petersbourg*, Maistre
attacked Rousseau's concept of the noble savage, claiming that the "savages" of
the New World, for example, were not primitive men but the late-stage, wicked
remnants of formerly grand civilizations, degraded by some original sin to the
point of being unrecognizable as human. "Barbarians," on the contrary, were
"halfway between the civilized man and the savage" and capable of civilization even through initiation into non-Christian religions.[33] According to this

bizarre typology—a characteristic blend of Enlightenment developmentalism and Christian and Classical notions of a golden age—Muslims, though not specifically referenced in the passage, would seem to belong to the category of sub-human, fallen savages. Unsurprisingly, Maistre had concluded his discussion of Islam in *Du pape* by insisting that Islamic states have no claim on international law: whoever conquered the territory of such an incorrigible enemy would be "universally" recognized as its legitimate sovereign.[34]

Writing a generation later, though, Veuillot revived the rhetorical ambivalence and sympathy toward Islam of the earlier Enlightenment. In the terms of Maistre's "savage"-"barbarian" typology, Veuillot seemed to move Muslims out of the category of savage enemies and into that of civilizable barbarians—barbarians perhaps even able to graft onto the French stock and reinvigorate it, the way primitive Northern Europeans had supposedly reinvigorated the decadent Roman Empire. Just as Maistre's understanding of Islam's place in history and its relationship to Christendom was in part a reflection of late Enlightenment trends, so too was Veuillot's more sympathetic treatment far from unique in the context of the 1840s. Veuillot's writings on Algerian Islam were, to be sure, primarily motivated by his reactionary and ultramontane concerns—his intention was to beat his secular enemies with the rhetorical stick of Muslim religiosity. On a deeper level, though, his writings were situated within conditions and mentalities he shared with contemporaries of varying political persuasions: the post-1830s reality of Algerian conquest, with its increase in firsthand knowledge of Islam, accompanied by endless debates about the methods and meaning of France's new empire; the "Oriental Renaissance," or the Romantic interest in Eastern cultures and religions; the widespread anxiety in postrevolutionary France that the relationship between state and society was broken and that a new civil religion was needed to restore a feeling of community and to resacralize the body politic; and, above all, a missionary desire to re-Christianize France by Christianizing Algeria.

Edgar Quinet, Postrevolutionary
Romanticism, and Islamic Theocracy

Given the common misconception that Islamic societies were theocracies—not distinguishing between civil and religious spheres—it is not surprising that Veuillot looked to Algeria as a model for French society, albeit an imperfect one that would need to be appropriated and superseded. In the postrevolutionary context of the 1840s, in which many French viewed their society as lacking legitimacy and organic unity, Veuillot was not alone in his admiration for the purportedly theocratic character of Islam. Edgar Quinet, one of the fathers of the "Oriental Renaissance" in France, similarly believed that Islam's ability to realize its spiritual ideals in the political sphere was something that historical Christianity had lacked.[35] In Quinet's Romantic philosophy of history, wherein each succeeding civilization had made some spiritual contribution to the future world religion, this theocratic unity would be Islam's historic contribution. The long-standing view that Islam was essentially theocratic was perhaps most famously employed by Rousseau in the concluding section of *The Social Contract*. In contrast to Christianity's encouragement of divided loyalties between church and state, Rousseau wrote, "Mahomet, in his wisdom, knit his political system into a strong whole... it was completely unified, and, in so far as unified, good."[36] Of course, the political and religious landscape of nineteenth-century Algeria—Veuillot and Quinet's primary window onto Islam—was in fact quite diverse and even contentious, as tribal leaders and religious reformers negotiated their responses to French encroachment.[37] Nevertheless, both men, like Rousseau, relied upon an essentialized image of Islamic unity in order to critique a divided Christendom.

Many Europeans of the 1830s and 1840s self-consciously saw their epoch as constituting a crucial turning point in world history—a time of "great world-historical parallel" with the early Roman Empire and the birth of Christianity.[38] For most observers, this sense of cyclical return led to the optimistic belief that "the Christian era had come to an end" and that the institution of a "new Christianity" was imminent. Invocations of this great parallel were common, especially among socialists like Henri de Saint-Simon and Pierre-Joseph Proudhon who characterized their systems as the much-anticipated new religion.[39] This historically self-conscious search for a revitalized civil religion was a reflection both of the fractured politics of the postrevolutionary period, as well as in the advent of the "Social Question"—the rise of industrialism and with it the creation of a new, marginalized class of industrial laborers and urban poor.[40]

There was no more divisive issue in the revolutionary years than the place of Catholicism in the public sphere. The Revolution's seizure of church lands and reform of the Catholic Church—transforming clergy into employees of the state and bishops into elective offices—was perhaps the turning point of the Revolution. Above all, the "oath" of loyalty to the new constitution, required of all clergymen in France, alienated millions of Catholic faithful who might otherwise have supported the gains of the early Revolution, pushing them into the camp of the counterrevolutionaries. With these battle lines drawn and France descending into civil war and terror, some Jacobins concluded that the Church was an entrenched enemy of progress and ramped up the violence of their de-christianization efforts. After Robespierre's fall and the reaction against the Terror, the Directory repressed Jacobins and royalists alike, but one continuity was that the Ideologues of the Directory maintained and even intensified the dechristianization campaign, attempting to replace Christianity with their own, deistic civil religion.[41] Napoleon pragmatically negotiated a concordat with the Catholic Church, "disarm[ing] the counterrevolution" of its most effective rallying cry—the defense of the Church—thus leaving only the most reactionary devotees of monarchism to resist his peace.[42] In one stroke Napoleon reintroduced formal, public Catholic worship to France and conceded to the Pope once more the right to appoint bishops and other clergy. But he drove a hard bargain: clergymen remained employees of the state and subject to vetting and surveillance.[43] With the institutional power of the Church irrevocably fractured and an entire generation raised (in the 1790s) without the catechism, the stage was set for some to return to a more combative Catholicism, while others sought "new paths to salvation."[44] The advent of a seemingly unchurched industrial working class by the 1830s—to some observers these workers were godless "barbarians," to others, they embodied the closest thing to the sufferings of Christ on earth—only made the quest for a "new Christianity" more acute.[45]

Postrevolutionary France's obsessive search for a new civil religion—a new sacral legitimation of society—was also inextricably tied to its colonial confrontation with the East and, specifically, with Islam. On the crudest level, the Restoration and subsequent regimes hoped the Algerian conquest would generate domestic unity and "political legitimacy" through military glory at the expense of an agreed-upon foe.[46] Even the liberal Alexis de Tocqueville famously supported imperial aggression as a way of shoring up support for the embattled July Monarchy.[47] But while such military aggression might produce an ephemeral unity, more Romanticized observers believed it was not conflict but reconciliation between East and West that would heal France's political divisions. The Saint-Simonians, for example, looked to the "Orient" as terrain for their utopian projects, even after the failure of Egyptian reform under Muhammad Ali. Many of the military officers tasked with administering Arab tribes in Algeria were Saint-Simonians and saw their work there as an opportunity to engineer an ideal society—an "alternate modernity"—among the "*indigènes*" and colonists.[48] Similarly, Quinet and Veuillot each hoped in their own way that Algerian colonization would enable France to tap the spiritual resources of Islam and become politically and religiously unified once more.

Quinet's Romantic orientalism emerged in this context of postrevolutionary disillusionment with Enlightenment rationalism, when many Frenchmen
looked "across the Rhine" to German Romanticism for a sensitivity to the
spiritual that they felt they lacked.[49] Quinet's *Génie des religions* is a kind of
Hegelian account of human progress through religious revolution, in which the
rediscovery of Eastern religions constitutes a crucial stage, a return to the cradle
of communal religion by a modern individualistic spirit whose *Bildungsroman*
is thus completed.[50] Quinet's belief that history was moving inexorably toward a
reconciliation of world religions—a reconciliation of reason and spirit, of individual and community, of man and nature—makes him a prime example of the
postrevolutionary, Romantic quest for a new religion.[51] For Quinet, "Oriental"
religion—defined and experienced chiefly through France's contact with Islam
in Algeria—held the key to the "new Christianity."[52]

Quinet's *Christianity and Revolution* lectures of 1845 devote far more attention to Islam than had earlier documents of the "Oriental Renaissance," to the
point of reducing the spirit and significance of the Orient entirely to the religion
of Muhammad.[53] According to Quinet, the spiritual revolution accomplished
by Islam represented a vital step in humanity's circuitous progress toward a
higher unity. The very essence of Islam, in Quinet's view, was its apocalyptic
activism. The Qur'an is full of evocative descriptions both of temporal and final
judgment and of indications that those judgments are near. Accordingly, Islam
suffers from none of the temporizing and accommodationism that has plagued
Christian churches. The Qur'an is marked by a sense of "haste"—"since the signs
are so near, so palpable . . . one must act."[54] Islam owes the success of its early
and precipitous conquests to this constant fear of chastisement. For Quinet, the
fundamental point of contrast between Christianity and Islam was that "the
first defers its promises until after death," while "the second, without losing a
day, wants to bring its doctrines into the constitution of civil and temporal society."[55] Islam's world-historical innovation lay in its commitment to the temporal,
earthly actualization of its ideals. Quinet cited the fact that Islam abolished
caste systems as soon as it had the rule over Asiatic societies. An emancipation
that took the West 1,800 years to implement—from ideal (primitive Christianity) to realization (French Revolution)—took the Orient a single instant. Muhammad was at once "the head and the arm, the Christ and the Napoleon of
the modern Orient."[56] So immediate was the application of Qur'anic ideals that
Islamic societies lived in a kind of ahistorical present. Some might accuse the
Orient of immobility, but only because it had experienced "in a single day . . . its
Messiah and its Social Contract, the preaching of its apostles and its Revolution

of '89 . . . its primitive Church and its Constituent Assembly."[57] The active apocalypticism of early Islam, unlike that of early Christianity, had already succeeded
in ushering in its posthistorical millennium.

Of course, Islam was not history's ultimate religion; but whatever the short-
comings of its creed, its devotion to the temporal actualization of that creed was
an attribute which France's new religion would need in order to reconcile France
and Algeria, West and East, self and society. Quinet suggested that Muslims had
noticed the discrepancy between France's church and state, between its ideal
and its actions, and had taken it for a weakness. Since "the Mohammedans have
reached religious and social unity before us," Quinet asked, why would they
want to revert to a state of contradiction?[58] In fact, the Orient would never be
subdued or conciliated as long as it observed France's missionaries teaching a
Gospel that the French themselves did not live by. This conclusion, expressive of
a desire for a new unity between church and state, was something the counterrevolutionary, pro-missionary Veuillot would have agreed with. However, the
two men could hardly have differed more in their envisioned bases for that unity:
Quinet promoted a civil religion that equated primitive, pre-institutional Christianity with the liberal principles of the Revolution, while Veuillot harked back
to a (fictional) golden age of corporate unity and absolute fidelity to the Pope.
But Quinet's description of Islam's genius represented an attribute both men
considered indispensable for France—"this suppression of time, this striking
simultaneity of the idea and the fact, this identity of religion and politics, this
flash of lightning which at once illuminates the sky and the earth, the church
and the state."[59]

Veuillot's *Les français en Algérie*: Theocracies and Noble Savages

The view that Islam did not distinguish between civil and religious spheres was
a commonplace of orientalist discourse in nineteenth-century France, and this
was often understood to be a harmful characteristic. This perception was sufficiently entrenched for Ernest Renan, in his inaugural speech at the Collège
de France in 1862, to compare the "state religion" of Islam to that of the papal
territories, concluding that both religions were irrevocably opposed to modern
European civilization.[60] But Veuillot's references to Islamic civil religion were
significant not only because, like Quinet's, they were relatively sympathetic but
also because, in the context of his counterrevolutionary culture war, he willingly
accepted this association of Catholicism and Islam and turned it against his sec-
ularist enemies. Unlike later proponents of the "Kabyle myth"—the "triangular

comparison" between French, Arabs, and Kabyles that was designed to divide the "*indigènes*" into fanatical, uncivilizable Arabs and civilizable Kabyles—for Veuillot it was not Algeria but metropolitan France itself that was divided. Algerian Muslims and French Catholics were closer to each other and to civilization than either of them were to the truly "savage" secular French.[61]

For Veuillot, as for Quinet, Algeria presented a world-historical opportunity for religious rebirth in which both East and West would participate.[62] In Veuillot's understanding, though, France's confrontation with Algeria was inscribed in a historical narrative that was specifically Christian. Because of the impending success of France's colonial venture, "the last days of Islam have come," confirming "calculations established by the Apocalypse of Saint John" that "assign a duration of thirteen centuries to Mohammed's reign." But despite his faith in God's guidance of history, the precondition for a French Algeria was nothing short of a national revival of (and state support for) Catholicism in France, attended by unqualified support for missionary endeavors in Algeria. Until then, the conquest would be neither successful nor justifiable, and the "Moors and Arabs" would continue to "reproach us . . . because they never see us pray."[63] At the level of state and society, Veuillot accused, the effects of France's irreligion were manifested in the fact that colonial administrators made no provision for Catholic worship or for the propagation of the faith.[64] Under such conditions, the Arabs were "right to call us impious."[65] Success in Algeria could only come from emulating Islamic society: rather than sending the orphans, deportees, and the offscourings of French society to work in agricultural settlements, Veuillot criticized, what the settlements of Algeria really needed were "Christian families" led by priests who would make of them a "theocratic" republic able to "respond to Muslim holy war with a Christian holy war." His readers may scoff at such a religiously inspired vision, Veuillot admitted, but a Christian theocracy would succeed precisely because it would be more intelligible and acceptable to the devout Algerians, ultimately rendering subjugation unnecessary. Transforming the agricultural villages into theocracies would "strike the Arabs with that respect and admiration [that they have] for all that is sincerely religious, which God has left them as an open channel for their return."[66]

Algerian Muslims' good faith and religiosity not only meant that they would more willingly accept a colonization that was openly and aggressively Christian; for Veuillot, in his pro-missionary polemic against colonial administrators, it also meant that they were susceptible to religious conversion. Because humans are "made in the image of God," however dehumanized by false religion, they retain the "intuition of the good and of the beautiful" and can always be saved.

But "unbelieving Europe," faced with a choice between converting and destroying the unfortunate Muslims, "prefers to annihilate them," effectively denying a universal human nature and giving the lie to its own vaunted humanitarianism. "It does not please God that we kill men before having tried to convert them."[67] Veuillot's commitment to proselytization even led him at times to openly criticize France's imperial atrocities. In one article, Veuillot gave a surprisingly frank description of the repressive tactics used in General Bugeaud's "pacification" campaigns, including the infamous *razzias* (raids), with their burning of crops, villages, and even burning alive of villagers who escaped into caves.[68] For Veuillot, the fact that so much blood had been spilled made missionary work a necessity. He believed it would be truly reprehensible for France to have caused so much suffering for mere commercial or political interests.[69]

For Veuillot, in a Catholic revival of the Enlightenment's rhetorical ambivalence toward Islam, the Muslim functioned as a kind of religious noble savage (indeed, even more "civilized" than secular Frenchmen). Veuillot's purpose was not only to prove that Muslims were open to religious dialogue and conversion but especially to denounce the empty irreligion of the metropolitan and colonial French.[70] The opening chapter of Veuillot's travel account is subtitled "A Savage." Significantly, though, this chapter takes place in France and relates the stage of his journey between Paris and Marseille, the subtitle referring to a well-fed fellow Frenchman who shared Veuillot's coach. By beginning his trip to Algeria with this encounter, Veuillot framed the entire book as a comparison between "savage" metropolitan French and admirably devout Algerians. While the two men rode together, their conversation turned to religion; Veuillot's companion became embarrassed and admitted that he remembered none of the prayers or religious teachings of his childhood. Incredulous, Veuillot lamented, "This man... did not know a single word of the Catholic religion, within which he had been born and had lived a half-century. He asked me questions that a savage could have asked."[71] Algerian Muslims, Veuillot discovered by contrast, had pride in their religion.

A favorite trope of Veuillot's, to which he would return in later writings on Algeria, was that of the French soldier who, shamed by the piety of his Muslim allies or enemies, pretended to be a practicing Catholic or, better yet, sincerely returned to the Church.[72] Veuillot related the story of a "brave officer" whose acquaintance with Algerian Muslims restored to him his religion. "What is your religion?" they had challenged the soldier; "Do you ever pray, fast, give homage to God?" Veuillot quoted, approvingly and at length, these Muslims' condemnation of French pretensions to civilizational superiority: "The least among us is not impressed by the wonders of Paris.... You have artillery pieces, steam ships, wire suspension bridges ... you set yourselves up in life like people who would want to stay there forever." Yet French soldiers were regularly found drunk in the streets and were so "afraid of dying" that "they convert to Islam" when captured: "We want no part of what you are."[73] Veuillot's rhetorical and missionary affection for Algeria's pious Muslims would even take him beyond the simple, traditional affirmation that all humans made in the image of God were theoretically amenable to proselytization; rather, the Arabs' natural credulity and instinct for veneration made them not just potential but ideal candidates for Christian faith.[74]

If the "Oriental Renaissance," Algerian conquest, and postrevolutionary malaise were necessary conditions for Veuillot's sympathetic approach to Islam, conditions shared by Catholic and freethinker alike, it was his specifically Catholic concerns—the polemical struggle against July Monarchy anticlericalism and the optimism of the "Catholic missionary awakening"[75] in its initial confrontation with Islam—that directly provoked his sympathetic representations and gave them force. Veuillot was not the only Catholic critic of the July Monarchy to raise the issue of the church's place in Algeria and to attack the Orléanist regime on this front. In the 1840s, many Catholic writers were united in a loose conglomeration of opposition to the July Monarchy and its educational policies.[76] The battle over educational liberty for Catholic secondary schools, especially over the status of unauthorized teaching congregations such as the Jesuits, was far and away the major "culture war" of the 1840s, the crucible out of which nineteenth-century Catholic journalism was forged.[77] It should come as no surprise, then, that other Catholic writers also found the July Monarchy's tepid support for the Christianization of Algeria to be a convenient club with which to beat the regime.

Charles de Riancey's 1846 pamphlet, *De la situation religieuse de l'Algérie*, was published by Charles de Montalembert's *Comité électoral pour la défense de la liberté religieuse* and was available for purchase at the offices of Veuillot's *L'Univers*. The immediate context for Riancey's pamphlet was the resignation of Algeria's first bishop, Antoine-Adolphe Dupuch, in December of 1845, and the publication of Dupuch's report to the Pope, which openly accused the July Monarchy and its colonial administrators of obstructing his work. Riancey clearly shared Veuillot's perspective on the Algerian problem: France's conquest of Algeria represented a sacred obligation to bring the colony into the fold of *civilisation chrétienne*, to "found a new Christendom"; yet "the Arabs themselves were astonished at the impiety of their conquerors," and their will to resist was empowered by the thought that their enemies were "a nation without God."[78] Far from resenting the Catholic element among the French, Riancey claimed, the Muslims themselves were pleased upon learning that some French were religious after all and magnanimously understood that some mosques would have to be seized and transformed into churches.[79] Yet the anticlerical colonial administration, more pro-Muslim than the Muslims themselves, had left numerous towns without churches and priests, building mosques instead. The Arabs, however, scorned these government-built mosques as profane. "I cannot prevent myself from admiring these Arabs," Riancey wrote, finding himself, like Veuillot, in solidarity with Muslims who were too noble and devout to accept the pandering tolerance of a "godless" government.[80] "Fortunately," congregations such as the Jesuits, "those persecuted priests who always respond to humiliations and slanders with new services," had come to the aid of the secular clergy.[81] Whether because Riancey's main purpose was to accuse France's administration of not giving sufficient financial support to Algeria's first bishop, or because Riancey, unlike Veuillot, had not encountered Algerian Muslims firsthand, his pamphlet did not engage in the kind of extended philo-Islamic reflections that marked Veuillot's work.

The same year, in 1846, Jacques Lecoffre, the Catholic publisher of Riancey's pamphlet, also published an anonymous tract "by an officer of the Army of Africa" with the much more explicit and crudely pragmatic title, *De la conversion de musulmans au christianisme, considerée comme moyen d'affermir la puissance française en Algérie* (The conversion of Muslims to Christianity, considered as a means for affirming French power in Algeria). The anonymous pamphlet was not a salvo in the educational debates but rather a contribution to the broader genre of utopian plans for how best to colonize Algeria. It again showed the currency of ideas akin to Veuillot's. Basing his argument on the same false dichotomy posed by Veuillot and Riancey—large-scale Muslim conversion to Christianity as the only alternative to endless conflict—the anonymous officer followed this line of reasoning to the extreme, advocating that the army escort and protect priests as they proselytize, that enemy women be entrusted to female religious congregations until they convert or are married to Christians, and that children be forcibly sent to French schools for their education.[82] He also added his own awkward take on the advantages of Muslims' natural religiosity. "Even today," he wrote, "the Muslims accept as holy writ the absurd tales of their marabouts. Let us be certain, then, that our priests, by preaching Christian truths with eloquence, will obtain the greatest successes." [83] In other words, the Muslims of Algeria were such superstitious simpletons that they would even

become Catholics! Catholic philo-Islamists like Veuillot would not have put this
argument so clumsily, but their hope was the same—that Catholic missionaries
like the Jesuits would be able to transfer the Muslims' religious allegiance over
to Christianity, without damaging any of their noble devoutness and credulity
along the way. This was not the only similarity between the "officer" and Veuillot. The anonymous pamphleteer suffered from the same confusion of priorities
that plagued Veuillot's thought and that would plague Catholic Orientalism for
decades to come—the confusion between Christianity's truth value and French
civilization's worldly success: "How can we fail when we fight for the truth, and
when we have . . . the advantage of knowledge and force?"[84]

Eugène Boré: Apologetics, Mission, and Analogy

One Catholic figure whose trajectory in thinking about Islam closely mirrors
Veuillot's was the orientalist-turned-Lazarist missionary Eugène Boré.[85] Boré was
of the same generation as Veuillot, the generation of "Romantic Catholics" who
came of age during the Catholic revival of the 1830s and 1840s, in the shadow
of the famous apologists Joseph de Maistre, François-René de Chateaubriand,
and Félicité de Lamennais—a time when discussion *cercles* and *conférences* for
Catholic students, charitable associations, and missionary congregations proliferated.[86] When Boré undertook his first "voyage en Orient" in 1837, he saw his
mission as sharing in the scholarly-apologetic project that sought to use history,
philology, and even the study of other religions to confirm the "universal" truth
of Catholic revelation and the historical benefits of "Christian civilization."[87]
Boré met Veuillot in 1842, when he was back in France after his first expedition
in Turkey and Persia.[88] Boré's closest friend, Eugène Taconet, was throughout
the 1840s the director and financial supporter of Veuillot's *L'Univers*, and Boré
would remain an avid reader and supporter of Veuillot's journalism for the rest
of his life.[89] Boré even contributed articles to *L'Univers*.[90] Though his academic
and missionary efforts focused on the Ottoman Empire rather than on Algeria,
Boré's writings on Islam—geared toward a French Catholic audience—were
conditioned by the same Romantic, apologetic, and evangelistic motives that
influenced Veuillot. Moreover, despite the Turkish context of Boré's personal
missionary labors, Algeria loomed large in his Islamic imaginary—as a place
where, thanks to the French conquest, a breach had been opened against Islam's
resistance to Christian missions. Boré stayed informed of the evangelistic attempts of his Lazarist missionary colleagues in Algeria, twice visiting the colony
and touring its missionary establishments.[91]

Like Veuillot, Boré was deeply impressed with the piety and apparent decency of Muslim culture, even confessing to experiencing a "seductive doubt" about the superiority of Christian civilization when he saw how infrequently suicides, murders, and other vices seemed to occur in Turkish society.[92] Writing in 1845 for the missionary journal *Annales de la Propagation de la Foi*, Boré summarized "the nature of the Muslim," emphasizing how noble and devout Muslims were in comparison to the unbelieving skeptics of France: "You admire in him his disposition to adhere to the constituent dogmas of all religion; you are not frightened by this rationalist audacity which among us denies and sneers at the beliefs of others; on the contrary, the word or deed which honors God is always respected and approved by him . . . and the only fault which his good sense finds unpardonable and incomprehensible is the monster of philosophical skepticism."[93] Implicit in this passage are the same motives that drove Veuillot's reflections on Islam—the desire to criticize by comparison the perceived anticlericalism of France's liberal July Monarchy and the hope that Muslims, with their natural credulity and religious sense, might themselves make ideal Christians.

Indeed, it is precisely because global Islam was presumed ripe for conversion that the work of missions in Algeria remained close to Boré's heart and intimately linked to his own Ottoman context. Boré was the animating spirit behind the Catechumenate of Algiers, a refuge directed by the Lazarists of Algeria with the purpose of welcoming converts to Catholicism who were escaping persecution in the Ottoman Empire. According to the overly optimistic logic of early nineteenth-century missions in their initial encounters with Muslims, Christianity was so obviously superior to Islam that all that was needed for Christianity to prevail was for the persecutory laws of the Ottoman Empire to be abolished, leveling the playing field. The unfolding conquest of Algeria, then, with its prospects for an unhindered Christian apostolate to Islam, was a source of great hope for Veuillot and Boré alike. In October 1842, Boré reported to the Paris Council of the Œuvre de la Propagation de la Foi (Association for the Propagation of the Faith; France's foremost funder of Catholic missions) that Muslims as well as Jews and "schismatics" (Orthodox Christians) in the Orient were ready to convert to Catholicism. All that prevented them was the lack of some haven where they could be safe from persecution, Boré claimed. Fortunately, "Providence offers us a natural outlet in Algeria." The important thing was that the converts not be sent to Europe because "European civilization has, among all its advantages, dangers and excesses which it is good to hide from oriental neophytes"—dangers that included "lessons in immorality and corruption."[94] Though the Council responded favorably to

Boré's proposal, allocating 20,000 francs to the Lazarists to begin the catechumenate, the work was a failure.[95]

Echoing Veuillot's polemics, Boré later blamed the "deadly prejudices" of
the July Monarchy's colonial administrators for this setback.[96] Some eight years
later—with the arrival of a new Bishop of Algiers and a new political regime—
Boré optimistically tried again, still believing the philo-Islamic idea that Muslims would be especially easy to convert because of their good faith: "The Arabs
are more sincere than the Greeks [Orthodox]."[97] Indeed, Boré's utopian view of
Muslim openness to Christian conversion had only grown. If they knew they
could apostatize from Islam safely, "The Arabs, which simple good sense, aided
by grace, has led to recognize the superiority of Christian institutions, would
lose the fear that holds them back" and would convert and become French, "saving their souls" and "rehabilitating their social position" at the same time.[98] The
refuge at Algiers would even grow into a force for reform across the entire Orient, Boré believed, since Muslim governments would be forced to offer liberty
of conscience domestically in order to prevent the mass exodus of converts.[99]

One reason Veuillot and Boré felt justified in seeking continuities between
Islam and Christianity was the commonplace that Islam was only a heresy of
Christianity. Hence, analogies between the two religions abounded.[100] For
Veuillot and Boré, of course, Islam would always be a false religion; yet its
truths—vestiges and analogies of Christianity—meant that Muslim-Christian
dialogue could be pursued, even perhaps that "Islam was not a demonic belief
but rather a 'preface to the Gospel.'"[101] In a letter Veuillot wrote from Algiers in
1841—which would form the basis for one of the concluding chapters of his book
on Algeria—he recounted a religious debate he had with a "zealous Muslim,"
which lasted "until two in the morning" and ended amicably.[102] This experience
more than any other seems to have confirmed Veuillot's "conviction that the
Muslims despise us and hate us less for being Christians than for our impiety."
After all, Veuillot's interlocutor had "an excellent soul, an upright sense, a naturally religious mind, and a predisposition to receive the truth that I have very
rarely met at Paris among the *Scholars*." Here, though, the reason for the Muslim's natural religiosity and capacity for good faith dialogue was explicit: "Islam
being nothing but a Christian heresy, there are many points of contact."[103]

Boré was also a proponent of the view that Islam's status as a Christian heresy
had created productive "points of contact." In 1836, even before his voyages gave
him firsthand experience of the Islamic world, Boré wrote an article on Islam for
the *Annales de philosophie chrétienne*, a quintessential journal of July Monarchy
Catholic apologetics that sought to publicize "whatever the human sciences . . .

contain in the way of proofs and discoveries in favor of Christianity." Boré's article was published as part of a series on "Christian Heresies" and endeavored to point out the important analogies that existed between Christianity and Islam. Boré's opening lines read almost like a frontal attack on the Maistrean idea of Islamic enmity: "It is commonly believed that Mohammedanism is opposed in all points to the Christian religion. . . . However, if we open the *Alcoran* . . . we are astonished to see . . . an appearance of kinship so striking, that Muslimism seems to be really only a bastard son of Christianity."[104] Boré noted that Muslims, as descendants of Ishmael, would certainly have retained some of the upright traditions of Abraham and that the *"Alcoran* . . . deploys a wealth and magnificence of images which recall the inspired pages of our prophets."[105] Boré's penchant for making analogies between Christianity and Islam was at its most systematic with his analysis of the relationship between Sunni and Shi'a Islam. According to Boré, the Shi'a are to Sunni Islam what Christian heretics are to Catholicism: "We see that for Muslims, as for Christians, there is only one church or communion considered orthodox. This is also the one that rests on tradition and the general authority of the faithful."[106] It was the recognition of such family resemblances and, most importantly, the specific analogy between Sunnism and Catholicism, Boré believed, that would lead Sunnis—the majority of Muslims worldwide—to return to the true, original faith of Catholicism. Since Sunnis, based on their own experiences with Shi'ism, could understand the relationship between orthodoxy and heresy, "it would be easy to prove to the orthodox church of Islam that it is itself only a branch detached from the great tree of life of the Catholic or universal church, and that all the fragments of truths that it contains are only scraps borrowed by their prophet from Judaism or Christianity."[107]

Despite the fanciful, deluded nature of these hopes for Muslim—and specifically Sunni—conversion, Boré's ideas about Sunni and Shi'a Islam would remain unfazed by his later firsthand experiences. While visiting a cemetery in the Black Sea region of central Turkey, Boré was accosted by a Sufi mystic (a "sect . . . extremely common in Persia").[108] The Sufi assured Boré that according to Sufism there was no need for him to convert from Christianity to Islam, since specific religious confessions were only the lowest level of religious development. "[T]he true believer is he who tramples the literal interpretation of the law. . . . Religion is in the thought and not in the act," the Sufi continued; "it is enough to want to love God and to unite oneself to him with a strong passion, in order to find him and to penetrate into his essence. . . . So when you are worshipping, do not say 'I' or 'me' or 'him' anymore; everything has become one."[109] True to his belief in the kinship between Sunnism and Catholicism and his attendant disdain for Shi'ism and Sufism, Boré interrupted this mystic "coldly," casting himself as a defender of orthodoxy—both Christian and Muslim orthodoxy—as he perceived it. Boré accused the mystic of "[contradicting] the unanimous faith of the human race. Can evil and good be one? Man and God merge into a single substance? No. . . . Faith and the works that fulfill it: that, according to the Gospel and the *Alcoran,* is the way to approach God."[110] Boré, the devout, practicing Catholic, reserved his respect for the most straightforwardly orthodox, practicing Muslims.

Boré's confrontation with Sufism shows the remarkable extent to which some conservative Catholic observers of Islam in the 1830s and 1840s were willing to respect the religious devotion found in Islam. For Boré as for Veuillot, Muslims who believed and practiced the basic doctrines of Islam—however corrupted those doctrines might be—were commendable inasmuch as they were people of faith and sincerity. But Boré's version, explicitly tying the image of Islamic piety and faithfulness to the Sunni branch and withholding respect from the "margins" of Islam, highlights—even more strikingly than Veuillot's—just how exceptional their view of Islam was, especially in light of later developments. As the evangelistic optimism of the first half of the nineteenth century endured failure after failure,[111] missionaries and observers alike would become convinced of the "inconvertibility of the heart of Sunnite Islam" and turn instead to Islam's "spiritual or geopolitical margins"—Alawites in Syria, Kabyles in Algeria, Shi'ites in Persia—in the hopes that such heterodox minorities would be more susceptible to conversion and cultural assimilation.[112] At the same time, orientalists from Ernest Renan to Louis Massignon and beyond were guilty of constructing an image of marginal Islam—Shi'ite, Sufi, "Indo-European" Islam—that was more approachable, more analogous to Christian, Occidental spirituality.[113] If, for these and for many Western observers of Islam today, "the only good Muslim is a bad [or heterodox] Muslim,"[114] for the conservatives Boré and Veuillot, the best Muslims were precisely those who followed Muhammad's precepts most literally and diligently.

Of Steamships and Theocracies

Veuillot's view of Islam was deeply contradictory. Despite his sympathy for Muslim unity and religiosity, his anti-Islamic rhetoric at times reached a pitch more violent and fevered than Maistre's. For one thing, he did not share Quinet's more Romantic respect for the person of Muhammad. According to Veuillot, the prophet was at best a new breed of Christian heretic, at worst a fraud and deceiver who, unlike his later adherents, was not in good faith. In contrast to Quinet, Veuillot separated Islam's admirable theocratic element from his account of the religion's origins, instead falling back on traditional anti-Islamic slurs. Muhammad's initial successes and conquests were due not to a genuine belief in coming judgment, nor to the social unity produced by this doctrine, but to the simple fact that "this Arab camel driver" promised plunder and women, appealing to humanity's basest instincts.[115] The Qur'an, like all the deceptive works of the devil, "apes" the Bible, stealing its forms in order to preach its opposite.[116] Slavery and misogyny were among the negative effects of Qur'anic teaching.[117] Islam had "plunged [Africa] into an irremediable barbarism" and had made of the Moors an "incurably stupid" and "fallen race." Indeed, if North Africa had not been drawn into the French orbit in 1830, but rather had been allowed to continue its inevitable decline for several more centuries, it would have sunk to a state analogous to that of the "degraded beings who vegetate in the solitude of the New World."[118] In stark contrast to his constant affirmations of the inherent piety and humanity of Algerian Muslims, Veuillot's reference to "New World" degradation recalls Maistre's more famous rejection of the very concept of the "noble savage," and includes Muslims in that rejection.

Worst of all, even Veuillot's admiration for Islam can be seen as cynical and entirely complicit with the violent conquest of Algeria.[119] Veuillot eagerly endorsed and echoed the mythic justification for conquest—that Algiers had been a nest of pirates tempting Christian captives to apostasy. He was in Algeria, after all, as the secretary of the governor general, accompanying him on expeditions, playing at soldier, and bragging about his newfound horseback riding skills.[120] His rhetoric of admiration for Islam was ultimately aimed not at defending Algerians against colonization but rather at bullying France's leaders into greater support for the Christianization of Algeria. His sympathy for Muslim religiosity, in other words, coexisted with his desire "to make Islam disappear."[121] Still, Veuillot's desire for a more peaceful, apostolic conquest seems to have been sincere enough. He was shaken by the sight and smell of the dead the day after a skirmish, and he was especially haunted by the image of an amputated leg. He ultimately concluded that he would rather serve Algeria as a missionary than a soldier, that he preferred the war of "ideas" to that of "sword and canon."[122] His criticisms of colonialism's damaging impact on Algerians (and his calls for a more devoutly Christian settler population) were not merely a cynical ploy to score points against the July Monarchy. He also promoted these views in his private reporting, even while still in Algeria and in Minister Guizot's employ.[123]

The inconsistencies in Veuillot's orientalism are reflective of deeper contradictions in his thought between Enlightenment models of progress and the Romantic embrace of religious feeling; between legitimations of empire based on European superiority and those based on the salvation of souls; between loyalty to France and loyalty to a spiritual community; between nationalism and ultramontanism. Veuillot's selective use of civilizational justifications for empire illustrates this ambivalence well. His account of his voyage to Algeria contains a lengthy paean to the steamship, which had rendered the crossing of the Mediterranean so much easier: "When one considers that it takes only two days to reach Africa from France, one must conclude that the last days of Islamism have come. . . . This is how Fulton, who probably hardly expected it, has served the Gospel."[124] At once guaranteeing and validating the success of France's mission, the technological superiority exemplified by the steamship counted for as much as the favor of God. Since European civilization was the product of Christianity, norms and tools that were illustrative of European superiority could be used as pragmatic defenses for missions, European practices and technologies substituted metonymically for Christian revelation. Muslim conversion was a certainty, because "the advances of civilization have made it impossible for them to believe in Mohammed."[125]

Veuillot is often portrayed as having "[detested] the innovations of the age,"[126] but when it came to justifying intervention in North Africa, Veuillot, like many French Catholics, set his traditionalism aside and pronounced the imperial password, *civilisation*.[127] By praising and invoking the steamship and French civilization in general, Veuillot identified himself with a secular view of history as a "race" to modernity, where the fastest and most powerful would get to define what the end goal was for everyone else.[128] Yet, Veuillot quoted approvingly the Muslim Algerian who mocked the France of steamships and suspension bridges. Incredibly, the steamship could—within the same text—stand for the liberating and inexorable march of French civilization as well as for the laughable hubris and hypocrisy of secular France's colonial mission. France's colonization of Algeria was justified and sure to succeed a priori on the basis of French modernity; simultaneously, it would remain nothing but an unjustified and unsuccessful aggression—a confirmation of France's own post-civilizational degradation—unless it brought Frenchmen and Arabs together and into the Christian fold.[129]

Beyond the immediate context of July Monarchy culture war and missionary Romanticism, Veuillot's two-fold rhetoric—at once appealing to France's technological superiority and to Algeria's religious superiority—may be illuminated by a consideration of his place in the longer history of nineteenth-century

French Catholicism. As French society became increasingly polarized in the nineteenth century, French Catholicism took on an apocalyptic cast, preferring apparitions and eschatological predictions over constructive engagement in the compromises of temporal politics.[130] Veuillot himself was exemplary of this process. After his journal was suppressed in the last years of the Second Empire, his writings reached a fever pitch of apocalypticism. In a diatribe against a plan to build a statue of Joan of Arc on Haussmann's new Avenue de l'Opéra, Veuillot wrote that Paris was no longer worthy of the Maid of Orléans. Since Paris stood for Revolution, irreligion, and decadence, Veuillot hoped that all statues of saints might be removed from the city.[131] Like righteous Lot fleeing Sodom and Gomorrah before the cities' biblical destruction, Veuillot believed Bernard of Clairvaux and Martin of Tours would want to leave Paris's pedestals to the saints of the Revolution. Unsurprisingly, given such biblical resonances, Veuillot went on to predict the violent destruction of "Parisian civilization" and the survival of only a righteous remnant.[132] Of course, Veuillot's desire to bring about a violent, revolutionary end—to make the boundary between good and evil clear and uncomplicated, once and for all—went against traditional understandings of Christianity's "prohibition . . . to 'set the time' of the End"[133] and against the biblical command to let the "wheat and tares" grow up together until that final judgment.[134]

Veuillot's rhetorical appeals to both "steamship" and "theocracy" betray an unstable and contradictory discourse, a sort of falling between the two stools of progress and reaction, "civilized" France and "devout" Algeria. Yet there is a kind of perverse unity in the pairing, at least when viewed through the context of French Catholicism's increasing apocalypticism. Both images appealed to Veuillot, despite their conflicting implications, perhaps because both spoke to his hope for a revolutionary Christian theocracy, to his rejection of the traditional slowness and accommodationism of institutional Catholicism, and to his more sectarian desire to see the wheat and tares separated immediately. Both the steamship and Islamic theocracy, as Veuillot appropriated them, symbolized radical new possibilities for the ubiquity of French power, for the Christian unity and uniformity of the world. Veuillot's admiration for the steamship—for the literal and historical speed that gave France the power to impose its values on others—was the flip side of his appreciation for the eschatological "speed" with which Islamic theocracy had imposed its own timeless unity. Perhaps a final reason, then, why Veuillot went beyond Maistre in his sympathy for Islam was that in the less than two decades between their writings, some French Catholics had already become more embattled, more pessimistic, and more willing to grasp at eschatological intervention. Maistre, criticizing the Revolution from the relative security of the Restoration, had affirmed Christianity's traditional, antirevolutionary gradualism, its "deferment of promises," as Quinet would say. "Christianity," according to Maistre, "which acted by Divine power, for this reason also acted gently and slowly.... Wherever there is noise, tumult, impetuosity, destruction, etc., it may be relied upon that crime or folly is at work."[135] In contrast, Veuillot—writing under an anticlerical July Monarchy that had even imprisoned him for too vehemently defending the right of a priest to lecture in a state school—no longer felt that time was on the side of the Catholic cause.[136] Instead, with Quinet, he looked to the example of Islam's revolutionary, near-immediate actualization of its ideals: "this suppression of time... this flash of lightning which at once illuminates the sky and the earth, the church and the state."

In view of how Veuillot employed these contradictory discourses, it is not surprising that his entire model for success in Algeria was impractical, to say the least. In a convoluted passage that should have made the utopian nature of his project apparent even to himself, Veuillot wrote, "The Arabs will only belong to France when they are French; they will only be French when they are Christians; [and] they will not be Christians as long as we do not know how to be Christians ourselves."[137] In order to successfully and peacefully assimilate Algeria, in other words, a decadent and nearly post-Christian France would have to return to a former stage of its own development—purging the original sin of the Revolution and rejoining Christian civilization—while at the same time bringing Algeria up to that same historical stage. Yet in arguing that France's rights over Algeria were derived in part from "civilization"—from the historical progress Christianity had brought to Europe—Veuillot subordinated Christian revelation to secular history and was left with no criterion on which to evaluate the normative endpoint of that progress.[138] He was left with no reason why a civilization should not progress beyond Christianity. The rhetorical triangulation between Muslim, Christian, and secular civilization was indeed a complicated operation.

Veuillot and his milieu's conflicted orientalism contained at its core a contradiction that would haunt Catholic encounters with Islam through the course of the nineteenth century. On the one hand, the rhetorically ambivalent use of Muslim piety to condemn metropolitan unbelief became almost a commonplace of counterrevolutionary discourse.[139] Émile Keller, legitimist Catholic deputy to the Second Empire's Corps Legislatif and theorist of Social Catholicism, claimed that, in their sincerity and loyalty to the traditional values of their society, Muslims were superior to the traitorous Rationalist and Protestant "Muslims of within."[140] Léon Gautier, a prolific Catholic apologist and historian of medieval literature, wrote that Muhammad—though a debauched, violent, hallucinatory idol-worshipper—nevertheless had the good sense to borrow heavily from Christianity and to be "full of respect for the person of Jesus Christ." Especially in his acceptance of the miracles of Christ, Muhammad demonstrated that he had undergone "divine influence."[141] In the introductory essay of *La Croix*—the Assumptionist journal founded in 1880 that would later become famous for its vocal anti-Dreyfusism—Emmanuel d'Alzon wrote that, in advocating for religious liberties such as those of public prayer and processions, he and his colleagues were only demanding what was permitted "at Constantinople." "Is it too much to ask," he quipped, "to claim a freedom *à la turque*?"[142] These apologetic versions of the trope, though, divorced from the kind of direct contact with Muslims that had inspired Veuillot and Boré, did not communicate any real sympathy for Muslim religiosity; on the contrary, the comparisons seem intended to demean Muslim and freethinker alike.

On the other hand, for many French Catholics, the lost and longed-for community of the French nation and civilization—"the eldest daughter of the Church"—would always exert a powerful temptation away from the ideal of an international community based on religion, dialogue, and conversion. Over the course of the nineteenth century, pragmatic and patriotic justifications for missions, intended to prove the efficacy of Christianity to a secularizing France, would increasingly displace traditional discourses of the salvation of souls.[143] In the context of domestic culture wars, many Catholics found it more advantageous to emphasize their patriotic alliance with the civilizing mission rather than their religious critique of it: a kind of anti-Islamic "clash of civilizations" ideology, it was believed, would unify all French of good faith. This shift was accompanied by "a more blatantly racial conceptualization of evangelizing."[144] At the same time—inspired by the new "sciences" of philology and racial demography, and ever more entangled with the pragmatic imperatives of colonial surveillance—academic orientalists and colonial ethnographers (Catholic and "free thinker" alike) began moving away from Romantic narratives of reconciliation with Islam and toward a view of Islam as a "Semitic," static object suited only for investigation and control.[145] Missionaries themselves would begin to write of Muslim Algerians in openly denigrating, racialized ways.

But before this disillusionment with philo-Islamism set in, some missionaries in the first decades of Algerian conquest would sincerely and diligently try to convert Algeria's Muslims. In the flush of missionary excitement that accompanied the conquest of Algeria, and in the environment of admiration for Islamic religiosity fostered by Veuillot, Boré, and other pro-missions culture warriors, some missionaries seemed to believe the philo-Islamic rhetoric—that the Muslims' natural devoutness would be an advantage rather than an obstacle. Missionaries did not necessarily arrive in Algeria with an ahistorical, a priori belief in Muslim fanaticism and resistance to Christianity. Some were quite optimistic about Muslim missions. It was only through concrete, personal, and sometimes deeply bitter failures to convert any Algerian Muslims that they eventually came to reject this optimistic view. When, in the waning decades of the nineteenth century, these missionaries needed an explanation for their failures, there was one at hand: the Arab race.

CHAPTER 2

God and Caesar

Missionaries and Militaires in Colonial Algeria

The commissaire civil at Constantine—one of colonial Algeria's provincial capitals—was concerned. Reporting to his superiors back in France in 1847, he described the Catholic personnel in his city. Ever since Napoleon's Concordat with the Catholic Church, churchmen in France were employees of the state: appointed, paid, and surveilled by the Ministry of Cults, to ensure their qualifications and political acceptability. The Diocese of Algiers, instituted in 1839, formed part of that hierarchy. This assimilation of the Algerian Church into metropolitan France gave French officials a measure of control over the clergy in Algeria. And in 1847, Constantine's commissaire civil, M. Lapame, felt the need to exercise that control. His complaint: "The clergy of Constantine belong entirely to the Society of Jesus." They were Jesuits.

No religious order was more symbolic of conflicts between church and state in nineteenth-century France than the Jesuits. The controversial order was a favorite target of anticlerical politicians and writers. It was often alleged that the Jesuits' real loyalty was not to France but to their superior in Rome. Because little was known of their internal organization, the Jesuits were the object of deranged conspiracy theories that greatly overestimated their actual strength, influence, and radicalism. Even under the Old Regime monarchy, in 1762, the Jesuits had been expelled from France because of their allegedly outsized influence as "a political corps" hiding "under the veil of a religious institute."[1] After the Revolution, the Jesuits began to trickle back into France, but they would continue to be feared for their political influence and intrigues and targeted by political leaders who hoped to profit from popular hatred of the Order. Under the Restoration of the Bourbon Monarchy in the 1820s, opponents of the arch-Catholic and reactionary Charles X accused the king of being a creature of the Jesuits, secretly colluding with them to reverse the liberal gains of the Revolution. One feverish conspiracy theory even had it that the Jesuits were using their *maison* at Montrouge, just south of Paris, to train a counterrevolutionary militia, and that an underground passage linked this novice-house to the king's palace at the Tuileries.[2] The Jesuits were barred from teaching in French schools in 1828; targeted throughout the 1840s by anticlerical liberals of the July Monarchy and, finally, expelled from France by the emerging Third Republic in 1880.[3] Summing up this century of anti-Jesuit polemic, French historian Jacqueline Lalouette writes: "Republicans, democrats, and anticlericals of the nineteenth century" had a "veritable obsession with the Jesuits," as evidenced "by the great number of publications, novels, essays, [and] satires directed against the famous Society." In the anticlerical mind, the Jesuits often stood for everything hated about the Catholic Church as a whole.[4]

In one sense, then, in his denunciation of the Jesuits at Constantine, the commissaire civil there was simply acting on anxieties and anti-Jesuit clichés imported from the culture wars of metropolitan France. Indeed, his first accusation was a conventional one: that the Jesuits were unpatriotic, loyal to Rome rather than to the French Church hierarchy. But there was another problem with the Jesuits at Constantine, a problem unique to the Muslim-dominated context of the Algerian colony: "They seem more occupied with the desire to propagandize in the army and indigène population than to exercise this action on the European civil population, which they hardly take care of." Even worse, since the colonial administration "finds their inclination for a General Conversion [of the Muslims] premature ... [they] set themselves up as martyrs." In other words, not only did they attempt to proselytize among the Muslim population against the colonial administration's wishes; they whined about any opposition. The commissaire ended his report by asking that the Jesuits be replaced by priests belonging to no religious order.[5] The minister of war was concerned by these revelations and received assurances from the bishop of Algiers that he would replace the Jesuits as soon as there were enough "secular" priests to fill Algeria's parishes.[6]

Missionaries' attempts to convert the Muslims of French Algeria have sometimes been minimized, on the grounds that either the colonial administration did not look favorably on such proselytization[7] or the clerics in Algeria were not truly interested in missionizing "*indigènes*"—at least until around 1870 and the missions of the White Fathers (Pères Blancs).[8] According to one recent study, missionaries and administrators alike cared more about presenting a colonial unified front against Algeria's Muslims than they did about converting Muslims to Christianity. Churchmen and colonial officials, according to this interpretation, knew better than to bring the culture wars of the metropole with them to Algeria.[9] Although there is a great deal of truth to this portrait of routine church-state cooperation in the colony, in fact, since the beginning of the Algerian conquest in the 1830s–40s, some missionaries (and their ultramontane supporters back in France) regularly clashed with colonial administrators and attempted to evangelize Algeria's Muslims.

To frame the context of the Jesuits' Arab mission, this chapter will explore the conditions of colonial Constantine in the 1840s and 1850s, when the Jesuits first arrived there. It will recount the complex dialectic of cooperation and conflict that characterized the Jesuits' relations with military and civilian authorities in the colony. Colonial authorities were not always opposed to the Jesuits and other religious congregations. Some officials were devout Catholics themselves, some were admirers of the Jesuits' scholarly or charitable efforts, and some sought to present a civilizational unified front against Muslim Algerians. Still, whenever the question of public evangelization of Algeria's Muslims arose, administrators were regularly and almost uniformly opposed to such missions.

This chapter culminates with the Jesuits' 1850 request to be permitted to live among and missionize Arab tribes that resided on military territory—lands protected from colonist encroachment—in Constantine Province. This request was transmitted by the governor general to the officers of the Bureaux arabes (Arab Bureaus), specialists in the management of the Muslim populations on military territory, and their responses were unanimously negative. Even in cases where missionaries were denied contact with Arab populations, though, they cannot simply be taken as proof that missionary aspirations did not matter. Arguments deployed by missionaries and colonial administrators in these early debates are rich in insights about how missionaries viewed Islam and how their missiological approach both coincided and conflicted with the colonial state's own secular "civilizing mission." This question of a potential Jesuit mission among the tribes in 1850 would surpass the confines of Arab Bureaus and ministerial offices and reach even to the Parliament and press of Second Republic France. The refusal of the Jesuits' mission was bitterly commented upon by ultramontane Catholics, and it became instrumentalized in larger debates about colonial policy and the place of religion in French society.

Church, Colonial State, and the Jesuits in 1840s Algeria

The story of the Jesuits in Algeria begins early on in the French conquest. They were called in as "auxiliaries" by colonial Algeria's first bishop, Monseigneur Antoine-Adolphe Dupuch, in the 1840s. In addition to serving as military chaplains, orphanage directors, and educators, as they had in France, the Jesuits were put to work by the short-handed bishop as parish priests in Constantine, the most overwhelmingly Arabic of early French Algeria's urban centers, and the same city that Abbé Suchet had first visited in 1839 and had seen as so admirably devout and patriarchal.[10] Perhaps unsurprisingly, given the famous missionary vocation (and infamous aggressiveness) of the Order, the Jesuits made attempts to launch a mission among the Muslim populations of Algeria with more frequency and with a higher public profile than other missionary congregations such as the Lazarists. In mid-nineteenth-century France, the Jesuits were the bogeymen of the anticlerical party—a flash point for debates about the place of religion in society and in education.[11] Indeed, their arrival and establishment in Algeria was carefully surveilled by authorities in France and in Algeria, and seen by many as a backdoor ploy to achieve the recognition and educational prerogatives in Algeria that they had lost in France.[12] The history of the Jesuits in Algeria is significant, on one level, simply as an illustration of the form that metropolitan culture wars could take in colonial and Muslim contexts. Hounded from anticlerical France, the Jesuits epitomized Claude Prudhomme's description of the ideological significance of nineteenth-century missions—"simultaneously a refuge . . . a Christendom transferred from Europe overseas, and a laboratory for the Christian reconquest of the metropole."[13]

But the Muslim-dominated context of colonial Algeria—combined with Algeria's special status as a settler colony, politically assimilated to the metropole—added a complicating factor that was not present in domestic debates about religious congregations. General Louis de Bourmont, upon disembarking at Algiers in 1830, had famously promised that the French invaders would leave the Algerians free to practice Islam.[14] Colonial administrators of Algeria throughout the nineteenth century worried that Catholic missionaries—especially if they were perceived by the Muslim population as having the support of the authorities—would provoke religiously motivated insurrections or jihads. In a sense, then, the Jesuits' plans and efforts to evangelize the Muslim populations of Algeria only made their rapport with colonial administrators more volatile. Conversely, the Jesuits' proselytizing efforts only increased their symbolic prestige for conservative Catholics back in France, who enjoyed accusing the July Monarchy and subsequent regimes of antimissionary obstructionism. Even in a Muslim context, France's culture wars—clericalism and anticlericalism—could be "articles for export."[15] Whatever their desire to present a unified, civilizational front in the face of colonized populations, the French could not help but bring the heterogeneity and conflicts of metropolitan modernity with them.[16]

But missionary-administrator conflicts were not simply motivated by varying levels of religious devotion or by varying commitments to the Christianization of North Africa. These conflicts were sites of competing representations of Islamic society: debates about Islam's capacity for civilization and of the role that religion—Muslim or Christian—might play in that civilizing process. The Jesuits' "Arab mission" in Algeria offers fertile ground not only for understanding domestic debates about the role of Catholicism in France, but also for understanding colonial debates about the nature of Islam.

The story of the Jesuits at Constantine suggests that French missionaries initially relied on a deeply ambiguous representation of Muslims—a philo-Islamism that was particular to mission-minded French Catholics in the first, hopeful decades of the Algerian Empire and of France's "missionary awakening."[17] According to this view, Muslims were people of great piety and faith, who would make ideal converts to Christianity; yet, simultaneously, they were fanatics incapable of coexisting with the French unless they converted. Muslim children especially could still be converted. Their natural (Muslim) capacity for religious devotion would be transferred seamlessly to Christianity, making them better Christians than many Europeans and ideal missionaries back to their own Algerian countrymen.

In addition to this kind of cautious philo-Islamism, the Jesuit mission was also informed by some of the culturally adaptive methods for which earlier Jesuit missions in India and China had been famous: attempting to respect and adopt local customs as much as possible and offering a minimally invasive version of Christian doctrine. The Jesuits were the first missionaries in Algeria to start learning and preaching in Arabic, and to translate prayers, catechisms, and songs. In Constantine, they regularly invited Arab notables to their house, shared meals of couscous and coffee, and exchanged gifts. The Jesuits encouraged their Muslim friends and students to think of them as "marabouts," Muslim holy men bearing a kind of spiritual power or charisma. Of course, this philo-Islamic sympathy and cultural adaptation could only go so far. The Jesuits' goal was to convert Muslims to Christianity, so theirs was a sympathy like Louis Veuillot's, that ironically worked in tandem with their "project to make Islam disappear."[18] But in the context of the mid-nineteenth century, where colonial administrators and jurists debated whether to culturally "assimilate" Muslims before allowing them the rights of citizenship or whether instead to allow them to maintain some measure of cultural autonomy, the missionaries' sympathetic approach placed them, perhaps unwittingly, in the more culturally respectful camp.

In 1845, French Algeria's first bishop, Monseigneur Dupuch, having spent himself into bankruptcy in his attempts to build up the new diocese, was forced to resign and unceremoniously decamp back to France to escape his creditors.[19] Attempting to deflect the blame for his failure, Dupuch addressed an open letter to the pope, summarizing his brief career in Algeria and exaggerating the extent to which he had been opposed by the colonial administration. Especially on the question of an apostolate to the Muslims, Dupuch claimed, the administration had constantly "thwarted" him. Among other things, he maintained that he had been "officially warned" not to minister to anyone but Catholics; that he had been ordered to "repress" a priest who had dared to tell a Muslim that Islam was "absurd"; and that his seminarians had even been prohibited from study- ing Arabic.[20]

While Dupuch was likely overstating the administration's opposition to de- flect the blame for his own financial failures, state archives make clear that Du- puch and other Algerian clergy were carefully surveilled by the government for any sign of evangelistic contact with Algeria's Muslims. Indeed, even the creation of a Catholic diocese in Algiers in 1839 was roundly criticized by the parliamen- tary Left in France. According to some deputies, making Algiers into a Catholic diocese risked dangerously offending Muslim consciences and allowing clerical "encroachments" and "invasions" back into French politics. Far from dismissing these fears of Catholic encroachment, the minister of justice, in defending the institution of an Algerian diocese, accepted the anticlerical terms of the debate. It was precisely because a *concordataire* (state-employed) clergy would be bound to the government in ways that missionary congregations and Rome-appointed apostolic prefects were not, the minister argued, that a French-controlled dio- cese was the right model for Algeria's pluralistic religious terrain. "We are not sending missionaries to convert the Arabs, that has to be made quite clear; we are sending a few priests and a bishop in order that the religious needs of the European population might be satisfied."[21]

Shortly after Dupuch's arrival in the new diocese, the minister of war heard that the new bishop had allowed a religious procession, the Corpus Christi, to take place outside the walls of his palace, and also that members of religious congregations were offering (unwanted) ministrations to non-Catholics in the hospital. Given the risk of "alarming" the other "cults," the minister demanded of Governor General Maréchal Valée that his administration "exercise an assid- uous surveillance" of any such events.[22] When both Bishop Dupuch and Gov- ernor General Valée responded that the procession had been insignificant, the minister of war nevertheless reiterated his general point: Paris should always be kept informed about such matters, because "in a country where religious fanaticism . . . is the main strength of our most dangerous enemy, nothing that concerns religion is unimportant."[23] Even more than the security of the colony, the minister admitted, it was the political climate of metropolitan France that had to be taken into account. As the government attempted to navigate its way through debates about the place of religion at home in France, the acts of careless clergy in Algeria might be taken up by "malevolent" left-wing observers and used against the government in the coming elections.[24]

The colonial administration was especially concerned with monitoring the presence of religious congregations in Algeria. One functionary at the Ministry of War, writing in 1846, put the department's position on religious congregations this way: "The motives [for denying official status to congregations] come down to just one: the fear of religious proselytization." Since "the need to proselytize is inherent to every Catholic congregation," the administration thought it best to simply tolerate, at its discretion, such dangerous entities, making it easier to control and expel them if need be. Female religious congregations whose members worked in hospitals and schools, and whose proselytization took place only on the individual level in the context of charitable work, might be granted authorization, since they did not engage in open preaching, and since they fulfilled a necessary social function that the state could not afford to take up. But authorizing provocative and socially useless male congregations, it was implied, was out of the question.[25]

The Ministry of War echoed the general sentiments of this report in its correspondence with the Algerian administration: even those congregations that were legally authorized in France (the Jesuits were not) should not, as a rule, be given official authorization in Algeria, so the government might be "ready to suppress immediately the abuses which could occur . . . on the pretext of charitable work."[26] Suspicion of missionary contact with Muslims was not confined to the Jesuits. The Lazarists (the "Congregation of the Mission") were also present in Algeria from early on in the French conquest. Despite their reputation for being more patriotic and less conspiratorial than the Jesuits, some Lazarists did run afoul of the administration over attempts to make evangelistic contact with Algeria's Muslims. Père Girard, a Lazarist who spent his entire career in Algeria, later reminisced that he and Algeria's bishops met with much opposition because the government "feared [Catholic] proselytization" and preferred to pander to the sensitive Arabs.[27] On one occasion, Girard was almost prosecuted for "corruption of minors," for catechizing some Algerian Muslim children without their parents' permission.[28] Girard would later leave an embittered testimony of his hopes for Muslim missions, hopes that had been dashed by both administrative obstruction and the resistance and alleged inconstancy of the Arabs themselves: "Upon arriving [in Algeria], I hoped to see the Arabs soon convert, and it has taken me fifteen years to abandon this illusion. . . . [W]ith a population without faith, with an atheistic legal regime, with a government indifferent to religion . . . what can one hope for?"[29]

This was the context into which the Jesuits inserted themselves in 1840s Algeria, a context of anxious government surveillance of any public Muslim-Christian contact, of especial suspicion toward congregations, and of "fear of religious proselytization"—to use the Ministry of War rapporteur's own words—to say nothing of the contentious and symbolic position of the Jesuits themselves in the debate then raging over religious education back in France.[30] Perhaps it should come us no surprise that when Bishop Dupuch originally called on the Jesuits to help him serve his vast, new diocese, he referred to them simply as "auxiliary priests"—because, the Jesuits' own historian tells us, "it would have been impossible to obtain the pères openly."[31] Seven Jesuits—five priests and two brothers—arrived in Algeria near the end of 1840. Two pères and one frère were sent eastward to Constantine, which had only been conquered some three years before, to serve as parish priests or military chaplains to the soldiers and colonists there. The rest stayed at Algiers, quickly taking up positions as directors of orphanages, hospital and military chaplains, and directors of various religious œuvres and associations among the colonists. The Order soon added a post in the coastal town of Philippeville, and another at Oran—the heavily Spanish-influenced provincial capital of Western Algeria. By 1849 there were already some seventy Jesuits in the colony.[32]

Among the Jesuits' ministries, the one that would take on the highest profile in these early years, at least from the perspective of the French authorities, was their orphanage at Ben-Aknoun, near Algiers.[33] After 1842, when Dupuch entrusted his diocese's orphanage to the Jesuits, its director was the ambitious Père Ferdinand Brumauld. Brumauld was soon caring for some two hundred children with the help of several other Jesuits. Other Jesuits in Algeria would grow to resent Brumauld's autocratic style or to disapprove of the extent to which this orphanage swallowed the resources of the Order and took priority over other ministries, but Brumauld knew how to maintain good relations with the military authorities for the use of government property and finances.[34] General Bugeaud, governor general of Algeria throughout the early and mid-1840s, especially respected and admired Brumauld and the orphanage. Brumauld's various utopian projects for populating Algeria with orphans-turned-farmers seem to have caught the imagination of the general.[35] The social utility of the orphanage and the goodwill Brumauld had garnered among colonial authorities would shield the Jesuits from anticlerical attacks emanating from France.[36]

In 1844, an article in the *Journal des Débats* exposed the presence of the Jesuits in Algeria and charged that they had already taken control of the diocesan *petit séminaire*, that they enlisted children in a secret congregation and used them to spy on the public school, and even that they supported royalist conspiracies in the colony, in favor of the ousted Bourbon dynasty.[37] Alarmed, the minister of cults wrote to the minister of war, reminding him that the "Jesuits' houses existing in France are watched with great attention by the government" and that it was illegal for them to involve themselves in education—even clerical (seminary) education. He asked the minister of war to verify the details of the story and even suggested that the Jesuits be banned entirely from Algeria.[38] The minister of war transmitted these concerns to Governor General Bugeaud and to the procureur general of Algiers.

It was only at this point that Bugeaud discovered that his friend Brumauld was a Jesuit. Despite his surprise, Bugeaud still defended the Jesuits.[39] General Bugeaud responded to the Ministry of War, acidly, that the *Débats* article had been sent in by a jealous educator. The General mocked the absurd idea that a political conspiracy of any kind could take place in a colony surrounded by Arab enemies, a colony entirely dependent on the metropole for survival.[40] Finally, Bugeaud launched into a glowing description of Brumauld's orphanage, explaining that it served a vital function that the administration could not yet afford to take up on its own and that its pedagogy, both vocational and religious, was entirely unobjectionable.[41]

Authorities back in France were not so sanguine. The Ministry of War went so far as to send someone to Algeria to investigate. This functionary complained that the Jesuits must have found out about his confidential mission and abruptly sent their seminarians back to the bishop, feeling more legally secure on the terrain of orphanage work alone. Unable to catch them in the act of education, he nevertheless gave a full, alarmist report on the number and functions of the Jesuits in Algeria. He concluded that the governor general's appreciation of their usefulness was irrelevant; as a "question of legality and social order," the Jesuits should not even be allowed to operate an orphanage.[42] Throughout the duration of the July Monarchy, authorities in Paris would worry about the presence of the Jesuits in Algeria—and the possibility that the Jesuits were seeking a back door to the official recognition that had been denied them in France. In the context of the July Monarchy's culture war, the administration's view of the Jesuits in

Algeria had been fixed: "It is a notorious fact in Algeria that [Brumauld's orphanage] at Ben-Aknoun served as a mask for the installation of the Jesuits."[43]

But Brumauld's orphanage and the Jesuits in Algiers were oriented almost exclusively toward the European population. These early accusations against them were driven more by general anti-Jesuit sentiment and by anticlerical education laws back in metropolitan France than by any uniquely colonial fears of proselytization to Muslims.[44] It was at Constantine, far to the eastern interior of the country, that the Jesuits felt most deeply their contact with Algeria's Muslim populations and their obligation to missionize these wayward offspring of Abraham.

"True Descendants of Ishmael": Colonial
Constantine as Mission Field

The choice of Constantine as a possible center for a wider missionary effort was not a random one, nor was it due exclusively to the aspirations of the Jesuits there. Geographically and demographically, the city seemed ideal for a mission. Conquered by the French in 1837, Constantine, the capital of Algeria's eastern province, was a crossroads to the east, and Tunisia, and to the south, with its plains and desert.[45] The precolonial city was a center of Turkish administration and a "flourishing *entrepôt* between Tunis and the Sahara, trading gold and silver thread, embroidered clothing, gilded pipes, perfumes, ostrich feathers . . . silk from Syria, precious fabric from Constantinople, and moka coffee."[46]

The shock of France's invasion and colonization transformed the social and demographic composition of Algeria's cities drastically, as expropriated Algerians migrated out of cities like Algiers and European populations quickly achieved a majority there.[47] Constantine survived an initial French attack, but in 1837 a second expedition breached the city's walls and subjected its people to violence and plunder the survivors would remember for generations: women and children fell to their deaths attempting to flee down the rock-perched city's iconic ravine.[48] But while it is true that Constantine, like Algiers, saw its religious endowments confiscated, many of its mosques and chapels appropriated,[49] and its indigenous population decrease in the days after French occupation, the city was exceptional in retaining an overwhelmingly Arab population and much of its precolonial layout (see figure 2.1).[50] For one thing, to maintain the "Arab . . . character" of the city as a symbol of France's paternal care for its new subjects, Governor General Bugeaud ordered European settlers to cease buying up property in Constantine's "indigenous quarter."[51]

FIGURE 2.1. "Constantine in 1837." From Ernest Mercier, *Histoire de Constantine* (Constantine: J. Marle et F. Biron, 1903). Courtesy Bibliothèque nationale de France.

Both before and after the French conquest, the province of Constantine maintained strong traditions of influential Muslim religious confraternities and ongoing contacts with the seats of Muslim learning farther east.[52] The small number of European colonists made the creation of an alternative, European city center unfeasible.[53] Even when European immigration into the city picked up in the 1850s and 1860s, Constantine's unique topography, perched like an "eagle's nest"[54] on the *"Rocher"* (Rock) and bounded by cliffs on three sides, limited development and transformation (see figure 2.2). French planners could not simply expand the city by annexing neighboring communes, nor could they reduce the traditional city center to a peripheral, ghetto-like *casbah* by building a new, European city, as they had at Algiers. To be sure, there was no shortage of "symbolic violence" in the French takeover of Constantine, with Arab homes

FIGURE 2.2. "View of a Part of Constantine." From Ernest
Mercier, *Histoire de Constantine* (Constantine: J. Marle et F.
Biron, 1903). Courtesy Bibliothèque nationale de France.

demolished, the principal mosque transformed into a church, and—with the
arrival of the first civilian settlers in the mid-1840s—a measure of segregation
imposed between the French and Arabs.[55] Still, the minority Europeans, though
they had their own *quartier*, were forced to live in close proximity to a large Arab
population.[56] It was only in the last third of the century that European architecture, facades, and urban planning became predominant, and that homogenously
European *faubourgs* began expanding beyond the ancient city center.[57]

From the very first, Algerian clerics viewed Constantine as a more fertile
mission field than Algiers. In addition to demographic and urban factors, this
may also have been because, at a time when much of Algeria was ignited by
Abd-el-Kader's rebellion in the west, the traditional aristocracy of Constantine
in the east had allied with (and been propped up by) the French.[58] Abbé Jacques
Suchet was delegated by Bishop Dupuch to travel to the newly-conquered Constantine in 1839 and establish the Catholic religion there. Suchet was especially
struck by the religiosity and receptivity of the population: "The Arabs come in
droves to our ceremonies. . . take holy water and kneel like us, and also move
their lips when they see us pray. They are very curious."[59] Muslim notables, even,
attended Suchet's services and asked him many questions about the Christian
religion. Like Louis Veuillot, Suchet wrote, "Truly the dispositions of these good
Arabs, the respect, the affection that they bear for priests and nuns astonishes us

and fills us with admiration."[60] The contrast with Algiers—already much more of a European settler colony, and much less of a missionary outpost—was unavoidable: "Monseigneur [Dupuch], who has just left us to return to Algiers, is delighted [with the receptivity of Constantine's Arabs]; he told me that he thought he was dreaming, since the things he saw seemed so incredible."[61]

The comparison between colonized, jaded Algiers and the virgin soil of Constantine was a theme that would continue throughout Suchet's letters, as well as in the writings of the Jesuits assigned there in the decades to come. For missionaries, this theme was linked, implicitly and sometimes explicitly, to the philo-Islamic conviction that sincere Muslim religiosity was superior to "civilized" religious indifference—the conviction that bringing European civilization and customs without Christianization would be a loss for these religious noble savages. Upon learning that he had been appointed one of Dupuch's vicar generals, and thus recalled to Algiers, Suchet wrote that he preferred to "stay at Constantine," with "my good Arabs." In contrast to the urbanized "Moors" of Algiers—corrupted by contact with European civilization—these Arabs of the inland were "true descendants of Ishmael; they have pure and completely patriarchal values."[62] And if "Moors" were bad, the Europeans themselves were even worse. Suchet seems to have believed that the main factor in determining a city's ripeness for missionary work was the presence or absence of irreligious French settlers: "If the province of Constantine is the best in the whole colony, that is because it has fewer *colons*."[63] The Jesuits and other Catholic observers of missions in Algeria would continue to evoke this tension—between the unspoiled mission field of Constantine, and Europeanized (and thus already post-Christian) Algiers; between the civilization of the metropole, simultaneously the fruit but also the corruption of Christianity, and the noble naïveté of these "true descendants of Ishmael."

The first two Jesuits accredited by Dupuch to serve as parish priests arrived in Constantine in December 1840—Père Lasserre as curé, and Père Brumauld tasked with serving surrounding outposts of European colonists.[64] Like all French clergymen serving "secular" state functions in Algeria, they were supposed to focus their efforts on the European populations and, in the heavily-garrisoned Constantine, on the spiritual needs of the soldiers.[65] Indeed, Lasserre as much as admitted to his superior at Lyon that, since there were only five or six hundred European colonists, who had not exactly "come to Africa out of piety," his work among the soldiers took up the largest part of his time.[66] As for the Muslim population, which was nearly ten times the European civilian population, Lasserre was initially more skeptical than Suchet, writing that "in addition to [our] ignorance of their language, an insurmountable obstacle to all good will, I do not believe the moment [has] come for their conversion.... After all the nice things that have been said about their dispositions toward Christianity, I am not quite convinced.... The Arabs are naturally dishonest; they easily deceive Frenchmen with poetic imaginations."[67] The Arabs' interest in Christian tableaux and medals, Lasserre claimed, was motivated only by wonder and greed, and they retained a fanatical devotion to their marabouts and a concomitant hatred for Christians. "The mercy of God has not yet come for this unfortunate people. It will come, I am sure of it...but little by little and imperceptibly."[68]

In casting himself as a realist, though, Lasserre's letter confirms the currency of such views among Catholic observers of Algerian Muslims. Lasserre's recommendation to postpone missionary efforts likewise implies that expectations of a *mission arabe* were inescapable for the Jesuits at Constantine. In 1844, an Arabic-speaking *père* from the Jesuit mission in Syria arrived to make some attempts at proselytization, and two scholastics were sent from France to direct the colonists' primary school and to devote themselves to study of the Arabic language.[69] But not until 1847, with the arrival of the Arabic-speaking Jean-Baptiste Creuzat as curé of Constantine, did opportunities for Muslim-Christian contact begin to proliferate. By 1848, Creuzat was preaching in Arabic to a "rather numerous" audience every Sunday.[70] In 1848 Bishop Pavy also entrusted the curé of Sétif, west of Constantine, to the Society of Jesus, thereby setting the stage for the Arabic-speaking Père Schembri's visits to the surrounding tribes. Despite Schembri's lack of success in establishing meaningful contacts (due, he claimed, to the opposition of the military authorities there), the hope remained that Constantine might become a "center from which missionaries might spread far around."[71]

The year 1850 would be a pivotal one for these early Jesuit attempts at a *mission arabe*—a year ripe with hopes and plans, but also full of disappointments. The efforts of Creuzat and the other Jesuits at Constantine seemed to be bearing fruit. Bishop Pavy visited Constantine in 1848 and, according to Jesuit historian Jules Burnichon, what Pavy saw in this city, "the citadel of Islamism in Algeria, had filled him with hope. While at Algiers the administration had placed a sentry at the door of Notre Dame des Victoires, to prevent the Muslims from entering,[72] [the Muslims] of Constantine crowded into the church, more numerous than the Christians themselves, and to satisfy them, it had become necessary to translate into Arabic the litanies of the Holy Virgin and other prayers, which they sang to tunes in use at the mosque."[73] Pavy also observed Creuzat preaching in Arabic.[74] The following year, Creuzat wrote in a cautiously optimistic letter that the mission would be slow-going, but as long as missionaries did not aggressively "rail against the *Coran*" because "this would be to lose all their confidence and to become unable to help them," he could always find opportunities to educate and teach Muslims to appreciate Christian dogma: "Generally, the *'ulama* [*eulamas*] admit that it is praiseworthy to study the Gospel."[75]

These allusions to the regular use of Arabic and even the borrowing of traditional Muslim tunes for Catholic liturgies afford a tantalizing glimpse of the Jesuits' methods at this early juncture. Jesuit missionaries in earlier periods, notably Matteo Ricci in China and Robert de Nobili in Madurai (India), had been famous for attempting to respect and adapt Christian doctrine to local customs as much as possible.[76] Some scholars have suggested that nineteenth-century Jesuits avoided the kind of cultural accommodation practiced by earlier Jesuit missionaries, whether out of fear of finding themselves again under papal condemnation, or perhaps simply as a reflection of the increasing conservatism of nineteenth-century Catholicism.[77] Such suggestions are reductive in their view of nineteenth-century Catholicism, which though explicitly "antimodern" in many ways, was plural and always in the process of selectively modernizing. More than that, this view underestimates the extent to which the missionary encounter tends by its very nature to relativize religion and to call forth a measure of dialectical adaptation. For the Jesuits in Algeria, "inculturation" was an ideal toward which they still strove. In 1847, Père Jordan, the superior of Algeria's Jesuits, had outlined his vision for a potential *mission arabe*, describing the Arabs as the "great purpose of our mission in Africa" and recommending "a means similar to that [used by] P. Nobili in the Indies: to live among the Arabs, to take up their customs."[78]

Parallel to the efforts of Creuzat at Constantine, Jesuits at Algiers established a seminary near Brumauld's Ben-Aknoun that was devoted to "the study of Arabic and the teaching of French to the indigènes," who were "touched . . . by the care that the *pères* [took] to treat them after the fashion of their country."[79] Brumauld himself visited the Council of the Association for the Propagation of the Faith in Lyon to seek an allocation for this seminary, which the Jesuits hoped could become a training ground for candidates destined for other Arabic-speaking countries. The Association's Council was not optimistic about the chances of success. "The *pères* of the Society do good in Algeria," the Council noted, "But the conversion of the Arabs will be the work of forbearance, of patience, and of charity, if it is even possible. The lack of effect of Christianity on Mohammedanism is a mystery."[80] Nevertheless, the Association offered a measure of financial support to the seminary and to the Jesuits' hopes for increasing contact with the surrounding Arabs. This seminary, however, lasted no more than three months. Its brief duration may be attributed to several issues: the *pères* tasked with directing it could not agree on its exact purpose and missiological method; Brumauld's heart seems not to have been in it, and he may even have cynically viewed the seminary as a pretext to get more funding for his orphanage; and finally, perhaps, Bishop Pavy resented that he was not informed of this new ministry in his diocese and that his own allocation of funds from the Propagation of the Faith was reduced in order to support it.[81]

Whatever the financial or interpersonal reasons for the failure of the seminary at Algiers, the more interesting revelation is that the Jesuits were themselves divided in their views of Muslim potential for conversion and how best to overcome the Muslim challenge. Those Jesuits who believed most in the *mission arabe* and who had entered into sustained contact with Muslims were convinced of the merits of a culturally accommodationist approach—"to treat them after the fashion of their country." For Père Baulard, the director of the short-lived seminary and one of the most vocal supporters of Muslim missions, the Jesuits at Brumauld's orphanage were not focused enough on the necessary preparation—study of the Arabic language and customs—since they were too absorbed by their own work with orphans. At the other extreme, some wanted the mission and large-scale contact with Muslim tribes to come all at once.[82] The following year, a dejected Baulard complained that all the *pères* seemed to be "in agreement that there [was] nothing to be done" for the Arab mission, and he even accused a fellow Jesuit of refusing to baptize an Arab and of referring to the Arabs as a "cursed nation."[83]

In 1853, a second catechumenate near Ben-Aknoun was attempted, funded by the pious Baroness de Coppens and directed by Baulard and the German Jesuit Père Meyer. Again, the catechumenate was closed after only a short time. Brumauld, the controversial orphanage director, sent a report to his superiors in France criticizing the catechumenate's approach to Arab missions. Brumauld argued that the best way to convert Algerian Muslims was first to re-Christianize Algeria's Europeans, as his orphanage purported to do, so that the Muslims would have true models of Christianity to emulate.[84] Until then, Brumauld maintained, it was better to leave the Muslims alone. Brumauld was far from alone in prioritizing ministry to Europeans; most clerics in Algeria concentrated on the European, settler population.[85] Brumauld may have sincerely believed in this strategy, but he also may have hoped to consolidate the power of his own European-focused institution. Indeed, when his advice was followed and the catechumenate for Muslims was suppressed, his orphanages absorbed the funding as well as the fledgling catechumenate's few Algerian students.

In the wake of this disappointment for the more mission-minded Jesuits, Père Meyer wrote a defense of the methods of the catechumenate and included a scathing critique of Brumauld. Meyer claimed that the Jesuits who had experience working with Algeria's Muslims agreed that the Muslims' education and evangelization must happen separately and distinct from European models, following the famous example of the Jesuit "reductions," the hinterland missions in eighteenth-century Paraguay. Meyer insisted, "In order to succeed it [is] necessary to know the Arabs, to speak their language . . . to raise their children not *à la française* or *à l'Européenne* . . . but after the fashion of the country, it [is] necessary to conserve their customs, their language and only change their beliefs and their *mœurs*." This was the accommodationist model advocated by Jordan, Baulard, and Meyer. Following the suppression of the Muslim catechumenate and its absorption into Brumauld's European settler-focused orphanage, the remaining Muslim children found this "completely French education" was ill-adapted to their needs. Some asked to leave; others simply snuck away.[86]

The 1850 Proposal for a "Mission among the Tribes"

Though Bishop Pavy had felt some resentment about the Jesuits' unilateral attempt at an Arab seminary at Ben-Aknoun, he remained encouraged by Père Creuzat's progress among the Muslims of Constantine, "the citadel of Islamism in Algeria," and by the good reports brought back from Père Schembri's work around Sétif. Inspired by the seeming openness of the Muslims at and around Constantine—those Muslims most preserved from unhealthy contact with godless Europeans—Pavy agreed to speak to the colonial authorities on the Jesuits' behalf.[87] In 1850, the same year as the first unsuccessful attempt at an "Arab Seminary" near Ben-Aknoun, Pavy made an official request to the government for a Jesuit Arabic mission among the tribes on the military territories surrounding Constantine.[88] Pavy addressed his proposal for the mission directly to the minister of war, asking that the Jesuits be permitted, "to begin . . . under my personal responsibility, [an Arabic Mission] in the tribes of the province of Constantine." No other congregation, Pavy added, "can successfully do what they are capable of in this *genre*."[89] As motivation for his request, Pavy cited his Christian desire to see the Arabs converted. However, in an effort to prove his patriotism to this military audience, he also emphasized the pragmatic, political benefits of conversion: since Islam teaches interminable war with Christians, no assimilation of the Muslims would be possible without their conversion. The Jesuits were ready to begin their apostolate, but they were asking for three guarantees from the

government: "(1) that the Arab Bureaus raise no opposition to their communication with the tribes; (2) that the military leaders look on them sympathetically
and favor them"; and (3) that the government give them a house at Constantine
as a base of operations.[90]

Minister d'Hautpol responded that such a sensitive political question would
have to be put to the officers of the Arab Bureaus, the military specialists in
indigenous affairs who administrated Algeria's tribal territories.[91] Algeria's governor general at the time, the Baron Viala Charon, sent a *circulaire* around to
his provincial bureau chiefs, who in turn transmitted it to their local subdi-
visions and *cercles*, asking for their views on the Jesuit proposal. The resulting
responses from these officers ranged from polite respect for Pavy's sincerity to
open anticlericalism. Some focused on the pragmatic side of the question, while
others waxed philosophical. But the officers' responses were unanimously negative. The officers' reports show how entrenched the military administration's
position against missions was. Perhaps more importantly, the reports reveal a
kind of institutional orthodoxy that Arab Bureau officers shared: on Islam and
its capacity to civilize, on the relationship between Christianity and Islam, and
on the role of religion in the civilizing process.

The officers' objections to the mission were often expressed in terms of the
concern that missionaries would provoke unrest and jihad, like Bu Ziyan's revolt
at the southern oasis of Zaatcha that had been bloodily repressed only the year
before.[92] Such concerns were premised on the idea that the Muslims were, at least
for the moment, helplessly, irrationally fanatical. The officers were also afraid of
losing the slight progress which their own civilizing initiatives—such as vacci-
nations, judicial reform, and schools—had made. Over and above these particular reasons, though, stood the unique institutional role, sociological make-up,
and ideology of the Arab Bureaus. The Arab Bureau officers were motivated by
the desire to protect their exclusive status as mediators between France and the
Algerians, and they were firmly rooted in Saint-Simonian notions of historical
progress and of Islam's place therein.[93]

Saint-Simon's social thought, as filtered through Prosper Enfantin and his co-
terie of followers at the École polytechnique, was widespread among Bureau officers, many of whom had been students together there.[94] For some among these
Saint-Simonian "apostles of modernity," Algeria was a chance to construct an
ideal society, an "alternative modernity" that would reconcile East and West.[95]
Above all, the historicism of Saint-Simon—his belief that societies progressed in
stages, but not necessarily along identical tracks—disposed his followers in Algeria's military administration to prefer "association" (indirect rule and sensitivity

to Algerian customs) over "assimilation."[96] Algeria had been "divided into civilian, mixed, and military territories" in 1845, and in the years following, the officers who managed the military territories began compiling massive reports on Algeria and its populations that would guide subsequent policy. By 1850, when they were called upon to set down their views on the Jesuit mission, the officers were beginning to enter a period of "ascendance" in French colonial policy-making: Ismaÿl Urbain, the Saint-Simonian convert to Islam, would eventually gain the ear of Napoleon III and directly inspire the protectionist, "Arabophile" policies of the emperor throughout the 1860s.[97] Urbain crystallized the culturally protectionist beliefs of the Arab Bureaus in a remarkable book published in 1860, entitled *L'Algérie pour les Algériens* (Algeria for the Algerians). According to Urbain, "It is not a matter of knowing if the Muslims will one day become Christians... we only want to establish that it is not impossible to make them French.... [E]very race, every people, every man as it were, departs from a specific point and goes toward a specific goal."[98]

One officer at the Philippeville Arab Bureau gave lucid expression to the Bureaus' worldview in his reaction to the Jesuits' 1850 missions proposal. Since, at their current educational and civilizational level, indigenous Algerians would not even understand what the Jesuits were trying to teach them, the officer wrote, "Let us develop therefore the faculties of the Arabs by a religious education in keeping with the dictates of the *Coran*, for in following [those dictates] with understanding, one finds the principles of all good. Let us force the Muslims to practice them . . . and we will have done more to lay the foundations of the Christian faith than all the preaching" with its inevitable "trouble and disorder."[99] In the Saint-Simonian worldview of these officers, Islam was appropriate to the social and moral level of Algeria's Muslims and, properly followed, could serve as a prelude to modernity just as well as Christianity had served to civilize Europeans.

The harshest critic of the potential mission, whose response was sent along to Charon but summarized more tactfully by his subdivisional commander at Bône, was an officer by the name of Devoluet: "I consider the idea of the conversion of the Arabs as a utopia, and if this were the occasion . . . I would seek to prove that the dogma of the *Coran* is simpler, more sympathetic to the senses of the Arabs than Catholic dogma. I would show the Catholic faith losing ground every day in Europe and forced to come plunge its dull weapons into the sands of Africa." The only fruit of this utopian delusion would be martyrdom.[100] Devoluet's furious anticlericalism made him something of an outlier in the responses: most Arab Bureau officers were not against the eventual assimilation of Algeria's

Muslims to something approximating European and even "Christian" civilization. Yet he and other Saint-Simonians viewed Islam, properly understood, as a
legitimate stage of development along a path to an "alternative modernity" that
would fuse the best of Orient and Occident.[101] From this perspective, aggressive
Catholic proselytization was a delusory attempt to transplant the particular, or-
ganically developed values of one culture into the alien ground of another.

Finally, in their responses to the 1850 proposal, many Arab Bureau officers
in the province of Constantine also criticized the fact that Catholic priests had
seemingly been unable to convert any Muslims in the cities of the civilian territories, despite having preached Catholicism "for more than thirteen years . . . in
complete freedom!"[102] Should not city-dwelling Muslims, who were more "enlightened," be easier to convert?[103] The subdivisional commander at Bône, one of
Constantine Province's main coastal cities, took this line of argument in another
direction, putting his finger on the reason why missionaries had optimistically
deceived themselves—"The Arabs have respect and consideration for everything
that is religious"—before presenting his counterarguments: The Muslims of the
province of Constantine had been less influenced or corrupted by "conquest and
civilization" than those of the other provinces, and they "[followed] the precepts
of their religion with more regularity. . . . The Arabs are not idolaters, they have
an even more extensive religion than our own. They cling to it even more than
the majority of those who bear the name of Christian do to theirs." For this
reason, he added in a gratuitous parting shot, the Jesuits would do better to concentrate on restoring the religious practice of their fellow European settlers, or
even on attempting to convert the "Israelites," since neither of these populations
would pose security risks.[104]

It is interesting that this officer put his finger on the missionaries' alleged failure to convert Algeria's "Israelites." Given the place of Jews in French Algeria's
racial hierarchy, the Jesuits' conspicuous neglect of Algeria's Jews placed them
at odds with the priorities of the civilizing mission and may indeed reveal some
latent anti-Semitism on the missionaries' part. Though many Jewish Algerians
participated in a wider North African culture, consuming "Arab" food, dress,
music, and—like Algerian Muslims—practicing polygamy, colonial leaders and
ideologues chose to ignore these facts and portray Jews as distinct and higher on
the racial hierarchy than Arabs.[105] According to this colonialist "mythology,"
Algeria's Jews had been persecuted and degraded by the Muslims and were in
need of French liberation and protection. In their gratitude to their French benefactors, they would be more susceptible to assimilation, worthier of citizenship
than the Muslims, and would become "useful allies" in the pacification of the

country.[106] Like the similar claim that Algeria's women needed to be protected, liberated, and unveiled by French dominance, the myth of Algerian Jews' oppression under Islam functioned as a "colonial hierarchy" that "[helped] to justify a wider system of exclusion" and colonialism itself.[107] The sticking point was that no "*indigène*"—Jew or Muslim—would be allowed the rights of citizenship unless they agreed to submit to French "personal status law": agreed, in other words, to renounce polygamy, divorce, and the religious courts that regulated family law and inheritance. Yet hardly any Jews or Muslims were willing to renounce the "personal status law" of their respective religions, until Algeria's Jews had citizenship forced upon them en masse by the Crémieux decree.[108]

In the officers' emphasis on the failures of missions in the cities of the civil territory, they were taking their cue from Governor General Charon's initial request for their opinions. Charon had set the tone for the responses by asking the officers to use missionary success or failure in the cities as an indicator of what might be expected among the tribes.[109] And yet this framing of the question—where the missionaries' failure to convert "enlightened," urban Muslims would inevitably translate into a similar failure among military-administered tribes—was a gross misunderstanding of the Jesuits' strategy. It was also a misunderstanding of the clear similarities between the missionaries' proposed method and that of the Arab Bureaus' own civilizational project. What the military administration saw as an obstacle to missions—that the Muslims surrounding Constantine were less touched by "civilization" and therefore less willing to give up their religious practices—was likely what the Jesuits imagined would be key to their success. It was the Muslims of the rural tribes, with their presumed simplicity and piety, who the Jesuits hoped would make ideal converts.

Distinguishing sharply between the Jesuits' religious mission and the officers' civilizing mission—the former culturally invasive, the latter culturally protective—underestimates the Jesuits' commitment to philo-Islamism and culturally adaptive methods. These Jesuit missionaries shared the philo-Islamic admiration and envy for Muslim religiosity expressed by Veuillot, Boré, Suchet, and others. Encouraged by the apparent religiosity of Algeria's Muslims, some missionaries even viewed Islam—in a sense similar to the views of Bureau officers—as a possible step toward rather than away from Christianity and civilization. Behind their mutual opposition and competing goals, the Bureau officers and the Jesuit missionaries in fact had surprisingly similar visions for the future of Algerian Islam and for how best to usher in that future. Much like the military officers of the Arab Bureaus, the Jesuits put less stock in their influence over the supposedly atomized, uprooted Muslims of Algeria's cities, who had grown callous and corrupt through contact with European colonists. Much like the officers—with their military territories and civilizing experiments—the missionaries wished for a "hinterland" mission, where they might serve as the sole interpreters of French civilization, the sole mediators of French modernity and power.[110] A "utopia" this may have been, as the officer Devoluet perceptively accused, but only in the sense that the officers' own Saint-Simonian, Romantic model of civilization-by-association was itself a utopia.[111]

Despite these similarities between their culturally protectionist intentions, the approaches of the Arab Bureaus and the proposed Jesuit mission could not have been further apart. Of course, the officers rejected the missionary argument that conversion to Christianity was a necessary stage toward the civilization and political assimilation of Muslim Algerians. The governor general even pointed to the historic example of Muslim civilization in Spain to prove that Muslims could be civilized without ceasing to be Muslims. But behind this pragmatic disagreement was a deeper ideological one: the military administration aimed to secularize Algerian Islamic society—to leave Islam intact but to interiorize and domesticate it. By contrast, what the philo-Islamic missionaries most admired about Algerian Islam—and what, to them, was most worth saving in indigenous society—was the all-encompassing social force of religion.

Governor General Charon finally responded to the minister of war's question about the Jesuit tribal mission in January of 1851, summarizing his Arab Bureau officers' various objections to the mission—an "idea so completely outside of [the ideas] which have until now dictated our policy . . . vis-à-vis the Arabs." He stressed the Muslims' fanatical attachment to their religion and argued that this was why, whatever other aspects of Algerian society the French might overturn—whatever lands the French expropriated or customs they suppressed—they must always leave the Muslims the personal practice of their religion—since it was their only possession which had "remained . . . sheltered from every attack." The Muslims needed to be taught that France's economic, military, or civilizational dominance would always be kept separate from the question of religion, to be taught that "religion is independent of the temporal power." Their "submission will only be definite on the day when we have completely persuaded the indigènes that, while protecting our interests, we will do no harm to their religious belief," and that their "personal belief" will be respected.[112] Submission would only be complete, in other words, when Algerian Islam had been "secularized"—when it had accepted the French colonial administration's own definition of what counted as "religion" and what did not.[113]

Nothing could have been more at odds with the Jesuit (and ultramontane Catholic) vision of Algeria's future, where Muslims, though converted to Christianity, would still retain their "Muslim" religious fervor and be organized into theocratic settlements led by Jesuit missionaries. At the very moment when—in the wake of the *Mahdi* Bu Ziyan's apocalyptic revolt the year before—the military administration and Arab Bureaus were more suspicious than ever of marabout and Sufi models of piety and "socioreligious" leadership and more concerned than ever to surveil and contain these local saints, the Jesuits were fervently hoping that Algerian Muslims might think of them as marabouts, with all the political and religious authority that entailed.[114] Charon, in his summary to the minister of war, had warned that even if the Jesuits were somehow successful in converting large numbers of Muslims, this would not decrease but rather exacerbate colonial violence, since Christian and Muslim "Sharifs" would then wage "holy war" against each other. In Charon's view, "the Arab"—even once converted to Christianity—could still not resist his own fanatical, irrational attachment to jihad.[115] Algeria's military administrators in the 1850s and 1860s seemed to believe paradoxically that Islam was in need of privatization but also that Muslims were almost biologically incapable of being anything but fanatical.[116] Jesuit missionaries and their supporters would have disagreed with Charon's negative assessment, but in a sense they were counting on this very possibility: that Muslim "fanaticism" and fervor would remain, even once converted to Christianity. But blocked by Algeria's military administrators, the Jesuits were never given the chance to attempt this tribal mission.[117]

The question of a Jesuit mission on Algeria's protected tribal lands surpassed the confines of the Arab Bureaus and ministerial offices and became instrumentalized in larger parliamentary and journalistic debates about colonial policy and the place of religion in French society. The debate about the best way to missionize or "civilize" Muslims—whether Christianity was a necessary stage of progress toward civilization or whether Christianity was wholly unnecessary to the process—was a sensitive question in the colony in part precisely because it was a terrain of intense apologetic and political debate back in metropolitan France.[118]

For one thing, the question of a Jesuit mission among Algeria's Muslim tribes pitted Catholic against Catholic in an internecine battle between the conservative-ultramontane wing of French Catholicism and those who were more liberal or simply more cautious and pragmatic. These larger divisions resembled the local tensions between the ultramontane Jesuits and state-employed ecclesiastics like Algeria's Bishop Pavy. When one devout colonist and missionary supporter accused the bishop of being in the colonial administration's pocket, obstructing the Jesuits and other missionaries and concentrating only on his European parishioners, Pavy and this pro-Jesuit critic fought out their battle in the pages of Veuillot's influential *L'Univers*.[119] Pavy proved adept at a kind of rhetorical double-game, emphasizing his commitment to Muslim missions whenever he needed funds from the Association for the Propagation of the Faith and other supporters of missions, but avoiding the subject when addressing larger, mainstream colonial and metropolitan audiences.[120]

Beyond the debate between Bishop Pavy's supporters and critics, in the broader context of France's culture wars, the refusal of the Jesuits' tribal mission set conservative Catholics against both mainstream Catholics and Republican anticlericals. During parliamentary debates on Algeria's religious budget, Émile Barrault, a Republican deputy representing Algeria, revealed the story of the Jesuits' request to evangelize the Muslims in Algeria's "cities of the interior." This plan was just one more sign of the "Church's and religious corporations' system ... of invasion in Algeria." Barrault claimed that although the government had had the "wisdom to refuse" Pavy's request for a Jesuit mission, it felt obliged to concede more land and funds for the bishop's other projects as a kind of consolation prize.[121] The General d'Hautpol, minister of war and former governor general of Algeria, disingenuously denied such accusations, claiming that only a "mental aberration" would lead one to think the Muslims could be converted to Catholicism: "no one is thinking of [the conversion of the Arabs], no one is asking for it."[122]

L'Univers, Louis Veuillot's ultramontane journal, published the text of this debate, along with indignant commentary; but what angered the journal's staff most was not Barrault or other anticlerical deputies' opposition to the Jesuits. Rather, *L'Univers* decried the fact that not even the parliamentarians on the Right had supported the idea of a Jesuit mission in Algeria. Instead, even on the Right, the deputies had "applauded" d'Hautpol's assurances that no one was attempting the conversion of the Arabs. Even these conservative deputies had affirmed their respect for "religious freedom" in Algeria—or at least their pragmatic concern for the security of the colony. *L'Univers* fulminated bitterly against this fetishization of tolerance taking root even among conservatives: dithering between Christianity and Islam instead of openly supporting Christianity, the state would only succeed in "inoculating [the Arabs] with apathy in religious matters" and in "sowing anarchy" in the name of order.[123] *L'Univers* concluded its discussion of the missionary debate: "Our society," after all, despite its "contemporary impieties, only survives by leaning on the blessings ... amassed by Christian generations." Even if the French found it convenient to deny how much their civilization owed to Christianity, they should not deny Algeria the same Christian civilization that Catholic religious orders had brought to European history.[124]

Here, in distilled form, was the argument of Veuillot's *Les Français en Algérie* of five years earlier: the only solution to the "Algerian question," the only chance for unity between France and Algeria, was for France to reverse its decadent course and return to the civilizational roots of Christianity, while simultaneously leading the Algerians historically forward to that same *civilisation chrétienne*. Parallel to wider debates about the existence of the Jesuits in general, the issue of Catholic proselytization in Algeria was becoming a bone of contention even between French Catholics—a cause only the most extreme Catholics would openly defend, while mainstream and liberal Catholics applauded the policy of "tolerance" in Algeria.

CHAPTER 3

White unto Harvest

Religion, Race, and the Jesuit Mission Arabe at Constantine

It was June of 1872 when Henri Ducat—a Jesuit missionary in French Algeria—put pen to paper to write to one of his former disciples, an Arab youth from the city of Constantine named Louis Khoudja. It was the feast day of St. Louis Gonzaga, patron saint of Catholic youth, so naturally Ducat's thoughts turned to his former convert, who had been baptized years before and named "Louis" in honor of this saint. Ducat had spent some fifteen years in Algeria, concentrating his efforts especially on Muslim youth, teaching them French, putting on magic lantern shows, distributing sugared almonds, and catechizing these children in the doctrines of the Catholic church. He had also been one of the most vocal advocates of the idea that Algeria's Muslims were not unconvertible fanatics but in fact potential Christians. Louis and his brother (whom the Jesuits christened "Stanislas," after another famous saintly youth) had been Ducat's star converts. The brothers had even traveled to France in the 1860s to train for the priesthood.

On this day, though, Ducat was writing to reproach Louis and to express his sense of betrayal. Ducat had heard through the grapevine that Louis had "taken up Arab dress again," and the missionary was worried: Did this sartorial choice indicate a rejection of Catholicism or, even worse, "a Muslim marriage"? Ducat reminded Louis that he loved him and his brother as if they were his own children and that they had once thought of him as a father, too. Ducat saved the real twist of the knife for the letter's postscript, where he wrote: "Attached is a picture [of Our Lord] in the garden—with the caption 'then all his disciples abandoned him and fled.'"[1] Yet God was still merciful: Ducat also enclosed a picture of the prodigal son returning home. The story of the Jesuits' failure to retain these two brothers—converts in whom they had invested so much—is a fitting illustration of the larger rise and fall of missionary hopes for Algeria's Muslims in the nineteenth century.

Like other Jesuits interested in proselytizing among Algeria's Muslims, Ducat was a believer in the missiology of cultural accommodation; he also exemplified the Catholic philo-Islamism of conservative culture warriors like Veuillot. He hoped that Muslims' inherent religiosity would survive their conversion to Christianity, reinvigorating Christendom with their premodern piety and leading them to serve as indigenous missionaries throughout North Africa. Ducat took this cultural respect and philo-Islamic optimism further than most. In one report to his superiors, Ducat sketched out a plan whereby the Jesuits would establish a special congregation specializing in Muslim missions. The Jesuits would also offer schools and catechumenates, orphanages, medical care, "excursions . . . among the tribes," and even create parishes wholly populated by indigenous Christians (supplemented, if need be, by Arabic-speaking Maronite Christians imported from Lebanon). The plan was animated by the kind of inculturation recommended by previous Jesuit missionaries. For example, Ducat advocated intermarriage between Europeans and (Christianized) Arabs, and—remarkably—even insisted that the Jesuits should "warn" the European partner-in-marriage "that [this mingling] not be to the detriment of [those customs] of the Arabs, even Muslims, which are much preferable."[2] On a later occasion, Ducat composed a song in Arabic in which the verses consisted of the Lord's Prayer, but the chorus was the *shahada*, the Islamic profession of faith—"there is no God but God"—repeated over and over. Of course, Ducat left out the second half of the profession: "and Muhammad is his prophet." Ducat's students would sing this song to the tune of the well-known French carol "Les anges dans nos campagnes" (Angels we have heard on high).[3]

Throughout the 1850s, the Jesuits' Arab Mission had become pervaded by a sense of discouragement, not only because of the government's refusal of their bid in 1850 for a mission to the tribal territories but also because a series of individual attempts in and around Constantine had met with failures, false starts, and governmental obstruction. The Père Jordan, the Jesuit superior in Algeria, initially hoped, along with Jean-Baptiste Creuzat, that the failing Arab seminary of 1849–50 could be relocated from Algiers to Constantine, and that some Jesuits might, "in the manner of the P.[ère] de Nobili [in India]," live and dress like the Arabs of Constantine and earn the reputation of "scholar-marabouts" specializing in "languages, poetry, astronomy, [and] medicine." These Christian marabouts would only broach the topic of religious conversion much later, after winning the Muslims' respect.[4] Such grandiose projects, though still in keeping with the ideal of cultural accommodation, always seem to have run into obstacles such as shortage of funds and personnel. Lacking the hoped-for wider mission among the Arab tribes, the *pères* at Constantine restricted their missionary efforts to smaller-scale educational and orphanage work in and around the city.[5]

In 1856, the Jesuits were relieved of their parish duties at Constantine by
Bishop Pavy. Pavy had finally recruited sufficient personnel to do without these
"auxiliaries" and had grown tired of tolerating independent priests within his hierarchy.[6] Thus the Jesuits had more reason than ever to concentrate their efforts
on the non-European population of Constantine. Not only did they now have
fewer responsibilities toward the European colonists and the secular Church hierarchy, but their new house in Constantine was more conducive to contact with
the Muslims. Following their ouster from the cure of Constantine, they had
been obliged to move into a *maison* in a less Europeanized neighborhood, "in the
middle of [the Infidels]."[7] They hoped to continue their educational outreach, focusing especially on the children while not neglecting any adult Muslims whose
"natures" had not been too "tainted."[8] Still, in 1857, one Jesuit superior in Algeria
bemoaned the "sad truth" that even those missionaries who had believed in the
mission arabe the most, like Creuzat and Père Baulard, were "discouraged" and
in need of more youthful replacements.[9] The superior also wondered if they had
erred in thinking that Constantine, "the center of infidelity," was indeed the
best location for their missionary attempts, since it was becoming clear how difficult it was for potential converts and catechists to resist the constant influence
of their families and other Muslim coreligionists.[10]

For Henri Ducat, an enterprising young Jesuit who first arrived at Constantine in the mid-1850s and who felt a particular vocation for Muslim evangelization, the Jesuits would only begin to have success when more Catholics around
the world were praying for Muslim conversion: "We prayed . . . but these prayers
seem not to have been universal enough, not insistent enough, not relentless
enough. The Muslims are generally viewed as a cursed race, and discouragement and indifference make Christians insensitive to the eternal loss of so many
souls."[11] While on leave back in France in 1857, Ducat had the idea of organizing
an "Association of Prayers to Our Lady of Africa for the Conversion of the Muslims" to pray for the spiritual awakening of Islamic Africa. Members committed to saying an Ave Maria every day, with the invocation "O Mary, conceived
without sin, pray for us and for the Muslims." Confessing and partaking of the
Eucharist at Easter was also a prerequisite for membership.[12]

Ducat had particular success publicizing his new Association of Prayers in
and around Besançon, where he had family connections, and around Lyon and
the Rhône valley, within his own Jesuit province. France was divided by the
Jesuits into four "provinces," and Lyon was the province charged with missions

in North Africa and elsewhere in the Mediterranean. Lyon was also known as the most ultramontane or "intransigent" Jesuit province. Moreover, in the 1860s, the idea of an "Apostolate of Prayer" that would knit Catholics around the world together into a wider mystic community—addressing its prayers to the "Sacred Hearts" of Mary and Jesus—was a trend associated with the sentimental devotional practices of ultramontane Catholicism.[13] These intransigent and emotive sensibilities may have made Ducat's new prayer association especially attractive to congregations throughout the Lyon province.

Nevertheless, tensions with Bishop Pavy in Algiers continued. Bishop Pavy approved the Association of Prayers, but with the caveats that the Association help raise funds for the new cathedral he was constructing at Algiers and that the Jesuits refrain from publicizing the Association until after he had completed his own fundraising campaign, because "the idea of proselytization" might alienate moderate Catholics.[14] Pavy decreed that any moneys given to Ducat's fledgling prayer Association would go toward the completion of his cathedral and not toward the actual work of catechizing the Muslims of Constantine. Pavy also revised the Association's prayer to read "Immaculate Heart of Mary, pray for us and for the poor Infidels," instead of "for the poor Muslims."[15] The Jesuits protested this rewording and were reassured that this had only been "by mistake."[16] Perhaps the Jesuits were concerned about the sensibilities of the Muslim population of Constantine who might hear the prayers: one Jesuit insisted they would need to change "Infidel" back to "Muslim" before they could "read [the prayers] in public."[17]

These early misunderstandings with Bishop Pavy suggest that Pavy's commitment to Muslim missions was halfhearted and pragmatic at best and that tensions continued to fester between the Jesuits and secular clergy in the colony. Pavy seems only to have spoken of his support for Muslim missions when he needed to justify receiving funds earmarked for missions, funds disbursed by the Lyon-based Œuvre de la Propagation de la Foi (Association for the Propagation of the Faith). Bishop Pavy's approach to the Muslims of Algeria was not at all in the philo-Islamic mode of Louis Veuillot and the Jesuit missionaries who tried to portray the Muslims as noble, devout, and susceptible to conversion and civilization. On the contrary, as Catholic observers of Islam would increasingly do in the second half of the nineteenth century, Pavy preferred to drum up support and financial contributions by denigrating Islam to his European audiences.

For example, on the occasion of Lent in 1853, Pavy preached a fiercely polemical sermon "On Mohammedanism" to his European parishioners of Algiers. According to the bishop, only the Arabs could have been so stupid and credulous as to believe that someone like Muhammad, without performing any miracles or fulfilling any prophesies, was a prophet of God. Unlike Eugène Boré, Pavy found nothing of literary value in the Qur'an. And he repeated the old slur that Muhammad and his followers were consumed by fleshly pleasures, and that unlike Christianity, Islam made no moral demands on its followers and allowed all manner of sexual vices.[18] In 1858, Pavy's fundraising appeal on behalf of his cathedral construction project emphasized opposition and enmity between Christianity and Islam. For Pavy, this new Chapel of Notre Dame d'Afrique would serve primarily as a commemoration of France's victory over the "Barbary" pirates of Algiers and of the Virgin Mary's role in that victory. Pavy's rhetorical strategy in his fundraising efforts was to emphasize just how evil these Muslim pirates had been to show that their defeat was great cause for celebration (and financial contribution).[19] Pavy's vision of the chapel as a pilgrimage destination for French Catholics thus grew out of a stance of total opposition to Islam that left no room for the rhetoric of Muslim religiosity or of future conversion and reconciliation.

Despite Pavy's tepid support for the prayer association, Ducat was back in Algeria by October 1858, announcing that the association had already grown to some 10,000 members. The missionary quickly received some encouraging results. For one thing, the missionaries back at Constantine reported having been able to baptize more dying Arab children than usual—without the knowledge of their parents, of course.[20] But the real "first fruits" of the Association's prayers were two young Muslim converts to Christianity, the Khoudja brothers, Garmi and Mouloud.[21] As many as thirty other children "from the best families of the city" quickly followed these brothers, perhaps attracted by the opportunity to learn French by way of Catholic liturgical texts and prayers. These children fit neatly into the sympathetic Catholic discourse about Muslim religiosity and receptivity to the Gospel: the Jesuits claimed they were initially cautious about broaching religious topics, but their students wanted to discuss religion and "already [seemed] to believe firmly in several important points of the Catholic religion."[22] From reports Ducat and others sent back to France, which were hand-copied by Jesuit scholars in Lyon and distributed to Jesuit houses across France, it is clear that the Jesuits hoped some of their catechists might themselves become priests and return as missionaries to their own people: the beginnings of an indigenous clergy.[23] One promising student had even expressed a desire to become a missionary to the Kabyles, but was withdrawn by his family after a prominent Muslim theology teacher in Constantine protested that the Jesuits "wanted to make him a Christian."[24]

In 1861, the Khoudja brothers were baptized and renamed "Louis" and "Stanislas" in the chapel of the Jesuits.[25] The Jesuits were careful to record in French and in Arabic the "formal consent" of the boys' father, with the father's signature not only authorizing the boys' baptism but promising to leave them "perfectly free to practice the Catholic religion."[26] The Jesuits and Ducat in particular made much of this consent—whenever Ducat recounted the story of the boys' baptism, he would often add some variation of the phrase "with the formal consent of their father." The Jesuits at Constantine would baptize a number of other Muslims in these early, heady years of the catechumenate; and in each case, Ducat kept careful records of parents' permissions and of baptismal certificates signed by witnesses.

These baptismal contracts were probably meant as insurance against the accusation—sometimes made by anticlerical enemies of the Jesuits or other missionaries—that the missionaries were kidnapping Muslim children. At a moment when the Pope himself had just ignited the anticlerical scandal of the century by seizing a Jewish child—Edgardo Mortara, who had been baptized without his parents' knowledge—the Jesuits of all congregations, and above all in colonial Algeria, could not afford the accusation that they had kidnapped Muslim children.[27] After all, the Lazarists at Algiers had been accused of the "corruption of minors" only a decade earlier, for their attempt to gather Muslim children into a catechumenate.[28] And some years later, in 1877, the Jesuits would find themselves attacked in the anticlerical press for having allegedly kidnapped "two new Mortaras"—two Kabyle youth sent to join the Trappist monks at Staoueli without their parents' permission.[29] But more than a defensive caution against European critics, Ducat's obsession with these "formal consents" could also be seen as a mark of his anxieties about Muslim conversion—anxieties about the Muslim influence the boys' family might still exert on these young Christians, that the boys would lapse and that their conversions and callings to the priesthood might fail.

The choice of saints for whom the brothers were named seems likewise significant: the saints Louis of Gonzaga and Stanislas Kostka had both from a young age received divine calls to the priesthood. More significantly for the anxieties and hopes of the *mission arabe*, both had met with some parental resistance, yet both had gone on to become Jesuit novices—Stanislas even fled his Vienna home to join the Jesuits in Rome. Ducat seems to have made the stories of these two saints a recurring part of his teaching to Muslim youth;[30] perhaps he even saw them as patrons of the Constantine catechumenate.[31] Years later, writing about Constantine in the pages of the French weekly *Les missions catholiques*, Ducat would recall a scene from the hopeful days "when we would give French lessons to some young Arabs": "the room which served both as our parlor and school" was decorated with engravings of "Our Lord, the holy Virgin," and of "the two young marabouts (saint Stanislas and saint Louis of Gonzaga)."[32] In taking these two Jesuit novices as the boys' saints, Ducat no doubt hoped the Arab brothers would display the same perseverance the young Jesuits had, forsaking even their own families for the sake of the gospel.

The social position of the Khoudja family in Constantine suggests they stood to gain from a relationship with the Jesuits. The boys' father, Mohamed ben Amin Khodja, was a *spahi*, or indigenous cavalryman, in the French colonial troops—an indication that he had already in some sense opted to better his social or financial position by "collaborating" with the French. Mohamed was away from Constantine on military exercises the day his sons were baptized, but the boys' uncle and head of the family, El Hadj Othman, represented the family and signed the baptismal certificate as a witness (perhaps their father signed a separate permission, before or after the day of the baptism). In fact, this "El Hadj," as the Jesuits called him, was an important indigenous functionary and the Jesuits' primary "native informant" in Constantine. Much of the Jesuits' contact with the Khoudja family and other Constantine Arabs was filtered through him, and he may even have smoothed over some initial objections from the boys' father. Until the mid-1860s, "*indigenès*" who lived in French Algeria's major cities were governed and policed by their own community or "corporation." These corporations were linked to ethnic or regional origin and were also associated with a given profession. El Hadj was the *amin*, or chief, of the corporation of the *Biskris*, residents of Constantine who hailed from the southern town of Biskra and had the monopoly on porterage in the city.[33] Although Ducat and the Jesuits referred to their disciples as "Arabs," at least some laborers from Biskra may also have been perceived as ethnically "other" in Algeria's cities. Some of the earliest travel writers and ethnographers in Algeria believed that migrant laborers from Biskra were darker skinned than other Algerians—Berbers, one rung above Black African laborers, if not Black themselves.[34]

Biskra, an oasis town perched at the southern end of Algeria's Aurès Mountains and a "gateway" to the Sahara and the caravan trade, was the center of the date-producing oases of the Ziban region and a source of seasonal labor migration that flowed along the trade route to and from Constantine to the north.[35] Back in the mid-1840s, as the French managed to subdue Abd-el-Kader's resistance to the west, Biskra and its surrounding oases in the southeast had become the center of a new kind of popular resistance led by a messianic *Mahdi*

FIGURE 3.1. "Constantine—Arab Families, from a photograph."
From *Les missions catholiques*, March 9, 1877.

figure, a divinely-appointed leader destined to appear at the end of days. A revolt near Constantine in 1845 was led by Djamina, an apocalyptic liberator who had spent time around Biskra. Algeria's most successful and widely followed claimant to the *Mahdi* title, Bu Ziyan, also hailed from the Biskra region and made his legendary last stand in 1849 in the nearby oasis of Zaatcha. The French subjected Zaatcha to vengeful annihilation—men, women, and children "put to the sword," its walls and date palms razed—a punishment exacerbated by the cholera French columns carried with them into the region. Perhaps the violence of 1849 drove even more Biskris to emigrate to Algeria's northern cities. But French authorities continued to worry that the mobility of Biskri laborers helped spread anti-French "rumors" and agitation.[36] In short, Biskris in Constantine were likely confined to manual labor and were social and ethnic outsiders.

Perhaps even religiously, they may not have been as integrated into the Islamic institutions of Constantine, but rather more attuned to the populist spirituality of rural saints and brotherhoods. Biskris were also not necessarily permanent residents of the city.

The Khoudja family head, El Hadj Othman, was himself a former student of the Jesuit Père Creuzat during the latter's time in Constantine, and his second wife was a former student of the Sœurs de la doctrine chrétienne at Bône. Though El Hadj was not a convert to Christianity—according to Ducat, because he had profited from the provisions of Islamic law in order to divorce his first wife—he "[felt] the benefits of an almost entirely French education." Indeed, it is possible he owed his administrative position as spokesman of the Biskris to his knowledge of French. El Hadj's positive experience with Catholic educators had disposed him to send his own son Moustafa to "the *frères*" rather than to one of the colonial administration's recently instituted *écoles arabes-françaises*. This son had already "expressed several times the desire . . . to go to France and be baptized." In a feat "almost miraculous for an Arab," according to Ducat, Moustafa had won prizes for his "diligence" and "daily exercises" and was even using his vacation to come to the daily French lessons at the Jesuits' house.[37] But conflict with the family of Moustafa's mother (El Hadj's ex-wife) erupted when El Hadj accepted a scholarship for the boy to study at Bishop Pavy's *Petit séminaire* in Algiers. El Hadj asserted his paternal right to educate his son however he wished, even after his wife appealed to the highest Muslim court of law in Constantine. He won this case, but at the expense—according to Ducat—of being considered by his fellow Muslims as someone who wanted to become "completely French (in other words Christian)."[38] Moustafa would follow one of the few career paths open to French-educated Algerians, studying at the military school at St. Cyr in France before being commissioned an officer in the Tirailleurs indigènes.[39]

There are a number of possible reasons why El Hadj, the Khoudja family, and others in this orbit might have opted for a Catholic education for their children. In the late 1850s, when Louis, Stanislas, and the other children first began attending the Jesuits' catechism class, French education for indigenous Algerians was at its most embattled and embryonic.[40] In 1850, as an experiment in winning hearts and minds, the military administration had opened several *écoles arabes-françaises*, where Algerians students could learn French, alongside traditional Arabic and Qur'anic studies from approved indigenous instructors.[41] One of these schools was at Constantine, but it never attracted more than a handful of students. Perhaps this failure was due to the school's symbolic association with the still-recent military violence or to the fact that in the 1850s and

1860s, *zaouias* and other independent Qur'anic schools were still widespread and popular enough to create very real competition with the colonial state.[42] At the same time, though, it was clear that a French education would soon be the only path to secure employment. In 1854, for example, the colonial administration began cracking down on its indigenous interpreters, in principle requiring them to pass a literacy test, rather than merely be able to speak French and Arabic.[43] To cut down on competition with its own schools, the colonial administration in 1857 shuttered "half of the 24 religious schools" in Constantine.[44] The same year, perhaps to save money, the administration also halted its policy of "[paying] students 2 francs a day to attend" its own Arab-French school.[45] Perhaps these factors combined with El Hadj's own friendship with the Jesuits and made the catechism class an attractive option for these children. In some Algerians' minds, the Jesuits' house might not have been as tainted with the violence of colonialism as the military administration's school was. The catechism class seems to have met for only an hour a day, so these children also could have continued working and contributing to their households. They might even have continued attending a Muslim school while they used the Christian catechism to learn French.

The fact that the most promising catechists were boys is unsurprising, given that the Jesuits were a male congregation hoping to train indigenous missionaries and that alternatives for female Catholic education existed. But the focus on male rather than female children was also in keeping with the broader "tone" of educational initiatives in Algeria by the end of the 1850s. The colonial administration briefly experimented with including girls in its Arab-French schools, but in Algiers, "book learning" was soon deemed inappropriate for Muslim girls as future wives. Muslim women were thus denied the "assimilation" promised by the civilizing mission, confined to their religion and race in the name of tolerance for Muslim family life.[46]

The Jesuits depended on El Hadj as their primary mediator with Constantine's Arabs. Not only did he witness Louis's and Stanislas's baptisms, but he represented the families of a number of other catechumens baptized around the same time. These other children likely came from Biskri families as well, and one wonders how El Hadj exercised his authority over his corporation in these instances. How did he explain the significance of the baptismal ceremony to his compatriots? Were his motives insincere all along, only a strategy to acquire lodging and education for these children?

In the early 1860s, however, the Jesuits were optimistic that these conversions were sincere. Louis and Stanislas were only the most encouraging signs of a much larger movement among the children of Constantine: the Jesuits' students were inviting friends to join them at their daily lessons, memorizing Christian prayers and repeating them at home in the evenings, wearing religious medals and crucifixes, even playing at "baptizing each other."[47] According to a suggestive entry in the Jesuits' diary, some European *dames* who came in their finery to worship in the Jesuits' chapel "complained that our chapel is *filled* with Arabs" taking up all the space.[48] The children even slept over one Christmas eve, to participate in the Vigil, midnight mass, and *réveillon* feast. During this period, El Hadj was visiting his Jesuit friends regularly, either to participate in the Jesuits' religious services or to dine or drink coffee with them. He would bring a pastry or some other local delicacy or give tours of the city's mosques and religious figures to a visiting Jesuit. He even invited the *pères* to his house for coffee on the Epiphany, "because that [was] the day," he said, "when the King of the Arabs went to worship Our Lord Jesus Christ."[49]

One little boy—probably Louis Khoudja himself—was asked to serve as a kind of junior missionary to help the Jesuits convert an Arab man who was dying at the hospital and who had successfully resisted the efforts of French priests and nuns. Louis, with his "childlike candor," debated religion as skillfully as any missionary, using the Qur'an's own teachings on Jesus Christ to trap this poor man in his words and lead him to admit the superiority of Christianity over Islam and be baptized.[50] Louis's success must have been a tantalizing demonstration of the potential for an indigenous clergy to communicate in ways the Jesuits could not. Soon after, the Jesuits marked Louis and Stanislas for the priesthood by beginning their instruction in Latin.[51] When, at the beginning of 1863, the boys' family—perhaps in financial difficulties—left them entirely to the Jesuits' care, Ducat took the boys to France, to a *maîtrise* (a Cathedral school) in the Jura, France's alpine foothills.[52]

Before entrusting his young charges to the school, Ducat took them on a tour of religious congregations and parishes in France, raising money to support the mission and the boys' education. These visits by Ducat and the Khoudja brothers were such a success that they led to "enrollments en masse" in Ducat's Association of Prayers for the Conversion of the Muslims, to the extent that "the peaceful Crusade now counted around *80 thousand* soldiers."[53] What Ducat and others still found most striking about the young Arabs was their natural propensity for religion. "Their simplicity—pious and full of affection—their naïve and precocious intelligence, everywhere aroused a benevolent sympathy," Ducat wrote.[54] The missionary was pleased to hear from the brothers' teachers the following year that, "even in an entirely religious establishment," the boys continued to distinguish themselves by their "piety . . . and their spirit of faith,"

FIGURE 3.2. Arab student of the Petit séminaire (?). Henri Ducat, "Diaire: Mission Arabe Consantine, 1871–72," RAl 81, ACJF.

and by "that naïveté, that simplicity [which is] so rare now."[55] Here is a reminder that, back in France, Catholic admiration for Muslim religiosity was not just a reflection of missionary optimism; it also always functioned as a veiled critique of France's own alleged decadence. As it had for Veuillot, the trope of the Muslim as a kind of religious noble savage could still serve as a stick for beating Catholicism's godless enemies at home. In Ducat's extensive notes and sketches, there is a drawing not of Louis or Stanislas, unfortunately, but of an Arab student he encountered some years later. The sketch is almost loving in its detail, and it is tempting to wonder whether Ducat still had his two dearest and most promising converts in mind (see figure 3.2).

In 1864, the brothers' cousin—El Hadj's daughter "Louise," who had studied with the Sœurs de la doctrine chrétienne and been baptized in 1861—was sent to a girls' school in Besançon, Ducat's hometown. For Ducat, the real danger was that contact with France would destroy these children's native innocence and credulity. Despite the dangers of subjecting the young converts to French civilization, such a method would remain necessary, as long as there was so little social support for indigenous converts in Algeria.[56] Ducat's repeated fears that the boys would lose their "innocence" and piety while in France speak to his recognition, however dim, that traveling to France for an education might serve to increase the cultural alienation experienced by converts or destroy the very links with their indigenous compatriots that were supposed to make them such effective missionaries.[57] In short, isolating the brothers from their indigenous milieu for an education in France seems at odds with some of the more culturally adaptive impulses of the missionaries, at odds with the Jesuits' desire for Arab Christian settlements untouched by European decadence. Similarly, Eugène Boré and the Lazarists sought to relocate potential converts from the Ottoman Empire to Malta or to Algeria; he saw France as too culturally or morally compromising or alienating for indigenous seminarians.

Yet, in the absence of fellow Arab Christians—to say nothing of fully formed Arab Christian parishes—to shelter and support indigenous converts in Algeria, the cathedral school in Jura may have seemed the next-best thing from the missionaries' perspective. At the *maîtrise*, students lived essentially as if already in a religious community, complete with cassock, daily liturgical chants, and annual spiritual retreats.[58] The school counted at least two other Arab Christians, young Maronites "who had escaped the massacres of Lebanon" in 1860, one of whom would end up a vicar general for the Maronite archbishop of Beirut.[59] Dom Gréa, the director of the school, planned to found a congregation of "Canons Regular"—priests who ministered publicly in parishes yet who lived in cloistered community like monks—and he and his followers believed this monastic model could also contribute to the formation of indigenous clergy in missionary contexts, since the regular, communal life would protect native converts from "the inconstancy of the infidel countries."[60]

Despite the promising beginnings of Louis's and Stanislas's education, in 1865 the fortunes of the "Arab mission" began to fade.[61] Ducat was recalled from Constantine to take up a new position at Algiers, and his main assistant at Constantine passed away. Ducat had naively hoped that, once he was nearer to the Cathedral of Notre Dame d'Afrique—theoretically the spiritual center of his Association of Prayers and of Bishop Pavy's pilgrimage—he would be able to exercise his influence more effectively. On the contrary, at the center of colonial Algeria's ecclesiastical and governmental hierarchy, he felt pressure *not* to proselytize.[62] An even worse blow fell in the fall of 1866: in a symbolic setback for the Association of Prayers and a personal heartbreak for Ducat, Louis and Stanislas's family demanded the boys' return from France and their circumcision, which to the missionaries signified their abandonment of Christianity and embrace of Islam. "Charmed by maternal caresses . . . intimidated by the threats of their father, our two poor children, Louis and Stanislas, were circumcised at the age of 14 and 15," Ducat wrote. "[T]he younger, Stanislas, protests against the violence which was done him, and still claims to be a Christian. But his brother [Louis] seems to have formally apostatized."[63] For Ducat, the family was guilty of long-term deceit after their father's promises to leave them free to practice Christianity. Even more disheartening, El Hadj had himself served as witness to the circumcision ritual and had "held them down during the operation."[64] Ducat accused El Hadj of having conspired against the Jesuits with what he called "Arab dexterity."[65]

One possibility was that the boys' family had always had a different understanding of their arrangement with the Jesuits and of the baptismal "contract" in which Ducat had put so much faith. El Hadj and the Khoudjas may have been more syncretistic in their understanding of the relationship between Muslim and Christian practices, seeing no inherent conflict between the rite of baptism, for example, and that of circumcision. Practices of Maghrebi Islam that later Muslim reformers would condemn as unorthodox or superstitious—veneration of saints or marabouts, praying for miracles at maraboutic shrines (perhaps even non-Muslim shrines), the use of amulets to heal and protect—may have predisposed some Algerian Muslims to believe they could adopt Christian venerations or practices.[66] The popularity of medals of the Virgin Mary among Algerian Muslims, for example, was one oft-cited reason for missionary optimism. Perhaps a certain measure of this syncretism was also encouraged by the missionaries' own strategy of adapting the Gospel in ways that emphasized its commonalities with Islam and of encouraging the Muslims to think of them as marabouts.

Even those Algerians who converted later on and who openly identified as Christian often "[played] with the rituals of either religion," according to Karima Dirèche-Slimani, combining religious practices that might seem "logically incompatible." The vast majority continued to practice circumcision; some even practiced Christianity their entire lives yet still refused to receive last rites, effectively dying as Muslims.[67] In short, it is possible that even if the Khoudjas never intended to "convert" in the full sense the Jesuits would have wanted, they may not have been conscious of perpetrating any deception. Another possible explanation for the family's decision to recall and circumcise the brothers could be that French Algeria's municipal governments may have begun eliminating official positions for "corporation" spokesmen like El Hadj, and perhaps he ceased to see the benefit of a French education for his nephews.[68] Finally, it is also possible that Ducat's accusations were correct: that the Khoudja family, driven by poverty and skillfully advised by El Hadj, had looked for some material advantage; that their actions had always been a ploy to acquire lodging and education. In any case, as Dirèche astutely observes, missionaries could not allow a situation of "double religious-belonging." For them, such behavior would always have to be evaluated according to the narrow calculus of "sincerity" versus "bad faith" of the Muslims.[69]

In the end, the Jesuits were able to convince the boys' family to let them return to France, where they spent another two years. The Jesuits agreed once again to fund the brothers' education and stay in France, but the family would have to pay for any return trip if they wanted the boys back.[70] Under the circumstances, one père worried that the parents had once again only consented out of "interested motives," because they were in "extreme poverty" and unable to support the brothers.[71] Still, Ducat was heartened to hear reports from France that "these dear children are still the same. . . . If they may have weakened for a moment, they did not cease to be what Baptism and Communion had made them."[72]

But in 1869, they returned to Algeria, this time for good. Ducat was no longer stationed at Constantine, but one colleague there wrote to him that "Louis is dressing in the Arab style. . . . He does not even greet us, if we by chance run into him—he works . . . as a [Lawyer's] clerk and interpreter. . . . Stanislas still has his European clothes, but in an almost destitute style. . . . He still half-greets us if he is alone; but not if he is with some friends."[73] One Jesuit in Constantine wrote that "both of them live a life worthy of a Muslim and worse."[74] Ducat's bitter remarks in 1866 about El Hadj's "Arab dexterity" in conspiring against the missionaries, as well as the snide implication of these later comments—that living a life "worthy of a Muslim" was somehow a reprehensible thing—seem a swift and bitter reversal of the missionaries' earlier belief that Muslims, inasmuch as they had a natural respect for all religion, were to be commended.

It was in the wake of this second apostasy that Ducat wrote the letter to Louis imploring him not to abandon the missionaries, not to abandon Christ. Ducat would continue to write, receiving no response from the brothers until, in June of 1876, he "hazarded" another letter. Hoping to appeal to Louis's self-interest and to "cause him to break [his] silence," Ducat suggested that he might be able to find Louis a job. Louis responded immediately. He was still working as a clerk-interpreter at Constantine and claimed to be married; he urged Ducat "in the name of the Sacred Heart" to help him find a post in the government, preferably in Algiers. A second response from Louis was even more insistent about the job and "even more Christian" in its language. After inquiring into Louis's conduct—he was in fact not married but living with a French woman, and still wearing "Arab clothing"—Ducat and his superiors decided that they should try to help. Even if Louis's motives were insincere, God might still use the circumstance to draw him back to the Jesuits. Ducat advised Louis to go back to wearing French clothing and to "regularize his [marital] position." Ducat then arranged for the colonial administration to offer Louis a low-level, rural post as an interpreter. It was not much, Ducat admitted, but perhaps it would come with opportunities for advancement and even relocation to Algiers. Louis accepted, and then seems to have once again stopped responding to Ducat's letters.[75] It is interesting to observe, on the one hand, how adroitly Louis mimicked the particularly emotive devotional vocabulary of ultramontane Catholics ("in the name of the Sacred Heart") and, on the other hand, how Ducat and other Jesuits were well aware of this potential for insincerity yet still tried to use their resources and influence to regulate Louis's moral behavior. The Jesuits' fixation on the brothers' European clothing and relationships also illustrates the period's ambivalence between cultural and racial thinking about difference.[76] No matter how culturally adaptive the missionaries claimed to be—because religious affections are not "observable"—the missionaries seem to have insisted on a visible display of the young men's conversion and civilization.[77]

Although there are a number of explanations for the Khoudja family's behavior—poverty, desire for education and advancement, the shifting politics of Constantine's municipal administration, and even a sincere but syncretistic admiration for Christianity—Ducat and his colleagues immediately leaped to racialized, collective explanations. "Commitments and even promises, what are they for the Arabs? Nothing at all. Whoever believes them is quite a dupe!!!" one *père* moaned.[78] In the years to come, Ducat would become even more inclined to see all Arabs through the lens of his personal disappointment with Louis and Stanislas. Throughout the 1870s, even as he still attempted to renew contact with the brothers, Ducat complained frequently, and with increasing dejection, about the "inconstancy" of the Arabs and other Algerians—former students or orphans—who returned to the missionaries only when they needed something and who could never stay in one place long enough to keep a job once it was offered. "These poor people," Ducat commiserated with his colleagues, had an "inconceivable . . . inconstancy"; they were "limited in their intelligence beyond a certain point and a certain age"; and they were "almost without gratitude...only thanking when they hope for something more."[79]

Later on, when another convert seemed hesitant to announce his conversion to his family, Ducat suggested that "these Arabs ... have a weak understanding for the things of religion."[80] What a reversal this was: at the beginning of the Arab mission, the missionaries had imagined that Muslims' respect for Christian priests, rites, and practices was an indication of their admirable capacity for belief in general and even of their imminent conversion. In a newly racialized discourse poisoned by personal disillusionment, that exact same syncretism proved that Arabs were not smart enough to understand that the two religions should be mutually exclusive.

Ducat did not keep these judgments private. He went on to publicize them and to elevate them to the level of ethnographic knowledge in a series of articles he coauthored for the metropolitan weekly *Les missions catholiques* in 1877. Ducat self-consciously inscribed this work in the discipline of colonial ethnography, claiming that at the beginning of the Algerian conquest, the French had known very little about the indigenous populations, but that his articles—concentrating especially on the Arabs—would contribute to the project of distinguishing the "diverse races" that inhabited Algeria.[81] In this series of articles, Ducat described the "physical constitution of the Arab" as consisting of "black hair, beard, and eyes ... oval face, and long neck," an "ovoid" head, and an "aquiline" nose.[82] According to Ducat, when it came to the humors the Arab temperament was especially heavy on the bile, though more "bilious-lymphatic ... in the plains of the Tell" and more "bilious-nervous in the Sahara." Finally, among other dehumanizing observations, Ducat noted that Arabs had especially keen senses of sight, smell, and hearing; were hopelessly dirty and smelly; and, although able to survive for months on a handful of dates alone, could also engage in gluttonous acts that would "frighten a European stomach."[83]

Following these pseudo-scientific claims about Arab physiognomy, Ducat shifted seamlessly to an evaluation of the Arab character, implying that Arabs' moral values were just as static and universal as their physical characteristics. His readers back in France could not have known just how deeply contingent and personal the circumstances were that had produced these generalized judgments: "The Arabs are liars... .. They are inconstant in their affections and in their relations. An Arab will be seen to frequent a house, to overwhelm the people who live there with consideration and good wishes; then, suddenly, without [a] plausible reason ... he will stop going there, and will pretend not to recognize his friends if he meets them.... When [the Arab] studies, he reaches a certain level of knowledge more quickly than the European: but there his efforts will stop.... More than forty years of French domination have changed

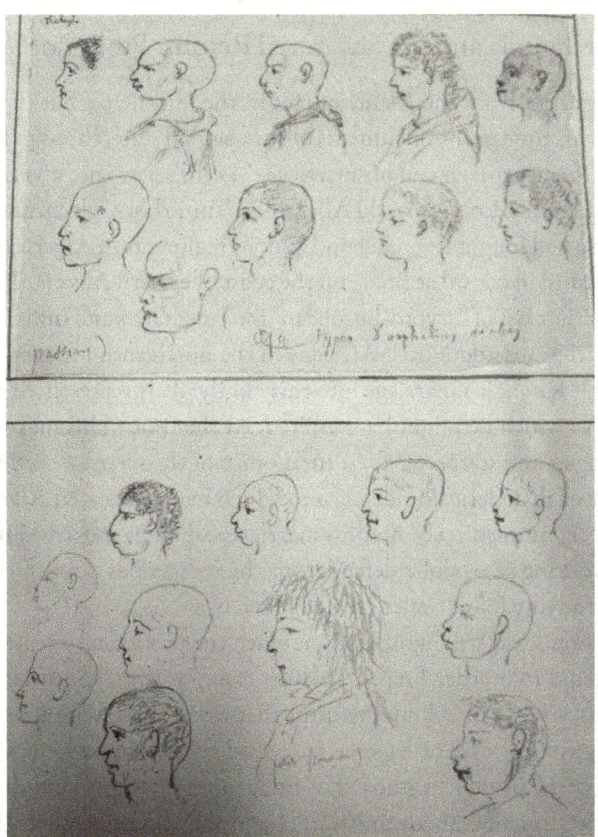

FIGURE 3.3. "Some types of Arab orphans," with a "petit français" in the middle.
Henri Ducat, "Diaire Mission Arabe Constantine, 1871–72," RAl 81, ACJF.

nothing of the beliefs of the Arabs. They are as rigid observers of their rites, as fatalistic and superstitious as the day we disembarked."[84] As Ducat bitterly described this abstract, universal Arab who supposedly always forsakes and ignores his friends, it is impossible not to think of Louis, Stanislas, and their Uncle El Hadj. In the bitterness of apostolic failure, no longer would Ducat and other missionaries speak the philo-Islamic language of admiration for Muslim morality and devotion. No longer would Ducat describe Muslim customs as being "preferable" to the decadence of European civilization. Ducat's hopes for Arab conversion had been utterly dashed. Arabs, he thus reported to Catholic readers back in France, were inherently inconstant, spiritually nomadic, dishonest, unstable, fanatical.

Louis Khoudja and the Senatorial Reform Project of 1891–92

The brothers fade from the Jesuit sources in the mid-1870s, but in 1886 Louis reemerges, this time in the documents of the colonial state, through his naturalization as a French citizen and his marriage.[85] Louis's new wife was Léonie Allegro, the daughter of Louis-Arnold Allegro—a Tunis-born adventurer of Italian descent, who had fought in French indigenous regiments in Algeria before serving as the Tunisian consul at Bône, on the coast of eastern Algeria. The Allegros were part of the class of "crypto-European" intermediaries and influence brokers between Europeans and North Africans in the nineteenth-century Mediterranean world.[86] Khoudja's marriage into this family likely represented the highest social level to which he might have aspired. At the time of his marriage he was still working as an interpreter for a rural office of the *service de la propriété indigène*, part of that clerical underclass to which many educated Algerians were consigned. Yet, immediately after his marriage, Khoudja moved to Bône where he began working as a public defender for the indigenous poor in the Muslim court and studying for entrance to the French bar.[87]

In 1892, Louis was still living in Bône when the prominent French politician Jules Ferry and two other French senators came to town to gather testimony in support of a series of colonial reforms that would lessen the abuses endured by the indigenous people of Algeria. Ferry had formed his senatorial "commission of eighteen" in 1891 to study the "indigenous question" and distributed a questionnaire to colonial administrators and Algerian notables. This reform commission was a signal that after two decades of metropolitan neglect and colonialist autonomy metropolitan France was once again taking interest in the management of Algeria and in the fate of its Muslim populations.[88] At Bône, Khoudja gave the senators a deposition that placed him "at the forefront" of "the orators of the *indigènes*."[89] In this atmosphere of reform, Louis Khoudja also published his thoughts on the Algerian Question in the form of an address to the eighteen senators of the commission.[90] Khoudja's publication was an indication of a rising class of Algerian *évolués* caught between their desire to vindicate Islam, on the one hand, and their readiness to profit from French education and the benefits promised by France's civilizing rhetoric, on the other. Khoudja, like the later Young Algerians and reformist 'ulama of the early 1900s, appropriated the "vocabulary" of France's Republican, civilizing mission in order to turn that rhetoric against colonial abuses.[91] He believed that the resolution of the "question indigène" was to be found in French education and full legal and political assimilation. Like other French-educated Algerian reformers of his time,

Khoudja was no anticolonial agitator; he accepted, as James McDougall has put it, that "the only possible future lay in emancipation *through* [not from] colonial modernity."[92] Yet despite this sincere or tactical belief in French Republicanism and schooling, Khoudja was still deeply sensitive to Algerian, Muslim difference.

While arguing eloquently and forcefully for the rights guaranteed by French republicanism—education, political participation, trial by jury—Khoudja still insisted on respect for Algerian difference, respect for tribal land ownership, and respect for Muslim belief.[93] The Algerians' problem was not their religion, Khoudja argued; in fact, the Qu'ran encouraged education and friendship with Christians. The problem was that France had not yet fulfilled its civilizing and emancipatory promises. Turning his knowledge of Islam and of French history against the colonist-critics of Algeria's Muslims, Khoudja made a trenchant historical and social argument: "I have read and re-read the Koran, in its original text; I know what it contains, and I am justified in saying that to make the Koran responsible for the oddities of the *indigène* mind, would be equivalent to attributing the massacres of the crusades, the horrors of the inquisition, St. Bartholomew's, and the Wars of Religion to the Gospel. Let us therefore cast such an absurd theory far away, and let us say that today it belongs to France, that enlightened society, to raise the *indigène* up to [France's] social level."[94] In short, Muslim traditionalists and anti-Islamic Frenchmen were both wrong: one could be "a good Frenchman and a good Muslim at the same time," as long as social and political equality were assured.[95]

Nowhere is Khoudja's balancing act between Republican universalism and indigenous difference—between universal and particular, "assimilation" and "association"—more effective than in his nuanced argument for allowing "*indigènes*" to serve on juries. Citing several real-life examples of the habitual "injustice" and "severity" of all-European juries toward accused Arabs, Khoudja argued that indigenous Algerians should have "the same guarantee as the Europeans," the right to be "judged, they too, by their peers."[96] Even though Khoudja was laying claim to one of the universal norms achieved by the French Revolution—jury trial by peers—and despite the universal, egalitarian character of his claim, the logic of his demand relied on and even enshrined indigenous difference. The reason European colonists could not stand in judgment of Arabs was precisely that they were not the Arabs' peers: they did not share the same values; they had "opposing interests"; and they could not avoid, even "unconsciously," treating the "*indigènes*" as "the vanquished."[97] Republican equality, in this case, necessitated the acknowledgment of cultural and racial difference, necessitated the intentional inclusion of Algerian jurors in cases involving Algerians. Like the

anticolonial movements studied by Priyamvada Gopal, Khoudja "at once asserted cultural specificities and made insistent claims upon shared humanity."[98]

One famous historian called this pamphlet the work of a "'young-Algerian'
avant la lettre."[99] Yet Khoudja's pamphlet and brief career as an Algerian spokesman are even more interesting for the light they shed on his early years with the
Jesuits. Historians of colonial education have written about the sense of alienation and disorientation experienced by indigenous students, as they found
themselves stuck between their need for family support and belonging, on the
one hand, and their genuine interest in the seemingly superior knowledge of
the colonizers, on the other.[100] This gap between indigenous society and French
civilization constituted the entire predicament of colonial education: how do
you create an indigenous elite assimilated enough to French civilization to be
trusted as representatives of the civilizing mission, yet not so assimilated as to
have lost all influence over their compatriots?[101] The usual result of this predicament was what one scholar has called "double alienation," the experience of no
longer feeling at home in either milieu.[102]

It is often assumed that this experience of alienation would have been even
greater for those who, like the Khoudja brothers, were educated by missionaries
and encouraged not only to embrace French language and civilization, but even
to abandon their religion.[103] In one moving passage from his political pamphlet,
Louis Khoudja sketches out this double alienation. Without letting on that he
is likely speaking about his own family, he describes the disappointing experience of Muslim Algerian parents who "sent their children to the *collèges*, the
lycées, and sometimes even the religious institutions of Algeria, others even... to
France... unfortunately, these [parents] have come to regret the sacrifices which
they forced themselves to make. Their completely assimilated children became
the object of the most total neglect on the part of the Algerian Administration.
. . they even served as a laughing stock for their compatriots [since. . .] there
was no need for them to go so far to study and work in order to acquire a position which was refused them."[104] These lines recall the pathetic image of Louis's
younger brother, Stanislas, back in the early 1870s, in his threadbare European
clothes, lukewarmly greeting the Jesuits when he was alone, yet ignoring them
when with friends. The passage also seems to confirm the Khoudjas' hope that
a Jesuit education would lead to positions in the colonial administration and to
social advancement.

Notwithstanding the cultural disorientation endured by Louis Khoudja and
his brother, the Jesuits may have played an important—albeit accidental—role
in making him into the nuanced Muslim spokesperson he became. Not only

had the Jesuits helped him acquire the French language, but with their initial sympathy for Muslim religiosity and adaptation to Muslim customs, they had "unwittingly relativized the concept of religion itself."[105] It is a paradox of the missionary encounter that it tends to undermine and reduce religion to a relative choice, perhaps even more so when "religion" is divorced from external cultural markers in the name of adaptation.[106] From his Muslim upbringing to his years in a Jesuit catechism class, from his time in France to his career in the offices of the colonial administration, Khoudja had a great deal of practice creatively toggling between the language of French ultramontane Catholicism, Republican universalism, and his Muslim faith. "In the name of the Sacred Heart" he asked Ducat for help in acquiring a job; in the name of the French Revolution he asked France's senators for universal, compulsory education and for trial by a jury of his peers; and in the name of the Qur'an he argued that Islam should not be seen as an impediment to becoming French.[107]

But the tide was turning against sympathy for Islam and for Algeria's indigenous peoples, even among the missionary congregations. At the end of the nineteenth century, Jesuit and other Catholic observers of Algerian Islam would begin employing an ever harsher rhetoric of inherent Muslim inferiority and enmity to Christianity.[108] Indeed, in 1892, in response to the very same reform commission that had prompted Khoudja's pamphlet, Jesuit editor and historian Joseph Burnichon wrote a pair of articles on the history of Catholic missions in Algeria, the Jesuits' own answer to the *"question indigène."*[109] Burnichon emphasized all the ways colonial administrators had obstructed missions to Muslims in the past.[110] But for him, this kind of missionary-administrator conflict was unfortunate not so much because it resulted in the loss of Muslim souls, but because it prevented the success of assimilation and colonialism. The *"indigènes"* could never hope to assimilate as long they were Muslims: "Mohammedanism . . . digs an abyss between the *indigènes* and ourselves that neither education, nor a common political and social life, nor clemency and benefits, nor time itself could fill. 'The disciple of Mohammed, says J.[oseph] de Maistre, does not belong to us in any way: he is foreign, *innassociable, immiscible* to us.' This is the lesson which results from the experience of ten centuries . . . . Antipathy for the Christians has entered into the marrow of the Muslim; it survives the weakening and even the loss of his faith."[111]

For Burnichon, placing one's hopes in education, as Khoudja did, was especially naïve: not only would education never succeed (since Muslims "will always draw their moral education from the Koran, and the Koran will always teach them that they must hate the *Christian dogs* and kill them whenever they can"[112]), but education would even serve to provide techniques and skills which these inveterate enemies of France would then turn and use against their bene-factors. Burnichon paid lip service to the traditional, conversion-focused goal of mission work: that Algeria might be transformed into a new Christendom. But his virulently anti-Islamic rhetoric made him an enemy of reform and an ally of the anti-Arab settlers who hoped to maintain the racialized indigenous code and prevent any indigenous education that would go beyond agricultural-vocational skills.[113] Signifying how far the Jesuits had departed from their earlier admira-tion for Muslim religiosity, Burnichon even commended Louis Tirman—the political leader of the settler-colonists—for being one of the few to "[recognize] that, against the Koran, assimilation runs into an insurmountable object."[114]

In the face of such growing animosity, perhaps it is no surprise that Khoudja never became the indigenous missionary the Jesuits had hoped for and never returned to his Muslim compatriots as an emissary of Catholic France. Yet if any Algerian learned to play the part of a cultural intermediary, it was he. In Bône, he garnered esteem both among Republican colonists and the more activist proto-Young Algerians around the journal *El hack* [*La verité*].[115] Indeed, the na-ture of his pamphlet, with its respectful references to France's civilizing goodwill and acknowledgments of indigenous ignorance and fanaticism but also its valo-rization of Islam and careful cataloging of legal abuses of the "*indigènes*," meant that sections of it were cited and commented upon favorably in both colonialist and Young Algerian journals.[116] Still, even as skilled a navigator as Khoudja must have found this a difficult course to steer. Both to be nearer his wife's family, but also in search of professional advancement, he would ultimately emigrate to Tunisia, whose "protectorate" model of colonization—a more indirect and collaborative rule over the Tunisians—had inspired the reforms Ferry had vainly hoped to see implemented in Algeria.[117]

CHAPTER 4

Crusade of Charity

Liberal Catholic Roots of the Civilizing Mission

Over the course of several weeks in June of 1860, bands of Syrian Druzes launched attacks on Maronite Christians throughout Mount Lebanon, in Ottoman-controlled Syria. In the early months of 1860 leading up to June, assassinations and smaller clashes had already begun to erupt between Maronites and Druzes. But when Maronites from northern Mount Lebanon began gathering and preparing to march on the Druze-dominated south, the Druze, fearing themselves the target of a Christian conspiracy, rose up preemptively to kill the Maronites and other Christian minorities in their midst. More unified and "superior in military tactics," the Druze quickly achieved victory in open battle. Throughout early and mid-June the Druze proceeded to massacre their Maronite enemies—first in smaller villages around Damascus, then in the sacking of Zahleh (a Melkite, or Arabic-speaking Greek Orthodox, city), and then Dayr al-Qamar, a previously tolerated Maronite enclave in the majority-Druze south.[1] Finally, in early July, as refugees poured into Damascus, swelling the Christian quarter there, Damascene Muslims saw a chance to vent their frustration against French-backed Christians whose social and commercial fortunes were on the rise in this era of Ottoman reform and increasing European intervention. Tensions in the city exploded into carnage, and some two thousand Christians were killed.[2] As the massacre and pillage spun out of control, local Ottoman garrisons, often staffed by underpaid irregulars, either stood idly by or even actively participated in the killing.[3] Among the thousands dead were numerous European religious, including a Jesuit missionary (and French national) "martyred" at Zahleh, Edouard Billotet.[4]

The Maronites were an ancient Christian sect that had united with Rome around the era of the Crusades and had kept their own rites, making them perhaps the oldest Catholic-affiliated rite in the Middle East.[5] The Maronites and Druze had coexisted for much of their history, despite tribal rivalries. But the Egyptian and European interventions of the nineteenth century stoked the flames of "sectarianism." Ibrahim Pasha ruled Syria in the 1830s through a policy of divide-and-rule, arming Christians against Druzes when the Druze refused to submit to conscription.[6] At the same time, France was cultivating commercial contacts with the Maronite Christians and posing as their protector, in order to "justify [its] involvement in the Ottoman Empire."[7] Following Ibrahim Pasha's ouster from Syria in 1840, violence broke out between Christian villagers and Druze notables seeking to reestablish their rights. But the European Powers, ignoring the social dimensions of these conflicts and "[taking] communal identity for granted," advised the Ottomans to separate Mount Lebanon into two districts, or *kaimakams*, thus "sectarianizing the landscape" and breaking with the more feudal coexistence of the past.[8] European missionaries were also doing their best to cultivate sectarian difference by creating more "purely Christian spaces," isolating their protégés and converts from the corrupting influence of unbelievers.[9] Maronite Christians, encouraged by Maronite clergymen and European mentors, began laying claim to religious or social parity with Muslims and Druzes. Indeed, in the years leading up to the violent events of 1860, it was often the rising Maronites who instigated sectarian clashes with their traditional notables, both Maronite and Druze.[10]

It would be difficult to overstate the uproar in Europe when news of the massacres began to trickle in from across the Mediterranean. In France, which prided itself on its role as the protector of Ottoman Christians, and particularly among French Catholics, the outrage and concern for the Christian victims was palpable. No orientalist trope was too hackneyed, no martyr narrative too excessive for recounting the horrors: Muslim fanaticism had been unleashed, directed against both local Christians and European Christendom as a whole, aided by the criminal indifference or open cooperation of the degenerate Ottomans. As a result, children had been murdered in front of their parents, defenseless victims had been struck down as they begged for mercy, women had been raped or pressed into Harem service, and bodies had been left stacked and mutilated in the streets.[11] Charitable subscriptions and calls for military intervention sprang up almost immediately. By early August, backed by public opinion and grudgingly approved by Britain and the other Great Powers, Napoleon III had decided upon a military expedition, ostensibly to help the Ottoman Sultan's own special commissioner to Syria punish the guilty and reestablish order.[12]

Especially vocal in raising funds for the victims and in drumming up anti-Ottoman outrage was the Catholic charitable association the Œuvre des écoles d'Orient (Association of Oriental Schools, also known simply as the Œuvre d'Orient), whose director was the abbé Charles Lavigerie. Many of the Œuvre's members—the cream of French Catholic notability and academia—possessed contacts in the Levant. These Catholic notables took on a guiding role in French Catholic responses to the massacres. They also seized the occasion to circulate information, through the Œuvre's bulletin and other Catholic journals, about alleged Muslim oppression of Christians—not just in the Ottoman Empire but around the world. The Œuvre d'Orient had only been established at the close of the Crimean War in 1856. The Œuvre's goal was to support the education and conversion to Catholicism of Ottoman Christians and to take advantage of new freedoms granted to Christians under the Ottoman reforms of the period.

The Œuvre's successful fundraiser and publicity campaign in response to the events of 1860—from an annual budget in the tens of thousands to over two million francs—catapulted the fledgling association to national prominence.[13] More than a landmark in the Œuvre's own institutional history, though, the 1860 massacres were a landmark in French Catholic thinking about Islam in general. The rising prominence of the Œuvre d'Orient and its response to the Syrian events of 1860 represent a larger shift in French Catholic views of Islam, away from the philo-Islamism of early Algerian missions and toward a hardened, essentialized portrait of Muslims as hopelessly and belligerently backward, fanatical, and politicized.

Claiming that the sectarian violence in Syria had been secretly plotted and directed from Istanbul or even from Mecca, members of the Œuvre were at the forefront of constructing fears of a global "pan-Islamic" conspiracy—long before the pan-Ottoman policies of Abdulhamid II, for example, or the rise of Young Turks or Young Algerians made such anxieties more believable at the turn of the century.[14] Catholic notables at the Œuvre also introduced a new level of reductionism into European views of Islam. Despite earlier missionaries' depictions of the Druze as non-Muslim, pagan idolaters (and despite accounts of the massacres that distinguished between the motives of the mountain-dwelling Druze and the urban Muslims of Damascus), Œuvre accounts assimilated the actions of Druzes and Muslims together into one Muslim monolith. Finally, in arguing that the only solution, the only security for the Maronites—more civilized, more industrious, more independent, and more democratic than the Ottoman Empire's Muslim subjects—would be found in an autonomous state,

Œuvre publicists discredited Muslim civilization and planted the seeds of Maronite exceptionalism.[15]

This chapter examines the social and political context behind the Œuvre d'Orient's ideas. It is striking that many of the elite Catholics who participated in the Œuvre—and thus in constructing harsher, civilizational denigrations of Islam—were what their contemporaries and later historians have called "liberal Catholics." Despite varying political persuasions, the founding members of the Œuvre were largely supporters of the liberal Catholic campaign against "intransigent" Catholics like Veuillot. They were advocates of mainstream scholarly respectability; active in the Academies and in the diplomatic corps; readers of the liberal Catholic *Le Correspondant* and not of Veuillot's *L'Univers*; patriotic Frenchmen; and loyal believers in a French imperial "civilizing mission." In their "aristocratic liberalism," their charitable associations, fashionable salons, and academic work, the men of the Œuvre were not populist critics of French secularization, like Veuillot. Rather, they were comfortable in the halls of intellectual and governmental power, rubbing elbows with Catholic and non-Catholic elites alike. Indeed, numerous Œuvre members were well-connected to secular academic networks that were anathema to more reactionary Catholics like Veuillot and were deeply involved in the production of orientalist knowledge—knowledge intended to belittle Islamic history and to bolster French claims in the Mediterranean world.

Above all, as classical liberals in the Tocquevillian mode, they were outspoken partisans of religious liberty.[16] Thus they accused their ultramontane rivals of theocratic tendencies, since Veuillot and his ilk supposedly wanted preferential treatment for the Catholic Church rather than true liberty for all. Elite liberal Catholics prided themselves on their commitment to progress, "civilization," and tolerance. Unlike the philo-Islamic conservatives, they tended to consider Muslim missions in the Algerian context dangerous and impolitic. But liberal Catholics were also quick to denigrate Islam as backward and fanatical. Not only did the notables of the Œuvre, as devout Catholics, condemn Islam as a false religion, but they also condemned Islam for its alleged theocratic fanaticism, precisely what Veuillot and other ultramontanes admired most about it. Their orientalism was liberal and Catholic, and thus doubly opposed to Islam—informed by liberal-nationalist values and inventing and judging Islamic "fanaticism" accordingly—but still every bit as committed to the traditional apologetics of proving Christianity's superiority. This combination would be a potent one. "Liberal Catholics" did much to introduce a more civilizational and racial mode into French Catholic views of Islam.

Domestic Politics, Elite Sociability, and the Founding of the *Œuvre d'Orient*

The Œuvre des écoles d'Orient was a Catholic charitable association founded in 1856, in the immediate aftermath of the Crimean War, a war in which Britain and France had allied with the Ottoman Empire to protect it from Russian encroachment. The Treaty of Paris, which ended the war, extended new freedoms and protections to the Christian subjects of the Ottoman Empire, as an Ottoman concession to its European Allies. As French troops began to withdraw from the Empire, the Œuvre hoped to take advantage of these reforms—to redeem France's wartime sacrifices by replacing France's "military occupation" of these regions with an "intellectual occupation."[17] European Catholics viewed the *Chrétiens d'Orient* (Christians of the Middle East) as hopelessly divided by heresies and degraded by centuries of contact with Islam. Orthodox Christians were of course deemed "schismatic" and heretical, but even rites that had united with the Catholic Church, such as the Maronites and Melkites, were seen as shamefully ignorant of their own religion.

This jaded view of Eastern Christians was partly inspired by the apologetic desire to rationalize Muslim ascendancy. If Islam was a false and wicked religion, then what accounted for its success? According to a common Catholic understanding of history, Middle Eastern Christians had been overwhelmed by Muslim and Turk invasions precisely because they were already weakened and divided by their own heresies. For Eugène Boré, the Muslim invasions of these ancient Christian regions had been a "punishment" for the "indomitable pride" of the "schismatics and heretics."[18] Similarly, because of their ignorant and degraded religious practices and petty rivalries, they were in no position to impress their Muslim overlords with Christianity or to convert them. In conversation with an Orthodox Armenian woman, Boré was shocked to learn that she could not read and that her priests had taught her nothing of Christianity. He sputtered, "The little children of Islam know unshakably the false doctrine of Mohammed, and [yet] you Christians make no effort to know your religion? Must we be surprised, after that, that God has punished you by allowing you to fall under the yoke of the Muslims?"[19]

In line with this prevailing attitude, the Œuvre's strategy was clear—above all, financing of missionary schools where heretical, "schismatic" Christians would be encouraged to "convert" and unify with Rome, and where Christians from already-united rites (such as the Maronites) would be educated and "civilized." In its emphasis on the power of education to revitalize the benighted

Christians of the Middle East, the Œuvre d'Orient's approach was strikingly similar to that of the Alliance israélite universelle, founded by French Jews in the wake of the Crimean War to educate and enlighten the Jews of the Ottoman Empire.[20] As for the possibility of converting Muslims, unlike the zealous Veuillot and Jesuit missionaries in Algeria, from the very beginning "the Committee [of the Œuvre] was of the view that there was hardly any hope" of it, not at least for a long time, and not before bringing the "indigenous Christians" back into the fold.[21] The regeneration of Eastern Christianity had to come first. Only then, with the improved example and reputation of Christendom, might they begin to attract and convert some Muslims to Christianity. This was a convenient justification for postponing the Muslim challenge—a challenge to missionary methods as well as a challenge to confidence in Christianity's superiority.[22]

If the Œuvre d'Orient was the product of a particular, post-Crimean moment in French Catholic hopes for reconquering the "Holy Land," domestically it was also a product of a momentary "entente" between church and state in Second Empire France, and it was the work of Catholic notables, with their elite modes of action and sociability.[23] Unlike the much larger and older missionary fundraiser the Œuvre de la Propagation de la Foi—which was centered in Lyon and managed by a largely bourgeois board, and which encouraged even the smallest of donations—the Œuvre d'Orient's founders and earliest directors and associates came from the academic, diplomatic, and military elite of Catholic France, many of them nobility.[24] The animating spirits behind the group's first meeting were Augustin Cauchy, a celebrated mathematician, and Charles Lenormant, an archaeologist, archivist, and professor at the Collège de France—both members of the Institute, both devout Catholics and legitimists, and both known defenders of Catholic education.[25]

One attendee at the inaugural meeting of the Œuvre recorded that the new committee was made up of men all "belonging to the luminaries of science and of the army."[26] The rear admiral Pierre-Louis-Aimé Mathieu served as the president of the conseil d'administration; Henri Wallon, a historian and member of the Académie des inscriptions et belles-lettres (AIBL), was its first secretary. Other members comprised a "who's who" of Catholic notables, many of them actively engaged in diplomacy or scholarship in the Orient. Eminent figures included Armand de Melun, one of the architects of "Social Catholic" concern for the poor, and Louis de Mas-Latrie, historian of medieval Mediterranean diplomacy and official archivist for the Second Empire.[27] Among the liberal Catholic statesmen were the Comte de Montalembert, the Comte de Falloux, and Albert (future Duke) de Broglie. From the Ministry of Foreign Affairs came the undersecretary Prosper Faugère and the Baron d'Acher de Montgascon, later joined at the Œuvre by their fellow diplomat Adolphe d'Avril. From the field of orientalist studies was the professor of Turkish Abel Pavet de Courteille. From the world of Catholic journalism came Henry de Riancey. Finally, a man representative of all these threads—the Comte Melchior de Vogüé, scion of an ancient noble family, philanthropist, a moderate legitimist engaged in politics, diplomacy, and industry, an accomplished orientalist and archaeologist in his own right, and future member of the AIBL.[28]

Although the Œuvre quite intentionally assembled a diverse group of actors and prided itself on its apolitical unity, its predominant political influences seem to have been moderate royalism; a kind of "neo-Gallican" desire for close cooperation between France's Church and State; and the paternalism of Social Catholicism—the view that domestic societal divisions were best healed through elite leadership and charitable policies rather than through worker agitation.[29] The first two religious directors of the Œuvre, Charles Lavigerie followed by Pierre Soubiranne, were both recruited from the neo-Gallican orbit of Felix Dupanloup at Orléans.[30] Dupanloup was a noted theologian and educator, and as Bishop of Orléans, he was quarreled with openly by Veuillot. When Pope Pius IX published his notoriously antiliberal "Syllabus of Errors," condemning all the thought crimes of modernity, Bishop Dupanloup did his best to contain the damage and promote a more moderate interpretation of the Pope's anathemas.[31] The president of the Œuvre in its early years was the Admiral Mathieu, brother of the Gallican Bishop of Besançon.[32] As for Lavigerie, although he would eventually side with the ultramontane camp and support the infallibility of the pope during the Vatican Council of 1870–71, in the 1860s he was seen by Rome as just another liberal Sorbonne academic.[33] Above all, the Œuvre prided itself on its patriotism. Its mission seemed so effortlessly to meld French and Catholic prerogatives, since the importance of religious politics in France's Ottoman diplomacy was universally recognized even by non-Catholics. From the very beginning, this patriotism translated itself into a rhetoric shot through with the words and images of the Crusades, expressed in the Œuvre's motto: "Dieu le veut!" (God wills it!).[34]

The Œuvre d'Orient was distinguished from other missionary fundraising associations not only by the high status of its board members and associates, but also in its fundraising methods, which relied heavily on networks of elite sociability, including committees of *Dames patronesses* in the salons and parish churches of Paris's fashionable Faubourg Saint-Germain. Many Parisian nobles already felt a historic connection with the Maronite Christians of the Ottoman

Empire, a sense that predated the founding of the Œuvre and the massacres of 1860. In the collective memory of the French nobility, the Maronites were the ancient allies of Frankish crusaders, symbols of a more Christian era of French history. As early as the 1830s, the presence of French missionaries in Syria had alerted the Maronite clergy to "the advantages to be drawn from cultivating the attention of . . . the devout and Legitimist [French]." In 1844, Nicolas Murad, the representative of the Maronites at Rome, published in Paris a "Notice historique sur l'origine de la nation maronite," which emphasized France's long-standing role as religious protectors of the Maronites and encouraged the French to think of the Maronites as the "Frankish-Maronite Nation."[35] And in 1847, after a violent conflict between Maronites and Druzes following Ibrahim Pasha's withdrawal from the region, the Maronite Père Azar toured France raising funds and consciousness for the Maronites and making exaggerated claims about Maronite exceptionalism and autonomy from the Turks.[36] The French government contested Azar's credentials and his right to collect funds in French dioceses, but in the salons of the Faubourg Saint-Germain, Paris's noblewomen heard him out and considered him a "new Peter the Hermit" calling for a new Crusade.[37] Led by the Comtesse Anquetil, a "crusader's daughter" who wanted to support "this heroic and martyred people," Parisian noblewomen established a Société de secours en faveur des Chrétiens du Liban.[38] In their meetings, they read letters from Maronite churchmen who claimed that the Maronites were even related to the French nobility by blood, since their ancestors had supposedly intermarried with Frankish crusaders. This charitable society was dispersed in the upheaval of the 1848 Revolution, but the Œuvre d'Orient took up the baton in 1856, replacing "the pious and charitable *dames* of the first society" with "men as distinguished by their knowledge as by their virtue."[39]

The new Œuvre likewise made use of these elite female social networks.[40] The *Dames patronesses* who supported the Œuvre were members of society who would canvass their friends for subscriptions, host meetings and charity sales, pass the collections plate after a sermon in favor of the Œuvre, and handle correspondence with missionaries.[41] In Paris, there were to be some fifteen of these women's committees. Each committee was presided over by a clergyman, council records specify, because of the "radical incapacity" of women to direct their own meetings.[42] It seems the Œuvre exercised the same paternalistic civilizing mission toward its female associates as toward its protégés in Syria, but this did not stop prominent women like Amélie Ozanam from seizing the chance to organize Christian charity within this framework of male supervision.[43]

In addition to relying on these Parisian committees of notable ladies and their networks, Lavigerie also traveled around France visiting dioceses, preaching sermons about the Œuvre, soliciting donations and subscriptions, and establishing diocesan subcommittees, charged with publicizing the Œuvre and gathering funds. Since charitable associations required the permission of the bishop to collect funds in a given diocese, the Œuvre d'Orient could thrive only where bishops were favorably disposed toward them and not overly jealous of their charitable resources. Yet it was an indication of the Œuvre's growing popularity that it prospered in many of France's dioceses, a popularity likely helped by the fact that it was approved and recommended by the Pope and that membership came with various opportunities for indulgences.[44] Following the Pope's brief in early 1858, which recommended the Œuvre and granted indulgences to its members, a wave of bishops, "more than fifty" in all, signaled their willingness to support the creation of local committees in their jurisdictions; and Monseigneur Dupanloup of Orléans, Lavigerie's former teacher and leader of the liberal Catholic party, offered his cathedral's pulpit on a weekly basis for a representative of the Œuvre to preach in its favor.[45]

The Œuvre d'Orient, then, was the association of choice for Catholic elites and their modes of sociability. Shot through with crusader rhetoric and distant memories of noble, ancestral links to the Holy Land, relying on elite networks derived from salon and parish life, and animated by amateur, gentleman-scholarly interests—the Œuvre gave its members an outlet for political and social action denied to them by the Second Empire, and allowed them to reproduce a certain image of themselves and of their leading role in the Catholic world.

"Liberal Catholicism"?

The category "liberal Catholicism" has been used to describe a range of disparate movements or figures over the course of the nineteenth century.[46] As a simple rubric for distinguishing the varieties of liberal Catholicism across the nineteenth century, historian Georges Weill posited the existence of three waves. The first wave was represented by the democratic movement around Félicité de Lamennais in 1830 and ultimately condemned by the Pope; the second wave of liberal Catholicism comprised the struggle for educational and other religious liberties under the July Monarchy and Second Empire, led by Lamennais's disciple Charles de Montalembert; and the third wave, a faint revival of moderation at the end of the century, was prompted by Leo XIII's cautious acceptance

of Republicanism and of Social Catholicism in the 1880s.[47] The liberals of the
Œuvre d'Orient arose out of the second wave, advocating for the liberties of
religious educators in the 1840s; and under the Second Empire, they embraced
the "liberal" identifier in order to distinguish themselves from ultramontane
reactionaries like Louis Veuillot and company.

Given the political diversity of these Catholics, Weill and subsequent scholars
of liberal Catholicism have found it helpful to consider the movement less as
a coherent set of political or theological commitments and more as a particular "sensibility" or "socio-cultural" position.[48] According to Weill, the liberal
Catholic sensibility was simply that Catholics' stance toward an increasingly
post-Catholic culture should not be one of "isolation" but of "friendly relations."
The men animated by this sensibility were "rich, well-educated, academicians
or future academicians . . . royalists by taste, sympathetic to the parliamentary
regime, far from democracy," and having "influence . . . especially in the salons."[49]
This preponderance of academics among the liberal Catholics should not be
surprising. After all, the liberal wing of the Catholic party had first begun to
extricate itself from Veuillot's intransigence because of his tasteless attacks on
University scholars and administrators and because of his anti-intellectual campaign against the use of "pagan" Classics in education.[50]

Liberal Catholics tended to accept and even praise the individualistic civil
liberties enshrined by the early, "Bourgeois" phase of the French Revolution.
It was above all their religious liberalism (their belief in freedom of conscience
and Church-State separation) that set them apart from Veuillot and company.
Montalembert's "Free Church in the Free State" address, given at the Catholic
Conference at Malines in 1863, is probably the most famous and eloquent expression of this position. Under the July Monarchy's anticlerical educational policies,
so the liberal narrative went, all members of the Catholic party—from Veuillot
to Montalembert—had called for greater liberties, turning the liberal rhetoric
of 1789 against the regime's secular "monopoly" of education. It was only after
the 1848 Republic, when elite Catholics such as Falloux, Montalembert, and
Dupanloup came to power and were given the chance to draft an educational law
in cooperation with sympathetic liberals like Alexis de Tocqueville and Adolphe Thiers, that the cynicism and bad faith of Veuillot's wing of the party was
revealed. Intransigent Catholics, it seemed, had only asked for liberty insincerely
and were not willing to offer it to others if the positions of power were reversed.
In contrast to the intransigents' alleged hypocrisy, liberal Catholics perceived
themselves as having called for religious neutrality in good faith. They remained
committed to neutrality, in other words, even when Catholics gained a position

of relative power. The shibboleth of "Liberal Catholicism," according to this narrative, was sincere belief in the liberty of conscience.

The Comte de Falloux, a liberal Catholic journalist and politician in the 1850s, wrote a history of the "Catholic party," at once a defense of his own moderate educational law and a counterattack on Veuillot, who had so acerbically criticized that law for not going far enough in its support for Catholic education. In the process of retelling the birth and eventual schism of the Catholic party, Falloux elaborated his own vision of the liberal Catholic sensibility. For Falloux, the 1789 Revolution had been right to establish freedom of religion. The revolutionaries had betrayed their ideals, however, in restricting the educational prerogatives of the Church.[51] Falloux, like Montalembert, believed the fortunes of the Church rose and fell on whether it was too closely linked with a political regime. After aligning itself with the Bourbon Restoration, for example, the Church had suffered in the anticlerical backlash of the July Monarchy, but then the Church was popularly acclaimed and welcomed by the Second Republic, in part because of its distance from power under the July Monarchy.[52]

Thus, upon entering Louis-Napoleon's cabinet as minister of public instruction, Falloux was eager to compromise with non-Catholics—not to impose Catholic education immediately on the nation or to substitute a clerical monopoly for the university's monopoly, but rather to decentralize the university's administrative councils and open them up to clerical influence, as well as to allow the creation of "free" schools directed by religious congregations.[53] Falloux described his approach to educational reform in liberal Catholic terms: "to look for gradations between the *collège* and the world, harmony between the *collège* and society, between society and the Church." Against Veuillot, Falloux insisted that Catholics should be open to working together for educational legislation with men like Tocqueville and Thiers, men of good faith who recognized the social utility of Catholicism.[54]

As for differences in political doctrine between himself and Veuillot, Falloux insisted that he was the more faithful monarchist, a "moderate monarchist," and that Veuillot was the real revolutionary, since Veuillot's authoritarianism went beyond anything the ancien régime, with its decentralized provincial parliaments, had ever dreamed of.[55] Interestingly, Falloux charged that Veuillot's authoritarianism was more comparable to that of the "Turkish regime" than to any ancien régime French precedent.[56] For Falloux the liberal Catholic, Veuillot was so illiberal as to be like a Muslim. Veuillot—the admirer of Muslim religiosity—was used to being called a theocrat by liberal Catholics, as he complained in his *Liberal Illusion* of 1866. But if wanting the civil power to encourage the triumph of Christianity, if believing that there are "rules of faith that we cannot keep apart from our rules of political life" made one a theocrat, Veuillot retorted, then he welcomed the insult.[57]

Falloux published his history of the liberal Catholic party (with its attack on Veuillot) in 1856, the same year the Crimean War came to an end and the same year the charitable Œuvre d'Orient was founded. It is no coincidence that Falloux used the concluding lines of *Le parti catholique* to outline his vision for liberal Catholic leadership in domestic French politics as well as in foreign policy. Contrary to Veuillot's apocalyptic predictions, Catholicism was not on the decline, neither in France nor in the world. "Society is returning to religion," Falloux prophesied, but this revival had begun not with populist journalists but at "the heights" of society, as any change that hoped to be "efficacious and durable" must. France's intervention in the Orient, where its army had comported itself so admirably, was only one evidence of this elite return to Catholic faith and policy.[58] Providence was at work, "the Orient is on the move, the Latin cross and the Greek cross find themselves face to face" with the possibility of Catholic-Orthodox reunification. Only the spirit of liberalism, elite leadership, and conciliation—not Veuillot's ultramontanism, populism, and proselytory aggression—could bring about the long-awaited reconciliation between East and West, Orthodoxy and Catholicism.[59] The Œuvre was the quintessential expression of this desire of elite liberal Catholics to have a hand in French foreign policy and in the creation of a global Christendom.

Catholic Patriotism and French Cultural Policy in the Ottoman Empire

It is not surprising that liberal Catholics would direct their patronage and missionary activity toward the Ottoman Empire, since intervention in favor of Catholic education there was absolutely aligned with French foreign policy. It was a "Gallican" foreign policy, a cause that enabled these men to act both as Catholics and within the mainstream of French patriotism. All throughout the nineteenth century, French governments, no matter how secularizing at home, financially supported mission schools in the Ottoman Empire. Missions in other parts of the world were viewed ambivalently, sometimes as furthering French interests, sometimes as hindering them. But in the Ottoman Empire France's long-standing, official policy was predicated on open financial support for Catholic missionary schools. Cultivating and protecting the Ottoman Empire's Christian populations gave France a pretext to intervene there. The goals of the

Œuvre d'Orient—continuing France's protectorate of Ottoman Christians and French cultural predominance there through the financing of education—were thus entirely in keeping with French foreign policy under the Second Empire and even long into the more secularizing Third Republic.

In 1887, for example, when the Œuvre distributed some 300,000 francs to Catholic schools primarily in the Ottoman Empire, the Ministry of Foreign Affairs gave twice that much to the same end.[60] That year was no exception for the Quai d'Orsay, which annually gave funding to Catholic educational establishments throughout the Ottoman Empire. Likewise, even at the high tide of the Third Republic's anticlericalism, the Œuvre's third director, Félix Charmetant, was named an officier d'académie by Jules Ferry, in recognition of his leadership in exporting French education.[61] And as late as the early twentieth century, "fully 5 per cent (if not more at times) of the Quai d'Orsay's budget" went to the approximately five hundred French (predominantly Catholic) schools in the Ottoman Empire,[62] in part to counteract the cultural influence of other Great Powers and in part as an inevitable product of the numbers of French missionaries and other "private French organizations" in the Levant.[63] Moreover, French commercial and economic interests, especially those centered on the Lyon-Lebanon silk trade connection and the demand for French-speaking subalterns, increased the demand for French education.[64] As a result of this cultural policy, by which subventions were given to schools (missionary or otherwise) that taught French, French remained the language of choice for Europeans in the Ottoman Empire until the time of the Great War.[65]

In 1859, inspired by the example of the newly founded Œuvre d'Orient, France's minister of Cults openly advocated a religiously driven use of foreign policy moneys among the Ottoman Christians.[66] The French state had not only a "moral obligation" to "maintain [its] ancient patronage" of these Christians and to serve the "interests of religion and civilization," but also its "political and commercial interests would be profoundly damaged if the rival powers" were able to supplant France's consular and cultural influence. Finally, in addition to serving "the interests of religion and civilization," the minister recognized that financial support for Ottoman Christians had the virtue of being a popular cause at the moment, one that was supported by the upper echelons of the episcopate as well as by the emperor himself.[67] The members and publicists of the Œuvre never tired of proclaiming that their association was a patriotic one, a quintessential melding of the political interests of France and of the spiritual interests of Catholics. A common fundraising refrain was that to give to the Œuvre was to give to France itself.[68] As one religious put it, in the Levant at least, "the question of

France merges necessarily with the question of Catholicism."[69] Indeed, France's "soft power" goals in the Ottoman Empire "merged" so closely with Catholic education that not only the Lazarists but even the normally suspect Jesuits eventually received France's full financial and political support. Jesuit houses were "[authorized] to hoist the French flag" and were under the protection of French consuls.[70] Especially in the aftermath of the 1860 massacres, French diplomats worked closely with the Jesuits to take advantage of the crisis and extract "reparations" from the Ottomans: more than 100,000 francs for the Jesuits alone and a new property on which to build an orphanage. In addition to generous funding from the French government, the Jesuits also received free passage on French boats, preferential shipping costs for their supplies, and an "exemption from Turkish tariffs."[71]

The liberal Catholics of the Œuvre were also in agreement with the French foreign policy consensus on France's right to intervene in the Ottoman Empire. France's prerogative to intrude in Ottoman affairs (which it would exercise after the massacres of 1860) was based both on its previously mentioned cultural and educational connections and also on France's supposedly traditional role as the protector of Ottoman Christians.[72] Even more fundamental than these cultural or religious affiliations was the European consensus that the Ottoman Empire—that "sick man" of legal and ethnic pluralism—was not modern, egalitarian, or liberal enough to have its sovereignty guaranteed by international law. The very system of international law developed in the nineteenth century to guarantee a state's sovereignty was only ever meant to apply to European nation-states and was predicated on the omission of the Ottoman Empire—an "uncivilized" entity on Europe's borders whose imminent collapse threatened European peace.[73] It was there that the bulk of nineteenth-century "humanitarian" interventions took place.

The inconsistencies in this civilizing-interventionist view of the Ottoman Empire were manifold: on the one hand, European empires were in many cases more violent and inequitable than the Ottoman Empire.[74] France's "protectorate" and right to intervene on behalf of Christians was premised on the idea that the Ottomans' treatment of Christian minorities was unjust and that Christian France had an obligation to support, missionize, and educate these Christians. Yet in French Algeria, Muslims were considered "subjects" with none of the legal rights of citizens. Moreover, French colonial authorities in Algeria knew better than to allow missionaries—whether Christian or Muslim—to stir up interreligious strife. Thus, there is a special irony in France's willingness first to send missionaries to cultivate sectarianism in the minority communities of the

Ottoman Empire and then to intervene in the name of progress when interreligious conflicts inevitably arose.

Not every contemporary observer was blind to this bad faith. The orientalist-turned-Lazarist missionary Eugène Boré was idiosyncratic among midcentury Catholics for his Turcophilia and his faith in Ottoman progress. In his days as a layman and scholar in the late 1840s, Boré was delegated to report to the French Foreign Ministry on the "Question of Lebanon" in the wake of the expulsion of Muhammad Ali and creation of two separate *kaimakams* for the Druze and the Maronites. With French public opinion already disposed in the 1840s against the Ottomans and in favor of independence for the various Christian nations, Boré warned, the Ottomans had a right to wonder whether France's "sympathies" were self-interested. Boré warned that instead of provoking the Maronites and other Christians to think only of their "rights" and not their "obligations," instead of inciting them to resist and obstruct Ottoman reform—a dangerous game that could easily end in the Christians' destruction—France should encourage them to bring their Christian civilizing capabilities to bear and to help the Ottomans along their modernizing path. "Let us have the patience to wait," Boré cautioned, "let us not be so unjust as to refuse a few years for developments which took us centuries." Boré also pointed out that Druze animosity against Maronites had nothing to do with religion but rather with the "purely political" divisions and "anarchy" artificially introduced during the Egyptian occupation, the increasing Maronite migration into the formerly Druze southern districts, and the new economic ascendancy of the French-backed Maronites.[75] But when Boré publicized some of these reflections in Veuillot's *L'Univers*, cautioning against blind support of the Maronites, he was attacked in the pages of the more liberal Catholic *Le Correspondant* and even accused of being an agent of the British government.[76]

The Œuvre d'Orient and the Production of Orientalist Scholarship

A significant number of the Œuvre's leaders and members were themselves orientalists and archeologists. Indeed, among the laymen on the council, the most common thread linking them was an academic interest in Mediterranean and Oriental history, languages, inscriptions, and other artifacts—the kind of scholarship that would gain many of them membership in the Académie des inscriptions et belles-lettres (AIBL). The AIBL was the section of the French Institute devoted to orientalist and antiquarian studies, and in this period, it was a bastion of noble dilettantes. The mid-nineteenth century was an "age of specialization"—a time when academic disciplines were being invented, institutionalized, and circumscribed.[77] Some aspects of the older field of antiquarianism were being rechristened as the more scientific-sounding "archaeology," while amateur gentleman-antiquarians and collectors were gradually supplanted by "more boring but less destructive professors."[78] This transitional culture where the methods of amateur antiquarianism and professional archaeology still "overlapped" was crystallized in the AIBL, where highborn amateurs of antiquity presented their own findings but also patronized the work of professional academics.[79] One member of the AIBL who typified this milieu was the fabulously wealthy archaeologist-collector, Honoré d'Albert de Luynes.[80]

By the mid-1800s, more narrowly nationalistic archaeologies were beginning to supplant the traditional pan-European search for the Classical heritage of the West as a whole. Earlier in the century, De Luynes had helped bankroll the foundation in 1829 of an international archaeological institute at Rome, the Instituto di corrispondenza archeologica, which assembled orientalists and archaeologists from various European countries with the apolitical, "cosmopolitan" purpose of bringing together all those who had a "feeling for the Beautiful."[81] But, with the rise of liberal nationalism and national revolutions, archaeologists and classicists of different nations began competing with each other and attempting to monopolize the Classical heritage for their own respective nation-building historical narratives. Many archaeologists turned their attentions away from Greece and Rome and toward understanding their national architectural traditions at home, foregrounding the Middle Ages instead. The search was on for each European nation's own particular "Golden Age."[82] Moreover, the scholars and dilettantes of the AIBL were no strangers to working hand-in-glove with French military expeditions, producing orientalist reconnaissance that would justify and aid France's humanitarian interventions and colonial expansion around the Mediterranean. Members of the AIBL, including Charles Lenormant, participated in the "scientific commission" that accompanied the military to support the Greeks against the Ottomans in 1829, and the Académie was also connected to the "Exploratory Commission" sent to draw maps, uncover antiquities, and describe the populations of Algeria in 1839.[83]

One final influence of the rise of nation-states on the discipline of archaeology was that after the 1830s the newly independent nation of Greece was finally able to enforce legislation against the "export of antiquities," thus leaving the Ottoman Empire as the only quarry left for European hunters of Classical sites and objects. In the second half of the nineteenth century, European archaeologists descended on Ephesus, Pergamon, Rhodes, and Cyprus in search of Classical or medieval antiquities. Of course, these archaeologists were by and large uninterested in Islamic history.[84] Decentralized, with less of an institutional or nationalistic interest in preserving its cultural sites, and finding itself at a disadvantage compared to many of the European Powers, the Ottoman Porte normally granted the necessary permission for European archaeologists to excavate sites within its Empire. Although the Ottomans often demanded at least a portion of an excavation's findings for their own museums, these agreements were not always honored. When Heinrich Schliemann famously broke his agreement with Ottoman authorities and smuggled the treasure of Troy back to Germany, he justified his theft with an appeal to civilization: "By keeping them all to myself, I saved them for . . . science. All the civilized world will appreciate what I have done."[85] Ottoman sovereignty, it seems, was not worthy of respect either in military or in cultural matters. Just as military and "humanitarian" violations of Ottoman sovereignty were justified because the Empire was judged insufficiently modern or liberal to benefit from the protections of international law, so too were violations of Ottoman cultural sovereignty justified because the Empire was not civilized enough to be trusted with the care of its own antiquities. Seen in this light, it is not surprising that so many Œuvre d'Orient members—supporters of humanitarian and missionary involvement in the declining Ottoman Empire—also happen to have focused their scholarly efforts and antiquity-plundering expeditions on that same Empire.

In some ways, the academic composition of the Œuvre resembles a smaller, more exclusively Catholic cross section of the AIBL. The Œuvre was a place where Catholic notables with amateur scholarly or diplomatic interests in the Mediterranean world could network with professional Catholic academics. Members of the Œuvre who were (or would eventually become) members of the AIBL included Charles Lenormant and his son François, Henri Wallon, Louis de Mas-Latrie, Pavet de Courteille, Félicien de Saulcy, and of course, Melchior de Vogüé.[86] Other members of the Œuvre, though never rising to the ranks of the Académie, entertained similar scholarly interests, stemming from diplomatic experiences, research, and travel in the Orient.

The archaeological and philological scholarship produced by Œuvre members was certainly representative of the midcentury shift toward nationalistic and imperialistic histories. Œuvre members' scholarship betrayed very definite ideological commitments, in the service both of French colonialism abroad and of a conception of France as essentially Catholic—the "eldest daughter of the Church"—at home. In the context of their work as historians, archaeologists, and orientalists, these men promoted French and Catholic claims on the Orient and often made degrading attacks on Islam, blurring the line between their scholarship and Catholic apologetic. In 1845, for example, Œuvre founder Charles Lenormant delivered a series of lectures at the Collège de France in a course intended to prove the "divinity" and superiority of Christianity over other religions. Lenormant offered three well-worn answers to explain Islam's historic successes: the best parts of Islam were stolen from Judaism and Christianity; it owed its appeal to the way it pandered to man's worst vices; and finally, Islam was a punishment permitted by God.[87] Islam would remain inferior to Christianity, though, because Muhammad's view of divine revelation—a series of prophets each sent to repeat the same message—encouraged inertia. Islam's lack of civilization and development, according to Lenormant, had theological roots.[88]

Another Œuvre d'Orient council member who produced orientalist scholarship was Louis de Mas-Latrie. Mas-Latrie trained at the École des chartes, a school for "archivist-paleographers"—specialists in the study and treatment of documents—who were then certified to work in the libraries and archives of the state. Mas-Latrie went on to teach at his alma mater, and a nucleus of devout Catholic chartistes formed around him and Catholic apologist and literary historian Léon Gautier.[89] Mas-Latrie and his fellow Œuvre member Melchior de Vogüé shared a scholarly interest in medieval contacts between Latins and Muslims, especially in the history of crusader states in the Mediterranean world.[90] Mas-Latrie devoted much of his research to the House of Lusignan, Frankish nobles who remained Kings of Cyprus for centuries after the rest of the crusaders were driven from the shores of the Holy Land. In Mas-Latrie's telling, the rise and fall of Frankish Cyprus offered lessons for nineteenth-century Christian civilization. Predictably, Mas-Latrie argued that the era of "European" control of Cyprus was much less oppressive than the subsequent regime of the Turks.[91] But Mas-Latrie implied that one reason Cyprus ultimately succumbed to the Turks was that the Greek inhabitants had resisted assimilating to and allying with the Europeans. If present-day Orthodox clergymen would only learn from this failure and allow European education to proliferate throughout Ottoman lands, the "ancient union in the faith . . . will be able to be reestablished, and Christian populations [of the Orient], supported by civilized Europe, will soon have conquered the emancipation, independence, and guarantees which are due them."[92] The lessons of history, conveniently, served to confirm the educational and imperial goals of the Œuvre d'Orient.

Another of Mas-Latrie's lifelong scholarly interests, intended to serve "the expansion of French interests abroad," was the history of medieval Mediterranean commerce between Muslims and Christians.[93] With his training as a *chartiste*, Mas-Latrie compiled and edited publications of medieval commercial treaties between North African Muslims and European merchants in Pisa, Genoa, Venice, Marseilles, and Sicily. Begun in the 1840s at the request of the Ministry of War, he would continue this research into the 1860s, dedicating it to Napoleon III and his plans to bring the Muslims of North Africa into closer collaboration with France. Mas-Latrie used this history of medieval commerce to argue that North African Arabs had once cooperated peacefully with European powers, guaranteeing the protection of commerce and the free exercise of Christianity for merchants and consuls. It was only with the arrival of the Turks in the sixteenth century that the "worst times of barbarism" in North Africa appeared, including a surge in piracy and in the persecution of Christians.[94] Mas-Latrie's conclusion heaped discredit on the Ottoman regencies in the Maghreb as nothing but an illegitimate interlude between two periods of European–North African concord. As if the ideological stakes of his scholarship were not already clear, Mas-Latrie republished his edition of medieval treaties again in the late 1880s to commemorate France's annexation of Tunisia (another Ottoman regency). For Mas-Latrie, North African history was now "part of the general history of France," and his history of Mediterranean commerce proved "that France is at home at Tunis, as at Algiers."[95]

Melchior de Vogüé—the most socially prominent of the Œuvre's active council members—was both a collector of antiquities and an accomplished orientalist of some distinction. His primary interest was archaeological history, but the ideological function of his research, like that of his colleagues at the Œuvre, was to minimize the history of Muslim civilizations and to emphasize French and Christian claims to the Mediterranean world. After resigning a nascent career in diplomacy in protest at Napoleon III's coup d'état, he spent the year of 1853–54 traveling across the Ottoman Empire and Holy Land, "roaming the ruins, measuring, sketching, copying inscriptions," and finding nationalistic and spiritual inspiration in the sites and memories of the Crusades and of biblical Jerusalem.[96] Vogüé spent the next five years studying and gathering his notes and sketches from this trip into a volume well-received even by specialists, *Les églises de la Terre Sainte*, a study of religious edifices built by the crusader kingdoms. Vogüé was a skilled draftsman, and one of the merits of the book—part travelogue, part compilation of sketches and analyses of religious edifices—was the rigor and detail of its illustrations.[97]

The work was also a sharp polemic. Running all through his tour of crusader churches was Vogüé's argument—that, contrary to some romantic historians of archaeology, Arab or Oriental techniques had exerted no significant influence on Europe's Gothic architecture. On the contrary, Gothic architecture, despite being transplanted to the Holy Land with the Crusades and despite its interaction with the Orient, had never ceased to be essentially northern European. Reflecting the disciplinary shift toward nationalistic narratives, Vogüé claimed that the crusaders were of predominantly French origin, and that their churches were examples of "our national architecture," "monuments that our fathers raised [in the Holy Land] at the price of their blood."[98] These crusaders, who had been able to build so many structures even in the midst of constant war, were like the followers of the ancient Jewish leader Nehemiah, who rebuilt Jerusalem's walls even while defending themselves from the Samaritans, a "trowel" in one hand and a "sword" in the other.[99] The rhetorical effect of such biblical comparisons, identifying crusaders with ancient Israelites (and, by implication, Muslims with Israel's Samaritan enemies), further strengthened the Christian West's cultural claims to these sites and delegitimized the intervening centuries' possessors.

In being transplanted to the Holy Land, Vogüé argued, Medieval society and architecture may have been affected by "local necessities," but only superficially. After all, what defined European architecture was not its strict adherence to any one form, but its creativity and suppleness.[100] The forms crusaders ended up using—especially the *ogive*, or pointed arch, so prominent in Arab architecture—were already known and available to European architects, and so should not be cited as evidence of Arab influence. Certainly, there had been various "parasitical" additions made throughout history to the Church of the Holy Sepulchre, for example, but its essential structure remained characteristically Latin and Gothic.[101] The "Arab influence," Vogüé concluded, "played only a very secondary role in the development of Gothic architecture."[102] Muslim "parasites" might come and go, Vogüé implied, but Christendom would continue to march independently forward in the path of progress.

Another lesson Vogüé drew from his studies was that the Christians of the Levant were at that moment too divided and heretical to effectively put Islam to shame. Like Mas-Latrie in this respect, Vogüé's scholarship served the Catholic-Orthodox reunification hopes of the Œuvre. The Greek Orthodox Church, by opting for schism, "had forever sacrificed to its vanity the spirit of union ... which would have saved it from the Turks."[103] As for the hotly contested "Question of the Holy Sites"—Catholic and Orthodox disputes over possession of biblical sites of memory—Vogüé argued (somewhat tautologically) that the "Franks" had "consecrated their right" to the Holy Sites by their "presence ... on the soil," while the Greeks had forfeited their rights by leaving the Christian fold. With those churches in a state of degradation, they had harmed the "dignity of the Christian name." Like Boré and other critics of Eastern Christians, Vogüé wrote that the indigenous Christians' petty divisions "[scandalized] even the Muslims."[104] Catholic, nationalist, and imperialist: the ideological function of Vogüé's focus on crusader monuments was clear. These "churches built by French hands" belonged to France and to French memory. In leaving the Holy Land to return to France, Vogüé felt like he was leaving home, like one of the "exiled children of Israel."[105]

For Vogüé, other works on Holy Land inscriptions and edifices would follow—in particular, a research expedition undertaken during a trip to Syria in 1861. Vogüé planned to use this trip both to check on establishments funded by the Œuvre, such as the orphanages founded in the wake of the 1860 massacres, and to take part in the French archaeological expedition organized by the philologist Ernest Renan, which had accompanied France's military intervention in Syria in 1860. As in the case of the first Napoleon's more famous "scientific commission" in Egypt, Renan's expedition to "Phoenicia" on the coattails of a civilizing army underscores the link between colonial power and colonial knowledge. With consular letters and Ottoman permissions in hand, Renan conducted his excavations with the help of a detachment of French soldiers and relied on the French expeditionary corps' mapmakers.[106] After finishing in Syria, Renan had planned but was unable to go on to Cyprus to excavate the Phoenician Citium. Vogüé had already been planning a trip of his own to Syria and was sufficiently respected as a scholar for Renan to ask him to detour to Cyprus and copy inscriptions on his behalf.[107] Renan passed on the necessary Ottoman permission for excavations and, predictably, advised Vogüé to concentrate on Classical antiquity rather than on the Muslim relics.[108]

In a report on his Syrian and Cypriot findings, Vogüé took to its extreme this tendency to value only the presumed forebears of Western and French civilization. On Cyprus, he had documented Cypriot, Phoenician, and Greek inscriptions, but also "all the monuments from the time of the Lusignans, French monuments, like the dynasty that birthed them." Vogüé also claimed that he had discovered intact ruins of ancient, pre-Islamic Christian villages in the Syrian Hauran—still preserved because the Christians had dropped everything to flee from Muslim invaders in the seventh century and because the Druze, who had not occupied the area until quite recently, "do not build," but rather simply take up residence on another's foundations. Thus, "the *Haouran* shows us unalloyed Christian civilization."[109]

Besides scholars and clergy, the other professional milieu most heavily represented on the Œuvre's council was the diplomatic corps. The Baron d'Acher de
Montgascon, like Vogüé, was from a royalist family and entered the diplomatic
service under Tocqueville's ministry.[110] Prosper Faugère was an undersecretary
in the Foreign Ministry's archives department and a patron to young diplomats
who began their careers in that department.[111] Like other Catholic diplomats,
he seems to have used his influence to lobby for French support for Christian
populations, notably on behalf of the Montenegrins against Turk invasion in
1858.[112] Finally, among the diplomats of the Œuvre, there was Adolphe d'Avril,
who began his career working in Faugère's office before being assigned to various
missions in the Orient.[113] D'Avril and d'Acher de Montgascon both joined the
Œuvre early on, and both had already been involved in the Œuvre des pèlerinages de Terre Sainte, a Catholic association that organized annual trips to the
sites of the Holy Land.[114] In their capacity as diplomats, both had occasion to
work under Vogüé some years later, when he served the conservative Republic of the 1870s as the ambassador to Constantinople. Vogüé recommended
d'Avril warmly to his superiors, which suggests that ties of Catholic patronage,
cemented in the context of social networks like that of the Œuvre d'Orient,
could be just as valuable to career diplomats as they were to antiquarians and
orientalists aspiring to the Académie.[115]

Other members of the Œuvre d'Orient similarly lent their scholarly expertise
to encouraging French interventions in the Ottoman Empire. But this sampling
of the scholarly production of key members—Charles Lenormant, Mas-Latrie,
Vogüé—is sufficient to show the constellation of orientalist themes that reinforced the charitable and foreign policy vision of the Œuvre. These themes included that the Mediterranean world was above all a site of French history and,
thus, of future French action; that the Christians of the Orient needed to reunite
with Rome, under the guidance of France, if they were ever to resist Muslim persecution and to protect Christianity's reputation; and that Muslims were only
momentary interlopers in the history of the Orient, immobile "parasites" with
no creativity or civilizational gains to show for themselves.

A Liberal Catholic "Civilizing Mission"

Much has been written about the rise of the rhetoric of *civilisation* and the *mission civilisatrice* especially as it became the imperial justification of choice under
the Third Republic in the 1880s.[116] The "civilizing mission" justification for imperial or humanitarian interventions is generally thought to have become more

hegemonic under the Third Republic, as a secularization of traditional missions, a secular substitute for the religious justifications of colonialism.[117] Although these claims are true as generalizations, they can obscure the extent to which the civilizing ideology was widespread before the Third Republic and the extent to which religious actors, far from being supplanted by a secularized mission, participated wholeheartedly in the construction of this civilizing ideology. Against a "Republican teleology" that views the Third Republic as the successful culmination of secular Republican ideals and the highpoint of imperial expansion, the reality is that much of the vocabulary and groundwork of late nineteenth-century imperialism was laid by the Second Empire and previous, non-Republican regimes and actors.[118] Liberal Catholics were present at the birth of the civilizing mission and were some of its first and most vocal articulators. Liberal Catholics did not view "civilization" as a replacement for religious justifications of Empire; rather they brought their Christian commitments with them into their understanding of the civilizing mission. They would not be the last Christian activists to weaponize "civilization" or "secularism" against a rival religion, nor would they be the last to portray their own Christian commitments as neutral or secular.

Liberal Catholic advocates of intervention in the Ottoman Empire were at the forefront of those who used the universalizing rhetoric of civilization. In their attempt to claim the terrain of mainstream patriotism, they were also eager to prove that there was no Catholic sectarianism behind their actions. They sincerely believed, and wanted their anticlerical adversaries to believe, that there need be no conflict between France's traditional policy of protecting Ottoman Christians and the wider liberal goals of human progress and emancipation. This was especially true in the context of the Ottoman Empire and in the kinds of educational missions prioritized by the liberal Catholics of the Œuvre d'Orient. For example, one project patronized by the Œuvre was a Jesuit-run printing press at Beirut, which was in the process of printing a French-Arab dictionary. As a Jesuit missionary proudly explained in 1862, the printing press would be able "to spread through all of the Lebanon, along with religious truth, the French spirit and the benefits of civilization."[119] Here the Gospel seems quite overshadowed by the importance of civilizational progress. There was an undeniable patriotism in the Jesuits' (and the Œuvre's) intentions here: that the "French language" and influence, and not Italian or English, would soon be "universal in Syria."[120] Indeed, no one, the Jesuit correspondent insisted, was better placed than these missionaries to spread both "faith and Christian civilization."[121] The press published primarily religious works and catechisms but also Arabic poetry and other literature, and thus it hoped to cause a "[renaissance] of intellectual life in the Lebanon."[122]

Similarly, the Jesuit Père de Damas, who worked with the Œuvre d'Orient, wrote in 1864 that Jesuit missionaries in the Lebanon were there "to exercise a *mission civilisatrice*."[123] Given the ignorance and lack of "science" among the Christian populations there, it was only natural that the first obligation of the missionaries should be to "make themselves *instituteurs*."[124] Between their schools (including training schools for indigenous teachers) and the printing press, Damas hoped, "the tree of Christian science will grow and will bear [the] fruits of civilization on the banks of Asia."[125] In short, the Catholic scholars and diplomats of the Œuvre, and the missionary-educators they supported, were not at all opponents of the language of the *mission civilisatrice*, nor were they its main targets; rather, they were some of the primary diffusers of the concept. Liberal Catholics strove to characterize Catholicism as a necessary component of France's civilizing mission, and it was above all in the Orient, against an illiberal Islamic foe, that this civilizational unity was articulated.

The men of the Œuvre d'Orient were united by their elite professional and fundraising networks; their disdain for more populist, "theocratic" styles of Catholicism; their professed patriotism and commitment to religious liberty; their desire to "regenerate" and reintegrate Middle Eastern Christians into the Catholic fold, while ignoring the possibility of Muslim conversion; and their impressive corpus of orientalist scholarship that depicted the Levant as the birthright of Catholic France. In the wake of the 1860 massacres in Syria, no organization would be better placed to raise funds and consciousness on behalf of Christian victims, to promote France's "civilizing mission" in the Ottoman Empire, or to manufacture outrage against the Muslims of the Mediterranean World.

CHAPTER 5

Conspiracy to Massacre

Liberal Catholics and the Invention of Pan-Islamism

When news of the violent events of Syria began trickling back to France in early July of 1860, the charitable and ideological machines of the Œuvre d'Orient lurched into high gear. The Œuvre's council immediately convened an emergency meeting to discuss how best to help "the Christians of Syria so cruelly persecuted by the *Druses*."[1] The council voted to publish a note about the massacres and to make an appeal in all the "journals of Paris" to raise funds for the Maronite victims. At the close of the meeting, the members scattered to deliver the announcement to various journal editors. The Œuvre itself, having already distributed its available funds for the fiscal year, could only devote 1,000 francs to inaugurate the fundraising drive and pray that Catholic France would be generous.

In the Catholic press, early coverage of the massacres was heavily influenced by members and friends of the Œuvre d'Orient. Those among the Œuvre's members who had traveled or cultivated contacts in the Levant, especially Melchior de Vogüé and François Lenormant, took it upon themselves to write opinion pieces or transmit firsthand accounts of the massacres to Catholic France. Given the Œuvre's scholarly and missionary contacts in the Ottoman Empire, the association was in a privileged position to control authoritative accounts of the massacres. From the very first, it seems, the members hoped not only to convince Catholics to donate but also to influence the Second Empire's foreign policy, pressuring Napoleon III to intervene militarily. Emmanuel Guillaume Rey—Œuvre council member and historian of the Crusades—wrote to Vogüé that he was sure that "something useful and serious" would come from the Œuvre: "But publicity, publicity is more necessary to us than ever" since there still seemed to be resistance "in the high regions" of the government against an "armed intervention." Guillaume Rey proceeded to sketch out a publicity campaign that Vogüé and other Œuvre members would follow. The next mail delivery from Syria was sure to contain horrifying details of the Druze sack of Christian Zahleh: "Let us take advantage of the circumstance." Disseminating the accounts of missionaries and other contacts, "Let us unmask more and more the perfidy of the Turkish authorities and try to tear the [French] government away . . . from its last scruples toward the *droit des gens* [customary international law]; which scarcely exists in the Orient" anyway.[2] In other words, Guillaume Rey argued, France had every right to intervene militarily, since the Ottomans had not shown themselves worthy of sovereignty and the protections of international law. Œuvre publicists needed only to hammer away on the theme that Ottoman authorities were complicit in the massacres.

Throughout the late summer of 1860, Guillaume Rey would continue to pass on to Vogüé communications from Syria.[3] Even after Vogüé published his first article on the Syrian events, Guillaume Rey begged Vogüé to pen more articles to encourage an "energetic" French repression of the Druze. Amid discussion of the Œuvre's fundraiser and Lavigerie's plans to distribute the charity, Guillaume Rey remarked, "It is indispensable for the pacification of [Mount Lebanon] that our soldiers burn some cartridges against the *Druses*."[4] Moreover, as we will see, in the Œuvre's response to the massacres, the conflict in Mount Lebanon between the Druze and Maronite rivals was elevated as evidence of a wider Islamic conspiracy against Ottoman Christians. By September, the Œuvre council's proceedings would refer simply to the "victims of the Muslims," no longer distinguishing between the Druze and Muslim attackers.[5] In their charity and publicity campaigns on behalf of the Maronites—in their desire to articulate a common, patriotic cause between mainstream Catholics and the French state— the liberal Catholics of the Œuvre were among the first in France to depict the Islamic world as a unified geopolitical enemy and to call for a civilizational clash against an allegedly conspiratorial global Islam. In their desire to demonstrate their own commitment to liberty of conscience and separation of church and state—to demonstrate their distance from theocratic Catholics like Veuillot— they were also at the forefront of those who depicted Islam as hopelessly fanatical and illiberal, as incapable of disentangling religion from politics.

The *Bulletin* of the Œuvre d'Orient published the eyewitness accounts of the Jesuit Père Billotet and the letters of Œuvre associate François Lenormant, both in Syria. The Père Gagarin, a representative of the Jesuits in Paris and a member of the Œuvre's council, also passed on to Vogüé reports from Jesuit missionaries in Syria.[6] These and other missionary sources relied heavily on classic martyrological tropes: the Catholic victim, presented with the choice of conversion to

Islam or death, who invariably held strong to her faith. But what all the mission-ary and other sources agreed upon was the complicity of the Turkish authorities and soldiers in the massacres. Guillaume Rey passed along the accusation that Turkish soldiers had even come from Damascus to participate in the destruc-tion of Zahleh. And Père de Prunières, a Jesuit missionary in Beirut, engaged in some conspiracy theorizing of his own: the Ottomans must have secretly tricked the Maronites somehow into being aggressive first, intentionally entrapping the Christians into their own massacre by the Druze. Prunières claimed that the Ottoman Pasha's cannon fire—supposedly intended to disperse the Druze at-tackers—was in fact a prearranged signal for them to begin their bloody work.[7] This accusation of a long-planned conspiracy at higher levels of the Ottoman administration or even in Mecca would be one of the most persistent themes in French Catholic coverage of the events.

Another missionary reported that the massacres were a predictably Islamic reaction to the liberal reforms of the Ottoman Empire. The Qur'an commands that Christians must pay for the right to live under Muslim overlords or else be killed and forfeit their property, the missionary explained. The *Hatti Ha-mayoun* (the 1856 reform that equalized the status of Christians and Muslims, and which had so excited the hopes of French Catholics) had done away with Christian subjugation and taxes. Therefore, devout Muslims believed they had every right to kill them. This explanation of local resistance to Ottoman reform was redundant and even contradictory, though, since the same missionary also agreed with the conspiracy theory that "the order to massacre the Christians was given at Constantinople."[8]

One other recurring theme in these letters, in addition to the conspiracy the-ory about Ottoman complicity and the essentially "Muslim" character of the fanaticism and violence, was the supposed special hatred these allegedly enraged Muslims had for France—their intentional targeting of French symbols and protégés. These Muslim fanatics knew about France's support for the Maronites and associated France with Catholicism, French eyewitnesses claimed; and thus, they intentionally disrespected symbols of French authority. The fact that some Muslim notables were also among the massacred was not proof that there were nonreligious motives for the massacres; rather, supposedly, it was because these Muslims happened to be loyal to France that they were massacred. "The war of extermination," Guillaume Rey wrote, "is addressed to our country."[9] One Jesuit claimed that as the missionary house of the Lazarists burned, the attackers cried out "Where then is Napoleon? May he come deliver you from our fires."[10] Of course, some rioters doubtless did resent the "humiliating" way French consuls intervened in local conflicts to protect their clients and missionaries.[11] Far from denationalizing and adapting their Christianity, missionaries under France's "religious protectorate" in Ottoman Syria had strong political incentives to associate their Christianity with Frenchness. Yet when missionaries' embrace of the French flag and protection became the focus of resentment and violence in 1860, this supposedly proved that it was Muslims, not Christians, who followed a politicized religion. For the liberal Catholics at the Œuvre, intent on proving the patriotism and essential Frenchness of Catholicism, a politicized and France-hating Islam was the perfect shadowboxing partner.

The notion that Muslims' anti-Christian animus included a particular hatred for France, the patron of Eastern Christians, would permeate Catholic correspondence from the region and appear in Œuvre-affiliated coverage of the events. This was a popular theme among Catholics not only because it was hoped it might taunt France into intervening militarily but also because it reinforced—from a negative perspective—the Œuvre's view of itself as the patriotic charity par excellence. The attackers had desecrated crosses and French flags alike. In other words, even the Muslim enemy correctly recognized that France's true interests in the Levant were represented by Catholicism. Lenormant's letters, published in *L'Ami de la religion* and later republished in the Œuvre's *Bulletin*, waxed particularly eloquent on this reverse image of the identification between Christian and French interests. "The favorite joke of the *Druses* and Turks," Lenormant wrote, "was to slaughter on the cross the unfortunate Christians of Deir-El-Kamar, saying to them: 'Why does your God not save you now?' Others were killed on the French flag with analogous insults."[12] In other words, the Christians of Syria were dying like Jesus himself, on a cross and to the sound of the same jeers that had filled the crucified Christ's ears. But if they were martyrs for their love of God, they were just as much martyrs for their love of France: the flag of France their cross of suffering, Napoleon III the God who would avenge them, or so the Œuvre hoped.

These were the sources and themes Vogüé and his colleagues worked with in their campaign to raise funds and to incite a military expedition. The royalist-turned-liberal Catholic journal, *L'Ami de la religion*, was the primary outlet where the Œuvre publicized its special fundraising drive, including lists of donations received, and it was where Vogüé and Lenormant published their editorials and the correspondence from their missionary contacts.[13] What *L'Ami de la religion*'s own correspondents and the Œuvre's contributors sought to demonstrate, above all, was that the "Muslims" of the Ottoman Empire, from local Druzes and Arabs all the way up to Turkish authorities, were driven by their

"Muslim fanaticism" to conspire at the "extermination of the entire Christian race in Syria."[14] One of the more prominent aspects of this reductivism was to lump the Druze-Maronite civil war in Mount Lebanon (which had raged since May 1860) together with the "Damascus incident" of early July, even though the two events followed distinct logics.[15] In a similar vein, *L'Ami de la religion* quoted reports from the Jesuit missionary Père Rousseau posted at Saïda (Sidon), who insisted that the "Muslims" of his town had been incited by their muftis. Reflecting the paranoia among on-site observers and setting the tone for Catholic France's subsequent views of the events, the père insisted that this was "not a war between the *Druses* and the Maronites, it is a conspiracy hatched by the Turkish authorities and the *Druses* to exterminate the Christians," a conspiracy that "reaches everywhere in the Turk Empire."[16] Rousseau reported that in some villages the Christian populations had resisted valiantly up until the Ottoman garrison disarmed them, promising them official protection and then allowing them to be massacred.

The Œuvre's first director, Abbé Charles Lavigerie, did his part to promote the thesis of the essentially Muslim, religious character of the massacres and, by extension, of Ottoman complicity. In one of his appeals for funds, Lavigerie claimed that a Druze chief had "sworn" not to stop hunting down Maronites until he had "cut off the head of the last man who makes the sign of the cross." The Maronites, on the other hand, were "martyrs . . . persecuted for their faith."[17] Likewise, the archbishop of Bordeaux, a supporter of the Œuvre, published a *mandement* to the faithful of his diocese (and reproduced in *L'Ami de la religion*) that accused the Ottomans of having concocted a "general extermination plan" against the Maronites, the "French of the Orient, an inoffensive, modest, agricultural people."[18]

Melchior de Vogüé was quick to bring his expertise and missionary contacts to bear on the events, authoring a piece on "The Events of Syria" in the July 14 edition of *L'Ami de la religion*, as well as a series of subsequent articles. Vogüé's firsthand knowledge of the region and air of foreign policy savvy lent his contributions authority and sophistication; but the themes he developed were identical to those of the missionaries: "Muslim fanaticism," Ottoman complicity and conspiracy, and the perpetrators' targeting of French protégés and symbols. Vogüé's first intent was to contradict anyone still naïve enough to believe in the "good faith" of Ottoman reforms and to justify French military occupation. The Ottomans and the Druze were motivated in their hatred for the Maronites because of the latter's cultural and commercial contacts with Europe. Muslims resented the Maronites' new ascendance brought on by missionary education and the growth of silk production and especially their pretenses to equality after the Treaty of Paris and *Hatti Hamayoun* reforms. Vogüé, echoing the views of his missionary correspondents, accused the "Turkish authorities" of entrapping the Maronites, by allegedly tricking them into quarreling among themselves, and then provoking them into a fight against the Druze.[19] Throughout *L'Ami de la religion*'s and the Œuvre's publicizing of the events, this theme of general Ottoman complicity and centralized plotting coexisted somehow with the contradictory theme that the massacres were due to Ottoman weakness and inability to impose security in the distant Mount Lebanon. What these contradictory themes had in common, though, was the impulse to justify a French military intervention. In effect, French Catholic readers could pick their preferred pretext: either the Ottomans had wanted to murder their Christian subjects and had effectively orchestrated the massacres, or the Ottomans were spread too thin to do anything about the murders. Less than a week after publishing the accusation that the "conspiracy extends everywhere in the Turkish empire," for example, the same writer at *L'Ami de la religion* claimed that French troops were necessary in Syria because of the "irremediable, original, absolute powerlessness of the Ottoman government."[20]

Vogüé wrote another article for *L'Ami de la religion* on July 28, arguing the case for a forceful military intervention with the aim of establishing an independent, sovereign state for the Christians of Syria. For Vogüé, as for many Catholic observers of the *Tanzimat* reforms, the Ottoman Empire's right to sovereignty and territorial integrity was absolutely conditional on its following Europe "in the way of civilization" and on keeping its promise to improve the status of its Christian subjects. The massacres in Mount Lebanon proved that these conditions were impossible for the Ottomans to fulfill. Here Vogüé's rhetoric hardened markedly from the reformist optimism of 1856: "There is a radical incompatibility between the Turk and civilization: between Muslims and Christians there is an abyss which . . . the good intentions of the Sultan . . . cannot fill up."[21] The sultan quickly dispatched a special commissioner, Fuad Pasha, to mete out punishment and restore calm, but how could the French trust the same Turks who had allegedly been complicit in the massacres? In fact, Vogüé perfectly understood the stakes of Fuad Pasha's mission—his purpose was to enact vengeance in as exemplary a manner as possible, precisely in order to preempt European intervention and to render French troops superfluous. Ironically, then, Vogüé hoped Fuad Pasha would *not* be successful in restoring legitimacy and the veneer of justice and that French-dispensed violence would still be necessary.[22]

In his criticism of the Ottoman special commissioner, Vogüé, like other commentators on the Ottoman question, could not help mixing together contradictory justifications for intervention, arguing both that Fuad Pasha and his troops would only amount to "new enemies for the Christians," but also that the Ottoman government lacked "the strength or even the time" to save the last of the threatened Christians. Vogüé agreed with Saint-Marc Girardin, who had argued in the pages of the liberal Catholic *Le Correspondant* that France's policy in the Ottoman Empire should be to replace Turkish sovereignty with independent, Christian sovereignties. This was the only way to settle the Ottoman question, since "Ottoman integrity" was beyond saving and since partition between European powers would disproportionately advantage Russia. Vogüé's justification of a French occupation relied on the same redemptive logic that had motivated the Œuvre's founding in the first place. France needed to ensure that the sacrifices of the Crimean War might be "crowned by the emancipation of the Orient."[23]

Not all Œuvre-affiliated observers began with such an essentialized, monolithic view of Syrian Druzes, Arabs, and Ottoman Turks as Vogüé. François Lenormant was excavating a site in Greece when the massacres first began. Quickly raising some money among sympathetic Christians there, he set off for Syria to bring what help he could to the refugees gathering in the coastal towns. Lenormant sent long accounts of his stay in Beirut to *L'Ami de la religion*, accounts then republished in the Œuvre's own *Bulletin*. In his first letter, he distinguished between the religions of the Druze and the Muslims—the Muslims were inspired by their usual "fanaticism," but the Druze were motivated merely by a "pagan rage." Lenormant also admitted that both the Maronite Christians and the Druze were to blame, at least initially, for the conflict in Lebanon; that the Maronites had been the main source of trouble the year before, when some refused allegiance to the new Ottoman *kaimakam*; and that even in the present civil war, Maronites had made the first move (in an attempt to prevent their massacre, Lenormant claimed). Lenormant even insisted that—in contrast to the more sadistic Muslims—the Druze possessed a kind of tribal chivalry and rarely raped or killed innocents. It was the *bachi-bouzouks*, or Ottoman irregulars, who committed the worst atrocities.[24]

It is also worth noting that in the early years of the Jesuit mission in Lebanon (before the increasing sectarian tensions of the 1840s) missionaries had distinguished clearly between Muslims and the non-Muslim Druze. In fact, French missionaries in the 1830s believed that the Druze were simple idolaters, having no particular affiliation with Islam, and that they were ripe for conversion to Christianity. In 1834, the editor of the missionary journal *Annales de la*

Propagation de la Foi even paid them the bizarre cultural compliment of theorizing that they were the descendants of French Crusaders.[25] In 1839, just before European intervention against Muhammad Ali's occupation, Jesuit missionaries reported that they were baptizing Druzes left and right and that the Druze were on the verge of a widespread movement toward Christianity.[26] It was only in the mid-1840s, after Egyptian, British, and French interventions to divide and rule Lebanon on the basis of sectarian identity, that the Druze clashed openly with the Maronites and earned the suspicion of Catholic France. Following the even more violent events of 1860, in the short space of twenty years, the Druze would be rhetorically transformed from pagans ripe for conversion into fanatical Muslims. Distinctions between the Druze and the Muslims faded, and the sectarian clashes between the "Muslim" Druze and Christian Maronites were transformed into one more evidence of pan-Islamic fanaticism.

Despite Lenormant's initial moderation in describing the Druze, his description of the sectarian tensions in Damascus shows that even before the massacres in July 1860, French Catholic observers were already ideologically preparing to merge any Muslim-Christian violence there together with the earlier Druze-Maronite conflicts in Mount Lebanon, effectively erasing the distinction between Druzes and Muslims. Both conflicts were animated by the same Muslim fanaticism, the same mania for "holy war."[27] Defining someone as "Muslim" served a completely static and negative function: as long as the Druze had seemed like prospective converts in the 1830s, they were not considered Muslims, but killing Christians was enough to make them Muslims again.

When the tense atmosphere in Damascus eventually boiled over into a general massacre of Christians, French Catholics needed no further convincing: this was no tribal conflict between the Druze and Maronites in Mount Lebanon but an all-out, pan-Islamic religious war. (This claim was made despite the fact that even the Damascus events were almost certainly motivated by social resentment, since "Muslim craftsmen and shopkeepers" targeted rich Christians with European connections, leaving poorer Christian districts alone.[28]) In the wake of the Damascus massacres in July, Vogüé's rhetoric grew more agitated, demanding that French policy take the form of an explicitly Christian holy war in response to this Islamic jihad. The exterminatory "plot" that the Turks had set in motion (for which the Druze-Maronite conflict was "only a pretext") would soon "encompass all the Muslim countries," Vogüé feverishly claimed, including France's subjects in Algeria, with their mysterious connections to Muslims in the Ottoman Empire. But, Vogüé threatened, if it was a crusade the Muslims wanted—if religious identity was to be the primary marker of difference in the coming battle—then it was a crusade France should give them.

The violence, Vogüé claimed, had been inspired by Islam's resistance to Christianity and civilization, and the Muslims falsely believed themselves ascendant and crowned with success. Against such arrogance, France's military intervention would need to "humiliate [Islam]" intentionally and explicitly, "to prove... its powerlessness." Not only must Muslims be punished in an exemplary and demeaning way, but they must know that it was precisely as Muslims that they were receiving their punishment from Christian Europe: "We must fight in the name of the cross." And what better site than Damascus, with its famous Umayyad Mosque, for France's forces to perform a desecration that would radiate throughout the Muslim world? As a respected archaeologist and lover of religious edifices, Vogüé affected to plead for "mercy" for the physical structure of the mosque, but he nevertheless demanded that it be "humiliated [in its capacity] as a sanctuary . . . our soldiers must penetrate within it, take up residence there, and bear witness to all of Christendom's contempt for Islam." If, during the anti-European riots at Jeddah two years earlier, France and England had simply sent some troops to occupy Mecca and "insult the Kaaba," Vogüé argued, this public demonstration of Islam's weakness and subjection "on the very tomb of its founder" [*sic*] might have singlehandedly prevented the more recent massacres in Syria.[29]

Here was a surfeit of anti-Islamic rage that stands out in its extremism even among similar outpourings of that summer of 1860. But the good liberal Vogüé was no reactionary Catholic, he insisted. He was not yielding to "religious fanaticism," nor was he contradicting his position as a "strong supporter of the liberty of conscience." Tellingly, Vogüé even contrasted France's supposedly prudent, antimissionary policies in Algeria with the aggressively anti-Islamic intervention he was recommending for Syria. "[R]eligious toleration . . . was perhaps necessary" in the Algerian colony, since it was subject to France. In Syria, however, where France had no intention of assimilating or secularizing the Muslim populations, Vogüé claimed that this kind of religious neutrality would be unintelligible to the Muslims and taken as a "sign of weakness."[30]

Vogüé's energetic campaign in the French Catholic press culminated with a longer piece on the "Events of Syria" published in *Le Correspondant*—the high-brow, monthly organ of liberal Catholicism—and reproduced in a pamphlet. Here, even perfunctory distinctions between Druze, Turk, or "Muslim" had been erased. Whereas Lenormant had spoken in his articles of a kind of primitive chivalry among many of the Druze, distinct from the cruelty of the

Ottoman irregulars, Vogüé claimed that "*Druses* and *bachi-bouzouks* competed [in their] cruelty and barbarity." Moreover, Vogüé reported, once the massacres had been set in motion, the "*Druse* sheiks" began calling for "holy war," uniting against the Christians "everyone who was not Christian, without distinction of race or sect." The implication was that everyone who claimed the name of Christian should in turn unite against these fanatics. The attack on the Christian quarter in Damascus proved that the "quarrel between the *Druses* and the Maronites" was only "a local incident in the great struggle of Islamism against Christian civilization."[31]

In his efforts to pin the massacres not on local political or social conditions but on global "Islamism" (and in order to justify a unified Christian response), Vogüé described at length the supposed existence of a pan-Islamic conspiracy that threatened not only Eastern Christians but even the French Empire in Algeria: "Those who know the Muslim countries know the influence of these hidden networks, whose offshoots extend everywhere there is a sectarian of *Mahomet*. . . . How many times have we observed the coordination of Algerian insurrections with certain sermons from Mecca and some unrest in the Ottoman Empire!"[32] This grasping for proof of a universal Muslim plot directed from Mecca shows Vogüé at his most paranoid and anti-Islamic, but there was a method to his madness. For him, if it could be shown that the events were the result of an essential, inescapable Muslim antagonism toward Christians, then an intervention and a Lebanese settlement that was explicitly motivated by Christian and civilizational unity would be justified: "The cross has been outraged, may it be the crescent's turn [to be outraged]."[33]

As in his *L'Ami de la religion* coverage, Vogüé recognized that his rhetoric might come across as fanatically religious; thus, to combat this impression he once again explicitly appealed to his liberal credentials. The "cover of this volume" of the *Correspondant*, he insisted, should be sufficient to prove that his reflections were not "inspired by the fanaticism of another age." Like Montalembert and Falloux and other elite liberal Catholics, he professed his faith in "liberty of conscience" for all, because liberty for all was the most effective way to preserve it for Catholics. But, he argued, it was impossible to extend this liberal understanding of religious pluralism to the Muslims of the Ottoman Empire. The reason for Vogüé's double standard was simple: "People must be spoken to in the language they understand."[34] Because of the fanaticism of the Ottomans themselves, France could pursue more explicitly religious policies there than in her own metropole and empire. In France, supposedly, even devout Catholics understood the liberty of conscience—understood that the proper site of religion was the interior—but in Muslim spaces, because of the Muslims' backward religiosity, Catholicism could still be externalized and politicized. "Religious tolerance" was faring badly enough among the Muslims of France's colony in Algeria, who "leave empty the mosques we have built them," Vogüé claimed. But in Algeria, for better or worse, France was duty-bound to impose its tolerance. In Syria, by contrast, where the French had not gone "as conquerors, but as avengers," they owed no such lip-service to religious liberty.[35] The Muslims in Syria had brought Catholic fanaticism on themselves.

Of course, as Oissila Saaïdia, Judith Surkis, and other scholars have shown, the religious terrain of colonial Algeria was, in reality, anything but secular or neutral. The French state, from the moment of invasion in 1830, had indeed promised to respect Algerians' religion. But France's reasons for officially sponsoring and financing certain mosques and *medersas* were more pragmatic: to compensate Algerians for the Islamic charitable endowments the French had seized and, more importantly, to encourage the creation of a loyal and easily surveilled cadre of Muslim functionaries. This was not religious freedom, but "financial control"; predictably, these official mosques and schools were unpopular among most Muslims.[36] Moreover, even the discourse of "tolerance" toward Islam in French Algeria was far from benevolent, since it functioned primarily as a pretext to exclude Muslims from social and political equality. To the extent that Muslim civil law (polygamy, divorce) was "tolerated," Muslims were thereby unworthy of citizenship. Since France had left Algerians the sop of their religious and family law, the ideology effectively went, they could justly deprive them of their land and the rights of citizenship.[37] Meanwhile, the colonial regime also financed Catholic churches and schools in an attempt to encourage unity among the diverse settler population.[38] Still, Vogüé contrasted these seeming "liberties" of secular tolerance that France so generously offered to its ungrateful Algerian subjects with the holy war that France must unleash upon its enemies in Syria.

The goal of Vogüé's "exclusively *Christian*"[39] expedition—meeting jihad with holy war—would be to establish an independent Maronite nation. Vogüé's arguments for the necessity of Lebanese independence show that many of the myths that would nourish Lebanese nationalism and exceptionalism in the twentieth century were already current among pro-Maronite French Catholics.[40] In a metaphor that would only become more common among French Catholic observers of Muslim-Christian relations, Vogüé compared the Maronites to the Kabyles of Algeria, since both were allegedly descended from pre-Islamic Christian populations who had retreated to a "mountain refuge" to resist Islamization; "but, happier than the Kabyles," the Maronites had succeeded in "[conserving] the

integrity of their faith."[41] It was the refuge of Mount Lebanon that enabled the
Maronites to remain distinct from the Arabs and the Ottomans who allegedly
would have persecuted and assimilated them if they could have. According to
the "mountain refuge" idea, Lebanon was a place to which pre-Muslim Christian
populations had escaped in order to retain their primitive purity and exceptionalism from an illegitimate Muslim interlude. The myth thus falsely implied that
the Maronites had been subject to Muslim persecution rather than to the Greek
Orthodox persecutions that had actually played a much more significant role in
their migrations.[42]

Vogüé called the Maronites a "happier" version of the Kabyles of Algeria,
who had similarly sought mountain refuge from Muslim invaders. This myth of
Maronite exceptionalism may well have functioned as a sort of mental rehearsal
for Catholics who would later latch on to the Kabyles and invest them with the
same civilizing hopes for colonial Algeria. French Catholics and missionaries—
Abbé Lavigerie, the Œuvre's director and future bishop of Algiers, chief among
them—would become some of the loudest and most persistent disseminators
of the "Kabyle myth" in Algeria. For Lavigerie, later on, the Kabyles in Algeria
were the *"Lebanon of Africa....* Exempt of [Islamic] fanaticism," and retaining
vestiges of Christian law and custom. The Kabyles in Algeria, like the Maronites
in Syria, were thus "destined" to ally themselves with the civilizing French.[43]
Some Catholic observers even suggested importing Maronite populations into
Algeria, where they would not only be safe from persecution but also form the
nucleus of a civilized, Christian indigenous population, supplanting the more re-
fractory Muslims and serving the interests of French colonization. This utopian
project of forming Maronite refugees into "a vast network of Arabic-speaking
Christians devoted to [French] interests" in Algeria would never come to fruition, but it demonstrates that the search for an indigenous population that was
non-Arab, non-fanatic, and crypto-Catholic coexisted with and possibly reinforced France's obsession with the Kabyles.[44]

Vogüé's plans for Lebanese independence show the long-standing role played
by French Catholics in producing knowledge and historical narratives that made
an independent Lebanon—the "mountain refuge" from Islam—thinkable in the
twentieth century.[45] Vogüé had even mapped out the boundaries of his proposed
state. Despite his sectarian and nationalistic justifications for Lebanese independence, he recognized that an independent Lebanon, in order to be a viable
state, would need to lay claim to coastland far beyond the Maronites' historic
mountain refuge—"all the coast from Latakia [in present-day Syria] to Tyre"—
comprising Tripoli, Beirut, and other territory that was not homogenously

Christian. An independent Lebanon, continuing its advantageous commercial and agricultural contacts with Europe—especially in the domain of silk production—as well as its political and civilizational apprenticeship under France, would soon be powerful enough to emancipate itself from any subordination to the Ottomans.[46] In sum, the Ottoman Empire's Christian minority populations would be secure only when they had independent nation-states of their own.[47]

Liberal Catholics like Vogüé and Lenormant were far from the only journalists to call for an armed expedition to Syria. Observers from across the political spectrum—including the anticlerical newspaper *Le Siècle*—clamored for a "holy war" against the "fanaticism" and "intolerance" of the Ottoman Empire.[48] Fundraising for the victims of the massacres was also an ecumenical endeavor. The Alliance israélite universelle, led by Adolphe Crémieux, even announced its charitable campaign a few days before the Œuvre d'Orient did.[49] Given this wide-ranging consensus, undertaking a Syrian expedition made political sense for Napoleon III, perhaps even offering him the chance to win back the support of Catholics at the precise moment when many were angry at his abandonment of the Pope to the forces of Italian nationalism. Beyond these domestic political considerations, economic and foreign policy pressures also called for a humanitarian intervention: to shore up the Lebanese silk industry, which supplied much of the raw material to Lyon workshops; to insulate Egypt from Ottoman influence, as Ferdinand de Lesseps had broken ground on the Suez Canal only the year before; even to secure access to cavalry horses from Syria and Iraq.[50] As David Todd has argued, in the 1850s and 1860s Napoleon III largely turned away from formal imperial conquests, instead following Britain's example of the "free trade imperialism" of commerce, financial investment, and gunboats. France justified this "informal empire" by linking it to "the global promotion of Catholicism."[51] In short—unlike the divisive issue of the papal states, championed by ultramontane Catholics—an intervention in Syria enjoyed consensus support, a chance for liberal Catholics to unproblematically demonstrate France's traditional ties to Catholicism.

Patriotism and Paternalism in Liberal Catholic Fundraising

Parallel to the journalistic efforts of Vogüé and Lenormant, the Œuvre d'Orient's fundraising drive was a wild success. Whereas its annual budget in its first several years of existence had hovered in the tens of thousands, the charity appeal quickly raised over 2 million francs.[52] In this success the Œuvre was aided by its existing diocesan and parish committees, by prominent bishops (at Bordeaux and Paris, for example) who channeled their dioceses' collections to the Œuvre, and by the national network of the conferences of Saint Vincent de Paul, whose leaders were close to the milieu of the Œuvre.[53] Well-placed members of the Jesuit order, such as Père de Damas, toured the salons of France and even visited Belgium, England, and Ireland to give speeches in favor of the poor Maronites and the fundraising subscription.[54] The lists of the subscription's donors, published several times a week in the pages of *L'Ami de la religion* throughout the late summer and early fall of 1860 read like a "who's who" of Catholic notability. Certainly, the lists included people from various social classes, numerous anonymous donors, parish curés, and the occasional widow's mite, but nobles were also common especially among the larger gifts. The Comte de Chambord, the legitimist pretender, made a sizable donation, perhaps hoping to encourage the impression that a restored Bourbon King would be more qualified than anyone to enforce France's traditional religious protectorate of Ottoman Christians.[55]

With so much money suddenly passing through its hands, the Œuvre council continued to meet more frequently than was customary to debate "the most equitable" ways to distribute the aid. The council also elected a special commission to supplement the regular treasurers in this task.[56] Initially, after sending some aid to assist refugees and the religious establishments that were caring for them, the council followed the advice of its clerical members—especially Père Gagarin, the Jesuit procurer—and agreed to retain the majority of the funds for rebuilding the (primarily French) Catholic missionary and charitable establishments that had been destroyed.[57] In subsequent meetings throughout September—under pressure from bishops who had supported the fundraising drive—the council modified this view somewhat, deciding that "the sums gathered must be distributed partly to provide clothing and food to the victims of the Muslims; partly to help the poorest [victims] reconstruct their residences; [and] finally, partly to found orphanages."[58] Some mention was also made of getting Maronite silk production back up and running as soon as possible and of encouraging surviving families to adopt the orphans of their martyred compatriots.

Lavigerie himself traveled to Syria to supervise the aid distribution firsthand, and for this purpose the Œuvre's council entrusted him with one million francs to be distributed at his discretion, keeping broadly within the guidelines laid out.[59] But even Lavigerie's decision to supervise the distribution of funds on-site could not silence all critics of the Œuvre. The Maronite delegate at Rome wrote to the French Foreign Ministry to accuse the Œuvre of neglecting the material needs of the Maronite victims and of instead wanting only to "pay the incomes for the *maisons* of the Jesuits, Lazarists, [and] Sisters of Charity Houses" and to use these institutions to "Latinize the country." Vogüé, in a private letter attempting to block any threat to the Œuvre's reputation, fumed that anyone would dare impugn a charitable effort "so eminently French and Catholic."[60] Lavigerie, for his part, wrote to the Foreign Ministry protesting against this or some similar critique. It was only the anti-French elements of the Syrian population that resented him, Lavigerie claimed, because of how loyally he had sought the advice of French Consuls and authorities there. Parroting the Œuvre's usual civilizing patriotism, Lavigerie insisted that despite the criticisms, his "charitable mission" would be sure to have a "happy influence . . . even on our political action" in Syria.[61] In other words, Vogüé and Lavigerie defended the Œuvre against the accusation that they were favoring French and "Latin" establishments by bragging about how patriotic and politically useful their efforts were to France, essentially conceding the point.

Indeed, the Œuvre d'Orient's commitment to a politically pragmatic civilizing mission on behalf of French influence was never in question. In advance of his journey to Syria, Lavigerie sought and received official approval of his plans from the ministers of Foreign Affairs and of Cults. The minister of Foreign Affairs remarked that Lavigerie "offer[ed] all the guarantees" that his comportment would be politically correct and useful to France—"his character, his moderation, [and] his sincere devotion to the government of the Emperor" were well known.[62] And when Lavigerie, once in Syria, appealed to France for further donations to replace liturgical ornaments and vessels that had been plundered from churches, Edouard Thouvenel, the minister of Foreign Affairs, himself paid for three hundred new communion chalices. The following year the Quai d'Orsay hosted a *fête de charité* for the Œuvre's subscription, complete with a charity sale, lottery, "children's amusements," and a puppet show.[63] Upon Lavigerie's return, the emperor would honor him with the rank of *chevalier* in the Legion of Honor.[64] Clearly, the defense of "Christian civilization" against Muslim fanaticism inspired patriotic unity.

In Lebanon, Lavigerie founded two orphanages for survivors of the massacres (one directed by the Jesuits, and one by the Sœurs de la Charité), and he set up four local commissions to supervise the distribution of funds and the rebuilding of homes in their respective areas. The Œuvre approved the allocation of considerable sums to each of these commissions to provide Maronite peasants with new silkworms and to support the founding of new scholarships at the Jesuit seminary and Lazarist college.[65]

Viewing the budgetary deliberations of the Œuvre's council provides a window onto the civilizing paternalism of this elite milieu, the same paternalism that informed the domestic charitable work of the Social Catholics among them.

For example, perhaps to incentivize industriousness, the council members were careful to stipulate that the silkworms were only a loan that the peasants would have to repay once their businesses were profitable again.[66] The councillors also wanted to ensure that the education dispensed in the new orphanages would not be too advanced or alienating. Only the "simplest notions of education" were necessary, the council maintained, since anything beyond "professional or agricultural" training might harm "the future and the morality of our children."[67] Lavigerie shared this worry that civilization might go too far and deprovincialize the indigenous Christians. Many supporters of the Œuvre had suggested bringing orphans of the massacres to France to be educated or adopted, but Lavigerie worried that if uprooted from their traditional family networks, "especially in the large cities," they would allow themselves to be corrupted. If the orphans were sent back to Syria after such an education, "these children will have acquired habits of well-being which will render them unhappy for the rest of their lives," dissatisfied with the Levantine level of civilization, food, and lifestyle. At most the occasional gifted seminarian or a "few daughters of a prince or cheikh" might be permitted to study in France.[68]

Liberal Catholicism and the Invention of Pan-Islamism

Upon Lavigerie's return to France in the spring of 1861, he authored a lengthy report detailing his activities in Syria. The main purpose of the report was to give a detailed budget and narrative account of how he had distributed the subscription's funds and to respond to criticisms of his actions by some of the "bad journals."[69] But, after reporting the mundane financial details and defending the Œuvre's charitable reputation, Lavigerie turned to describing the threat of global Islam. Lavigerie's rhetorical goal was to encourage the continued contributions of French Catholic charity, but in the process, he made his own "liberal Catholic" contribution to the invention of pan-Islamism. Echoing Vogüé's pronouncements about a Muslim plot that stretched even beyond the borders of the Ottoman Empire, Lavigerie wrote that the Syrian massacres, far from being an "isolated event," were caused by a "general disposition of minds within Mohammedanism" toward hating and exterminating Christians. In defense of this conspiracy theory, Lavigerie cited a "learned" and "prophetic" article published in the liberal Catholic *Correspondant* some ten years previous on "Muslim Propaganda [Missions] in Africa and the Indies." This article described Muslim designs on Africa and proved that the global Muslim conspiracy against "Christian civilization" had been a long time in coming. The article was published by none other than Prosper

Faugère—the same foreign ministry official who had joined the council of the Œuvre d'Orient from almost the beginning and who assisted Lavigerie in editing the very 1861 report in which this "prophetic" article was cited.[70]

First published back in 1851, Faugère's article shows that the liberal Catholic ideological network played a pioneering role in manufacturing fears about a global pan-Islamism.[71] The *Correspondant* article, though presented by Faugère and including his commentary, was published anonymously; it was probably the work of one of Faugère's missionary contacts in Ethiopia. Faugère's commentary on this report was indeed "prophetic"—but not because it had somehow predicted pan-Islamic violence or the Syrian massacres, as Lavigerie implied. It was self-fulfilling in its articulation of a Catholic civilizing mission that Faugère's future colleagues at the Œuvre d'Orient would transform into a hegemonic cliché. Faugère wrote in his introduction to the article that it would be "useful for European civilization" to recognize the specter of Islamic expansion, a phenomenon "little known" back in France, and he reminded readers that when it came to "Africa and especially the Orient," "the interests of religion and. . . of French influence... are in fact inseparable."[72] Wherever the Islamic enemy was present, France's unity with a traditional Catholic foreign policy was clear.

This 1851 article on "Muslim Propaganda" endeavored to remind Europeans that global Islam involved much more than the Ottoman Empire and that by concentrating on Ottoman decadence, Europe was being given a misleading view of the threat Islam still posed. The Ottoman Empire may claim to be the political head of global Islam, but the true spiritual and intellectual center of Muslim politics was at Mecca.[73] Mecca was the "center of the world" for Muslims, the channel of all true spiritual and political power, the direction of their prayers, and the destination of their obligatory pilgrimage.[74] The prominence of Mecca was such that the "elite of fanaticism" had congregated there, supported by the "considerable riches" of the holy sites and their commerce. According to Faugère's anonymous correspondent, this Meccan aristocracy of fanaticism had observed with dismay the decline and attempted reforms of the Ottoman Empire and had devised an alternative plan to "prepare a new outburst for Islam in Africa and in the Indies."[75] The engine in this conspiratorial machine was the pilgrimage to Mecca, where the "sectarians of Mohammed" received their marching orders. Those returning from the pilgrimage were to preach against Egyptian and Ottoman reforms and civilization; those in India against European colonization; and those in Africa—already "a country almost entirely Muslim"—were to "prepare the great empire to come." In the Ottoman Empire this Meccan influence was unmistakable, given the "numerous plots uncovered at

Constantinople" and the recurring "revolts" in Syria. Once Mecca emancipated itself from the tottering Ottoman Empire and declared itself not just the spiritual but also the political center of Islam, the *Correspondant* warned, Muslims all over the world, regardless of race, would unite in a global jihad.[76]

It was in the supposedly blank, virgin territories of Africa that Islamic expansion was most daunting and dominant, where Islam had "the monopoly of education and . . . of commerce." Islam was propagated by thousands of "missionary-merchants," bringing the benefits of commerce and easy adherence to a religion that preached few doctrines and no moral demands. No intrigue was too dastardly for these Muslim missionary-merchants; "they understood better than the Europeans" how much was at stake for the future of Africa, how significant the battle over Christian Abyssinia was, and how important it was to pursue a religious policy in such regions.[77] The report's author called for a European colonial intervention in East Africa to put an end to the machinations of Muslim leaders in the African kingdoms there and to encourage the civilization of the Copts, Abyssinians, and other Christian nations. A colonial intervention that was openly supportive of Catholic missions would regenerate the poor savages of Africa, win for itself the commercial rights that came with that paternal responsibility, and stamp out the barbaric and degrading influence of Islam while the "gigantic monster" was still weakened and "under [Europe's] feet."[78]

If Christendom did not seize this opportunity to crush Islam in Africa—if it allowed itself to be duped into thinking that it could be "friends and allies" with Muslims—subsequent generations would be punished for this indifference. Even France's Muslim subjects in Algeria would never want peace, and here again the pilgrimage to Mecca and attendant radicalization was a primary cause: "The Muslim will not be able to call himself civilized and friend as long as he has not abandoned his faith, source of every barbarity and of every cruelty."[79] The Muslim Africa of the future, united in Qur'anic depravity, would "take up arms to make war against the 'filthy' children of Christ," and "what will unfortunate Europe say then," especially if its current secularizing trajectory were to leave it even "more divided and less powerful?"[80] Written decades before French commentators and Muslim reformers alike would invoke "pan-Islamism" or the geopolitical unity of Muslims, the article could hardly have been more prescient in its explication of the theme that would come to dominate the Œuvre d'Orient's publicity efforts and French Catholic views of Islam. Faced with the supposedly monolithic, global expansion of Islam, the interests of "civilization" and of Christianity were one and the same. Islamic expansion had to be met with an even more powerful expansion of Christendom.

This anti-Islamic vitriol is what passed for serious foreign policy discussion in the flagship publication of elite liberal Catholics. This was the "learned" and "prophetic" study cited ten years later by Lavigerie in his 1861 fundraising report. The article was "prophetic" in Lavigerie's mind because, given the alleged expansion of fanatical Islam—its diabolical networks stretching out from Mecca and its plots to resist Ottoman reform—the Syrian massacres of 1860 had been almost inevitable. In the paranoid style of Faugère's 1851 article and of other Catholic coverage of the 1860 events, Lavigerie went so far as to claim that the Syrian massacres had been plotted, beginning with meetings at Mecca, for a full two years beforehand, and that the anti-British riots at Jeddah in 1858 had likewise been a planned phase of the larger anti-European movement.[81] At least, Lavigerie crowed, thanks to the publicity work of the Œuvre d'Orient, French public opinion was unanimously in favor of the Maronites. "Every rank of society" sympathized with the poor Maronites, and this fact "[gave] everything we have done . . . for Syria a truly national character."[82]

One prominent exception that gave the lie to the Œuvre's theory of a pan-Islamic plot in 1860 was the widely publicized comportment of the Algerian emir Abd el-Kader ('Abd al-Qâdir), then living in Damascus. The most tenacious leader of Algerian resistance to French occupation in the 1830s and 1840s, Abd el-Kader was renowned in France for his chivalry, honor, and Sufi wisdom—manifested during prisoner exchanges and negotiations, and then in the "salon" of friends and seekers that gathered around him once he was finally defeated and placed under house arrest in France.[83] Released from France by Napoleon III, Abd el-Kader and his entourage settled in Damascus and were living there during the events of 1860. Abd el-Kader tried not only to appease Druze notables and warn France of the coming storm but, when the violence reached Damascus, he also personally led his men through the city gathering European consuls and other Christian refugees and taking them to his home for protection. These actions earned the emir "hagiographic" treatment in the French press.[84]

Catholic writers similarly lionized Abd el-Kader. Lavigerie, on his tour of Syria, even paid the emir a visit and listened "with admiration and joy" as Abd-el-Kader recounted his role in the events at Damascus in "language that Christianity would not have rejected." But for Lavigerie, as for other French admirers, Abd el-Kader was simply an exception, distinct from the fanatical Muslims he had led. Lavigerie went so far as to characterize the emir's heroic behavior in Damascus not as flowing from an Islamic ethic but rather as an unwittingly Christian act. "Emir, the God that I serve can also be yours," Lavigerie told him, since "all righteous men must be his children." The emir's "natural justice,"

Lavigerie told his readers, might make of him a Christian yet. Here was a kind of discursive imperialism: whatever was good in other religions was de facto Christian. The emir's virtuous actions belonged more properly to Christianity than to the Islamic beliefs in whose name he had acted.[85]

In the end, to resolve the question of Mount Lebanon's political future, the Great Powers sent delegates to a diplomatic commission at Beirut. Despite the presence of France's expeditionary force and the efforts of its delegate, France's most extreme demands for a predominant Maronite role in Lebanon were out-maneuvered by Fuad Pasha and the British delegate, Lord Dufferin. Against the bloodthirsty rhetoric of Vogüé and other French Catholics, French diplomats were committed to working within the "Concert" of European diplomacy and preserving the "integrity of the Ottoman Empire." Against the idea of a Muslim conspiracy throughout Syria and the Ottoman Empire, the commissioners con-centrated more realistically on stabilizing Maronite-Druze relations in Mount Lebanon.[86] The *règlement* hammered out by the International Commission was sent to a council of European diplomats at Constantinople for further debate and ratification, just as the French Expeditionary Force was withdrawing from Syria in the summer of 1861. Though each power sought to counter the influence of the other, all parties wanted a more modernized, centralized, and equitable administration of the Mountain. Accordingly, the 1861 *Règlement* did away with the system of dual Druze and Maronite *kaimakams*, instead uniting Mount Leb-anon under a single, semiautonomous administration. Despite French hopes, the first governor was not to be Maronite—or any native of the area, for that matter—but at least the Ottomans agreed to appoint a Christian. The first gov-ernor, the Armenian Catholic Daud Effendi, was assisted by twelve councillors, but—again to the disappointment of the Maronites—positions on the council were not apportioned on the basis of population; rather, there were simply two members "from each of the six major sects inhabiting the Mountain." This règle-ment proved surprisingly stable, managing to survive all the way until the First World War, despite the profound social and religious changes that continued to mark the Empire in these years.[87]

Many Maronites (and their most ardent supporters back in Catholic France) resented the terms of the settlement, since they were not given a role commen-surate with their perceived demographic and social dominance.[88] Nevertheless, interested Œuvre members like Vogüé and the Jesuit père de Damas encour-aged their Maronite contacts to accept Daud Effendi's administration. When the Maronite notable Joseph Karam, a friend of Vogüé's and one of the heroes of Maronite resistance to the Druze, refused to submit to the new administration,

Vogüé and Damas quickly became frustrated with what they saw as Karam's counterproductive ambition. To French Catholics, the important thing was to maintain the independence of the (Christian) Mountain from (Muslim) Ottoman interference. A Maronite rebellion led by Karam would force Daud Effendi to call on Ottoman troops.[89] In Vogüé's view, trying to unseat the governor whom the Powers had agreed on in 1861 would only jeopardize the chance that a Maronite would ever be permitted to succeed to the post.[90] French Catholics had spent years inflating the ambitions of their Maronite clients. The men of the Œuvre belatedly realized that it had become important to convince French opinion that Karam should not be allowed to conflate himself with Christian interests.[91] Still, such second thoughts about the motives and behavior of their Maronite protégés does not seem to have prompted members of the Œuvre to reconsider their one-sided narration of the events of 1860 in the first place.

Sincerity, Politics, and the Lives of Muhammad after 1860

Just how far Vogüé was prepared to go in generalizing the events of 1860 into an essentialized and global view of pan-Islamic conspiracy and violence would become clear some five years later, in the context not of fundraising and humanitarian intervention but of scholarly disputes over Islam's place in the history of religions. In 1865, as part of a series meant to popularize the history of the great world religions, Barthélémy Saint-Hilaire, a scholar and moderate Republican free thinker, published a book entitled *Mahomet et le Coran*. In the vein of earlier nineteenth-century treatments of the Prophet by Thomas Carlyle and Edgar Quinet, Saint-Hilaire's Muhammad was no longer the arch-heretic or impostor but the Romantic "Great Man"—sincere in his religious vocation and in his belief in the oneness of God and gifted as a leader of men.[92] For Catholic apologists, for whom the comparative approach to religion already seemed to be an attack on the singularity of Christianity, this apparent attempt to "rehabilitate" Muhammad was more than they could stand. In a review for the Jesuit journal *Études*, the Jesuit educator Eugène Marquigny complained that "the doctors of free thought" were lining up to write glowing reviews of Saint-Hilaire's book. This was only natural, Marquigny claimed, since freethinkers had so much in common with Muslims. "Be good Muslims, since you are such bad Christians," the Jesuit spat; "Praise the Arab prophet as you like; he, like you, was a deist, a rationalist, an eclectic, a partisan of independent morality."[93]

Vogüé took it upon himself to represent a more tempered, scholarly Catholic response to Saint-Hilaire's Muhammad in a review for the *Correspondant*. On the question of Muhammad's sincerity, and in his review as a whole, Vogüé's Catholic "liberalism" and apparent moderation were front and center. Vogüé began by acknowledging that the increasing "exercise of the liberty of con-science" had made scholars more sensitive to the "private meaning of beliefs" and more willing to grant the sincerity of other faiths.[94] Vogüé was prepared to accept, at least for the sake of argument, Saint-Hilaire's distinction between "the beginning of [Muhammad's] career" and his later career after Medina. Ini-tially, the prophet's sincere desire had been to replace the "religious anarchy" and idolatry of Mecca with "the religion . . . of the one God," an "entirely spiritual" message; later, at Medina, he was corrupted by political success and self-interest, by his role as a "military and political chief."[95]

This approach to dealing with the question of Muhammad's sincerity or im-posture (his mission was initially religious and sincere, but was corrupted by the post-hegira stage of political power and success) has since become familiar.[96] In the mid-nineteenth-century context, though, this narrative strategy addressed precisely the problem Vogüé posed: How, after centuries of Christian apolo-getics that cast Muhammad as the quintessential impostor, to account for the new Romantic view of Muhammad's genius and sincerity, all while retaining the apologetic defense of Christianity's superiority? In this sense, the simple solu-tion—positing Muhammad's "early" sincerity but still judging the history of post-hegira Islam as hopelessly violent and political—might seem nothing more than a crude attempt at a more scholarly and respectable dismissal of Islam, a falling between the two stools of the old apologetics and the newer, more plu-ralistic history of religions. And it was. But this way of breaking Muhammad's career in two can also be seen as a final product of the liberal Catholicism of Vogüé's milieu. The divorce between Muhammad's "moral" mission and his "po-litical" one and the conclusion that political power was corrosive of a religious mission had as its premise liberalism's distinction between public and private spheres, with religion properly belonging to the private sphere.

For Vogüé the liberal Catholic, the post-hegira stage necessarily signified a loss of the primitive simplicity and sincerity of Muhammad's religion. Dividing Mu-hammad's career and moral life this way, between Mecca and Medina, presumed that private morality and sanctity were incompatible with a politicized, estab-lished religion. At the very moment when Vogüé's friend and academic colleague Ernest Renan was inventing "a Jesus for the nineteenth century"—libertarian, politically quiescent, and emphasizing individual and internal spirituality rather than a will to social change—Vogüé seems to have accepted this liberal-individu-alistic view of Christianity and found Muhammad wanting.[97] Vogüé had begun his review by acknowledging that the "exercise of the liberty of conscience" had newly highlighted the importance of religion's "private meaning." Yet by beginning with the assumption that this interiorized mode of religious belonging was normative (superior to public or political expressions of religion), Vogüé begged the question of Muhammad's sincerity and religiosity. For Vogüé and other liberal Catholics, a political religion was necessarily an insincere religion. It is perhaps no coincidence that, given Vogüé's own liberal commitments and the readership of the *Correspondant*, he closed with a quote from Tocqueville (a man whose anti-Islamic liberalism is well known[98]). Islam, Vogüé wrote, quoting his former mentor, was nothing but a "skillful compromise between materialism and spiritualism," vice and virtue, demanding absolute obedience, and pervaded by "violent and sensual tendencies."[99]

Far from encouraging a more nuanced view of Islam, Vogüé's bifurcation of Muhammad's life resulted in an even more monolithic perspective. For it was precisely because Muhammad's career (and Islam itself) was shot through with this fatal contradiction between the spiritual and the political—sincere interior and corrupted, politicized exterior—that scholars of Islam had no choice but to make an essentializing, transhistorical move: "Mohammed, without the saber, is no longer Mohammed. . . . The man cannot be separated from his acts, nor the system from twelve centuries of application and of experience."[100] For Vogüé, because Islam was a religion that externalized itself in an illegitimate and politicized way, all that mattered about Islam was that externalization. (Because Christianity was a religion of the interior, Vogüé implied, its outward historical manifestations and failings could be dismissed as not essential to it.) And here the events of 1860 made their reappearance in Vogüé's book review, as the coup de grâce to Saint-Hilaire's argument. For history's verdict on Islamic morality, one only had to look "at Jeddah, at Damascus, at Delhi," where "true believers still commit holy war!" Elsewhere in the review, Vogüé appealed to his own encounters with Islam as a traveler in Syria and among the Druze for evidence: "We have seen too closely the evils caused by Islam . . . to delude ourselves about its merits. Christianity and Islam, cross and crescent, are . . . inevitably hostile. . . . We know by experience that [attempts at conciliation] are useless."[101]

Afterlives of Liberal Catholic Orientalism

Liberal Catholic inventions of a conspiratorial, monolithic Islam in the 1860s had less to do with shoring up support for any particular colonial project, or with fear of any actual threat of pan-Islamism, and more to do with convincing fellow Frenchmen of the need for Catholic unity at home and an explicitly Catholic foreign policy abroad.[102] In an early, French Catholic version of the "Clash of Civilizations," the notables of the Œuvre d'Orient used enmity with global Islam to signal their patriotic unity with France's civilizational superiority and religious liberty. In the process, they concocted a virulent new blend of liberal Catholic orientalism, which constructed Islam both as the theocratic, politicized, and fanatical opposite of the new liberalism yet still as the heretical, religiously fraudulent opposite of traditional Catholicism. Liberal Catholicism is often narrated as having been increasingly marginalized in the course of the nineteenth century, first theologically defeated by the intransigent ultramontanes at the First Vatican Council, and then politically discredited by the failure of liberal Catholic leadership in the early, conservative phase of the Third Republic.[103] But the liberal Catholic hybrid of orientalism—the Œuvre's strategy of claiming unity with France's liberal civilizing mission against fanatical Islam—would live on, along with the influence of the men of the Œuvre.

Vogüé, for his part, would continue to exercise his influence on French religious and cultural policies in the Orient as treasurer and eventual president of the Œuvre d'Orient, as a council member of the larger missionary Œuvre de la Propagation de la Foi (Association for the Propagation of the Faith), and as an ambassador under the conservative republic of the 1870s, first at Constantinople and then at Vienna. Vogüé's work at Constantinople echoed in interesting ways the Œuvre d'Orient's Ottoman anxieties of ten years earlier. As ambassador, one of Vogüé's main tasks was to defend France's traditional role as civilizational tutor of the Ottomans and as principal European defender of Christians in the Empire. With France's prestige weakened by the Franco-Prussian War, this was a difficult battle on two fronts: against other European powers, who were looking for more influence in the Ottoman Empire, and against the Ottomans, who hoped to escape all European tutelage.

At the same time, the papacy was attempting to centralize its control over the Eastern churches by appointing their patriarchs rather than allowing these churches to elect their own, as they had traditionally done. One effect of this new policy was that the Ottoman authorities would no longer view these patriarchs as civil functionaries in charge of dispensing justice within their own ethnoreligious communities; instead, they would become merely spiritual authorities. Rome claimed to be fine with this spiritualization of the patriarchs' role (this separation of the religious from the political) as it went hand-in-hand with the increased power of the pope. For Vogüé, however, if the Ottoman churches—whether Armenian, Chaldean, Melkite, or Maronite—lost their "theocratic" character, if they became purely spiritual modes of belonging within a legally homogenous empire of equal civil rights, France would lose any pretext for intervening on these communities' behalf. Once again, Vogüé's liberalism did not extend to the Ottoman Empire. However "liberal" his own Catholicism, the rights of the religious protectorate—the ability to cultivate an "ecclesiastical clientele"—were too important to allow the Ottomans to truly emancipate or secularize their different minority communities.[104] Of course, Vogüé protested, he wanted nothing more than for the Ottomans to become civilized enough to dispense with minority communities (and thus with France's protective interventions), but the liberal Catholic ideal of a "Free Church in a Free State" would long be a "chimera" in the Ottoman context.[105] Thus Vogüé opposed the very liberal reforms he claimed were the end goal of France's tutelage, because successful reforms would remove the need for that tutelage. Like colonial administrators elsewhere in France's empire, Vogüé pursued a strategy of "indefinitely deferr[ing]" the promised rights of civilization.[106]

Of course, France's interest in promoting religious coexistence or secularism in the Ottoman Empire was primarily a pretext for intervention.[107] Indeed, some Syrians believed in religious coexistence more genuinely than these European soft imperialists who claimed to promote "religious protection." In the aftermath of the 1860 massacres, Butrus al-Bustani, the Maronite convert to Protestantism and father of Arab nationalism and reform, thanked Europe and America for their charity and support. But he then called on his fellow Syrians not to rely on "foreign political intervention" or to seek sectarian advantage over each other, but rather to separate religion from politics and unite around their common Arabic language and Syrian "homeland."[108] Shortly after 1860, Bustani founded a school to put his reformist ideas into practice: students came "from all sects, *millets*, and races without discriminating against their personal beliefs" and without "any attempt at proselytizing." But Protestant missionaries, Bustani's former supporters, reacted with hostility to the school and deemed it insufficiently religious.[109] One imagines that French Catholic missionaries would have responded with similar hostility if any of their client-converts had tried to take the promise of religious liberalism literally.[110]

Another one of Vogüé's diplomatic tasks that reprised the themes of 1860 was that of keeping an eye on the rise of "Islamic Unity," a term that predates "pan-Islamism" but that stood for some of the same European anxieties.[111] For example, the Dutch, in the middle of "pacifying" anticolonial resistance in Sumatra, asked that Vogüé refuse recognition to the Atchinese [Acehnese] Sultan, who was visiting Istanbul to seek out the help of the Ottoman Caliph. Vogüé agreed, "It is in the common interest [of governments with Muslim subjects] to discourage all attempts . . . to reconstitute at Constantinople . . . a center of Muslim action." But far from stoking fears of pan-Islamism, as he had in 1860, Vogüé wrote that he considered these attempts at "Islamic Unity" to be illusory and confined to the "domain of abstractions."[112] It seems that the serious work of Vogüé the ambassador was not conducive to the flights of conspiracy theorizing permitted to Vogüé the Catholic journalist.

Finally, in his capacity as a board member of the massive missionary Association for the Propagation of the Faith, Vogüé was seen as an influential expert on the Ottoman Empire, and he used his position there to continue to advocate a missionary strategy identical to that of the Œuvre d'Orient: regeneration and reunification of Eastern Christians and continual postponing of any attempt to proselytize Muslims. "The purpose that we are pursuing in the Orient," he told the Association for the Propagation of the Faith in 1888, "is much less the conversion of the Infidels than that of the Schismatics." After all, Muslims were nearly impossible to convert and still very far from the "paths of grace"; "the conversion of the schismatics, on the contrary, is possible."[113]

Another figure who forged his view of the Islamic world out of the crucible of the Œuvre d'Orient's response to the events of 1860 was the charity's director, Abbé Charles Lavigerie. Lavigerie would become the archbishop of Algiers in 1866 and would establish a new missionary congregation there for the evangelization of Africa: the White Fathers. In this capacity, he would exert a more powerful influence on French Catholic ideas about Islam than any other alumnus of the Œuvre milieu. Lavigerie and his White Fathers congregation would attack Islam not only for traditional, religious reasons but also for its alleged illiberalism, lack of civilization, fanaticism, and inordinate religiosity: precisely the qualities Veuillot and earlier missionaries in Algeria had claimed to admire about Islam. Lavigerie and his hagiographers would later claim that it was his time spent directing the Œuvre that first inspired him with a vocation for Muslim lands.[114] One admirer recalled the effect of the events of 1860 this way: "The massacres of Lebanon . . . [which] laid bare the incurable barbarity of the Muslim world," had prompted Lavigerie to turn toward the Orient, thus setting him on "the glorious path wherein he would become archbishop of Algiers, Cardinal-Archbishop of Carthage, [and] Primate of Africa."[115]

Algerian Anxieties: Ismaÿl Urbain and the Massacres of Syria

Though they were few, there were critics of Catholic France's virulently anti-Islamic response to the events in Syria. One perceptive and incensed critic was Ismaÿl Urbain, the French Guyanese, Saint-Simonian social thinker, officer of the Arab Bureaus in Algeria, convert to Islam, and adviser to Napoleon III. Urbain's *L'Algérie pour les Algériens* (1860) can be read as the founding document of Napoleon III's so-called *Royaume arabe* policies, by means of which the emperor intended to prove his care and protection for Algeria's indigenous populations. Surprisingly, though, this document does not begin with any reference to Algeria. Rather, Urbain opened with a description of the "Massacres of Syria" that very year, and with a stinging condemnation of Europe's anti-Muslim reactions to those events. His criticism of these reactions was discerning. In the wake of the Syrian "events," he wrote, the European public had not been content to feel compassion for the Maronites, nor had they sought out and punished the actual perpetrators. To the contrary, self-proclaimed experts had proliferated, ready to stand in judgment over "kings, peoples, and the gods themselves. The sultan and his government, the Turks, the Druze, Mohammed, his Koran and his God, have been summoned to appear" before these writers' tribunals. Nothing was too extreme to be "printed about the fanaticism of the Muslims, about their fatalism, which dooms them to immobility, about the bloody excitations of the Koran, about the immense conspiracy hatched throughout all Islam against the Christians! The great aggregation of diverse races and peoples who follow Islam as [their] religious law has been disdainfully, scornfully, hatefully denounced, declared rebellious to progress and destined to be driven back into Asia, far from the *foyer* of civilization."

Urbain did not believe that this European "holy war of the pen" against Islam would be especially harmful to Muslim-Christian relations in Syria or elsewhere in the Ottoman Empire: Muslims there did not read European newspapers, and the Ottoman government, supervised by France and the other European powers, would find a way to successfully administer justice to the blameworthy. For Urbain, the real danger was in Algeria, France's overwhelmingly Muslim colony. The outpouring of anti-Islamic sentiment in France provoked by the events in Syria would endanger the chances for reconciliation and reform there. Some observers would doubtless "want to apply to our Algerian Muslims what is being said about those of Syria. . . . [A]lready brochures are linking the religious *confréries (khouans)* of Algeria to the immense conspiracy of Muslim fanaticism centered at Mecca; already the French government is being reproached for having treated the *indigènes* too gently, and are proposing to replace this perverse population with Maronites imported from Lebanon." Urbain, it seems, had been reading Vogüé, Lavigerie, and other liberal Catholics. For these anti-Islamic writers, Urbain presciently worried, the events in Syria were proof that Muslims would always be backward and would always hate the French. Indeed, Vogüé condemned all Muslims to just such an inability to reconcile with civilization. If subsequent wars and revolts broke out in French Algeria, Urbain angrily predicted, it would not be because of Islam and its backwardness; instead, all blame should be laid at the door of those "misguided sermonizers" in France who had stoked the fires of mutual hatred.[116]

But there was another observer who was also deeply worried about French Catholics' reactions to the massacres, someone whose motives were diametrically opposed to Urbain's. This was the Père Ducat, the Jesuit most involved in the Algerian *mission arabe* and most optimistic about the possibility of Muslim conversion to Christianity. Of course, Ducat did not share Urbain's desire to exonerate Islam. But he was concerned that the events in Syria would discourage Catholics from supporting the mission in Algeria. In light of the "horrible excesses" of the Muslims in Syria, according to Ducat, some members of his own Algeria-based "Association of Prayers...for the Conversion of the Muslims" were tempted to abandon the cause of Muslim conversion, saying, "This people is cursed forever . . . no conversion [is] possible. We will only be done with them when they are exterminated."[117] Ducat hastened to send out a circular to his association's members, wherein he recounted the horrors of the Syrian massacres but tried to frame them as the last death rattle of a toppling faith, not the conspiracy of a powerful enemy. He urged his associates not only to pray for the "Victory and Peace" of the *Chrétiens d'Orient*, but also to continue praying for the "conversion of their persecutors," so that, in the words of the prayer association's motto, there would one day be only "one flock and one shepherd" on earth.[118]

Like the majority of Ducat's publicity efforts on behalf of the *mission arabe*, this circular was barred from any official publication in Ducat's own home diocese of Besançon by an archbishop jealous of his diocese's charitable resources.[119] That archbishop was none other than the Cardinal Mathieu, the liberal Gallican and brother of the Œuvre d'Orient's lay president, Admiral Mathieu. Even as Mathieu was blocking Ducat's efforts to publicize the mission to Muslims on the grounds that his own charities needed the funds instead, he was supporting the Œuvre's appeal in favor of the persecuted Christians of Syria, allowing over 30,000 francs to be collected in his diocese.[120] It seems the cause of rallying Christian civilization against its ultimate enemy, Islam, was more popular than the cause of Muslim conversion and reconciliation. The profile of the Œuvre d'Orient would only continue to rise and to be supported throughout France, while Ducat's Muslim-focused prayer association would find no such lasting support. This contrast is one testament to the growing hegemony of anti-Islamic (rather than philo-Islamic) sentiment among French Catholics and to the role the "events of Syria" played in solidifying that sentiment.

CHAPTER 6

Worthy of His Hire

Charles Lavigerie, Algerian Muslims, and Missionary Fundraising

In 1866, Charles Lavigerie took up his new post as bishop of the massive diocese of Algiers. Lavigerie's arrival in colonial Algeria was followed shortly by a devastating famine. The fragile indigenous ecology and economy of Algeria suffered regular convulsions throughout the nineteenth century, and French violence and economic encroachment only exacerbated these crises. In a region where rainfall was often insufficient, where harvests periodically failed, or where plague struck people and livestock, the ruthless tactics of French military and colonialists had aggravated this agricultural insecurity by destroying crops and oases. Furthermore, in their attempts to "pacify" the Algerians, the French seized the charitable endowments and other institutions that had traditionally served as indigenous social safety nets and confiscated tribal lands, disrupting trade and migration networks as well as traditional usufruct rights. Land confiscations accelerated after 1865, reducing many Algerians to "rural proletarians or sharecroppers."[1] Levying taxes on Algerians also forced them to integrate into the money economy and to sell their surplus grain—which traditionally would have been stored and shared—in exchange for currency to pay taxes. In the period from 1866 to 1868, a perfect storm of these environmental and colonial disruptions converged to produce the most brutal famine colonial Algeria ever endured. A weak harvest and drought in 1866 resulted in a failed harvest in 1867. Locusts, cholera, and typhus compounded the misery. One Algerian demographer has estimated that no fewer than 820,000 Algerians died of starvation.[2]

Lavigerie's arrival in Algeria in 1866 ushered in a stark transformation of the Catholic Church's approach to colonialism and missions in Algeria.[3] More than the colony's previous two bishops, Lavigerie was ready to provoke acrimonious debates with the colonial administration about the allegedly antimissionary policies of the military administrators. He also engaged in public and dangerously offensive denigrations of Islam. Most infamously, in the wake of the famine and cholera epidemic of 1866–68, he fought the governor general of the colony, in a series of open letters, for the right to keep and raise hundreds of Arab and Kabyle orphans of the catastrophe. Indeed, the famine served as pretext and provocation for Lavigerie's highly public attacks on the military administration of the colony. The military had not always been favorable to the idea of Christian proselytization among Algeria's Muslims, and some missionary apologists had done their part to exaggerate this alleged anticlericalism of the military administration, offering up the red meat of culture war for consumption by Catholic audiences back in France. For Lavigerie, conveniently, the horrors of the famine seemed to prove not only that the military administration was incompetent but that the Muslims' own allegedly lazy and heedless way of life was killing them. In his zeal to raise funds for the new orphanages and to press his advantage against the military regime, Lavigerie indulged in flights of vehement anti-Islamic rhetoric. At one point, Lavigerie even claimed that Muslims were so barbarous and recalcitrant to civilization that they only had two options: convert and be civilized or be thrown "back into the desert" from whence they had come. When Governor General MacMahon pounced on this unfortunate phrase, Lavigerie claimed it was intended to be an absurd dichotomy, to point up the necessity of conversion.[4]

From Lavigerie's perspective, the famine and disease had been providential, presenting the first major breach in the colonial administration's long-standing opposition to a Muslim mission. This breach was both a discursive opportunity to criticize the administration and a practical opportunity to step in and claim responsibility of caring for the famine's Muslim orphans. Lavigerie quickly seized the initiative and, with the aid of his clergy and sympathetic military officials, gathered many displaced children into makeshift orphanages (see figure 6.1). Through the early months of 1868, hundreds of these children died of typhus or other lingering complications, sometimes as many as "20 per day," as did some of the religious *frères* and *sœurs* who cared for them. But since those "in danger of death" were usually given emergency baptisms, in the eyes of Lavigerie, these children were now in heaven praying for him and his charitable contributors. Many hundreds more children survived and needed to be fed, educated, evangelized, and put to work.[5]

Once he had secured an apostolic beachhead with these controversial orphanages, Lavigerie founded a new congregation of missionaries—the White Fathers (Pères Blancs)—to staff the orphanages and to begin training for missions elsewhere in Algeria and Africa. He also launched a vast fundraising network to

FIGURE 6.1. "The Famine in Algeria—Mgr. the Archbishop
of Algiers gathering orphans at the episcopal palace." From
L'illustration: Journal universel 51, no. 1299 (January 18, 1868).

support his orphans and missionaries, one of the first such charitable efforts
to use the dissemination of humanitarian photography and to offer European
supporters the chance to "adopt-an-orphan," complete with a photo and dossier.[6]
Significantly, it was Lavigerie's old liberal Catholic allies in Paris at the Œuvre
d'Orient who published his appeals for funds and his attacks on the colonial administration and who disseminated the White Fathers' fundraising newsletter.

This newsletter, the *Bulletin de l'Œuvre de Sainte Monique*, also produced and
transmitted anti-Islamic and increasingly racialized anti-Arab tropes back to the
metropole—whether by continually commenting on the inherent vices of the
Arab orphans (most often greed, laziness, ingratitude, and a prurient sexual precociousness) or by contributing to the rise of the "Kabyle myth," the idea that Algeria's Berber populations were more susceptible to conversion and civilization
than the purportedly backward and fanatical Arabs. In all these ways, Lavigerie
and his congregation brought a new virulence and a new racialization to previous anti-Muslim discourses, as well as a new willingness to collaborate with the
secular "civilizing mission" of mainstream France. This racialized orientalism

represented a convergence of the metropolitan and colonial trajectories identified in the previous chapters, a toxic blend of liberal and ultramontane Catholic approaches to Islam. On the one hand, Lavigerie and his fundraising public back in France were forged out of the liberal, patriotic, civilizing milieu of the Œuvre d'Orient. On the other hand, Lavigerie arrived in the colony at a moment when missionaries and secular imperialists alike had finally abandoned any hope of converting or civilizing (Arab) Muslims and had begun constructing an elaborate edifice of colonial ethnography intended to explain Arab backwardness and justify their preference for the Berbers.

At the same time, though, there is an interesting wrinkle in Lavigerie's missiological approach that has encouraged his sympathizers and defenders to depict him not as less but rather as more sensitive to Muslim consciences than his predecessors and contemporaries. Unlike previous missionaries to Algeria's Muslims, such as the Jesuits, Lavigerie strictly prohibited his White Fathers from openly trying to convert Muslims or from arguing about religion with them. Against the sociological and religious force of a unified Islam, he believed, all a missionary could hope for was to wear down Muslim resistance through selfless, "disinterested" charity and medical aid, a task that might take generations. Lavigerie insisted scrupulously on this "charity first" policy, even punishing missionaries who engaged in proselytization. This policy, combined with his insistence that his missionaries learn indigenous languages and adapt themselves to indigenous ways of life, has led some of his hagiographers and defenders to claim that the archbishop was prefiguring the Church's later openness toward Islam.[7] On the contrary, Lavigerie and the White Fathers' use of "disinterested" charity and their postponement of evangelization, far from reflecting any shift toward interreligious understanding, was in perfect accord with the larger anti-Muslim tenor of Lavigerie's efforts. His missionaries' strategic deployment of charity was explicitly aimed at delegitimizing the Muslim religion and indigenous culture. And their claim to disinterestedness—in contrast to the Muslims' own, allegedly greedy marabouts—relied on European, liberal-secular notions of calculation and exchange.

Situated on a longer continuum of French Catholic views of Islam—both metropolitan and colonial—Lavigerie and the White Fathers' participation in a shift toward more racialized, more civilizational denigrations of Islam is unmistakable. In the history of French Catholic orientalism, Lavigerie's Algerian and African efforts represent the culmination of discourses inaugurated by the Œuvre in France—a religious discourse that battled Islam as the opposite of Christianity and a secular discourse that constructed Islam as the opposite of French civilization, tolerance, and liberal political economy. But Lavigerie combined these discourses with the disappointment of missionaries on the ground in Algeria. Indeed, for those back in France who had known Lavigerie in his earlier "liberal" days, his explosive, pro-missionary attacks on the colonial administration came as a shock. It also seems likely that Lavigerie's betrayal of the liberal camp and his embrace of the pope's authority at the Vatican Council two years later was at least partially motivated by resentment of the liberals' tepid support for his controversial Algerian orphan campaign.[8] But Lavigerie never lost the patriotic, civilizational, and "liberal" opposition to Islam that had served the Œuvre d'Orient so well. Though in 1868 it was momentarily expedient to attack the "tolerance" of the French colonial regime, à la Veuillot, Lavigerie never went so far as to admire Muslim "fanaticism" or theocracy, and he always remained willing to offer a civilizational alliance against Islam to any government that would support his projects. This chapter shows how Lavigerie and his missionaries articulated and spread harsher, disillusioned views of Arab Islam in the fundraising and publicity materials they transmitted back to France.[9]

Lavigerie, the Œuvre d'Orient, and Liberal Catholic Opinion

The main avenues by which Lavigerie and the White Fathers exerted influence on metropolitan French views of Islam were his fundraising networks and publications. Lavigerie's resources for publicity in France consisted, at first, of his contacts at the Œuvre d'Orient. White Father missionaries also regularly went to France to *quêter* (to preach about the mission and collect funds in churches and schools). In addition, there was a dedicated newsletter independent of the Œuvre's *Bulletin* but still printed and distributed by the Œuvre's Paris office. These overlapping methods were also supplemented as needed by Lavigerie's own periodic preaching tours in France. Lavigerie's campaign for the right to keep and evangelize the orphans of the famine burst onto the French metropolitan scene with a series of open letters published by his friends at the Œuvre—the charitable association he had formerly directed and whose current director, Pierre Soubiranne, was a friend and, like Lavigerie, a former protégé of the liberal Bishop Dupanloup. With these and other personal connections between Lavigerie and the Œuvre's council and membership, the Œuvre was ideally placed to do Lavigerie's publicity work in the metropole. In the early months of 1867, the Œuvre opened a special fundraising drive on Lavigerie's behalf and publicized the fundraiser among its associates and Catholic France at large.[10]

It was in the context of this campaign on behalf of the orphans of the famine that Lavigerie infamously provoked the colonial administration into a public relations dogfight. Lavigerie used the columns of the *Bulletin de l'Œuvre des écoles d'Orient* to publish letters accusing the administration of playing down the crisis and claiming to reveal the true extent of the catastrophe. Governor General MacMahon and his devout wife were known to be practicing Catholics and were well-connected to the Catholic notability in France. Lavigerie's public attacks on MacMahon's administration departed from the respectability of liberal Catholic salons, bewildering and dividing prominent Catholics in France. In the first months of the subscription, Soubiranne cautioned Lavigerie that there had been some resistance among the Parisian ecclesiastical hierarchy—some had hesitated to believe Lavigerie's breathless accounts of the famine as opposed to MacMahon's more measured accounts. Soubiranne respectfully advised Lavigerie not to keep linking his charitable efforts on behalf of the orphans, which were universally acclaimed in Catholic France, to his more politicized attacks on the military administration and its alleged antimissionary policies. This political debate, Soubiranne worried, would certainly compromise the success of the fundraising drive.[11]

But against the advice of Soubiranne and other allies, Lavigerie doubled down. Lavigerie's next letter to the Œuvre's subscribers is the most infamous and oft-cited documents of his public conflict with MacMahon.[12] Lavigerie pressed home his attacks on the administration by recounting an alleged scene of cannibalism, wherein a starving indigenous family had been reduced to murdering and eating passers-by and, finally, their own children. Not only did this sensationalist news convince shocked French audiences that MacMahon's administration had indeed been underestimating and mismanaging the Algerian calamity, but Lavigerie also used the cannibalism accusation to denigrate the Muslim population writ large. He claimed that such horrors were by no means rare, and that the "complete absence of a moral sense [among Algerian Muslims] undeniably promotes the multiplication of these heinous crimes."[13] It was not, then, because of Muslims' respect for religion, or their moral uprightness, or their intuition of some of the truths of Christian revelation—in short, it was not because of their potential to be good Catholics but rather because they were capable of the most horrible barbarisms that "France must raise this people up . . . or must drive it into the deserts, far from the civilized world."[14] This was one provocation too far for MacMahon, who viewed himself and his administration as responsible for maintaining peaceable relations between colonial Europeans and Muslim

Algerians. Such inflammatory rhetoric, he feared, would antagonize Algeria's Muslims, who far outnumbered the European population.[15]

Louis Veuillot intervened on behalf of Lavigerie, but the article he wrote in response reprised his themes going back more than twenty years—the natural religiosity of the Muslims and the likelihood that devout Muslims would have more respect for an outspokenly Christian government than for an "impious" one—rather than highlighting Lavigerie's dehumanizing anecdotes.[16] Eventually, Napoleon III intervened to put a stop to this internecine conflict between the governor and the bishop, two men who were both employees of the state. Lavigerie traveled to France to make his case before the emperor himself and succeeded in winning the right to dispose of the orphans as he pleased. He had only to promise not to baptize them before an appropriate age of consent. Meanwhile, MacMahon's superior, the minister of war, withdrew the colonial administration from the battle with a face-saving letter published in the official state journal, the *Moniteur*.[17] But what is especially significant about the debate over Islam and missions was how it corresponded to a modification of Lavigerie's position in the larger culture war between liberal and ultramontane Catholics in France and in Rome.

Indeed, as Soubiranne and Lavigerie's correspondence shows, some moderate Catholics in France were offended by Lavigerie's hostility toward Governor General MacMahon. Soubiranne not only worried that Lavigerie's political contest with Algeria's military administrators would compromise the seeming disinterestedness and success of the fundraising appeal; he was also concerned that by pandering to pro-missionary extremists and by attacking the tolerance and pragmatism of MacMahon, Lavigerie was alienating liberal Catholics. Most damaging of all was the competition for metropolitan charitable funds pursued by Lavigerie's fellow Algerian prelate, the well-born and well-connected bishop of Constantine, Félix de Las Cases. These concerns were tied together because many of Las Cases's metropolitan allies were found among France's more moderate Catholic notables. Recall that for liberal Catholics like Vogüé at the Œuvre d'Orient, the colonial administration's policy of religious toleration for Muslim consciences was sensible and right. In keeping with this sensibility, Bishop de Las Cases even wrote to Lavigerie to scold him for going "too quickly" and "making too much noise" in the journals.[18]

Lavigerie was perceived by some as betraying the liberal aristocratic sensibilities of the milieu that had educated and produced him. Soubiranne, who kept his pulse on the different representatives of French Catholicism and their reactions to Lavigerie's campaign, worried that influential "liberal Catholics" were siding against Lavigerie in his contest with the administration and would give their charitable donations to the less controversial Las Cases.[19] Melchior de Vogüé, the most long-standing and important member of the Œuvre d'Orient's council, expressed in private correspondence the embarrassment felt by mainstream Catholics at Lavigerie's vocal condemnations of MacMahon. Governor General MacMahon was himself a Catholic and his wife a devoted supporter of orphanages and other Catholic charities in the colony. This kind of internecine fighting between Catholics of good faith and breeding was anathema to the "liberal" or moderate sensibility. Lavigerie and MacMahon should have settled their differences behind closed doors; they should not have publicly aired Catholic dirty laundry. Vogüé was in a difficult position personally as well, since his brother Robert served in Algeria on MacMahon's staff and was a friend of both the governor general and his wife.[20] Vogüé even tried to use this connection to hammer out a "conciliation" between Lavigerie and MacMahon.[21]

Robert de Vogüé, for his part, wrote from Algeria to his brother in 1870 that Lavigerie even had the gall to ask MacMahon for financial support once the charitable funds raised on the basis of his unfair attacks against the governor had been spent. "The Marechal, instead of avenging himself, gave [Lavigerie] five thousand francs out of his pocket to keep the children that [Lavigerie] stole from their parents from dying of hunger." For Catholic notability like the Vogüé brothers, Governor General MacMahon was an honorable man of action, too noble to sully himself with public debate and journalistic recrimination.[22] Lavigerie, on the other hand, had used the press to publicize his accusations against MacMahon and had manipulated the growing rift between liberal and ultramontane Catholics. There is an unmistakable aristocratic element in these complaints about Lavigerie's underhanded tactics, complaints that recall how upper-class liberal Catholics like the Comte de Falloux had felt about Veuillot's lowbrow journalism.

However, despite Lavigerie's exploitation of ultramontane sensibilities and pro-missionary tropes, in his larger approach to colonial missions, to Islam, and to metropolitan public opinion he retained the civilizing discourse of liberal Catholicism. Like Veuillot and the conservatives, Lavigerie loudly demanded missionary activity even if it seemed to violate Muslim religious liberty—a demand for an openly Catholic foreign policy. Like Vogüé and the liberals, though, he denigrated Islam for its alleged fanaticism, economic backwardness, misogyny, and lack of religious liberty. Veuillot and the Jesuits had admired Muslims as theocratic noble savages; Lavigerie, using tactics honed during his days with the Œuvre d'Orient, derided Islam for precisely those allegedly theocratic tendencies.

Humanitarian Publicity: Muslim Orphans
between Distance and Proximity

Lavigerie and his supporters crowed that being allowed to keep the orphans against MacMahon's wishes constituted an unprecedented victory for missions in French Algeria. After settling the debate to his own satisfaction, Lavigerie took upon himself the role of the *quêteur*—the alms-collecting priest—traveling across France to preach about his orphans and take up offerings.[23] In addition to his fundraising drive, begun in early 1868 under the auspices of the Œuvre d'Orient, Lavigerie sent letters to France's bishops asking permission to collect funds in their dioceses. Lavigerie's discourse falsely linked the famine to Muslim Algerians' lack of agriculture, industriousness, and forethought. This strategy enabled him to blame the Muslims for their own misfortune, to delegitimize Islam as a religion, and to justify Christian proselytization. A letter from Lavigerie read from the pulpits in the diocese of Arras, for example, was full of the kind of Islam-blaming common among French colonial-settler observers of the famine. The famine and cholera took a far greater toll on the indigenous population than on the Europeans, Lavigerie explained to French Catholics, because the Muslims were not a civilized, agricultural people. The Europeans had "completely escaped the scourges" of the famine, since they were "more farsighted, more industrious, more moral, Christian, and, in a word, French."[24] The clear implication of this kind of rhetoric was not only that the Algerians had brought their deaths upon themselves but that industriousness, planning, and morality were exclusively Christian, even exclusively French, attributes. Against the more culturally adaptive hopes and practices of former missionaries in Algeria, Lavigerie thus foreclosed the possibility of accommodation between Christian doctrine and indigenous culture. To become "Christian" was to accept all the trappings of French modernity—including "agrarian capitalism"—as universal and normative.[25]

This narrative that the famine had been caused or exacerbated by the Algerians' own lack of civilizational, agricultural, or economic virtue seems to reflect the influence on Lavigerie of the emerging colonial-settler lobby in Algeria. Napoleon III's approach to colonial Algeria had emerged not only under the influence of Ismaÿl Urbain and the Arab Offices but also as a means of reconciling his political need for imperial glory with his sincere belief in the spirit of national development and liberation.[26] By the 1860s, Napoleon III was openly announcing his view that Algeria was an "Arab Kingdom" and that the national aspirations of its Arab population should be respected and cultivated—within a French imperial framework, of course. Napoleon III's paternal concern for his Algerian subjects would be short-lived, bringing mostly unintended consequences. A reform passed in 1863 and meant to safeguard tribal lands included "conditions and exceptions" that allowed the continued breakup and purchase of Algerian territory. Another reform passed in 1865—intended to create a path to citizenship for individual Algerians who disavowed their religious law—made official Muslim Algerians' status as second-class citizens and laid the groundwork for their later oppression as rights-less "*indigènes*."[27] But the most counterproductive legacy of Napoleon III's "Arab Kingdom" approach was that it provoked Algeria's European settler population into a vociferous resistance that was closely allied with Republican critics of the Second Empire back in France. Civilian settlers' desire for greater control over Algeria coalesced with Republican desires for greater political freedom back in France. Settler ideologues wanted Algerian land and labor and found it politically convenient to smear Algeria's military administrators (and by implication Algeria's Muslim peoples) for their slowness to "civilize" the Muslims.[28]

In the 1860s, settler ideologues launched newspapers, published pamphlets, and joined forces with the Republican opposition in France to demand representation and to attack Napoleon III's pro-"Arab" policies. Muslim society was "feudalistic," they claimed, and European settlers deserved the freedom to break up that society and seize its tribal lands. In the words of one settler spokesman who Lavigerie might as well have been quoting in his notorious letter, Algeria's "tribes must either 'be transformed or disappear.'"[29] The best way to civilize the Algerians, Lavigerie and the settlers agreed, was not to cordon off an area for them to live their nomadic lifestyle, as the military administration had done, but rather to break up this backward society and force them to associate with and learn from the colonists. Moreover, the settlers believed that land left to the Algerians was being wasted; only European landowners could make it productive.

In 1868, both because it served the purposes of missionary-fundraising rhetoric and of his momentary alliance with civilian colonists against the military administration, Lavigerie wholly shared this view of the Algerians' responsibility for their plight.[30] Lavigerie's papers preserve a stack of research notes he took during this period, the thoughts and citations he gathered to help him in his struggle against the military system of protected tribal lands. These notes range from accounts of the military administration's incompetence to condemnations of Islam on a religious and racial level, to political-economic explanations of European superiority and indigenous backwardness. One scrawled note states that there is "no [possibility of conversion] for adult Arabs[.] They are predestined to destruction." Another card explains that the "*indigènes*" are "inaccessible to all progress" because of their "Muslim fanaticism."

As part of this opposition research against the military administration, Lavigerie also jotted down quotations from the deliberations of Algiers's Chambre consultative d'agriculture on the famine. These leading colonists' views of the Algerians' agricultural backwardness surely inspired Lavigerie's *circulaire* to the French bishops. According to members of the chamber of agriculture, cited in Lavigerie's notes, the Algerians who lived far from the centers of European civilization and refused to learn from them were essentially choosing to die and had to be saved "in spite of themselves." It was their "feudal system," the "joint ownership" of their collective tribal lands, and their "forced separation" from colonists that were killing them.[31] Only individual, private ownership would incentivize agricultural production. More importantly, enacting individual ownership would enable European settlers and speculators to come in and buy up pieces of the land, completing the destruction of the nomadic economy. In relying on these colonialist discourses in his appeal for French charitable funds, Lavigerie thus emphasized the wide civilizational, political-economic, even racial chasm that separated the French from Algerians. Lavigerie was far from the Jesuit approach, which had hoped to preserve indigenous culture from the corruption and godlessness of European colonists.

Still, appeals for financial support had to avoid over-emphasizing the unbridgeable distance between receiver and donor. The paradox of missionary or humanitarian publicity is that it must both inspire pity (which borders dangerously on disgust, alienation, or resignation) toward those in need, while still somehow portraying the receivers as worthy of aid and capable of change. Donors need to be convinced that prospective converts are good investments.[32] For the purposes of indicting the colonial administration and Islam as a whole, Lavigerie had portrayed the Muslim victims as horrifying skeletons, reduced to acts of cannibalism through their own laziness and lack of foresight. For the purposes of fundraising, though, such a negative image had to be counterbalanced by the assurance that Lavigerie would be able to make Christians—or at least grateful and assimilated subalterns—out of them. Here, as in so much of the publicity and debates surrounding the orphans, it was important that the main victims focused on were children. Religious and racial difference intensified the empathy gap between Christian-French-donor and Muslim-Arab-receiver, but the conviction that Muslim children were "blank slates," still innocent enough to be converted, kept the pity from veering into disgust or complete indifference. Images of suffering childlike innocence could overcome the basic unworthiness of Muslims and Arabs, motivating sympathy and alms and inspiring a measure of optimism for the conversion of these children.

On a tour of France, Lavigerie's fundraising preaching strikingly illustrates this tension between pity/disgust and sympathy/worth, the play between distance and proximity. Lavigerie wanted to condemn and distance the Algerians from French civilization, while simultaneously encouraging a feeling of closeness with and sympathy for the children. According to one contemporary biographer of Lavigerie, who himself witnessed one of these sermons, Lavigerie vividly reported the story of the starving orphans and their pitiful state, but he also sketched an image of the improved future that awaited them as Christian protégés. Once French charitable donations had "knock[ed] down the barriers which separate us from these poor souls [ces malheureux]," it would then be possible to convert and improve them. Only then would missionaries be able to teach them about the true God, a Father God who (unlike their own immoral deity) "forbids them to hate, butcher, [and] destroy each other."[33]

To further "knock down the barriers" of distance and misunderstanding between French donors and these starving children, Lavigerie used not just words but images. Lavigerie circulated "photographic images representing poor children reduced to the state of skeletons, mothers with infants emaciated and close to death." These images afforded a glimpse of "the famine captured on the spot"—the illusion of proximity and eye-witness veracity.[34] For an idea of what these photographs might have looked like, the sketches reproduced in *L'Illustration* were based on photographs of famine victims taken in the environs of Constantine (see figure 6.2). They show parents seated on the ground, children—either in loincloths or entirely naked—in their laps, nothing but skin and bones, their heads hung low. The text of *L'Illustration*'s article exclaimed, "See, and pity these sad victims! Look at these faces tortured by the horrible pang of hunger; look at these bodies where the frightful form of the human skeleton emerges, and reckon the tortures of the long agony which tore apart [their] last days."[35] In the case of Lavigerie's preaching tour, the shocking realism of such photographs was effective in producing sympathy. In the words of Lavigerie's contemporary and biographer, Louis Baunard: "We wept, we gave. In the Cathedral of Orléans, for example, the collection which followed Lavigerie's sermon reached 8,000 francs. . . . In the month of May [1868], the œuvre des Ecoles d'Orient gathered 245,000 francs for the Arab orphans."[36]

Supposedly candid photos of starving indigenous families were not the only way Lavigerie and the White Fathers manufactured feelings of "proximity" and sympathy for the distant orphans. Lavigerie went one step further and

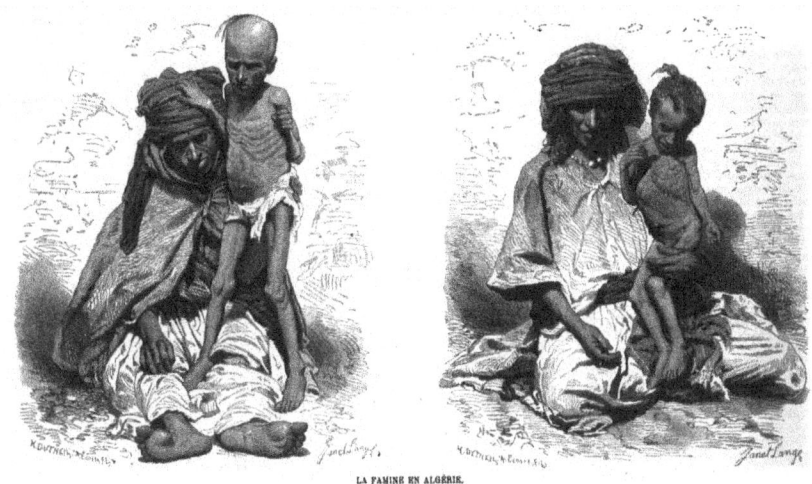

LA FAMINE EN ALGÉRIE.

FIGURE 6.2. "The Famine in Algeria." From *L'illustration: Journal universel* 51, no. 1322 (June 27, 1868).

produced examples of the orphans in the flesh. Throughout late 1868 and early 1869, he maintained missionaries in France to collect offerings in dioceses that were favorable to his projects. The missionaries were accompanied by one or two orphans who had been brought to France for the express purpose of inspiring donors. Bishop Dupanloup of Orléans, Lavigerie's old teacher, wrote Lavigerie in February of 1869 that "your little Kabyle is the delight of Orléans" and that Lavigerie's missionary had preached three fundraising sermons in one day. At least it was not the eloquent Lavigerie himself, Dupanloup joked, or all the charitable resources of his diocese would have been cleaned out.[37]

In the front of a little booklet published by the Œuvre d'Orient, where volunteer charitable women could write the names of those whose funds they collected, a photograph of two orphans was used to signal the transformative power of Lavigerie's mission (see figure 6.3).[38] Rather than the famine photographs of the previous year (pictures of downcast, skeletal forms, in rags or completely naked on the ground), we instead see two boys—the elder, larger boy, on a bench, with his arm draped over the younger boy, who sits in a lower position on a stool or step. They both appear bright and well-fed, and in one version of the photograph, they even seem to be on the verge of smiling playfully. Nevertheless, despite these signifiers of transformation and of relative dignity and autonomy compared to the abject helplessness of the famine pictures, the boys still needed

FIGURE 6.3. "Arab orphans gathered by Mgr. Lavigerie, Archbishop of
Algiers." From a fundraising booklet published by the Œuvre des écoles
d'Orient, dossier A19, document 282, Fonds Lavigerie, AGMAfr.

help. They gaze solemnly into the camera, with empty bowls in their hands,
waiting for the bowls to be filled with alms or with food.[39]

Lavigerie used the new medium of humanitarian photography to create the
illusion of proximity to Algeria's victims and to overcome the civilizational and
racial distance created by his own rhetoric. But even the most sympathetic, hu-
manizing photographs—of the clothed and dignified orphans in Paris—still preserved a strong sense of distance between French donor and indigenous receiver,
emphasizing the superiority of the "civilized, white community" over the "vulnerable, racial other."[40] Photography was thus a medium tailor-made for Lavigerie's
paradoxical representation of indigenous Muslims as savage but transformable.[41]
Algerian Muslims were geographically, racially, and religiously distant from
French Catholics; photography helped Lavigerie simultaneously confirm and
overcome the civilizational and racial chasm he himself had done so much to dig.

In addition to humanitarian photographs, Lavigerie employed rhetorical strategies that similarly inspired sympathy and optimism while nevertheless retaining superiority and distance. The most ubiquitous of these strategies— both in the orphanage campaigns of 1868–70 and in the later publications of the White Fathers—was the trope of indigenous gratitude. Lavigerie's letters and other publications constantly insisted on how grateful the little orphans were. Representations of the proper respect and gratitude of the Algerians served to inspire sympathy, build confidence in the mission's future prospects, and create the impression that the Algerians themselves were consenting to the missionaries' presence. For devout donors back home in France, there was a "social meaning of [the Algerians'] gratitude."[42] Too destitute to complete the gift exchange with a gift of their own, the children's gratitude was their repayment, and not an insignificant one, since it assured Europeans of their own goodness, rightness, and continued superiority.[43]

Since gratitude contrasted with how the allegedly ingrate Muslims normally behaved, this proved just how effective the donations and missions were. The children stayed at the orphanages of their own volition, Lavigerie claimed, out of gratitude and spiritual longing. Lavigerie boasted that he had instructed his orphanage directors to leave their doors unlocked and to keep no one by force. And his faith was rewarded—"barely a few deserted our houses." Even one child whose mother was still alive begged Lavigerie to let him stay, "because here I have found a father who is better than my mother." Lavigerie recounted this self-aggrandizing (and doubtful) conversation and then offered his official interpretation of it: "These children feel . . . the power of a virtue foreign to Mohammedanism: charity!"[44] Highlighting the voluntary gratitude of the orphans had the double benefit of gratifying donors back home in France and proving to Lavigerie's critics that the orphans were under no constraints, either to convert or even to remain at the orphanages. On the contrary, as a missionary recorded in his diary, one orphan had been so terrified by the prospect of being sent "*chez les français*" that the child became deaf and nonverbal from the trauma.[45] It is hard to imagine a more heartbreaking illustration of the archival silences of these children, even as Lavigerie reported their supposed words of gratitude.

According to Lavigerie's letter, the goodness of the orphanages was so well-known across Algeria that some parents even tried to get their own children admitted, despite the fact that these children were not orphaned.[46] Lavigerie did not admit to his metropolitan readers that some parents and other relatives had attempted to reclaim children that had found their way to his orphanages. The General de Wimpffen, a devout Catholic and one of the highest military administrators in the department of Algiers, had actively helped Lavigerie gather orphans and other children in early 1868 (a fact that seems to undermine Lavigerie's constant complaints of military and administrative obstruction). In the spring of 1869, the general was likewise using his position to intimidate parents and relatives who wanted their children back. Wimpffen was the gatekeeper through which parents had to pass; they had to prove their relationship to a child and, Wimpffen assured Lavigerie, he would not approve such reclamations lightly. He also supported Lavigerie's idea of requiring relatives who wanted their children back to repay the orphanage's costs of supporting their children.[47] Perhaps Lavigerie genuinely felt that this financial burden would weed out all but the most devoted parents. He also seems to have believed, according to colonialist and gendered views of Muslim society, that he had a special obligation to protect the girls whose relatives might claim them only to "sell" them. But Lavigerie's repayment policy would have made it extremely difficult for parents to reclaim their children, and it reveals that his charity was anything but disinterested.[48]

As if to punctuate the letter with examples of the miraculous transformations he was capable of performing, Lavigerie concluded with a series of evocative descriptions, painting scenes of how far the children had come from the skeletal forms he had initially saved. Here were the orphans visiting Algiers from their orphanage outside the city, well-dressed and well-fed, greeting astonished passers-by in French; they were no longer instinctively stealing whatever they could, but instead were overcome by the "sentiment of gratitude"; they had become cheerful, hard workers, "nearly transformed."[49] "I watch them sometimes from my windows, when they are at Saint-Eugène [the grounds of the Archbishopric], and I would wish that all of France might see them," Lavigerie wrote.[50] With a patriotic flourish practiced from his time at the Œuvre d'Orient, he called on all those who cared for the triple interests of the Church, of "Christian civilization," and of France's overseas "influence," to support him. According to Soubiranne, this letter (published in January 1869) marked a turning point away from the political battles and fundraising competitions of the previous year. The scenes of indigenous gratitude, the sense of proximity to these poor orphans, and Lavigerie's ambitious visions of future projects must have been irresistible. The letter was having such a powerful effect in France, Soubiranne wrote Lavigerie, that "even those who last year seemed to want to criticize you by acting sage and moderate cannot help praising you."[51]

1870 was a grim year for fundraising in France. Lavigerie himself was at the First Vatican Council, with Soubiranne in his entourage. Bishop Las Cases of

Constantine was competing for charitable funds. Moreover, with the coming of the Franco-Prussian War, charitable resources dried up, and Catholics in France fell behind in their support for the orphans. Trying to revive public interest in his efforts, while still at Rome for the meeting of the Vatican Council, Lavigerie found the time to launch another project in favor of the orphans, this one based on the insight that Catholics—especially Catholic women—longed for more personal, affective connections to the children. For 200 francs a year, for a period of five years, interested benefactors could "adopt" one of Lavigerie's orphans. Donors who adopted orphans were promised a personal dossier on their child, including a photograph and letters from the designated orphan. They would also have the right to choose the child's Christian name, taken at baptism. In addition, the pope had offered monthly plenary indulgences to anyone who supported Lavigerie's projects.[52] And the orphans would keep up their end of the bargain, Lavigerie assured: gratitude for France's gifts and prayers on behalf of their benefactors.

In keeping with the settler-colonial project of dispossessing Algerians of their land and reducing them to agricultural laborers, Lavigerie had emphasized Arab laziness and the wasteful misuse of Algeria's land. But, paradoxically, neither the settlers' agricultural capitalism nor Lavigerie's evangelism and fundraising could succeed unless the stereotype of Arab laziness was in some sense false—unless Algerians could be "transformed into rural proletarians," shown to be hard workers.[53] Thus, in their calls for donations, Lavigerie and his allies presented the orphans as "well disciplined," their "labor power a great resource" for the future. Even the "little girls handle the pickax" with "dexterity."[54] Another fundraiser described his astonishment at seeing "hundreds of young boys," many under the age of fifteen, working as hard as grown men in Lavigerie's fields. Given that Arabs were normally consumed with "the most voluptuous laziness," this was nothing short of a "miracle."[55]

Lavigerie encouraged mothers in France, especially aggrieved mothers of deceased or wayward children, to adopt these orphans, to earn the redemption of their own children. In a kind of global exchange of prayers and merits, mothers with their own prodigal children might benefit from the efficacious prayers of these "innocent" orphans. Perhaps they would want to name the orphan for their own lost child, creating a "living prayer" and monument; perhaps God would view their donation as a "ransom" to buy back their prodigal.[56] Here Saint Monica (devout mother of St. Augustine) was the reference of choice, with her many valences: the ancient saint of a bygone, Christian Africa that was now being restored; a member—as Lavigerie would argue—of the very same race as Algeria's

Kabyles; and a patron saint of all Christian mothers who prayed for prodigal sons. As St. Ambrose had famously assured Monica that her wayward Augustine would eventually become a Christian, so Lavigerie assured France's Christian mothers that their prayers and donations would be answered: "It is impossible that the son . . . of your tears [and] charity, should not be protected by God."[57]

This adopt-an-orphan campaign distilled a heady blend of emotional and cultural appeals and was carefully marketed to the sensibilities and "affective economies" of French Catholics, especially French Catholic women, in the late nineteenth century.[58] The Church was famously undergoing a process of "feminization," both in its personnel and in its sensibilities.[59] The century saw a dramatic rise in the number of female religious vocations, and even as French men became increasingly secularized, the vast majority of girls (even daughters of freethinking, Republican men) were left to the Church for their confirmation and education.[60] Thus was created a situation where many devout women may indeed have had a wayward husband, brother, or son for whom they prayed. Women also played an influential role in French Catholicism's global imaginary, with women religious on the front lines of missions—such as Emilie de Vialar in Algeria and Tunisia—and with laywomen at home in France founding and sustaining some of the most prominent charitable organizations—such as Pauline Jaricot and the Œuvre de la Propagation de la Foi (Association for the Propagation of the Faith).[61]

Finally, in conjunction with its growing feminization and internationalization, French Catholicism in the nineteenth century—shaken by the violence and martyrdoms of the French Revolution and by the embattled position of the pope—also witnessed a rising trend toward an emphasis on sacrificial, redemptive suffering.[62] The Christian notion of vicarious, redemptive suffering converged with the Catholic doctrine of the "reversibility," or exchange of merits, leading some devout Catholics (especially women) to believe that their own sufferings and privations could, like Christ's, be applied to someone else's account.[63] This doctrine encouraged French Catholics to imagine themselves as embedded in a global network of sufferings, sins, and merits that could be exchanged.[64] Devout Frenchwomen were thus primed to participate in the redemption not only of orphan children but of their own children in exchange for their monetary gifts, prayers, and privations.

Though some wealthy donors took on the onerous charge of supporting an orphan individually, one common arrangement was for a child to be supported collectively by an association, such as the Association of Christian Mothers or the Society of Saint Vincent de Paul. Glimpses of these various benefactors and their motives have been conserved in the White Fathers' archives. Individual donors sometimes wrote, following Lavigerie's recommendation, to request that their Algerian adoptee pray for a sick or wayward child back in France. But the most common theme in these letters from benefactors was a desire for more information about their particular orphan—in keeping with the longing for proximity Lavigerie had so carefully cultivated. Some showed disappointment with the sparse information provided by the White Fathers after the initial adoption booklet was sent. A couple from Rennes adopted a boy in 1870 and asked that he be christened Henri. Despite not receiving any updates thereafter, they continued to send the sizable yearly sum up through 1873, but they "[desired] intensely to have some news of our dear adoptive son."[65] An Association of Christian Mothers in Bayeux, unlike the couple from Rennes, did not feel comfortable forwarding more money until they had received some news of their child. If little "Edouard-Roger" had died or gone back to his tribe, they wrote, they were happy to see their charity applied to another child, using the same two names for christening, on the condition (underlined twice in the letter's text) that they receive this second child's photograph.[66] Another letter, from the Blois branch of the Society of Saint Vincent de Paul, described how happy these *Messieurs* were to have received a new photograph, of an orphan who was replacing another they had originally sponsored. "We examined this portrait with the sharpest interest, and hung it on a medallion from Our Holy Father the Pope." But they had not received any accompanying information: What was the child's age, baptismal status, or level of education in the French language?[67]

The White Fathers and the Kabyle Myth: From the Orphanages to the Sahara

Out of this fundraising work of "adoptions" grew the White Fathers' first periodical, launched in 1871. Like Lavigerie's other metropolitan publicity, this *Bulletin* was published in the offices of the Œuvre d'Orient and was managed by its director and secretary. Unlike the Œuvre's bulletin, it was dedicated to the Algerian orphans and Lavigerie's other missionary projects. This newsletter, the *Bulletin de l'Œuvre de Sainte Monique*, would eventually become the mouthpiece for all the White Fathers' endeavors in Africa.[68] Accordingly, the colonialist and orientalist scope of the *Bulletin* expanded: letters and updates from Lavigerie were published alongside travel narratives, ethnological reflections, and fundraising appeals written by various White Fathers. Lavigerie and the White Fathers' fundraising publicity clearly contributed to and articulated anti-Arab sentiment. The two most prominent themes that emerge from the *Bulletin*'s various letters and articles are, first, the oft-remarked "Kabyle myth," the missionaries' belief that Kabyles and other Berbers were more civilized and more susceptible to Christianity than the Arabs; and second, the contrast between the allegedly "disinterested" charity of Christian missionaries compared to the money-grubbing local marabouts. Both these themes demonstrate that the White Fathers' approach to Algerian Islam—more than that of previous missionaries and polemicists—partook of liberal, civilizational, even secularized modes of denigrating Islam.

The Kabyle missions of the White Fathers existed in a tight symbiosis with the discourse of the "Kabyle Myth," both basing their practice and confidence on the myth and, in turn, contributing to its further elaboration and transmission.[69] In the early 1870s, a number of factors converged to offer missionaries unprecedented access to the Kabyles. The new governor general of Algeria, Admiral de Gueydon, was a friend of Lavigerie's and a believer in the disciplinary and civilizing power of Christian education.[70] The Mokrani rebellion that erupted in the mountains of Kabylie during the Franco-Prussian War seemed to confirm Lavigerie's argument that the Algerians needed to be forcibly civilized and subdued, and Lavigerie used his influence to advocate for the colonization of Kabylie.[71] As early as 1871, then, the White Fathers began establishing mission posts throughout Kabylie. They also sent missionaries into the southern Sahara where, in keeping with the racial hierarchies of the "Kabyle myth," they searched especially for Berber tribes that would be similarly amenable to receiving missionaries. Thus, although the *Bulletin de l'Œuvre de Sainte Monique* grew out of the need to fund the orphans and related charities, and although it was initially distributed and marketed accordingly (to the Associations of Christian Mothers, for example), from its earliest issues the *Bulletin* also recounted the exploits of the White Fathers beyond the orphanages—in Kabylie and the Sahara.

In the columns of the *Bulletin* itself, a tension developed between its original emphasis on the work with the orphans—both Arab and Kabyle—and articles on the rest of the White Fathers' initiatives, which focused almost exclusively on Kabyles/Berbers and often stigmatized Arabs. In a letter authored by Lavigerie, for example, the archbishop described his missionary projects with such pro-Berber optimism as to erase even those Arabs who were children in his own orphanages and seminary. Kabyles, Lavigerie believed, had descended from Christianized North Africans such as St. Augustine and still possessed a dim collective memory of their Christian past. In addition, as other peddlers of the "Kabyle myth" would repeat, they were monogamous, sedentary in "villages similar to ours," and were "more hardworking, more sober, and purer in their lives" than the Arabs. "Therefore," Lavigerie concluded, "it is through the Kabyles that [the conversion of the "*indigènes*"] must commence."[72] For example, one reason for optimism was that Lavigerie's missionaries were in the process of making contact with Saharan tribes far to the south, which was especially promising because "they are Berbers also."[73] On the subject of his indigenous seminary, Lavigerie claimed that "the majority" of students there were Kabyles, with only "a few Arabs."[74] It is a testament to the power of the pro-Kabyle discourse that Lavigerie felt the need to emphasize that the seminarians were predominantly Kabyle. Erasing the existence of Arab children from his own indigenous seminary was in keeping with the claim that only the Kabyles showed any promise of conversion in the near future. The archbishop seemed to recognize, whether instinctively or intentionally, that he had so denigrated Arab-ness that it would be impossible to excite his donors about supporting the Arab orphans. Similarly, an update on the orphans three months later referred to them as "new Augustines . . . since they are of the same blood, the same people, for the most part" as the famous saint, thus foregrounding the Kabyle students.[75]

Denigrations of the children's Arab-ness were even more prominent in reports from the girls' orphanages. From one of the girls' *maisons* came a report, published in the *Bulletin*, which reveals that the word "Arab" was used as an insult there. The report's author, a Sister Marie-Cécile Brunet, described how one girl, "[sensing] by instinct the humiliation of the Arab woman," asked, "with a profoundly sad appearance," whether, once grown, "it will be seen that I am an Arab? . . . Oh! . . . I would like to remain young!"[76] Whether she was referring to the wearing of the veil or to some other marker of Arab female difference, this girl instinctively bore witness to the goodness of Christian France's gender regime. Sister Marie-Cécile went on to describe how zealously these girls wanted to be considered French: they looked on their lives before their salvation and baptism as a time where they had been merely "like the beasts." Thus, "when they have made some transgression, we cannot grieve them more than by calling them by their Arab names." Another girl, realizing (according to Sister Marie-Cécile) that it seemed especially difficult for her and her compatriots to be "well-behaved," asked if the devil was an Arab; and a dying child expressed "vigorous . . . disgust" at the mere idea that the heavenly choirs awaiting her might be singing in Arabic.[77] (See figure 6.4.)

These remarks, however racialized, were intended as sweet evidence of the girls' innocence and piety and of the mission's success in colonizing and Christianizing their young minds. But the remarks also reveal how closely Lavigerie

FIGURE 6.4. "A sick girl (Louise fatma)." Henri Ducat, "Diaires: 1.
Séminaire de Maison Carrée ... 1872–1874," RAl 105, ACJF.

and his missionaries had aligned themselves with gendered settler-colonial discourses about Muslim Algerian families. Settler activists criticized the ways the
military regime had "tolerated" Muslim family law and claimed to want to civilize Muslims and emancipate their women. Focusing on Algerians' oppressive
treatment of women offered settlers both the "civilizing" justification to intervene and the opportunity to break any remaining influence of the traditional
Algerian family and society, to render Algerians atomized individuals at the
mercy of the agricultural land and labor markets.[78] Lavigerie agreed with this
gendered civilizing mission, telling his supporters in France that Arab women
were "treated as slaves," regularly beaten, and kept in a state of ignorance, but that
"the conversion of this poor people ... will begin with her [the Arab woman]."[79]
    Beginning in mid-1872, the *Bulletin* began featuring another kind of report
in the ethnographic genre of the "Kabyle myth." These were travel narratives
about the Berber and Arab tribes in the southern Sahara. Such travel narratives

proliferated as Lavigerie's clerics and missionaries began setting out from the southern outpost of Laghouat to reconnoiter sites for new missions and potential routes to sub-Saharan Africa. Given the discursive importance that the White Fathers and their supporters had given to the "Kabyle myth," the main ethnographic yardstick used for evaluating the nomadic tribes of the Sahara became whether or not a given tribe was of Berber descent. In August 1872, for example, the *Bulletin* published a report from Père Olivier, a Jesuit who had been posted to France's most distant settlement, Laghouat. Olivier reported that the Mozabites (a confederation of the Saharan M'zab region), supposedly Berber like the Kabyles, "have stricter customs than the Arabs," and "polygamy is very rare among them. They are very hardworking, hate lying; and one notices in their religious practices several signs of Christianity, among others a sort of public confession ... which is a lot like the one practiced in the primitive Church."[80] Olivier also met some Touaregs in and around Laghouat, predictably describing them as "Muslims only in name, and consequently not very fanatical. They observe neither the fast of Ramadan, nor the pilgrimage to Mecca, nor the prayer prescribed by the Coran and preceded by ablutions." As was often remarked of the Kabyles, Olivier also noted that designs and tattoos resembling the Christian cross were everywhere in Touareg culture and that their treatment of women allegedly distinguished them from the misogynistic Arabs.[81]

With Père Olivier's encouragements ringing in his ears, Lavigerie dispatched Félix Charmetant—one of the original three White Fathers—on an exploratory journey into the Sahara beyond Laghouat, to make contact with the tribes there. Charmetant's reports, like Olivier's, were filled with his ethnographic speculations about these peoples and his impressions of their receptivity to the Gospel. Charmetant confirmed that there were "traces" and "vestiges of Christianity" that persisted among the Mozabites and that it was "precisely" these Christian elements that accounted for "the profound aversion of the Muslims for the Mozabites."[82] Like other amateur ethnographers of the colonial state, Charmetant set himself the task of establishing a careful gradation between the ethnic and social groups of North Africa. The Mozabite race, he wrote, was not as "pure" a type of Berber character as was the Kabyle. While the Kabyles were "tall, fair-haired, bony ... even the true Roman type," the Mozabite was "stocky and dark-haired," somewhat Jewish in his aptitude for commerce and finance, but "less untrustworthy" than "the Jew."[83] Despite racial gradations between them, though, the important point was that the Kabyles, the Touaregs, and the Mozabites had descended from the ancient Christians of Numidia and that, despite their "[isolation] from each other," had each succeeded in conserving at least "the cross, monogamy, hatred for the Arab, and . . . the canon or code of their former laws." The Berbers may have taken on a Muslim shell, but because of these remarkable vestiges, their "customs" were "entirely Christian."[84]

Pro-Berber rhetoric was applied in wide-ranging fashion—from the orphans, to Kabylie, to the tribes of the Sahara. The rhetoric alternated constantly between different iterations of the "Kabyle myth" and applied identical vocabulary and Christian comparisons to various Saharan Berbers as well as to Kabyles, but it mattered little whether metropolitan Catholics could keep the differences between Kabyles or Mozabites or Touaregs straight. All that mattered was that these people were not "Arabs." In the larger scheme of French North Africa, one missionary claimed, the Arabs did not matter anyway, since "Berbers" made up the majority of Algeria's population. "It is not Arabs that we have before us; it is, in very large majority, Berbers, Berbers who have been Christians, consequently our brothers in civilization and in faith."[85] The effect of such an overriding emphasis on descent was to racialize religion completely: one could only hope to become a Christian if one's ancestors had been Christian.

"Disinterested" Charity and the Secularization of Muslim Missions

Next to the "Kabyle myth," the most prominent motif in the White Fathers' accounts of missionary contact was the role of their charity—representations of the missionaries' own charitable and medical activities. The key interpretive component of this motif, ubiquitous in the missionaries' accounts, lay in the contrast between the disinterestedness of Christian charity, on the one hand, and the alleged venality and greed of the local Muslim marabouts, on the other. Like the "Kabyle myth," the "disinterested charity" trope served to denigrate North Africa's Muslims and to confirm the rightness of Christian and European religion, society, and political economy. Muslims, Lavigerie and his missionaries believed, were naturally ungrateful and crafty, so the true test of missionary charity would be if it could force even such ingrates to recognize the superiority of the Christian religion.

The superior charity of the missionaries was a preferred theme in the White Fathers' *Bulletin de l'Œuvre de Sainte Monique* for a number of related reasons. In the eyes of the French metropolitan audience, charity functioned both as an apologetic for the truth of Christianity (Christianity inspired charity more effectively than Islam did, and must therefore be true) and as a self-serving justification for their own feelings of goodness, for having supported these humanitarian efforts.[86] In addition, relating scenes of disinterested charity, and of Muslims' apparent shock and gratitude at this generosity, seemed to give reason for optimism about the prospects of the mission. Finally, charitable and medical activities featured so prominently in the *Bulletin* because they seemed to justify Lavigerie's controversial missiological strategy of prohibiting evangelism until charity had first worn down Muslim resistance. Beyond these rhetorical reasons, the missionaries' discourse of disinterestedness (contrasted with the greed of Muslim holy men) relied paradoxically on a capitalistic, calculating, liberal-individualistic understanding of charitable giving. This ideological baggage made it impossible for the missionaries to understand indigenous spiritual economies of gift exchange. Quite the opposite, the missionaries wielded their superior charity to discredit and disrupt the social authority of the marabouts and to create new, more individualistic tribesmen, ready to receive the Gospel.[87] The White Fathers' rhetoric of disinterested charity—like their discourse on Islam in general—was more indebted to the liberal-capitalistic ethos of the secular civilizing mission than to traditional Christian missiology.

Veuillot, the Jesuits, and other earlier missionary advocates had spoken admiringly of Muslim society—of how pervaded it was by religiosity, how full of respect and social prestige for its marabouts, and how theocratic and pre-secular it was in its linking of politics and religion. Veuillot and the Jesuits had no desire to uproot, individualize, and secularize indigenous culture; rather, they had hoped that Muslim Algerians would maintain their pervasive religiosity, but transfer that sacralized loyalty from their marabouts to the missionaries. At the same time, however, these "philo-Islamic" missionaries had openly challenged Muslim doctrines and preached Christianity in often offensive ways, refusing to separate their word from their deed. The White Fathers inverted this earlier approach. On the one hand, they made no pretense of admiring Muslim religiosity or "theocratic" qualities; on the other hand, they professed their allegedly disinterested willingness to postpone proselytization. The White Fathers' tactic of separating Christian charity from the creed that ostensibly motivated it is consistent with the liberal/secular separation of politics from religion. The White Fathers, unlike previous missionaries, sought to prove Christianity's superiority over Islam precisely by demonstrating how secularized and unfanatical Christianity could be.

"Islam does not even awaken in [its marabouts] the idea of charity," Charmetant wrote in one of his reports from the Sahara.[88] For Charmetant, it was in this arena of charitable activity that the contrast between the Muslim marabout and the "French marabout" was starkest. Charmetant claimed that the Algerians

themselves "invariably" remarked upon the generosity and disinterestedness of
the missionaries, contrasting the generous Christian priests with the venality of
their own marabouts. In the words of one Muslim cited by Charmetant, "The
French marabout only seeks to do [us] good and always freely, expecting his
reward only from God, while the Muslim marabout . . . always takes care to be
paid handsomely for both his services and his prayers." Placing this testimony in
the mouths of Algerians rather than in the missionary's own narration seemed
to justify the missionaries' territorial claim on the Sahara—it constituted a
kind of consent for the missionaries to take spiritual possession. Even among
the Arabic-speaking Chambas, whom he predictably denigrated for not being
as "civilized" as the neighboring (Berber) Mozabites, Charmetant believed he
had made a great impression by his disinterested charity, by refusing the gifts
traditionally offered to Muslim marabouts.[89]

Charmetant's charitable contrast with indigenous customs was evoked col-
orfully in one story he recounted, a story that may be read against the grain to
see how deeply the missionaries and their supporters misunderstood indigenous
culture. Back within the outpost town of Laghouat, after his excursion into the
southern Sahara, Charmetant was visited by one of the contacts he had made,
"Sliman, the most influential man of the Chambas."[90] This indigenous notable
hoped that Charmetant would attend to a sick relative he had brought with
him, but when he tried to press some money into Charmetant's hand as a token
of gratitude, the priest let the payment fall to the ground. "Why do you insult
me?" Sliman asked. "Why do you grieve me?" Charmetant retorted. And then
he explained, "If you pay us here on earth, we no longer have a reward to expect
in heaven." Sliman commended Charmetant's charity and single-minded focus
on heavenly reward: "Since the day you told me . . . that everything [Christian
marabouts] did was not for money but for God . . . you became as sweet to my
heart as sugar is to the mouth."[91] Missionary charity was so powerful that it
could overcome even the rigid ethnographic hierarchy of the "Kabyle myth":
even the uncivilized and normally ungrateful Arabic-speaking peoples of the
Sahara, according to this interpretation, could be impressed and seduced by the
supernaturally motivated charity of the missionaries.

This success shows how episodes of disinterested charity seemed to confirm
the wisdom of Lavigerie's long-term strategy: charity and medical aid first, proselytization later. Some missionaries had chafed under Lavigerie's temporary
prohibition of explicit preaching and conversion. The *Bulletin* seems to reveal
missionary writers in the process of anxiously justifying this policy not only to
skeptical supporters but also to themselves. "Care for the sick and education of

children," Charmetant gushed approvingly, would do more to soften the hearts of these Arabs than any direct challenge, because "charity," for the Muslim, was "a language full of persuasion." Certainly, Charmetant was familiar with accusations that Muslims were "profoundly ungrateful," that they professed gratitude only to turn around and "curse" their Christian benefactors behind their backs.[92] All this was true, he admitted, but the daily, persistent dedication and charity of missionaries, living among them, could not but succeed in winning them over.[93] At the same time, it is worth noting that Sliman, the indigenous notable, initially took offense at the rejection of his payment—a fact that survives even in Charmetant's triumphant narration. This insult suggests the possibility that Charmetant and other "disinterested" missionaries misunderstood indigenous rules of gift-giving and the "potential humiliation" they caused.[94]

The author of another letter, Père Paulmier, repeated the theme of how the missionaries' generosity and refusal of reciprocal gifts astonished and impressed the Algerians. Like Charmetant, he proudly recounted stories of how he refused gifts and payments, even to the point of offending his interlocutors. In exchange for his medical help, for example, the Muslims offered bandages, eggs, sheep, and cloths, but Paulmier and his fellow missionaries would always refuse, protesting that they would lose their heavenly reward if recompensed on earth. As in Charmetant's accounts, the indigenous Muslims praised the priests' generosity, and offered negative comparisons with their own greedy marabouts: "Truly [the French missionaries] are men of God!"[95] With medical assistance, the White Fathers were trying to wean the Algerians off their reliance on the amulets and talismans of the local marabouts with their allegedly greedy fees. One White Father—Père Pascal, stationed at Geryville—was offered fruit, milk, and money as a *marauf* (tip) for his labors, but like his fellow missionaries, he too "obstinately refuse[d]," in order to keep his "ministry of charity . . . disinterested," and to retain his claim on a heavenly rather than an earthly reward.[96]

In the concluding installment of Père Richard's account of his "voyage to Tuggurth and to Ouargla" published in 1875, Richard developed this theme of charitable contrast between Christian priest and Muslim marabout to an extreme that betrays the discourse's contradictions. At the oasis of Ouargla, the Arabic-speaking tribe of the Chambas (with whom Charmetant had made contact) put on a "fantasia" to celebrate the end of Ramadan—galloping on their horses, firing their guns, and simulating combat. Even before any exchange of religious or medical services occurred, Richard was already having some difficulty navigating between the gift-giving customs of the Chambas and his desire to retain a measure of independence: "I was offered eggs which I refused, [and] milk which I accepted, to please [them]." Three of the Chambas at the festival later approached the missionary and asked him to make it rain—on the assumption that this was one of the tasks proper to the marabout. Though the Christian priest could not guarantee the result, he agreed to pray for rain. Before his departure the next morning, several of the Arab notables of the tribe came to present him with monetary gifts. Richard demanded an explanation from his native informant, who explained, "They think you are like one of our marabouts, that you travel only to collect alms, and they bring you their offerings so that you might not curse the country." Of course, Richard indignantly refused, explaining that "French marabouts" performed their services not for riches but out of fear of God.[97]

With Richard's self-conscious refusal to be like the greedy marabouts—who only visited their parishioners when they needed to collect alms (*quêter*)—the inconsistencies in the White Fathers' comparisons between Christian priest and Muslim marabout are concentrated. A Catholic clergyman serving a parish back in France—not visiting temporarily as a missionary but providing solace and ritual passage through all stages of life—was understood to be "worthy of his hire," accepting gifts and fees from his parishioners. But the allegedly "disinterested" missionaries were closer to the marabouts than they would have liked to admit, since their very ability to do without gifts and payments was contingent on their incessant fundraising back in France. Here Richard's use of the word *quêter* to describe the practice of the venal marabouts—something a self-respecting missionary would never do—is a curious slip, because *quêter* was the term used to describe missionary fundraising back in France. Many White Fathers would take periodic tours to France as *quêteurs*; to *quêter* was of course the very reason for the *Bulletin* and the purpose of Richard's letter itself. Readers of the *Bulletin* would have seen the word employed regularly in connection with the missionaries and their efforts. Thus, Richard's use of the word *quêter* to condemn the marabouts discloses at once the unconfessed similarity between missionary and marabout and also the deep asymmetry of power between them in Europe's age of industrial, colonial, and missionary expansion. The missionaries relied on a system of spiritual economic exchange—alms received from devout French believers in exchange for rituals, masses, and other spiritual services—every bit as much as the marabouts did. The difference was that the global reach and surplus of Europe's charitable resources enabled the missionaries to disrupt the spiritual economy of Muslim Algerians. Because of the "*quête*-ing" done back in France, missionaries in Algeria could make a show of their superiority and disinterestedness—their detachment from the mundane concerns of local marabouts and their almost angelic spirituality.

The missionaries' constant accusations of marabout venality and claims of superior disinterestedness not only obscured their own debt to fundraising and remuneration from France but also relied on an understanding of charity that was in some ways more cynical and calculating than that of the marabouts themselves. As Pierre Bourdieu argued about Kabyle culture, the "game" of gift exchange was regulated by a "sense of honor," not of accumulation. Gifts offered to marabouts were given and accepted in a spirit of honor—out of a desire to fulfill customary obligations and show one's symbolic superiority—not out of a "spirit of calculation," as he elsewhere characterizes the capitalistic ethos. Only someone who did not understand the precapitalist ethos of Kabyle culture could call such gifts bribery.[98] Similarly, when White Father travel-writers suggested that a marabout who accepted honorable gifts was guilty of greed or partiality, they imposed their own spirit of capitalistic calculation onto the traditional exchange. In accusing the marabouts of greed, the White Fathers betrayed only how "economical" their own thinking was.

If the White Fathers' discourse and practice of charity were in some ways more capitalistic or calculating than those of the tribes and marabouts they visited, they were also, in a sense, more secular. Lavigerie's "charity first" strategy—the postponement of proselytization until after missionary charity had worn down the Muslims' alleged pride and prejudice—was a more secularized approach than that of previous missionaries. On one level this shift is obvious: the White Fathers' charitable and medical efforts were "secular" simply in the sense that these services were tactically divorced from the preaching of the Gospel. In other words, Lavigerie directed his missionaries to win the Muslims' hearts and minds through their deeds alone, independently of the word that motivated that deed. In this shift, Lavigerie was not only concerned with avoiding Muslim resistance but with avoiding criticism and anticlerical attacks from French and French-Algerian journalists and political leaders. But this missiological strategy was also "secular" in a deeper sense in that it relied on normative assumptions about the proper separation of religion from other spheres of society.

The *Bulletin* produced a great deal of self-congratulatory verbiage on Lavigerie's "prudence" in adopting this policy and would trot out anecdotes about how scrupulously the rule was observed. On this subject at least, the publicity materials did not exaggerate. In private, Lavigerie was, if anything, even more insistent on the rule. In 1873, alarmed by political opposition in Algeria and France, Lavigerie severely reprimanded a missionary for baptizing a sick Muslim child and, even worse, for talking about the baptism "in a letter which can fall into the wrong hands." He punished the over-zealous missionary by withdrawing for three days his right to say mass. Lavigerie sternly reminded the local superior of the Kabyle mission that under the political circumstances "a single impru-dence . . . *can ruin everything*."[99] Now, "more than ever," Lavigerie emphasized, they must abide by the rules: " Do not speak to the Kabyles about religion, under any pretext. . . . This is not the moment to convert, this is the moment to win the heart and the confidence of the Kabyles by charity and by kindness. . . . [I]t may take centuries."[100]

More than Lavigerie's own missionaries, it was the Jesuits—who had been lay-ing the groundwork in Kabylie for some time before the White Fathers' arrival—who chafed under Lavigerie's new anti-proselytization policy. In February of 1873, Jesuit Père Lagrange described a series of recent conflicts with Lavigerie. As a condition for keeping their post at Fort National, Lavigerie had demanded that the Jesuits agree to a "delimited radius" of action over the surrounding Kabyles and to a list of conditions (the anti-proselytization rules, chiefly) the Jesuits con-sidered "unacceptable." Between the jurisdictional rivalry, the postponement of open preaching, and a denial of the Jesuits' right to collect alms publicly for their mission, Lavigerie's conditions "take from us all liberty of action and make it impossible for us to create future projects," Lagrange complained.[101] Eventually, the Jesuits reached a compromise with Lavigerie—they could solicit funds on an individual, private level, and they could, similarly, teach prayers and catechism privately.[102] Despite this shaky compromise, the Jesuits would continue to kick against the pricks of the ban on preaching and conversion (albeit occasionally realizing the tactical wisdom of the policy).[103]

Félix Charmetant, one of the earliest White Fathers, seems to have observed the policy conscientiously and to have buzzed in Lavigerie's ear about the Jesuits' deviations from the prescribed conduct in Kabylie. In March of 1874, Charme-tant wrote to Lavigerie to warn him that the general residing at Fort National was troubled by the Jesuits' bluntness—"They are teaching the children of the *Fraoucen* to make the sign of the cross," ignoring "the prudent policy that Your Grandeur traced for us." Charmetant, like Lavigerie, worried that the Jesuits would, through their misbehavior, offer up a "pretext" to the administration for a more general persecution against missionaries, a blowback that might harm the White Fathers, too.[104] Charmetant reported to Lavigerie a few years later that he himself had told a Kabyle interested in conversion to keep these desires to himself for the time being. Charmetant's advice to this prospective convert was to live a God-fearing life within his community until conversion to Chris-tianity was more opportune, perhaps until Muslim desires for conversion were more widespread.[105]

It is unlikely that this caution (and its attendant "disinterested" charity) ever resulted in many conversions among the Muslim population, but it may have paid off in winning the toleration and even the support of normally missionary-averse colonial officials. When the White Fathers applied to the minister of Cults for official status as a teaching congregation in 1878, Admiral Gueydon wrote a glowing recommendation to the minister on their behalf. To illustrate Lavigerie's "extreme prudence," the admiral recounted an anecdote from his time in Algeria: A Muslim woman had brought a complaint against her local curé for refusing to baptize her, and the matter came across the desk of the Procureur General. Upon investigating the complaint, he learned that the curé was simply following Lavigerie's orders, which had strictly forbidden the baptizing of any Muslims without his express permission. How could the Ministry of Cults refuse recognition to such a pragmatic, politically sensible, and cautious congregation?[106]

The Jesuits, on the other hand, continued to complain about the new policy. In one instance, some children of the Beni-Yenni tribe (where the Jesuits had one of their posts in Kabylie) somehow got ahold of some catechisms on their own and began to teach themselves—or so the Jesuits innocently claimed. Of their own volition, these youths demanded to be baptized, but when Lavigerie got wind of this budding spiritual movement, he barred the Jesuits from baptizing any of them. Lavigerie ordered that any young Muslim desiring baptism would have to move to France, where a more suitable education awaited (and, one surmises, where they might be protected from conflict or from the temptation to apostatize and embarrass the mission).[107] Lavigerie worried that the imprudence of the Jesuits could jeopardize his entire mission. After all, it was because of the Jesuits' alleged "kidnapping" and baptism in 1881 of two young Kabyles without parental permission—publicized in anticlerical journals—that Lavigerie, spooked, was forced to recall the Kabyle students from his own indigenous seminary in France to make sure their papers and parental permissions were in order.[108]

The White Fathers' charity first approach was not only "secular" in the sense that it bracketed and postponed preaching. It was also secular in that it relied on the view that religion should only be spiritual and interior. By highlighting their own angelic, interiorized motives for dispensing religious, charitable, or medical services—by refusing the gifts that indigenous honor dictated were due them—the White Fathers sought to disaggregate religion and the priestly functions from the marabout's traditional embeddedness in every sphere of society.[109] The White Fathers' self-conscious disinterestedness aimed first of all to demonstrate the Christian religion's superiority over and separateness from indigenous society. It reflected the French missionary's haughty isolation from the entire complex of the gift-giving economy. But it also pushed a normative conception of religion in general: any religion worthy of the name would be similarly angelic and disinterested, concentrating only on interior and heavenly rewards and rejecting the social, political, or economic existence of the holy man.

In this connection, one more contrast with Jesuit missionaries' earlier approach is instructive. Not only had the Jesuits insisted on broaching explicitly religious topics whenever possible, but—on the more mundane level of gift-giving and spiritual exchanges—the Jesuits would not have dreamed of divorcing their apostolate from medicine and charity or of refusing the gifts to which custom and hospitality entitled them. Their strategy had been the perfect inverse of Lavigerie's: they preached Christianity openly and aggressively, but they also happily accepted the Muslims' gifts and meals, as any good marabout should. The diaries of the Jesuit missions in the 1850s and 1860s—both the *mission arabe* at Constantine, and Creuzat's pioneering mission at Fort Napoleon in Kabylie—are filled with allusions to gifts and meals offered by indigenous notables or students. Sometimes on Muslim holidays such as Ramadan (and sometimes even on Christian holidays) the families of the Jesuits' indigenous students at Constantine would offer a pastry or other gift for the *pères*. On Creuzat's first visit among the Kabyle tribes around Fort Napoleon back in 1862, he exchanged gifts and ate the large meals that were offered to him (and at the same time he did not hesitate to preach openly about Jesus and Mary).[110] As late as 1869, when Père Vincent had replaced the controversial Creuzat at Fort Napoleon, Vincent and his colleagues distributed gifts and tunics on a visit to the Beni-Frah, and in exchange they accepted a large feast that the Kabyles offered in their honor.[111]

The Jesuits had been happy to embed themselves into indigenous customs of exchange and obligation, instead of standing in detached opposition to those obligations. They had also been happy to usurp some of the religio-medicinal services of the marabouts. They offered medical and sacramental aid, but far from aggressively seeking to distinguish between their medical aid and the more "superstitious" remedies of the marabouts, they substituted their own sacral remedies, their own conduits of charisma. In one instance, five Kabyles from a neighboring tribe visited Creuzat's mission, seeking a cure for a "possessed" mother—Creuzat offered them a "medal of the Holy Virgin" to take to her (probably the ubiquitous "miraculous medal" of Catherine Labouré), and taught them how to say part of the Ave Maria.[112] In another evocative account, some Jesuit *frères*—auxiliaries to Père Vincent at Fort National—came across a sick man who was covered with the traditional amulets that the local marabout had tied all over his person. The *frères* tore off the amulets and administered some "Water of Saint Ignatius" to the sick man, who was immediately healed. There followed a public disputation with the marabout, first over whether the amulets or the holy water had actually healed the man and then moving on more explicitly to doctrinal disagreements.[113]

In other words, the earlier Jesuits were at once less accommodationist (more disruptive) when it came to open doctrinal disputation and yet more accommodationist with respect to local gift-giving customs and religious practices. The Jesuits swapped out the amulets of the Marabouts for their own miraculous medals and holy water. The Jesuits, unlike the White Fathers, had no desire to discipline or interiorize the all-pervasive religiosity of the Muslims. They wanted to play the role of the marabout in its entirety, to take full advantage of just how entangled indigenous society was with the sacred, without leaving their own religious motivations in the background. Jesuits had wanted to humiliate and discredit local marabouts every bit as much as the White Fathers would, but their field of combat was explicit doctrinal disputation, not the social conflict over whose charity was more detached and "disinterested."

The self-proclaimed disinterestedness of the White Fathers' charity can be seen as what literary scholar Mary Louise Pratt called a "strategy of innocence": the "strategies of representation whereby European bourgeois subjects seek to secure their innocence in the same moment as they assert European hegemony."[114] The missionaries attempted to obscure their own interested motives and position within France's imperial system, representing themselves as "taking possession without subjugation and violence," all while actively delegitimizing the Algerians' traditional culture and rights.[115] The missionaries hoped the Algerians would believe them when they claimed that their gifts were spiritually motivated, with no obligation or ideology attached. Perhaps, in the Algerians' reluctance to believe that the missionaries desired no gifts or religious conversion in return, they were implicitly (and accurately) rejecting the claim that the White Fathers' charity was completely disinterested, performed only for heavenly reward.[116] Like the military officers of the Arab Bureaus, the White Fathers' "disinterested" actions were configured toward persuading the Algerians that charity, medicine, and other civilizational improvements were neutral and could be accepted without compromising their Muslim faith. For the "disinterestedness" to be convincing, it had to convey that there was no necessary connection between accepting medical, charitable, or social improvements and compromising one's religious belonging. Ironically, though, in order to effectively prepare the ground for future proselytization, the charity also had to convey that only Christians could give such gifts.

Much would change in the course of the 1870s—despite Lavigerie's public spat with colonial authorities in 1868, he would later come to be viewed as a valuable ally in the colonization of Africa. The crowning achievement of Lavigerie's unique combination of "imperialist and missionary"—interested and disinterested—which definitively swung the balance of mainstream colonialist opinion in his favor, was his role in France's annexation of Tunisia in 1881.[117] Lavigerie used his missionaries to facilitate the conquest, even passing on information about fortifications and then using insider information and the disruptions and anxieties of the conquest to buy up Tunisian property for himself and his congregation at low rates.[118] In a letter addressed to the bishops of France on the occasion of his assumption of episcopal authority in the newly annexed Tunisia, he once again cited the disinterestedness, the "innocence" of his missionaries as the main reason they were a necessary, pragmatic complement to imperialist disruption. Lavigerie implied, paradoxically, that the reason Frenchmen should support clerics and missionaries in Tunisia was that this support, in seeming disinterested, would render the conquest less offensive. As with the Saharan missions of the previous decade, the illusion of apolitical impartiality would itself serve a political purpose. "It will be the campaign of charity after [the campaign] of arms; [a] campaign which cannot trouble or worry anyone, for it has only one purpose, that of bandaging the wounds" of all, regardless of race or religion.[119]

The tension between Lavigerie as imperialist (as a patriotic believer in the pragmatic benefits of his religious influence) and as missionary (as an apostle hoping eventually to convert the souls of Africa), does not necessarily imply that Lavigerie was conscious of any insincerity or opposition between these two identities.[120] For the most part, Lavigerie and his missionaries would have sincerely viewed their uprooting and individualizing impact on indigenous culture as part and parcel with the Gospel, the advancement of French modernity and "agrarian capitalism" as synonymous with the advancement of Christian interests.[121] Indeed, despite the apparent irony and bad faith of their claims to disinterestedness, there is a logic to their discourse. The obsession with appearing disinterested, apolitical, and purely spiritual was itself a feature of colonial, secularizing, and civilizing modernity. The luxury of disinterestedness was supported by charities from industrialized Europe; influenced by a capitalistic ethos that viewed gift exchange cynically and therefore rejected its social symbolism; and conditioned by the missionaries' acceptance of the secular distinction between the political and the religious, the exterior and interior life. Thus, the scrupulous policy of "charity first, proselytization later" ironically functioned to justify and "bandage the wounds" of France's continued colonial expansion, even as the policy denigrated Muslim Algerians as greedy and fanatical.

CHAPTER 7

Compel Them to Come

Algerian Students and Colonial Racism between France and Algeria

Lavigerie portrayed his success in gathering and keeping the orphans of 1868–69 as an unprecedented victory in the struggle for the rights of missionaries in Algeria. Shortly after this public triumph, the pope entrusted him with the new vicariate of the Sahara and the Sudan.[1] Lavigerie needed laborers for this new mission field and, as it happened, some of the clergy-in-training at Algiers's Grand séminaire, inspired by their director, the Lazarist Père Girard, had already felt a calling for Muslim missions. Moreover, the orphanages required personnel. At the beginning, Lavigerie relied heavily on the Jesuits (especially the Arabic-speaking Henri Ducat), the Sœurs du Bon Secours, and the Frères des Écoles Chrétiennes to manage the orphanages, instruct the children, and direct their agricultural labor. But these challenges also presented new opportunities—opportunities to evangelize a captive audience of Algerian Muslims for the first time and to practice language skills by giving religious instruction in Arabic and Kabyle to these young neophytes. In all these ways, then, it was the orphans and orphanages that offered both the demand and the occasion for a new missionary congregation. Lavigerie was never one to hesitate in launching a new project, nor was he one to delegate his own ministries to outside congregations when he might retain tight control himself.[2]

The Algerian orphans of the 1868 famine, were the original catalyst for the founding of Lavigerie's White Fathers (Péres Blancs) congregation. Even though the White Fathers soon came to focus their efforts almost exclusively on the non-Arab, Berber populations of Algeria and the Sahara, and then expanded to sub-Saharan Africa, their original mandate was to staff the orphanages and to train for Arab and Kabyle missions within Algeria. Indeed, the "missionaries of Africa," as the White Fathers are officially called, were known in their early years as the "missionaries of Algiers."[3] The White Fathers' pivot away from Arabs and toward the allegedly less fanatical Kabyles (and later, to sub-Saharan Africans) was partly a result of circumstances. In 1871, following the brutal suppression of a revolt in Kabylie (and the arrival of a more mission-friendly administration), the colonial government allowed the establishment of Jesuit and White Fathers missions and schools there.[4] The focus on Kabylie was also encouraged by the notion that the Kabyles and other Berbers were only superficially Muslim and therefore more susceptible to civilization and conversion than the fanatical Arabs.

Even as the missionaries turned their efforts away from the supposedly unconvertable Arabs and toward Kabylie and then sub-Saharan Africa, Lavigerie's missionaries attempted to Christianize at least some Arabs: the orphans who first called their congregation into being. Other apostolic efforts grew out of the orphanages: the *petit séminaire indigène*, where the most promising among the orphans were trained, first in Algeria, then in France; Arab Christian villages where older orphans, married off, were settled and given a plot of land to work; and the fundraising Œuvre de Sainte Monique whereby French Catholics could "adopt" these orphans financially and receive letters about and pictures of them.[5] These conversion efforts met with mixed success (in the case of the Arab Christian villages) and almost total failure (in the case of the *petit séminaire indigène*), but they are a necessary component in understanding the missionaries' increasingly racialized denigrations of Arabs. They allow for a comparison of discourse and practice, or rather they show how discourse was put into practice. The students and orphans at Lavigerie's indigenous seminary became the everyday, intimate targets of these racialized discourses.

In the end, the missionaries seem to have ended up believing that their experience had confirmed their preference for the Kabyles, and that the Arab students were less suited for the priesthood. In other words, the growing anti-Arab racism of the missionaries was not only due to an a priori, imagined cultural affinity with the Kabyles, but also—similar to Ducat and the Jesuits' experience with the Khoudja brothers—seemed to be supported by experiences of disillusionment with actual Arab seminarians that were often self-fulfilling. This chapter delves into how the mission actually treated the orphans in practice. Although the orphanages functioned according to a racialized aversion for Arab children almost from the beginning, eventually Arab and Kabyle seminarians alike were subjected to discrimination that provoked resentment and even flared up into episodes of open conflict.

Lavigerie gathered the orphans of the famine and disease by calling upon the priests of his diocese to send them to him at Algiers.[6] At first he kept them all on or near the grounds of his archbishopric in the Algiers parish of St. Eugène; but as their numbers grew, he rented Ben-Aknoun, the former site of Brumauld's orphanage, from the Jesuits, sending the boys there and the girls to Kouba. Lavigerie "kept . . . only the most robust to work in the gardens of St. Eugène."[7] Though he initially relied on female religious orders, Lavigerie soon called on the Frères des Écoles Chrétiennes to direct his fledgling orphanage in the hope that the latter would be more suited to directing the agricultural training and labor of the orphans.[8] Lavigerie wrote a long list of instructions for the *frères* that reveal a great deal about his pedagogical and missionary approach, as well as his expectations and anxieties for the indigenous orphans. The orphanage, he told them, was first a "work of charity," since it was necessary to save these children who were "images of God" from certain death. Second, and more importantly, though, it was a "work of apostolate," or of religious conversion. Here, Lavigerie was quite clear that he saw conversion to Christianity and assimilation to French civilization as two sides of the same coin. The colonial government had done "nothing for the conversion of the *indigènes*" and thus "[nothing] for their assimilation." Clearly, only Christian converts could truly be civilized and politically included. By this time such accusations had attained the status of cliché among missionary critics of the "tolerant" military regime. In Lavigerie's view, it was because of France's faux tolerance that "these poor Arabs were confined to their Koran, in their dissolute and cruel customs" and offered no chance to become "Christian [or] French."

What was especially exciting about the orphans was that they were children, relatively innocent and unspoiled, offering a providential opportunity to experiment with Christian assimilation. Lavigerie echoed the reigning childhood pedagogy of his day, which emphasized the innocence and impressionability of children: "They are without passion, without prejudices of any kind, without instruction. They are a blank slate on which can be drawn all the letters not only of our civilization, but also and especially of Christianity which is the basis [of that civilization]."[9] At least, to the extent that their youth made them innocent and somehow pre-Muslim, this view of childhood exercised a measure of restraint on French Catholics' growing anti-Arab sentiment. Lavigerie had brought with him from his time at the Œuvre d'Orient a fully articulated vision of a patriotic "Christian civilization," co-opting the "civilization" coined by Enlightenment writers. The main objective of the orphanage was to "make Frenchmen, Christians" out of these orphans—categories treated as one and the same. However, much like the missionary schools patronized by the Œuvre d'Orient in Ottoman Syria, geared toward training colonial subalterns, Lavigerie advised that the orphanage should restrict itself to teaching them the French language and some vocational training, only what was necessary for them to "make an honest living."

Lavigerie's approach, even at this early juncture, was already colored by negative ethnographic assumptions about Arabs. Despite the relative optimism of his
vision of indigenous children's potential, even the children were not free from
the corruption of their race and climate, as Lavigerie made clear to the *frères* in
a series of specific instructions on pedagogical method and organizational matters. For example, Lavigerie recommended a light, almost indulgent treatment
for the orphans, but this was because of the children's volatile, nomadic nature.
"If the work is not rendered attractive to them, with their dispositions to laziness, [and] the need of vagabondage which is innate in them, which is their very
nature ... they will take the first chance to run away." Thus, the *frères* should vary
the subjects and activities often and not spend too long with classes. Lavigerie
even ordered that they not punish the orphans for bad behavior, but only reward
them for good. As he explained, since the "self-regard" of Arabs was "excessive,"
awards and "flattery" would go a long way in preventing them from following
their nomadic instincts.

Finally, Lavigerie laid down explicit ground rules to protect against accusations of sexual impropriety, something that missionaries and other clerics usually
discussed in more oblique ways, if at all. Tellingly, Lavigerie put these ground
rules in place not to prevent the *frères'* misconduct or temptation but rather to
protect them from the vices and illegitimate insinuations of the children. "Show
them affection," Lavigerie wrote, "but avoid every kind of familiarity and caress.
These children are very perverted and they would easily misinterpret even the
most innocent things." Such instructions implied that any future scandal would
be the fault not of the missionaries but of the Arab youths, given the alleged
sexual precociousness of their race. Similarly, Lavigerie warned the *frères* to separate the older students from the younger ones. The little children may still be
salvageable, but the older ones were "already very corrupted" and liable to lead
the "poor little ones" astray.[10]

Lavigerie's missionaries seem to have shared this view of aberrantly premature Arab sexuality, almost as a truism. In 1871, Félix Charmetant, Lavigerie's
right-hand man in the early years, wrote to the archbishop what was supposed
to be an encouraging letter from the orphanage. Certainly, some orphans had
deserted the orphanage, he admitted, but given the "innate instability of this
race, its instincts of liberty." and "passions" that "develop more during adoles-
cence," the surprising and encouraging thing was that so many of the children
had stayed.[11] Such views of Arabs and of Muslims—as especially predisposed to
nomadism and sexual vice, whether because of their climate, religion, or race—
were present not only in Algeria but back in France as well. At one point when

the orphanages were in a particularly desperate financial situation, Lavigerie offered some of the older children up for adoption into Christian families in France as domestic servants or workers. One Norman farmer responded to this offer, writing that he would be glad to have an Algerian orphan to help with agricultural labor. But the farmer confessed to feeling "a certain anxiety" due to "the nationality and original upbringing of these children of Mohammed." Did not the sun and climate of Algeria make them "precocious and ardent [in their] passions"? Even after conversion to Christianity, was not natural "human weakness...even greater among these poor inhabitants of Algeria"?[12] The attempt to discipline and control the supposedly degenerate sexuality of the children would continue to be a major concern of the mission and would be the source of some of the most damaging conflicts with those orphans chosen for the indigenous seminary and later moved to France.

The first of Lavigerie's missionaries to begin working at the orphanages—Charmetant, Deguerry, Finateu—took on the religious instruction of the children, with the help of the Jesuit Henri Ducat, who was no longer at Constantine. Ducat seems to have brought the energy and cultural accommodation of his *mission arabe* to the orphanage. At the beginning, according to Charmetant, Ducat was the only one capable of speaking to the orphans. The fact that out of all the priests in the colony, only Ducat and a few others knew Arabic showed how neglected the Arab mission had been before Lavigerie's intervention.[13] Ducat "translated into vulgar Arabic" a little catechism and also composed some Arabic songs, or translated French hymns into Arabic, which the orphans sang as they worked the fields.[14] Charmetant and the other White Father novices would practice their own Arabic by teaching the catechism and songs. As he had done at Constantine, Ducat used magic lantern shows to "entertain . . . and instruct" the children.[15] Ducat also seems to have drawn up a list of "regulations" for life at the orphanage, including guidelines for surveillance and punishment of the children, but also forbidding teachers to promote Christianity or to criticize Arabs and Islam. Instead, the teachers were to emphasize the attributes the two religions shared.[16]

When the Jesuits hesitated to sell the property at Ben-Aknoun to Lavigerie outright, he bought property for himself at the Maison Carrée and sent the strongest of the orphans there to begin the work of clearing the land for cultivation and new construction. This was "difficult work," done with pickaxes in the "burning sun" (see figure 7.1).[17] Suitable clothing and adequate food were often lacking. The hardest lands to clear were the "vast terrains" where Lavigerie planned to build a monastery and to plant a recently developed breed

FIGURE 7.1. "Arab orphans in the fields." Henri Ducat, "Diaire:
Mission Arabe Consantine, 1871–72," RAl 81, ACJF.

of asparagus that he hoped would produce "large profits." Charmetant remembered that the work of clearing land that had remained "uncultivated for so
many centuries" took its toll on the children and missionaries alike, and many
developed malaria, which they treated with liberal amounts of quinine.[18] With
the coming winter and the orphanage lacking shoes and warm clothing, the missionaries relied on the services of an Arab tailor who was a convert of the Jesuits'
earlier mission at Constantine. They also appealed to friends in France to send
clothing. The orphans earned points through work and good behavior and could
buy the necessary clothes from their "bank" of points.[19] One reason this system
worked so well, Charmetant believed, was that the points were not a physical
currency that could be placed in the orphans' possession and thus functioned as
a safeguard against misuse, given "the pillaging instincts of their race."[20]

In one story from his memoir of the White Fathers' early years, Charmetant offered valuable details of the day-to-day management and disciplinary
regime of the orphanage, as well as of the perceived differences between Arab
and Kabyle that already governed the missionaries' rapport with the children.

Despite Lavigerie's recommendation to avoid corporal punishment, it appears the practice was not completely disallowed. On at least one occasion, because of the "scandalous" nature of a child's disobedience, Charmetant decided that a public, exemplary punishment was necessary. For maximum humiliation this punishment would be meted out with participation from all the orphans. Significantly, Charmetant justified the use of corporal punishment through a kind of projection—not as the missionaries' own preference, but as something appropriate for the Arab orphans. After all, he reasoned, one had to speak a language these Arabs understood. Among the Arabs, Charmetant claimed, it was customary for children to be beaten on the bottom of the feet with a rod. So, in a softening of this practice, Charmetant decided that each child would instead administer a blow with a "thick strap" to the "fleshy" part of the offending orphan's body (presumably the buttocks). One Kabyle orphan did not strike his blow as "conscientiously" as the others, because "the Kabyles have a profound aversion for corporal punishments, so frequent and so effective with the Arabs, because the Berbers consider them degrading."[21] Beatings, Charmetant implied, were more appropriate to the degraded Arabs than to the dignified Kabyles. Arab and Kabyle seminarians must certainly have been aware of these differences in treatment, divide-and-rule tactics that surely bred resentment.

The year 1870 was an especially trying one for the missionaries and the orphans, as charitable funds from France were reduced by the privations of the Franco-Prussian War. In addition, Lavigerie himself was away at the First Vatican Council. The livestock and harvest from the orphanage's fields were to be sold or used for the profit of Lavigerie's projects as a whole, so the orphans were reduced to eating potatoes, whatever creatures and fish they could catch in the environs, and even the pet cat of one of the missionaries ("unwittingly," since "Father Deguerry killed it secretly and served it as 'wild rabbit'"). Sufficient and seasonal clothing was hard to come by. It was of little surprise that "some of the orphans left us surreptitiously."[22] Later on, Charmetant reported that with the children "malnourished and almost without clothing," there were a number of "desertions" from the orphanage, including seven who had already received the sacrament of baptism.[23]

Clearly, preconceptions about Arabs' innate vices and sexual precociousness already governed not just the missionaries' discourses and publications but their daily rapport with the children. But there is even greater evidence of racial tension in the experiences of those orphans and students who were selected to attend the *petit séminaire indigène*. The orphans who would spend the most time in France—and whose experience would mimic in many ways that of the

Khoudja brothers a decade earlier—were those selected for the *petit séminaire indigène*, which was eventually moved to the diocese of Rodez in the South of France. Lavigerie hoped that seminary training would develop their vocations as missionaries. Like the Jesuits, Lavigerie and the White Fathers hoped to train an indigenous clergy, Christian Arabs and Kabyles who would have more success in communicating the gospel to their compatriots than European missionaries ever could.

Lavigerie and the White Fathers were far from unique in this ambition. Across the French and British empires, in Catholic and Protestant contexts alike, missionary leaders in the optimistic mid-nineteenth century anticipated that local churches would one day become "self-supporting, self-governing and self-propagating." At least in theory, the goal was for missionaries to render themselves superfluous. Mission territories were simply too large, the unreached too numerous; and European missionaries were too expensive, susceptible to disease, or compromised by alliance with colonial power. But the few African clergy given any real authority—most famously the formerly enslaved Anglican Bishop Samuel Ajayi Crowther in West Africa—were treated with disrespect by European colleagues and were, in the end, replaced "by white successors," the "experiment" aborted.[24] Catholic missions likewise defined success as the transformation of mission fields into regular, self-supporting dioceses, and both the mission hierarchy at Rome and missionary leaders on the ground like Lavigerie and Daniel Comboni expressed their commitment to the training of indigenous priests. But in practice—whether out of racism or simply out of reluctance to part with hard-won organizations—European missionaries regularly criticized native clergy as immoral, insufficiently orthodox, and not ready to take the reins.[25]

Unlike Ducat and the handful of other Jesuits who had been interested in Muslim missions, Lavigerie's missionaries seem to have framed the benefits of indigenous clergy in demeaning ethnic and environmental terms, ignoring any inherent good to be gained by accommodation to indigenous culture. For example, in the seminary's fundraising prospectus, the seminary director, Père Charbonnier, wrote that these children were significant because they would meet the need for "workers capable of enduring the rigors of the desert and of tolerating the vulgar customs of the Muslims or of the sons of Ham [Black Africans]."[26] This kind of language effectively reduced indigenous clergy to nothing more than their hardy constitutions and low material and moral expectations. In this sense, it can be said that the rationale behind the turn to indigenous clergy—often seen as a movement of progress toward indigenous initiative and cultural compromise—had a racialized component. Imperialists in the early half of the nineteenth century still believed it was possible for Europeans to acclimate to tropical climates if they remained long enough. Only near the end of the century did climatology and racial science alike dictate that European constitutions could never learn to survive in the tropics.[27]

The White Fathers' *petit séminaire indigène* is a rich site for uncovering concrete examples of racial conflict between French and Arabs. Lavigerie eventually decided to move the Arab and Kabyle seminarians to St. Laurent d'Olt in France, an establishment where they would live alongside French seminarians who studied at the White Fathers' École Apostolique, distinct from the indigenous seminary. Unsurprisingly, the story of the indigenous seminary is punctuated by a series of conflicts between indigenous students and their directors or European peers, conflicts where anti-Arab sentiment was only thinly veiled. The indigenous seminary began in Algiers as an annex to the work of the orphanage. Those orphans considered to have intellectual or spiritual gifts were separated from the others and were initially kept at St. Eugène, on Lavigerie's archiepiscopal complex. Once a week, one student later remembered, they would go up to his quarters, where he would personally read out the reports on their behavior and administer canings to those deserving of punishment.[28]

On another occasion, recounted by Charmetant in the popular metropolitan missionary newsletter *Annales de la Propagation de la Foi*, Lavigerie received the students at his episcopal palace to read their grades for the week and dispense or withhold commendation. "Those who have the best grades are allowed to kiss [Lavigerie's] ring . . . certainly the reward that they most covet," Charmetant gushed; but "this favor is refused" to any with a less than perfect record, which is "for them the most feared punishment." It is likely the poor seminarians were more afraid of the canings than of losing the privilege to kiss the archbishop's ring.[29] When the children eagerly followed Lavigerie off the terrace and into his office, crowding around his desk, Lavigerie scolded, "See that you don't take anything, because I am watching your hands." "Don't worry! We are Christians now," the children assured him. "So, in the past, one did have to be wary of you, then?" Lavigerie probed. "Oh! Yes, because we were little thieves," they replied, and then proceeded to confess to all manner of past thefts. Now, though, they realized that "theft offends God."[30] No doubt Charmetant included this little exchange because he thought it illustrated the bishop's stern but fatherly rapport with his charges, but also because it placed in the children's own mouths the testimony of how miraculous, how drastic was their transformation from thieving Muslims/Arabs to honest Christians/French.

The fear that the local colonial government would attempt to close the seminary or seize the children seems to have prompted the relocation to France, to the diocese of Rodez in the Aveyron, where Lavigerie's old schoolmate and close friend Monseigneur Bourret was bishop. Reading between the lines one can also perceive the well-worn fear that the impiety and scorn of French colonists might harm the converts' faith.[31] Indeed, the White Fathers chronicler Lucien Duchêne wrote about the sad fate that met orphans who abandoned the orphanage: "one runs into [these 'renegades'] on every road of the colony." Lavigerie's enemies loved nothing better than to point them out—in their rags, "dying of hunger, sometimes being led away by the police"—and to mock: "Behold the children of the Archbishop."[32] Here, as in the ban on proselytization, one can observe Lavigerie's finely tuned anxieties about public opinion in the colony and in France. Indeed, many decisions made about the orphans (sending them to Europe, attempting to force even the "renegades" from the seminary to remain in Europe, settling the adults in segregated "Arab villages") seem driven not only by the fear of the corrupting influence of unbelieving colonists but also by the fear that the children would end up embarrassing Lavigerie and his projects. On one occasion, Lavigerie advised one of his missionaries to get rid of the "bad subjects" at the Arab village by sending them back to their tribes. Under no condition, though, should they be allowed to have enough money to travel to Algiers, where they might create "very serious difficulties."[33]

A more unpleasant surprise awaiting the young seminarians was how cold the weather was in France and how often the students and priests were beset with sickness. As elsewhere in Lavigerie's establishments in the early to mid-1870s, resources were spread thin, and the *pères* at St. Laurent d'Olt, as the seminary in southern France was called, were forced to do much of their own fundraising to come up with enough clothing, bedding, and food. When one of the missionaries from the seminary would go on a fundraising trip, he would often take one or two of the indigenous seminarians with him to illustrate the mission's high hopes for these children and to inspire donors. But, according to Duchêne, the in-house historian of the White Fathers' beginnings, as profitable as this strategy may have been on the material level, it was spiritually damaging to the children since it gave them an inflated sense of themselves. Perhaps "the sight of the little African" prompted "more abundant alms," but "when the child—pampered [and] feted for several months—returned to St. Laurent he found the rules severe, the clothing rough, the food meager, and the bed hard. Did not this change in life bring [with it] a weakening of piety and disgust for the Seminary?"[34]

Between the lines of this complaint is implied that the children were treated better while out on alms-gathering tours, given better clothing and food, perhaps to create a more optimistic image of how things were going at the seminary. Perhaps the children's disillusionment upon their return to the seminary had less to do with having been spoiled and more to do with alienation by the fundraising tactics of their teachers. Perhaps the traveling alms-collectors depicted the conditions at St. Laurent in a falsely optimistic light, or perhaps they exaggerated some of the seminary's needs. If Lavigerie's and the White Fathers' published reports are any indication, it is not difficult to imagine that their depictions of Muslims and Arabs in fundraising sermons were extremely negative. Could the older seminarians have begun to resent their role as beggars or their obligation to travel from parish to parish constantly acknowledging their supposed former wickedness and barbarity? According to Duchêne, in any case, it was the "pampering" while out on fundraising trips that led to a growing spirit of rebellion among some of the older students at the seminary—a "conspiracy" to behave badly and to ruin the younger students morally, as another *père* put it at the time. This undercurrent of rebellion exploded in the summer of 1875, when the missionaries at St. Laurent felt it necessary to expel twelve students at once. On this occasion, sensing what a setback this was, Lavigerie was "pained" and angered that such a draconian measure had been necessary.[35]

According to Père Deguerry, the Superior of the White Fathers at the time, the expulsions were actually due to the students' immoral practices rather than to any arrogance bred on a fundraising tour. Deguerry's letters to Lavigerie, wherein he justified the expulsions and assured him of their chastening effects, offer a window onto the operation of the seminary, and especially onto the moral concerns of the missionaries. The main culprits in this "veritable conspiracy against the good operation of the house" were a group of students who had already been expelled the year before, it seems, for "immoral acts"—probably masturbation or even mutual sexual activities in the dormitories. These students had been allowed to return but showed no real signs of repentance. Instead, they associated only with each other, confessed seldom, and even "invented a jargon" of their own, so they might engage in "malicious conversations" without being caught. Reportedly, one seminarian named Gabriel Edmond had even "solicited one of his younger comrades to [do] evil." None of the others, fortunately, had succeeded in "doing evil" with each other, since they were surveilled constantly.[36] Indeed, precisely so that the "acts of immorality which unfortunately occurred last year" would not be repeated, the missionaries had been pursuing a tight regime of surveillance over every bodily function of the seminarians. At night the dormitories were locked, and each dormitory had a priest assigned to sleep there and hold the key. Any student needing to use the bathroom had to wake the father, ask for the key, and relock the dormitory door upon his reentrance to ensure that "two children may never leave the dormitory together." During the day, if any needed to go to the latrine during recess, they were accompanied by a "surveillant." It is difficult to avoid the conclusion that the subtext of these rules was an intense fear of sexual experimentation.

Other expelled children had simply been impious or insolent. One child, Emile, even went around telling "whoever would listen" that he was at the seminary against his will, "by force." Deguerry thought all twelve were such bad apples that they were in fact quite happy to have been expelled and preferred the "sad liberty of their *gourbi*" (Algerian hut) to the constant surveillance of the seminary. Deguerry sympathized with Lavigerie's discouragement and acknowledged that the expulsions had raised doubts about the future of the seminary. At least the public had no idea of what had happened, leaving open the possibility that these students could be shuffled off to another educational site rather than publicly embarrassing Lavigerie by returning to Algeria.[37] The following year, one of the missionaries on site reported to his superior that things were going much better with regard to the seminarians' morality since the *pères* had continued to be "very active" in their "surveillance." More significantly, the indigenous students had been humbled and frightened not only by the expulsions of the previous year but also by the spectacular failures of their former classmates who had run away from the seminary to make their way in the world. The fate of one former student in particular had recently been the talk of the seminary, since after trying his hand at "a thousand adventures" throughout France, he had been forced to return to the Aveyron, near the seminary, to find work as a "domestic or shepherd for a small farmer." "Now, thank God," one priest wrote, "[the seminarians] understand much better that without a serious education and good conduct they cannot even become a good farmer's domestic."[38] Clearly, one way the missionaries kept the indigenous students in line was to remind them of their natural "inferiority" and their social precariousness without the support of the White Fathers.

Though Deguerry had already been discouraged by the "immoral acts" and subsequent expulsions of 1874–75, according to Duchêne's later history of the seminary, it was not until 1877 that things took a definitive turn for the worse. Allegedly, the students were still happy to struggle through ill health and bad weather, and many continued to seek baptism. In part this was because the children were "still young . . . docile, submissive, pious," but "with age the passions appear [and] an unbridled love of liberty." These adolescent rebellions caused "more than one student" to be expelled.[39] Perhaps more significantly for the day-to-day experience of the seminary and the ongoing alienation of these students, 1877 saw the creation of an École Apostolique—a seminary for European postulants to join the White Fathers—at St. Laurent d'Olt, within the same *maison*.[40] More than any other development, the decision to locate a corps of French and other European seminarians among the indigenous students would signal the end of the indigenous seminary, as the indigenous students increasingly compared their situation to that of their European counterparts, finding themselves behind in their seminary courses or their treatment prejudicial. According to Duchêne, some of the Arab and Kabyle children lacked "a sufficiently developed intelligence" for theological studies; few, in any case, had shown sustained interest in a "sacerdotal vocation." Thus, in the early months of 1878, it was provisionally decided that the indigenous seminary would be phased out, with those who wished to continue their religious studies returning to the Maison Carrée outside of Algiers. As for the others, the White Fathers would do their best to "help them obtain a position in the world, which would permit them to earn their living and remain good Christians."[41]

Still, perhaps because of inertia or because some promising students remained, the *petit séminaire indigène* plodded on for three more years. More children died every winter, and periodic outbursts of misbehavior led to further expulsions. In February of 1878, some "papers" and "letters" of the students were discovered that revealed the existence of a "shameful commerce" between "a number of students." "Shameful commerce" might refer to a literal exchange of contraband items, but once again some kind of sexual experimentation is implied.[42] In reaction to this misbehavior, the *pères* decided to designate a room to be used as a kind of "isolation cell" where "rebellious spirits" would be placed under lock and key, and to redouble—"more vigilant than ever"—their surveillance efforts.[43] As during the expulsion crisis in 1875, these "grave disorders" merited a visit from the White Fathers' superior general. With the superior presiding, the council of the seminary decided to expel five more students—those who had been most culpable in the "shameful commerce." Reprising the theme that the adolescents were corrupting the purer little ones, the council also decreed that from then on, the older students would be absolutely separated from the younger ones. Even during recess and "promenades" they were not permitted to "play together," and the younger, still unspoiled students would be scrupulously quarantined.[44]

The *pères* viewed the indigenous students as so contagious in their vice and irreligion, or as so inferior in their race, as to keep them completely segregated from the European White Fathers–in-training. For example, in response to the high illness and death rate among the Algerian children, one missionary suggested removing them to the sunnier climate of Malta, where the White Fathers maintained a school for Black Africans redeemed from slavery. But in this case, of course, it would be necessary to keep the Arabs separate from the African students, just as they were kept separate from the European *apostoliques*.[45] Duchêne quotes one missionary stationed at the seminary who wrote a damning report in February of 1879, estimating that three-quarters of the indigenous seminarians were incapable of "acquiring the necessary science" for any "ordinary job." This missionary mocked the efforts of another White Father who was trying to teach Latin to "students who hardly know how to stammer in French." He also claimed that some of the children at the seminary were only "pretending to learn" so they might continue to eat and be lodged by the congregation. Such seminarians would inevitably become "idlers and *déclassés*"—a word commonly used in colonialist circles to criticize colonial subjects who had been uprooted and educated "above their station," then left without employment to become conductors of dissatisfaction and political resistance.[46]

As part of the plan to phase out the indigenous seminary, several of the oldest and most gifted students were selected to pursue medical studies at the Catholic University of Lille. Even if they could never become priests, they could at least further the work of the mission by providing medical services, Lavigerie hoped. Others opted to become interpreters for the colonial state or joined some branch of the military, and a precious few did join the congregation. Some medical students moved north to Lille from St. Laurent in 1880, and a few others followed in 1882, when the seminary closed for good. As for the indigenous seminary, Duchêne's explanation for its failure and disbandment was frankly racialized. No one among the White Fathers denied how essential an indigenous clergy was to the mission, "but the experiment done at St. Laurent seems to have demonstrated peremptorily that it is extremely difficult to bring converted Muslim children all the way to the priesthood. . . . They bear in their blood some ferment which demands to be purged." Only "after two or three generations" of Christianity in one's family could one ever hope to be a priest "deep down in the soul."[47] It is interesting, in this moment of failure, that the Fathers no longer distinguished between fanatical Arabs and civilized Kabyles; instead, they seem to have given up on Muslims in general. At the same time, the White Fathers were beginning to take stock of their missionary failures in Kabylie. Against the expectations of the "Kabyle myth," Charmetant would come to admit, the Kabyles were still "far from the kingdom of heaven" and just as "Muslim" as the Arabs.[48]

Another blow, which brought elements of anticlerical opposition from back in the Algerian colony together with the White Fathers' own ethnographic distinctions between Arab and Kabyle, fell in January of 1881. The anticlerical press accused the Jesuits in Kabylie of taking and baptizing two Kabyles—"two new Mortaras"—without their parents' permission. For Lavigerie, the Jesuits' indelicacy was even more inopportune, since it placed a weapon of negative publicity in the hands of his colonial enemies. As it turned out, not all of his own Kabyle seminarians at St. Laurent had received the necessary parental permissions either. Lavigerie, understandably spooked by the prospect of a public relations nightmare just as his plans for expansion into Tunisia and elsewhere were coming to fruition, quickly demanded the recall of every last Kabyle seminarian to their tribes.[49] Père Le Roy, then superior of St. Laurent, wrote that this order was like the "death warrant of the *collège arabe*," since the Kabyles were the "sole hope" of the seminary and, presumably unlike the Arab students, had never done anything worthy of "grave" reproach.[50] Some of the Kabyle children were permitted to return to the seminary later in the year, after their positions had been confirmed in their families and tribes, but one of those who returned had lost much of his "fervor" and "good spirit" in the course of his "ordeal"—perhaps exhausted by the travel or discouraged by the fleeting sight of his family and homeland.[51]

But what plagued the good spirit of the Algerian seminarians more than anything else was the European apostolic students. The very presence of these more privileged students reminded the Algerians of the unlikelihood that they would ever be allowed to join the congregation, since they were constantly playing catch-up in the required French, Latin, and theology lessons and were even receiving less food. In January of 1882, they collectively protested their inferior status by refusing to sign their "Christian" (French) names given at baptism, and only writing their original "Arab" names. According to one *père*, this was a concerted effort at opposition to the missionaries, apparently in reaction to some spiritual lecture they had received and resented.[52] What seems likely is that one missionary had used the daily time of spiritual teaching to berate them about their lack of submission to the priests or their lack of proper respect for their French co-seminarians. Finally, by that summer, Le Roy despaired that most of the remaining Algerians seemed to be trying to get themselves expelled, since their numbers had already been so reduced by death, expulsion, or escape and since the few who remained could not help but resent "their inferiority, when they compare themselves to the *apostoliques*" (European White Fathers–in–training).[53]

Duchêne, summarizing these conflicts some years later, wrote that the "bitterness" caused by their "manifest inferiority" in intellect and education resulted in a "disgust for studies and a desire to leave."[54] Those indigenous students who left a record of their time at the seminary did indeed express their resentment of the European seminarians, but perhaps more for the superior treatment the European students received than for their superior abilities. Père Louail, the seminary's last director, pleaded that the seminary be left open. Not only did its existence justify the donations that continued to be made on its behalf, but there was also still a spiritual benefit in the seminary, however meager. Despite the many failures of the indigenous students, Louail reasoned, and "however naughty they may be, are they not better than the Muslims![?]" Anticlerical colonists could mock the disappointing achievements of Lavigerie's converts all they wanted, Louail argued, but for "neophytes" they were doing quite well, as a simple comparison with the allegedly much less advanced "negro" orphans adopted by Spiritan missionaries could attest.[55]

The last indigenous seminarians were sent away in the fall of 1882—a few to join the medical students at Lille, some to Lavigerie's *école apostolique* for Black Africans at Malta, and some, finally, back to Algiers to continue their religious education in some reduced form. Louail announced that the students would have to leave but could choose, with the *pères'* guidance, between several possible future positions. One student whom the *pères* had designated to study medicine at Lille, named Leonce, "wept a lot, saying that he felt called to the vocation of missionary." Louail assured him that medical science would aid the mission too, and that, "by following [the missionaries'] desires," he could be "sure of following the will of God."[56] According to Duchêne's history, a few of the former seminarians were allowed to enter a special "Arab novitiate" at Lavigerie's archiepiscopal complex at Algiers. In order to encourage these persistent seminarians, the *pères* dispensed with the requirement that the students finish all "philosophy" courses before commencing their theology courses. Only two finished the course of studies and were still lacking in the required Latin and Classics. One indigenous student, in the end, made himself useful by teaching Arabic to postulants from France.[57] The final result of all the "most beautiful hopes" that the indigenous seminary had inspired could be summed up in "2 priests, a minor cleric, 5 doctors and a few teachers."[58] One reason for the orphanage and seminary's failures, Duchêne claimed, was that they had not been hard enough on the Algerians. Lavigerie had prohibited overly harsh treatments and physical punishments and sometimes even publicly reprimanded his missionaries in front of the orphans. According to Duchêne, "pride was . . . profoundly enrooted in the soul of these young catechumens," so that instead of respecting the priests for submitting to Lavigerie's rebukes, they learned to despise them and became insolent and spoiled.[59]

Historian Bertrand Taithe has traced the trajectories of some of the five Algerian students who went on to Lille and who succeeded in their medical studies
there—and of one, in particular, who even married a Frenchwoman, settled in
France, and enjoyed a happy career as a provincial doctor. For Taithe, the story
of these doctors is confirmation that France was in large measure "indifferent"
to race, unlike the more racist French Algerian colonists.[60] There is truth to this
narrative contrast between metropolitan and colonial attitudes toward indigenous Algerians. The indigenous medical students experienced something of
this heightened persecution when they were not permitted to practice medicine
in Algeria; the medical faculty of Algiers refused to accredit their degrees. But
there is also evidence in the trajectories of these medical students that, even in
France, they were subjected to anti-Algerian prejudice and they endured continuing differential treatment and alienation. From the beginning of their experience at the seminary at St. Laurent d'Olt, they suffered discrimination and
segregation, seemingly driven by European stereotypes about Arab inclinations
to corruption and indecency. As the few remaining medical students continued their careers in France, they continued to express the requisite gratitude for
the White Fathers' support. But at moments when conflicts arose between the
students and their directors or European counterparts, evidence of racialized
treatment bubbled to the surface.

One conflict in particular has left behind a substantial collection of disillusioned letters in the students' own voices: accusations against their religious
director, another canon with whom they lived and worked; and—once again—
expressions of their resentment of the European *apostoliques* studying at Lille
to prepare for entry into the White Fathers. The immediate provocation was an
argument between the Algerian medical students and the local abbé who had
agreed to lodge them in Lille. In January of 1883, soon after their arrival, several
of the Algerian students wrote (either to the superior of the White Fathers or
to Archbishop Lavigerie himself) to complain of an unfair change in their diet,
linking this change to resentments that were still festering from their time at the
petit séminaire indigène of St. Laurent. A medical student named Félix Kaddour
wrote that Père Louail had introduced "the diet of St. Laurent d'Olt," a meager
food allowance which—Kaddour damningly claimed—had already been responsible for the deaths of "more than one of my unfortunate classmates" back
at the seminary. At Lille this treatment made even less sense, Kaddour wrote,
since the climate was less healthy, and since medical students especially needed
to maintain strong constitutions to withstand the diseases they encountered on
medical visits and during autopsies. What rankled the most, though, was that

this cutback in nourishment had only been applied to the "African" medical students and not to the European seminarians. Kaddour linked this injustice to a larger pattern of mistreatment and disrespect toward the Algerians in the house, before concluding, plaintively, " Am I not, whatever one may say, your adoptive child?"[61]

Another medical student, Pierre Alexis, developed much further and even more indignantly the accusation that the European postulants were favored and the Algerian medical students discriminated against at Lille. Pierre seems to have felt more deeply than some of the others the humiliations of their position and the ways in which they were reminded of their unique status almost as perpetual minors in the congregation. For example, the Algerians—perhaps because of their training in singing at the orphanage, or because it gratified the paternalistic or orientalist sensibilities of the parishioners—were made to serve as cantors in the chapel, despite Pierre's feeling that this was beneath their station as doctors in training. He also claimed that he and his classmates had often heard "repeated . . . this same phrase: nothing can be made of the Arabs," and that this anti-Arab sentiment was the real reason behind the most recent dietary injustices.[62]

According to the Algerian students' accounts of the affair, the local abbé, who had been charged with lodging them, had told Père Louail that they were spoiled and ungrateful. He had raised funds for them in his parish but had kept the funds for his own needs. Then, when some of the students did not show up to sing in the parish choir and "scandalized the faithful," he made his accusations of ingratitude to Louail. The reduction in their diet was their punishment for ruining the good impressions of the parish choir and the connected fundraising effort. Louail removed not only meat but also beer from the students' diet, restricting them to water. Here the students deployed their newly acquired medical discourse and knowledge of contagion: beer was a necessity because scientific studies of Lille's water supply had found that it was tainted with tapeworm.[63] Finally, Louail had gone so far as to berate and humiliate them during their spiritual instruction time, not only repeating the well-worn clichés about how "inconstant" and "ungrateful" Arabs are, but also reminding them that they were less valuable to the mission than the European seminarians. Louail told them, allegedly, that he would "prefer one *apostolique* over eighty-six Arabs," or that, according to a different student's account, in cases of conflict between the two groups he would expel ninety Arabs before expelling a single European postulant.[64]

Even more tellingly, a student named Vital claimed that some version of this demeaning phrase—that one European student was more valuable than many Arabs—had been used against them even back in their days at the *petit séminaire indigène*. Pierre Alexis was the most acerbic, going so far as to question the evangelistic project itself in light of these racialized conflicts. "Why . . . pass on [to the missionaries-in-training] feelings of hatred against us[?] What use is it to the missionaries to pull the infidels out of an error that [the infidels] believe to be good, in order to lead them into another, much more terrible and serious error[?]"[65] The subversive implication of Alexis's accusation was that it is better to be an innocent Muslim than a prejudiced Christian. Louail, for his part, seems to have seized at least one of the letters and wrote across it that the accusations were "lies."[66] Whether or not the letters had their desired effect, or whether they were ever even seen by Lavigerie or the White Fathers' superior, it was not long before the medical students were back in place, expressing the proper levels of submission and gratitude, at least in their correspondence with Lavigerie.

Having earned the rank of *officiers de santé*, they returned to Algeria in early 1884. It was then that they discovered their degrees would not be recognized by the Medical Faculty of Algiers—perhaps to protect the careers of the faculty's own students or perhaps "because the colonists do not under any circumstances want Arab doctors."[67] Thus a few of the young men returned to Lille to pursue their full doctorates. As might be expected, another conflict arose with Louail. During their previous stay at Lille, they had been given two rooms, thirty francs' allowance, and the right to eat "at the *pères'* table." On their return, Louail greeted them "coldly" and denied these privileges, seemingly wanting to drive them away from the mission house and force them to find their own lodging in the city. The three students who had returned for their doctorates were confined to one small chamber with no desks or chairs, and they found it impossible to study under these conditions.[68]

Love in the Time of the *Indigénat*

The other major conflict involving the medical students at Lille might have been easily predicted: several of the students became romantically entangled with French women. In late 1883, Félix Kaddour announced his intentions to marry the daughter of Lille's *commissaire civil*, who lived adjacent to the White Fathers' *maison* and whose family was known for its "Christian virtues."[69] The girl signed her name "Baby Jeanne" in a letter she wrote him while he was in Algeria in 1884.[70] In late 1883, another medical student named Michel Hamed similarly asked for permission to marry a girl named Irma Dumarchez. Like Kaddour, he was careful to assure his religious directors that she was from a suitably Christian family. Irma had even promised to return to Africa with Michel.[71]

By highlighting his fiancée's intentions to return with him to the mission field, Michel surely hoped to show Lavigerie that he recognized the debt of service he owed back in Algeria once his education was complete.

Notwithstanding these assurances from Michel, Lavigerie exploded when he heard that his protégés were contemplating marriages with French girls. Judging from Lavigerie's angry reaction directed at Père Louail ("what folly and what treason on your part"), Louail had not nipped these proposals in the bud and had perhaps even encouraged them. Lavigerie's opposition was not based, at least not explicitly, on any aversion to interracial marriage but on his vision for the missionary future of these students. Still, implicit in the rejection was the view that these students were incapable of integration, that they were useful precisely because they would always remain better adapted to African ways. "I will never let them marry in France where they would remain useless for our works and where they themselves would be unhappy. . . . It is in Africa that they must marry and not elsewhere. They will never have my consent for marriages in France after all the sacrifices we have made for them."[72] Lavigerie seems to have recalled the medical students to Algeria to see if their training would be enough to gain them employment in the colony but also to ward off the specter of romantic entanglements in France and potential loss of their valuable status as colonial intermediaries.[73]

Sadly, while Lavigerie waited for their amorous feelings to blow over and tried to decide how best to use their gifts, these young men were subjected to a series of setbacks and insults in Algeria, insults clearly linked to their legal status as "*indigènes*," or subjects, rather than citizens. After they were refused the necessary medical accreditation to practice in Algeria, a few of the young physicians went on to Tunisia, where the recent creation of a French protectorate had enabled Lavigerie and his missionaries to speculate in land and build up a beach-head of missionary posts. As a protectorate and not a settler colony, Tunisia was not held as tightly by the repressive embrace of the "indigenous code" (Code de l'indigénat), nor was it populated by licensed French physicians fearing competition. This meant that, unlike in Algeria, the young men had every right to dispense (and be paid for) medical care. Yet, as Félix Kaddour complained, this also meant that any quack could hang out his shingle and compete for customers at "50 centimes a visit."[74] Before going to Tunisia, Kaddour spent the spring of 1884 with the White Fathers at Djemâa Saharidj, near Tizi Ouzou, in Kabylie.[75] At Djemâa Saharidj, the White Fathers and the local civil authorities had both recently opened rival schools to convert and "civilize" the Kabyles and were locked in a struggle for indigenous students. Félix Kaddour seems to have become a casualty of this culture war, discovering belatedly that the patronage and protection of the French missionaries were no match for the new legal weaponry of the "indigenous code." In his liminal status as a convert to Christianity and a French University student but also an "*indigène*," Kaddour was still vulnerable to the racialized surveillance of colonial administrators.

Passed by the Senate in 1881, the Code de l'indigénat, often simply called the indigénat, granted local administrators and commandants sweeping powers to punish, repress, and terrorize anyone belonging to the category "*indigène*": any "native" colonial subject lacking the rare privilege of French citizenship. Under the indigénat, local administrators gained the authority—summarily and without judicial oversight—to detain and restrain, mete out fines of up to fifteen francs, to imprison subjects for up to five days, and to impose forced labor.[76] The "infractions" leading to such punishments included traveling beyond the confines of one's village without a permit, failure or slowness to respond to an order, or any act or word deemed "disrespectful" by an "agent" of French power.[77] The granting of these powers corresponded roughly to the end of the military administration in Algeria and the passing of administrative power to civilian authorities: ironically, as the bulk of Algeria's indigenous population came under the control of civilian administrators of "mixed communes," those administrators vested themselves with military-style powers of swift and summary punishment.[78] In debates surrounding the law's passage, some parliamentarians worried that it violated France's Republican commitment to the separation of powers and singled out a category of noncriminal "infractions" that "only natives could commit."[79] Any cognitive dissonance was quickly overcome, however, through the fiction of making the law "temporary"—only necessary until such time as the Algerians were "evolved" enough to profit from French citizenship. In practice, this "temporary" suspension of Republican norms was renewed every seven years until well into the twentieth century.[80]

Despite his status as a Christian convert, a longtime student in France, and a protégé of the well-connected Cardinal Lavigerie, Félix Kaddour was to discover with humiliation that the recently passed law was a blunt instrument, intended to divide Algerian society into citizens and subjects and to acknowledge no intermediate categories of Frenchness. Djemâa Saharidj fell under the administrative authority of Camille Sabatier at Fort National, a political rival of the White Fathers and an aggressive "civilizer" of the Kabyles who had established laic schools throughout the region and even an orphanage for Kabyle girls.[81] Sabatier was also a vocal defender of the repressive arsenal granted by the indigénat.[82] According to the missionaries, Sabatier used his discretionary powers to bully Kabyles into attending his laic schools, to deny travel permits, and to fine and imprison the students of the White Fathers.[83] In the spring of 1884, when the village was suffering a wave of diphtheria cases, Kaddour, wanting to make himself useful and perhaps to support the influence of the missionaries, offered medical advice and treatment, including giving a vomit-inducing treatment to the child of the local schoolteacher. Kaddour scrupulously refused payment for these ministrations, since the medical school at Algiers had not granted him a license to practice in Algeria. Nevertheless, when the patient's condition worsened for a time before improving, Sabatier summoned Kaddour to Fort National, to punish him for traveling without a permit and for practicing medicine without a license.[84]

Interestingly, the *garde-champêtre* sent by Sabatier did not know or did not choose to ask for Félix by his French name, nor even by his correct Arabic name, and threatened him with a beating. Kaddour, believing himself above the *indigénat* and protected by the missionary (a French citizen) with whom he was staying, refused to respond to these "illegal" threats. Sabatier sent two more policemen to bring Kaddour back to Fort National in chains. Kaddour could not believe that he—a convert to Christianity, adopted by French missionaries at the age of four or five, and educated in France for the past nine years—should be treated as a "Muslim *indigène*," should be subject to a law passed while he was at the University of Lille, a law whose purpose was clearly to exercise colonial control over "vagabond Muslims."[85] Under Sabatier's interrogation, Kaddour initially refused to give the administrator his name or to acknowledge that he was considered an "*indigène*," denying Sabatier the power to classify him. But the administrator's line of questioning aimed to put Kaddour in his place, to expose the cold, binary facts of the situation: "Have you been naturalized French?" [Kaddour:] "I don't know." [Sabatier:] "You cannot be ignorant of such a fact. You must know if you are or are not [a French citizen]." [Kaddour:] "I am not."[86] No matter how culturally or socially French he had become, Kaddour had no right to travel without a permit, no right to resist the home intrusion and orders of Sabatier's agents, and no right to refuse to answer Sabatier's questions. Between Kaddour's "disrespect" and his resistance to two different orders to appear, Sabatier counted three separate violations of the indigenous code. These violations cumulatively permitted the administrator to fine the young physician forty-five francs and to jail him for fifteen days, a degrading experience that left Kaddour furious against this colonial "Robespierre," a man "unworthy to be called French."[87]

Lavigerie and his missionaries were livid and immediately began lobbying the governor general to reprimand and remove Sabatier from his post at Fort

National. Lavigerie's quarrel seems to have been not so much with the "spirit" of the indigenous code in general, but rather with Sabatier's literal application of the code to harass the White Fathers' converts like Kaddour.[88] Nevertheless, if the governor general would not reprimand Sabatier, Lavigerie threatened to expose Sabatier's alleged abuses in the press.[89] Kaddour, for example, prepared a statement to send to the Society for the Protection of the Indigènes, a group of reformers in Paris who tried to prevent colonial abuses throughout France's empire.[90] Lavigerie, the imperialist, was thus cast in the unlikely role of defender of colonized Algerians, and even of Muslims. But there was an ambiguity in Lavigerie and the missionaries' approach. On the one hand, Kaddour and his missionary allies tried to gather testimony of Sabatier's mistreatment of "*indigènes*" in general; on the other hand, they emphasized all the ways Kaddour was socially and culturally "French" and thus did not deserve to have the indigenous code applied to him to begin with. This latter approach—focusing on Kaddour's unique "Frenchness" and worthiness—implicitly reasserted the binary distinctions of the indigénat. Lavigerie and Kaddour's real complaint was perhaps not so much with the racialized system of colonial control, but with the targeting of converts to Christianity.

Lavigerie's converts presented a challenge to the binary logic of French/citizen and "native"/subject and thus "threatened the stability of the most basic categories of the colonial social order."[91] These converts also uncomfortably exposed the fictions and ambiguities beneath the racial thinking of the late nineteenth century. At a time when "biological, social, and cultural" understandings of race still blended together and vied for ascendancy, cases like that of Félix Kaddour, where culture and socialization did not correspond with apparent biological race, forced defenders of the indigenous code into more nakedly biological explanations of colonial difference.[92] The existence of people like Kaddour exposed the colonial project's own ambiguities between different ways of conceptualizing race, different ways of defining Frenchness. Sabatier's insistence on treating a Christian convert like any other "*indigène*" reveals that, at least in the "empire of law," biological race had begun to edge out social and cultural explanations of difference.[93]

Unfortunately for Cardinal Lavigerie's campaign against Sabatier, the administrator had acted well within his repressive rights. Kaddour had been in the care of French missionaries since the age of five, had embraced Christianity, become fluent in the French language, and had a French fiancée. But the code's authors had not contemplated the existence of this liminal category. To be sure, one prefect admitted, Félix Kaddour the converted Christian was a "very particular" case, probably not intended as a target of the "exceptional," "temporary" law of

1881. Nonetheless, in the eyes of the law, which made "no distinction between Muslim *indigènes* and those who profess[ed] another religion," Kaddour was merely an "*indigène*."[94] In punishing Kaddour, even in cumulatively penalizing him three times, Sabatier had followed the letter of the law "with an extreme rigor."[95] Sabatier would later go on to become one of Algeria's deputies in Paris, where he would remain a staunch defender of the Code de l'indigénat and a thorn in the side of Lavigerie's requests for government funding.[96]

    In brief, the young men were denied not only medical accreditation and jobs in Algeria but also acknowledgment of their Frenchness. Some went on to Tunisia, while three returned to Lille for further education. Again, one of the doctors in training—Frédéric Mohamed—fell in love. This time, Lavigerie could not in good conscience oppose the match nor the couple's intent to settle in France. After all, he had not been able to find posts for his protégés in Algeria and had, for the most part, given up on Muslim conversion by the 1880s anyway. As Lavigerie wrote to Michel Hamed in 1889, for the present "I cannot prevent you from establishing yourself in France"; however, he reserved the right to demand his return to Algeria if circumstances changed and if he could be useful to the mission, "for it is certainly not in the interests of France, but in that of your African compatriots that I had you educated at such great expense."[97] This time, though, resistance to the student's settling in France came from supporters in France. At the news of Frédéric Mohamed's 1889 engagement to a French girl, and his plans to remain in France as a provincial doctor in the Mayenne, François Guermonprez, a doctor on the medical faculty of the Catholic University, wrote to the White Fathers to complain. Much like the medical faculty in Algiers, he and his colleagues appear to have been concerned that the Arab doctors were competing with French doctors. The problem was that this competition was unfair, since the Algerians had been permitted to dispense with certain requirements before taking their exams. As long as the Arabs were supposed to return to Africa, these dispensations were freely given, but for them to turn around and practice in France would be a betrayal of French doctors. Also, unwittingly echoing the criticism Lavigerie himself had made in 1883, the first time the Algerians had talked about marrying in France, Guermonprez argued that allowing the students to stay in France would betray the confidence of those who had financially supported these students. Would not this misdirection of funds from their original African intent damage Lavigerie's reputation?[98] Though he framed his protest as sincere concern for Lavigerie's reputation and made no explicit mention of the young men's race, Guermonprez's letter reveals that integration of the indigenous doctors into French society was not seamless.

The White Fathers—through the discourses of their fundraising bulletin and the discriminatory practices of their missionary excursions, orphanages, and seminary—presided over a shift toward more racialized views of Arabs. Moreover, more than previous missionaries, they were instrumental in transmitting these anti-Arab sentiments back to metropolitan France. The White Fathers' *Bulletin de l'Œuvre de Sainte Monique* and other fundraising publicity promoted an unforgiving version of the demarcation between Berbers and Arabs by constantly referring back to a given tribe's Berber or Arab status to determine whether it was a promising mission field and by going so far as to ignore or obscure the presence of Arab children among the White Fathers' own indigenous orphans and seminarians. The missionaries' accounts of travel and transcultural contact highlighted how greedy, calculating, and worldly the conduct of Muslim marabouts supposedly was, in contrast to the more spiritual, individualized, and other-worldly religion of the French priests. In the missionaries' actual day-to-day supervision and contact with their orphan-students, they operated under a series of racialized stereotypes about Arab laziness, lack of intelligence, inconstancy, ingratitude, and deviant sexuality.

This new racialized Catholic Orientalism was a product of both missionary disillusionment on the ground and ready-made domestic discourses from the more "liberal," civilizational wing of French Catholicism. Lavigerie and his missionaries appeared on the Algerian scene at a time when missionaries in Algeria had already begun abandoning the possibility of Arab conversion and had pivoted toward the Kabyles. Lavigerie also brought with him to Algeria a virulent blend of anti-Islamic discourses: liberal-civilizational denigrations of Islam blended with traditional, religious anti-Islamic apologetics. This blend was concocted in part by the ideological machinery of the liberal Catholic Œuvre d'Orient milieu.[99] It explains, on the one hand, Lavigerie's constant, unproblematic use of civilizational, colonialist, patriotic language to deride Muslim fanaticism (something Veuillot and other conservative "philo-Islamists" had not done) and, on the other hand, his occasional willingness to challenge the colonial administration in the name of missionary prerogatives (something his liberal, patriotic allies could not understand).

In 1892, the same year that Lavigerie died, an anonymous White Father in Algeria filled a small booklet with reports on orphans who no longer lived at Lavigerie's "Arab villages" in the Attafs. The purpose of this record, beyond taking stock of these former students' whereabouts, was perhaps to keep track of what funds or resources the mission had distributed to each of them (each entry includes a notation about monetary gifts received by the subject). Former students often came to the missionaries asking for money, and the *pères* used this incentive of financial support paternalistically: to try to improve the moral situation of their beneficiaries. For example, the missionaries encouraged their wayward disciples to find suitable employment, to regularize their marriage situations, or to make sure their own children were receiving religious instruction and baptism. Overall, the booklet—with its brief, dismissive entries on orphan after orphan—produces a snapshot of the missionaries' disappointment and of their own ethnographic view of indigenous weakness and failure.

One former orphan was an "inveterate drunk," unable to find a job and reducing his family to poverty. Offered a loaf of bread by the missionaries, he refused and "went away threatening." Many of these ex-disciples were described as being "unhealthy" and also "lazy" and too reliant on the mission's support. Another was a complete hoodlum, "insolent," often drunk, even flinging "filthy insults" at the female religious. Still another had "not been able to last at the construction site" where the *pères* had so generously found him a job and was threatening to come back to the Arab village to reclaim his property there. One former student, who had even been in Europe at the *petit séminaire indigène* but had been expelled for "misconduct," was as "lazy," nomadic, and dishonest as the others. One who had served with the colonial troops had picked up the "the vices of barracks" and was more "debauched and corrupted" than most. Another had contracted various diseases "in his debaucheries." Laziness, drunkenness, and sexual deviance—these were the common accusations lobbed at the former orphans. Perhaps worst of all, these orphans were ungrateful and entitled, expecting handouts or engaging in thievery or fraud when handouts were not forthcoming. The "social meaning of gratitude" was that the mission's beneficiaries had an obligation to respectfully thank the missionaries—serving as living witnesses to the goodness of the Europeans' charity and the truthfulness of Catholicism.[100] The former students in this booklet had, by their alleged ingratitude and sense of entitlement, broken the contract of gratitude that they owed to the mission. Thus, they received perhaps the most bitter denunciation found in the reports: they were "insolent."[101]

The apotheosis of French Catholicism's rhetorical return to Islam-as-enemy, both in the life of Lavigerie's nascent congregation and in the larger context of imperialism and metropolitan Catholic apologetics, was Lavigerie's widely publicized "Antislavery Crusade" of the late 1880s and 1890s. As his missionaries penetrated farther into central Africa, they found themselves increasingly in conflict both with Muslim missionaries and with Muslim, Arabo-Swahili slavers.[1] Troubled by accounts of violent slave raids, believing that the evangelization of Africa could not proceed without the abolition of African slavery, and perhaps seeing a prime opportunity for raising the profile and fundraising capabilities of his new congregation, Lavigerie put his "crusade" into action.[2] His letter describing the scourge of African slavery and announcing the crusade to the readers of *Missions catholiques* was a string of ferociously anti-Islamic canards, animated by a deep anxiety about conspiracies of Islamic expansion in sub-Saharan Africa and by a hardened belief that Muslims were unconvertible, "irreconcilable [enemies] of Christian Europe."[3]

The founding of the Antislavery Society represents a high point both in French Catholics' anti-Islamic rhetoric and in their willingness to cooperate with the secular, imperial state—suggesting a correlation between these two phenomena. In the context of metropolitan French culture wars, the Antislavery Crusade functioned as a kind of proto-*ralliement* (a dress rehearsal for the Church's official ceasefire with Republicanism in 1892), as Catholics hoped that even anticlerical French would be forced to recognize the justice and goodness of their cause and ally with them against the Muslim foe.[4] Much like the Œuvre des écoles d'Orient's appeals to *civilisation chrétienne* in the 1860s, the unleashing of anti-Islamic rhetoric that attended the crusade was due as much to the desire for metropolitan, mainstream Christian unity and money as it was to any reality on the ground in Africa. Indeed, the liberal Catholics of the Œuvre d'Orient had already begun sounding the alarm about a Muslim "invasion" of Africa as early as the 1850s and 1860s.

The Archbishop of Paris hoped that this crusade would cause Europeans to "forget [their] quarrels" and unite in a "truce of God" for the advancement of

"Christian civilization," against what Lavigerie had called "Europe's natural born enemies."[5] The archbishop of Toulouse wrote that "to subscribe to the abolition of African slavery, it is not necessary to be Catholic, it is enough to have the true notion of human dignity and solidarity."[6] The archbishop of Besançon declared the crusade to be "the cause of humanity and of civilization as well as that of the Church and of souls."[7] The bishop of Chartres even noted that a common thread of Lavigerie's career was his role as protector of those oppressed by Muslims, comparing the Maronite Christians of Lebanon with the "poor blacks" of sub-Saharan Africa: "May God support you in this work of humanity and of Christian civilization, and give you back a little of the strength which, already a long time ago, allowed you to fly to the aid of our brothers of Lebanon!"[8] This "crusade" was more than rhetoric: Lavigerie planned to employ private missionary armies to protect his missionaries and to forcibly bring civilization to Africa. According to Bertrand Taithe, "These literal examples of missionary militarism"—much like the language that accompanied them—were motivated by the Catholic desire to be unified with the colonial state against a common enemy: "Islamism."[9]

The strategy of the Antislavery Campaign was thus identical to that of the mainstream, liberal Catholic Orientalism of the Œuvre d'Orient: the Campaign was supposed to be an anti-Islamic clash of civilizations that would unite Republicans and Catholics alike against the horrors of the "Muslim" slave trade. Lavigerie's civilizational-unity tactics paid off when he snagged the moderate anticlerical Jules Simon to serve as president of the Society's Committee of High Patronage. Simon was more suited than anyone to symbolize a possible rapprochement between well-meaning Catholics and secularists against the common Muslim foe.[10] In February 1889, Simon held a conference at the Sorbonne in favor of the Antislavery Campaign and gave a speech in which he blamed African slavery on Muslim polygamy, particularly on the "Ottoman" demand for more wives, and in which he dwelled at salacious length on the forced castration of slaves destined to be eunuchs.[11] At the climax of this discourse, which was liberally peppered with praise for his former student Lavigerie, Simon pontificated, "I do not ask you, *Messieurs*, if you are Catholics; I do not ask you if you are Christians; I am speaking to you as a man and as a philosopher," united against that enemy of the human race: Muslim slavery. For Simon, the Antislavery Campaign was "a crusade, a crusade against barbarism; it is the special crusade of humanity."[12]

Even as mainstream Catholics increasingly used their opposition to Muslim "barbarism" to signal an alliance with Republican France, some ultramontane Catholics still reflexively claimed to prefer Islam to agnosticism, as Veuillot had. By now this clichéd use of Islam as a rhetorical foil contained none of Veuillot's genuine admiration for Muslims. The closest thing to a successor to Veuillot's acerbic, ultramontane journalism in the 1880s and 1890s was the daily *La Croix*. The journal was run by the Assumptionists, a congregation that specialized in organizing pilgrimages to Marian shrines and to the Holy Land and in mission-ary work in the Ottoman Empire.[13] The journalist-priests of *La Croix* took up the torch of defending Catholic education against the secularizing Ferry Laws in the 1880s and portrayed themselves as engaged in a fight to the death with the conspiratorial forces of free thought, socialism, divorce, Protestants, Jews, and Satan himself. *La Croix* is most famous for its feverishly anti-Semitic coverage of the Dreyfus affair in the 1890s, which provoked a Republican backlash against the congregation and led to the final church-state separation laws of the early 1900s.[14] The Assumptionists, in other words, were no liberal Catholics. Unlike Lavigerie or the publicists of the Œuvre d'Orient, they sought no plaudits for their mainstream respectability or commitment to liberty of conscience, nor did they attempt to justify their support for imperial interventions on liberal or humanitarian grounds.

Interestingly, in their fight against the secularism of the Third Republic, the Assumptionists even preserved some of the philo-Islamic rhetorical instincts of Veuillot, Boré, and the Jesuits of Algeria. In demanding that the French state allow public Catholic prayer and processions, the Assumptionists maintained they were only asking for what was allowed at Constantinople, for "liberty *à la turque*."[15] The visibility permitted to Catholic rituals in the Ottoman Empire supposedly meant that there was more religious liberty "under the Muslim yoke" than in secular France and that private morality was superior in the Orient as well.[16] But the intention of these rhetorical comparisons was to humiliate the Assumptionists' secular enemies. There was none of the sincere respect for Islam, none of the missionary optimism of the first half of the century. On the contrary, *La Croix* accused Islam of somehow being in league with the satanic forces of secularism and republicanism. Its writers also pandered to French fears of pan-Is-lamic fanaticism and expansion. Muslims were "obstinate" and "do not convert"; and the Islamic world was a vast, mysterious network that France should dis-member with its "civilizing" and Christian influence in North Africa.[17]

The field of Catholic Orientalism back in France was also influenced by the rise of "scientific" racism. The Baron Carra de Vaux, a professor of Arabic at the Catholic Institute of Paris in the early years of the twentieth century, was relatively sympathetic to Islam by the standards of his day and in some ways an-ticipated Catholicism's more open attitude to Islam in the twentieth century.[18] Yet Carra de Vaux's understanding of Islamic history drew heavily on the racial distinction between Aryan and Semite popularized by philologists like Renan and by the demographer-orientalist Arthur de Gobineau. Carra de Vaux characterized the history of Islam as a struggle between the Semitic simplicity and despotism of primitive Islam and the Aryan creativity and individuality brought to the religion by the new blood of the Persians—thus it was no surprise that Shi'ism, Sufism, and other allegedly heterodox Islams emerged among the Persians, and not in Islam's Semitic homeland.

For Carra de Vaux, the most sympathetic Muslims were those seen as heterodox by Islam's static, oppressive mainstream. The only good Muslims were those who could be portrayed according to Christian norms of sanctity—those who favored a more mystical relationship with an immanent, loving God and who looked for the coming of a Christlike Mahdi or redeemer.[19] According to Carra de Vaux, such attributes were not just exclusively Christian but exclusively Aryan possessions. The history of Islam was a series of "Aryan reactions," or attempts from the Persian borders of the Islamic world to "move toward the moral conceptions of the peoples of Europe."[20] The lesson for Carra de Vaux's readers was that, in the future, they must be quick to support fellow Aryans in their efforts to reform Islam, efforts that would yield material and spiritual benefits for Europe: "[Every man] is, by birth at least, a member of one of those segments into which the world is divided. . . . Aryans that we are, we must take sides with those who are like us" and must "revive in the Orient the flame of our own genius."[21] Carra de Vaux's rehabilitation of some Islamic sects and figures, then, relied upon a racial divide that was more rigid and reductive than ever: whatever was good in Islam was by that same token Aryan, Christian, and European—and at odds with Islam's original, "Semitic" essence.

The fin-de-siècle fate of Catholic philo-Islamism is perhaps best exemplified by the spiritual trajectory of Ernest Psichari, the grandson of Ernest Renan. In his autobiographical novel, *Le voyage du centurion*, Psichari recounts his conversion to Catholicism while serving as a *sous-lieutenant* in Mauritania from 1909 to 1912. The story of Psichari's conversion could have come from the pages of Veuillot's newspaper, for Psichari, like the officers Veuillot loved to describe, was led back to the Church after being shamed by the Islamic faith and practice he observed in Mauritania. Islam's spirituality, severity, and submission to God impressed him and convinced him of the need for religion in his own life and in the national life of France.[22] At first Psichari, like Veuillot and Boré more than a generation before, was seduced by the beauty and spirituality of Islam.[23] But he quickly reminded himself that Christianity was the superior religion: it had, after all, produced the civilization that was overpowering Islam. In fact, it was the very inferiority of the Moors, Psichari decided, rather than their religion, that had restored to him a sense of his identity and membership in Catholic France.[24] No matter how degraded French civilization was, it was still infinitely more vital and active than that of Mauritania. Psichari was separated from the Moors by "twenty centuries of Christianity" and must remain separated, because he was the proud "envoy of western power." What began as a movement of analogy and openness broke down into total opposition; in restoring to Psichari a sense of his French-Catholic identity, Islam served only as contrast and enemy.[25]

Psichari's insistence on the unbridgeable divide between "Western power" and Eastern weakness illustrates the temptation exerted on Catholic writers by the paradigm of the civilizing mission, which held out the prospect of an even better social glue than Christian belief. According to Eric Hobsbawm, it was the technology of the late nineteenth century, so much more advanced than that of its victims, that definitively killed the trope of the noble savage: possession of the Maxim gun divided the world neatly into civilizers and recipients of civilization.[26] Veuillot, writing in the 1840s, had wavered between his respect for Muslim religiosity and his enthusiasm for European steamships, technology that seemed to justify "Christian" civilization's superiority and right of conquest. Perhaps this eventual resolution of the tension, the prevailing of admiration for "steamships" over admiration for Islam, would not have surprised Veuillot. After all, he had already linked Christianity's truth value to its civilizational superiority, making Catholic complicity with later, more secular civilizing missions thinkable. But in the context of the 1840s—provoked by an increasingly marginal and embattled position in his own culture, impressed with the tenacity of Algerian resistance, and inspired by missionary optimism and a sincere belief in the potential salvation of Muslim souls—the most illiberal man in France had identified with the colonized against the hypocrisy of the colonizer and looked to Islam as a model for French society.

In nineteenth-century France and Algeria, Catholics talked about "Islam" as a way of working through their own anxieties about secularism and imperialism. Some conservative Catholics like Veuillot purported to admire Islam for its unity and religiosity, but this philo-Islamic discourse could be a tactic for condemning the flaws and divisions of secular France or for justifying imperial violence through traditional evangelism. Liberal Catholics, by contrast, despised Islam for its supposed conspiratorial fanaticism. But this anti-Islamic discourse was a tactic for manufacturing Christian solidarity and for justifying imperial violence as the promotion of "civilization" and religious tolerance.

Both the philo-Islamic conservatives and the anti-Islamic liberals were guilty of exploiting "Islam" for their own rhetorical purposes rather than seeking genuinely to understand Muslims.[27] Both discourses also reduced Islam to an imaginary monolith, divorced from how it has been practiced by real individuals and cultures in history.[28] Finally, both the sympathetic and critical images of Islam were complicit, each in their own way, in sanctioning imperialist expansion and violence. But it was the anti-Islamic discourse that flourished. This liberal Catholic synthesis or something like it—defending France's Christian identity and foreign policy goals, all while attacking Islam for its alleged religiosity and intolerance—would continue far beyond its own time.

Much has changed in France since the end of the nineteenth century. Current tensions between the Muslim minority and the secular state have causes that should first be sought in more recent history—in the Algerian War and decolonization, in postwar and postcolonial immigration trends, in the social isolation and unemployment of the *banlieues*, and in the rise of a new, aggressive brand of secularism, or *laïcité*, that targets Muslims.[29] After Algerian independence in 1962, many on the far right—embarrassed and emasculated by the loss of the empire—pivoted to portraying Muslim Algerians as violent and virile anticolonialists, hell-bent on immigrating to France and violating France's women.[30] Muslim states in the 1960s and 1970s engaged in anticolonial struggle and secular nation-building, not primarily motivated by religion; but the Iranian Revolution in 1979 marked a return of Islam as a source of geopolitical concern to the West. With the rhetoric of the "War on Terror," this reflex of reducing the actions of Muslims to some imagined Islamic allegiance, has only intensified.[31]

But these current tensions also have more distant, nineteenth-century resonances. The complicated triangulation between Catholics, Muslims, and secularists this book has traced throughout the nineteenth century persists today. Right-wing agitators still occasionally pose as admirers of Islam in order to score points against the liberal, decadent West. In the United States, after the terror attacks of September 11, 2001, conservative provocateur Dinesh D'Souza argued that liberal Americans had brought the attacks on themselves with their "cultural depravity" and advocacy for gay marriage and birth control. Conservative Americans, D'Souza maintained, should see al-Qaida's hatred for liberalism as understandable and should seek out an alliance with "traditional Muslims." But the post-9/11 moment was not ripe for using Islam, Veuillot-style, to shame the godless left. Hostility toward Islam was too unanimous and D'Souza's argument too confused. His book was swiftly and roundly condemned, on both the left and the right.[32]

In France, more recently, cultural critics have pretended a similar admiration for the virility and unity of Islamic civilization. Michel Houellebecq's cynical novel *Submission* imagines a France in the near future, so rotted out by individualism, consumerism, and feminism that a Muslim takeover is welcomed as a mercy, restoring patriarchal order and reversing France's sexual and demographic decline.[33] But this Islamization is not a betrayal of France's Christian heritage, one character explains, channeling Veuillot: "For these Muslims, the real enemy . . . isn't Catholicism. It's secularism. . . . They think of Catholics as fellow believers."[34] Taking Houellebecq's satire too literally, far-right journalist Eric Zemmour has professed his "respect" for adherents of ISIS who, unlike the feeble French, are "ready to die for what they believe in." For Zemmour, "Islam" is a "holistic society" as opposed to the destructive individualism of post-1968 France. But a traditional France, "still steeped in Catholicism and patriarchy, would have offended [Muslim immigrants] less and integrated [them] more easily."[35] Veuillot himself could not have wielded these backhanded compliments for Islam any better. But such cynical far-right attempts to shame leftists by pretending admiration for Islam remain marginal. The "liberal Catholic" discourse is still dominant, claiming to detest Islam in the name of religious tolerance while simultaneously defending a culturally Christian vision of France.

According to a recent sociological survey of French Catholics, some of the most left-wing and socially conscious Catholics—those dubbed *émancipés*—can also be "the most hostile to migrants," perhaps because they fear that Muslim immigrants "threaten the emancipation of women and the liberty of homosexuals."[36] Figures on both the right and the left in France have embraced a "new *laïcité*" that enables the Republic to maintain a pretense of colorblind neutrality even as it stigmatizes Muslim practice—from headscarves to halal meat—more aggressively than the Republic ever regulated Catholics.[37] Even the far-right Front national (recently renamed Rassemblement national) has begun posing as a defender of Republican secularism to make its anti-Muslim, anti-immigrant agenda appear mainstream.[38] In perhaps the most striking echo of the nineteenth century, the charitable organization the Œuvre d'Orient still exists and still advocates for persecuted Christian minorities in the Middle East. To be sure, the precarious position of Christian minorities in the Middle East deserves concern. But in an effort to encourage French solidarity with "Christians of the Orient," the crusading language of the nineteenth century sometimes re-emerges. When ISIS militants murdered Coptic Christians in Libya, the Œuvre d'Orient's director warned, "By targeting the 'Kingdom of the Cross' as they put it, the Islamic State really wanted to strike at the heart of Europe."[39] In a replay of nineteenth-century soft power politics, the French Foreign Ministry has recently begun working with the Œuvre d'Orient to help fund Christian schools throughout the Middle East, as a way of spreading the French language and, ostensibly, of encouraging interreligious peace. And in the months leading up to his 2022 reelection bid, French President Emmanuel Macron rewarded the Œuvre's director, as Napoleon III had honored his predecessor, with the Legion of Honor. Some suggested that this ceremony was intended to shore up the support of Catholic voters (not unlike Napoleon III's expedition to Syria).[40]

However, unlikely alliances between Catholics and Muslims still occur, genuine encounters that go beyond the cynical "Islam envy" of Houellebecq or Zemmour.[41] After the headscarf ban was enacted in 2004, Catholic schools saw an increase in the number of Muslim students, in part because these schools are sometimes more flexible in allowing Muslim religious signs and observances.[42] Such Catholic schools "respect the spiritual dimension of the person" and aspire that their Muslim students, far from having to leave their faith at home, will be "respected in their capacity as Muslims."[43] And there were signs in the most recent debates over "communitarian" religious education that Catholic and Muslim schools may make common cause against invasive regulations.[44] One hopes that such interfaith encounters and alliances will lead more Christians to a knowledge not of an imagined "Islam" but of individual Muslims themselves.[45]

This book has shown some of the Christian and colonialist histories behind a series of negative stereotypes about Muslims and Arabs—their supposed religious fanaticism, lack of development, laziness, inconstancy, greed, and sensuality. Many of these stereotypes are still current and, despite their colonial past, purport to be neutral or secular even as they continue to demean and subjugate.[46] Resolving France's tensions will not be easy. If anything, recent events point in the direction of further division and alienation. Leaders will need the political courage to stop exploiting the culture wars around Islam and immigration and focus instead on offering genuine support and opportunities for the disadvantaged. But it is unrealistic to think people of faith can simply leave their religious lives and consciences at the door when they enter the public sphere.[47] Instead, Muslims, Christians, and secularists alike must come together to establish conditions for mutual toleration and understanding—not in a pretend neutrality that protects the privileged, but in an open and hospitable acknowledgment of difference, so that "*everyone* may live as a minority among minorities."[48]

NOTES

Acknowledgments

1. Gautier, *Études et controverses historiques*.

Introduction

1. Mercier, *Histoire de Constantine* esp. 414–40.

2. Suchet, *Lettres édifiantes et curieuses*, 24, 26.

3. Lambert, *L'Algérie*, 27. I owe this reference to Trumbull, *An Empire of Facts*, 36.

4. Lambert, *L'Algérie*, 52–53.

5. See the "Introduction," in White and Daughton, *In God's Empire*, 4–5.

6. For the British Empire, see Porter, *Religion versus Empire?*; and Porter, "An Overview, 1700–1914," 40, 51–53.

7. See Prudhomme, *Missions chretiennes*, 87.

8. Prudhomme, *Missions chretiennes*, 69–87; cf. Daughton, *An Empire Divided*.

9. Keith, *Catholic Vietnam*, 1–15, 65–87 [quoted phrase on 76].

10. Foster, *Faith in Empire*, 10 and ff.

11. This is the thesis of Daughton, *An Empire Divided*, 17-24. At present, this "missionary turn" in the historiography of imperialism is moving into the mid-twentieth century and the end of empires, producing sophisticated considerations of the role of Christianity and indigenous Christians' agency in decolonization movements. See Foster, "'Theologies of Colonization'"; Greenberg, "Protestants, Decolonization"; Fontaine, "Treason or Charity?"; and Walker-Said, "Wealth, Law, and Moral Authority." One forerunner of this interest in Christianity's influence on decolonization is Sanneh, *Translating the Message*.

12. Sessions, *By Sword and Plow*, 1.

13. McDougall, *A History of Algeria*, 89–90.

14. Like dioceses in metropolitan France, in other words, the diocese of Algiers was regulated by the Concordat negotiated between Napoleon and Pope Pius VII in 1801, which famously gave the French state power to appoint and surveil the political opinions of French bishops and parish priests. (In 1865, the diocese of Algiers split into three

dioceses, corresponding to the three departments at Oran, Algiers, and Constantine.) See Saaïdia, *L'Algérie catholique*, 33–61.

15. Daughton, *An Empire Divided*, 22; and Prudhomme, *Missions chretiennes*, 88. On the training and missionary vocation (or lack thereof) of parish priests in nineteenth-century Algeria, see Saaïdia, *L'Algérie catholique*, 42–45.

16. This point is from Saaïdia, *L'Algérie catholique*, 18. See, for example, Émerit, "La lutte entre les généraux"; Ageron, *Les algériens musulmans*; Rey-Goldzeiguer, *Le royaume arabe*. See also the historiographical discussion in Prochaska, *Making Algeria French*, 1–4; and Saaïdia, "De l'histoire de l'Orient," 207–8.

17. McDougall, *A History of Algeria*, 86–128.

18. Brower, *A Desert Named Peace*, esp. 4 and ff.; and Sessions, *By Sword and Plow*.

19. McDougall, *A History of Algeria*, 97ff; and Surkis, *Sex, Law, and Sovereignty*, 1–6.

20. Émerit, "La question algérienne en 1871," 256–64; Duffy, *Nomad's Land*, 148; Cole, *Lethal Provocation*, 38; Davis, "Colonial Capitalism and Imperial Myth," 165, 167–68.

21. The phrase is Saaïdia's *L'Algérie catholique*, passim.

22. Suchet, *Lettres édifiantes et curieuses*, qtd. in Brower, *A Desert Named Peace*, 86-89. Italics in original.

23. See, for example, Daughton, *An Empire Divided*, 22; Prudhomme, *Missions chretiennes*, 88; and Saaïdia, *Algérie coloniale*.

24. Saaïdia, *L'Algérie catholique*, 17.

25. Curtis, *Civilizing Habits*, 101–73 (the quoted phrases and words appear on 113, 127, and 170.) See also. Curtis, "Emilie de Vialar," 261–92. Clancy-Smith, *Mediterraneans*, 270. For the similar role of nonreligious women in the "civilizing mission," see Rogers, *A Frenchwoman's Imperial Story*. One other notable treatment of missionaries in nineteenth-century Algeria is the work of Kyle Francis, which explores Catholic missionary outreach to the non-French European settlers of Algeria (Spanish, German, Italian, Maltese, etc.). See Francis, "Catholic Missionaries in Colonial Algeria," 686.

26. See Direche-Slimani, *Chrétiens de Kabylie*; Claire Fredj, "Une Mission Impossible?," 163–229.

27. See letters from Girard to Étienne [Lazarist Superior General], Oct. 19, Nov. 24, 1851, dossier 108a: Alger; and the letter from Étienne to Boré, January 17, 1852, in Fonds de Saint-Benoît de Constantinople, Supérieurs généraux, carton VIII, dossier I, Correspondance de M. Étienne avec M. Boré, 1843–1865, Archives de la Congrégation de la Mission, Paris.

28. Baudicour, "Correspondance de particulière."

29. "Ultramontane" refers to one's allegiance to the pope, "over the mountains," rather than to national ("Gallican") church councils. Hastings, "Ultramontanism," 730.

30. Said, *Orientalism*.

31. See Burke and Prochaska, "Introduction: Orientalism," 1–71.

32. Bar-Yosef, *The Holy Land in English Culture*, 4, 9–10, 15.

33. Billie Melman, qtd. in Bar-Yosef, *The Holy Land in English Culture*, 9.

34. Mary Louise Pratt has coined the term "contact zone." See Pratt, *Imperial Eyes*, 7–8.

35. See, for example, Wilder, *The French Imperial Nation-State*.

36. This reductionist narrative has reigned from Adrien Dansette all the way down to a recent, popular treatment of Third Republic "culture wars." See Dansette, *Histoire religieuse*; and F. Brown, *For the Soul of France*.

37. Lagrée, *Religion et cultures en bretagne*.

38. Harris, *Lourdes*; and Kaufman, *Consuming Visions*.

39. On the connection between the Church's democratization and increasing apocalypticism, see Kselman, *Miracles and Prophecies*. For the shift "from a God of fear to a God of love," see Gibson, *A Social History of French Catholicism*, 265.

40. On the relationship between European fears of pan-Islamic unity and a racialized view of the Muslim world, see Aydin, *The Idea of the Muslim World*; on the view that Muslims bear their religiosity in their very bodies, see Davidson, *Only Muslim*.

41. See, for example, Prudhomme, *Missions chrétiennes*, 69, 79, 87; Daughton, *An Empire Divided*, 18–20; and Keith, *Catholic Vietnam*, 7, 56, 65 and ff. On earlier missionaries' more Christian appeals to "*civilisation*," see Curtis, *Civilizing Habits*, 13, 269–70; and Daughton, *An Empire Divided*, 42–43.

42. See Foster, *Faith in Empire*, 8, 10–12, 167. On the apologetic motives for the Catholic appropriation of Enlightenment *civilisation*, see Laurens, "La projection chrétienne," 39–55; and Derré et al., *Civilisation chrétienne*.

43. Weiss, *Captives and Corsairs*, 2–3; quoted words from Coller, *Arab France*, 13, 17.

44. Coller, *Arab France*, 9.

45. See Peterson, "Morality Plays," esp. 983–87.

46. Fogarty and Osborne, "Constructions and Functions of Race," 206–36, esp. 217–19.

47. Stoler, *Carnal Knowledge*, 17, 118.

48. Stoler, *Carnal Knowledge*, 43, and also 68, 70, 112, 114, 120–21, 131; and Saada, *Empire's Children*.

49. Fogarty and Osborne, "Constructions and Functions of Race," 206, 227.

50. Asseraf, *Electric News in Colonial Algeria*, 90.

51. Surkis, *Sex, Law, and Sovereignty*; Blévis, "La citoyenneté française."

52. Schreier, *Arabs of the Jewish Faith*.

53. Blévis, "La citoyenneté française," 30–32. See also Smith, "Citizenship in the Colony," 33–50.

54. Cole, *Lethal Provocation*, 26, 29.

55. Asseraf, *Electric News in Colonial Algeria*, 91. As Laure Blévis explains, indigeneity was fixed from birth and could only be escaped by applying for French citizenship, a "favor" rarely requested by Muslim Algerians and even more rarely granted. Blévis, "La citoyenneté française," 34, 37, 44–45.

56. Blévis, "La citoyenneté française," 43–44. For all these reasons, I will avoid the use of the colonialist pejorative "*indigène*" unless I am quoting or specifically discussing the racialized hierarchy produced by colonialist discourse and law. I am following the lead of scholars Arthur Asseraf, *Electric News in Colonial Algeria*, 14–15; and Surkis, *Sex, Law, and Sovereignty*, 4.

57. Arsan, "'There is, in the Heart of Asia,'" 80.

Chapter 1

1. See M. L. Brown, *Louis Veuillot*, 54–56.

2. L. Veuillot, *Les Français en Algérie*, 54–58; Brower, *A Desert named Peace*, 22–25.

3. See WorldCat for a list of all editions of L. Veuillot's *Les Français en Algérie*.

4. For a detailed account of the conflicts between the headstrong Bishop of Algiers, Monseigneur Dupuch, the congregations, and the colonial administration, see Émerit, "La lutte entre les généraux et les prêtres," 66–97; and Curtis, "Emilie de Vialar, 261–92.

5. For the biographical information in the preceding and following sentences, see E. Veuillot, *Louis Veuillot (1813–1845)*, 169–75, 229–30.

6. For the first quoted phrase, Clark, "The New Catholicism," 24. For the second phrase, McPhee, *Social History of France*, 244.

7. McMillan, "Louis Veuillot, *L'Univers* and the Ultramontane," [e-book, paragraphs 11 and 25].

8. L. Veuillot once wrote that, though God had made him a Catholic, "M. de Maistre made me Roman." Letter from Louis Veuillot to Comte Rodolphe de Maistre, February 9, 1847, in Nouvelles Acquisitions Françaises [hereafter NAF], Fonds Veuillot 24223, "Lettres copiées de Louis Veuillot, 1839–1849," Bibliothèque nationale de France, département des manuscrits; Pierrard, *Louis Veuillot*, 109.

9. See Gough, *Paris and Rome*, 80–102.

10. Maistre, *The Pope*, 291–92.

11. L. Veuillot, *Les Français en Algérie*, 8

12. L. Veuillot, *Les Français en Algérie*, 154–55.

13. L. Veuillot, *Les Français en Algérie*, 11.

14. Gildea, *Children of the Revolution*, 135–38.

15. For another example of how orientalist tropes were transformed by contact with North Africa and by the need to address the July Monarchy's cultural and political anxieties, see Lowe, *Critical Terrains*, 75 and ff.

16. See Lesourd, "Le réveil des missions, 52–71.

17. Two types of studying Islam in nineteenth century France that have been seen as distinct in outlook, method, and goals. Burke, "The Sociology of Islam," 155–56.

18. Saaïdia, "L'anticléricalisme article d'exportation?," 110. Cf. Conklin, *A Mission to Civilize*; and Daughton, *An Empire Divided*.

19. Carnoy-Torabi, "Regards sur l'islam," 472–82.

20. Cf. Mosher, "The Judgmental Gaze," 25-44; and Carnoy-Torabi, "Regards sur l'islam," 492–95.

21. Carnoy-Torabi, "Regards sur l'islam," 497–500.

22. And Maxime Rodinson points that in *Candide*, Voltaire's protagonists end up fleeing Europe and the Inquisition, like so many other religious minorities, for the relative tolerance of Constantinople. Rodinson, *Europe and the Mystique of Islam*, 46–49. For more on Voltaire's ambivalence towards Islam, see Fatih, "Peering into the Mosque," 1070–82; and Tolan, *Faces of Muhammad*, 155–83.

23. Carnoy-Torabi, "Regards sur l'Islam," 466.

24. With the exception of the atheist *philosophes* (Spinoza, d'Holbach) celebrated by Israel, *A Revolution of the Mind*.

25. Romilly, "Tolerance."

26. On this distinction between "liberty of conscience" and "tolerance" in the Enlightenment, see the excellent discussion by Kselman, *Conscience and Conversion*, 13–48.

27. Rousseau, *The Social Contract*, 427–28. Cf. Coller, "Islam and the Revolutionary Age."

28. Thomson, *Barbary and Enlightenment*, 1–2.

29. Thomson, *Barbary and Enlightenment*, 134–35.

30. Muthu, *Enlightenment against Empire*, 278–80. On anti-Ottoman sentiment in 1820s Europe, see Weiss, *Captives and Corsairs*, 155–71.

31. On some of the ways Maistre borrowed from Enlightenment thought, see Armenteros, *The French Idea of History*.

32. Maistre, *The Pope*, 258.

33. Maistre, *Les Soirées de Saint-Petersbourg*, 85–86.

34. Maistre, *The Pope*, 293.

35. Schwab, *The Oriental Renaissance*, 11 and ff.; 275–88.

36. Rousseau, *The Social Contract*, 427–28.

37. Clancy-Smith, *Rebel and Saint*.

38. Schmitt, "A Pan-European Interpretation of Donoso Cortés," 100–15. In spite of his own reactionary tendencies, his membership in the Nazi party, and his refusal to reckon honestly with that membership after 1945, Schmitt remains a useful interpreter of nineteenth-century counterrevolutionary thought.

39. Schmitt, "A Pan-European Interpretation of Donoso Cortés," 107–8.

40. Schmitt, "A Pan-European Interpretation of Donoso Cortés," 107–8.

41. Throughout this paragraph, I am influenced by Tackett, *Religion, Revolution, and Regional Culture*; Suzanne Desan, *Reclaiming the Sacred*; McPhee, *Social History of France*; and Helena Rosenblatt, *Liberal Values*.

42. The phrase, and the point, are from Englund, *Napoleon*, 182.

43. See McPhee, *Social History of France*, 79–80; and Englund, *Napoleon*, 180 and ff.

44. The phrase is Peter Gay's (in a different, late-nineteenth century context). Gay, *Schnitzler's Century*, 174.

45. McPhee, *Social History of France*, 134; and Andrews, "Selective Empathy, 3, 13–14.

46. Sessions, *By Sword and Plow*, 2.

47. See Tocqueville, *Writings on Empire and Slavery*.

48. Abi-Mershed, *Apostles of Modernity*. See also the "Romantic Socialists" studied by Naomi Andrews, in "Selective Empathy," 1–25.

49. For previous two sentences, see Crossley, "Edgar Quinet," 132.

50. Crossley, "Edgar Quinet," 133–35. For romantic philosophies of history in general, see Abrams, *Natural Supernaturalism*.

51. Cf. Collin, *Laïcité ou religion nouvelle*.

52. Crossley, *Edgar Quinet (1803–1875)*, 58. Edgar Quinet, *Le christianisme et la révolution française*, 161, 191.

53. Quinet, *Le christianisme et la révolution*, 13.

54. Quinet, *Le christianisme et la révolution*, 169–70.

55. Quinet, *Le christianisme et la révolution*, 176.

56. Quinet, *Le christianisme et la révolution*, 177.

57. Quinet, *Le christianisme et la révolution*, 179.

58. Quinet, *Le christianisme et la révolution*, 180.

59. Quinet, *Le christianisme et la révolution*, 178.

60. Renan, *De la part des peuples sémitiques*, 27–28. See also Laurens, "L'islam dans la pensée française," 525–26. George Trumbull has argued that this negative association of Catholic and Islamic politics could move in the other direction too, colonial administrators in Algeria considering Muslim religious orders a threat because they viewed them through the lens of their "anxieties" about religious orders in France. Trumbull, *An Empire of Facts*, 95, 103, 105, 131.

61. Lorcin, *Imperial Identities*, 3.

62. L. Veuillot, *Les Français en Algérie*, 132.

63. L. Veuillot, *Les Français en Algérie*, 17, 13.

64. On the contrary, various mosques were seized and given to Dupuch to convert into churches, for example, although administrators did try to keep Catholic processions and other public provocations to a minimum. See Émerit, "La lutte entre les généraux et les prêtres"; and Curtis, "Emilie de Vialar."

65. L. Veuillot, *Les Français en Algérie*, 147–48.

66. L. Veuillot, *Les Français en Algérie*, 154–55.

67. L. Veuillot, *Les Français en Algérie*, 168.

68. For a valuable discussion of the racism and hypocrisy underlying the French use of the term *razzia*, see Gallois, "Dahra and the History of Violence," 3–25.

69. Louis Veuillot, "La Croisade en Algérie," *L'Univers*, June 29, 1847.

70. On the missionary roots of the "noble savage" trope, see Healy, "The French Jesuits," 143–67.

71. L. Veuillot, *Les Français en Algérie*, 21.

72. See Louis Veuillot, "L'islamisme algérien en France," *L'Univers*, May 26, 1868.

73. L. Veuillot, *Les Français en Algérie*, 173.

74. L. Veuillot, *Les Français en Algérie*, 171.

75. Prudhomme, *Missions chrétiennes*, 67–68.

76. See Milbach, "Les catholiques libéraux," 9–34; and Moody, "The French Catholic Press," 394–415.

77. Milbach, "Les catholiques libéraux," 9–10; Moody, The French Catholic Press," 402.

78. Riancey, *De la situation religieuse*, 3–5, 22.

79. Riancey, *De la situation religieuse*, 13–14.

80. Riancey, *De la situation religieuse*, 28.

81. Riancey, *De la situation religieuse*, 17–20; qt. 18.

82. Anonymous, *De la conversion de musulmans*, 15–16, 26–27.

83. Anonymous, *De la conversion de musulmans*, 34.

84. Anonymous, *De la conversion de musulmans*, 36.

85. See Anonymous, *Eugène Boré supérieur général des Lazaristes*.

86. See Harrison, *Romantic Catholics*.

87. Boré, *Correspondance et mémoires*, 6, 11, 13, 101, 121. For other Catholic apologists who were romantic orientalists and used comparative religion, see Schwab, *The Oriental Renaissance*, 209, 216, 220–21.

88. Anonymous, *Eugène Boré supérieur général des Lazaristes*, 142. Even before the two met, L. Veuillot had already warmly reviewed Boré's travel writings in the pages of *L'Univers*, highlighting Boré's theme that the July Monarchy should take a more active role in supporting Catholicism in the "profoundly religious" Orient. See L. Veuillot, "Le Portefeuille de Louis Veuillot," in *L'Univers*, April 28, 1894 (reprint of an article from October 26, 1840).

89. See the admiring letters Boré wrote to L. Veuillot which were reprinted by Eugène Veuillot in the July 14, 1894, issue of *L'Univers*. And Pierrard, *Louis Veuillot*, 45, 52–53.

90. See "Lettres sur le Liban," *L'Univers*, August 30, 1848; and September 4, 8, 10, 18, and 25 September, 1848.

91. Boré visited Algeria in 1851 as a companion to then-superior general of the Lazarists Jean-Baptiste Etienne, and again in 1877, as superior general himself. On this latter trip, undertaken one year before his death, he was as preoccupied as ever with the prospects of an apostolate to the Muslims, reportedly taking every opportunity to speak to Arabs "in their own language," and bringing up the possibility of "the conversion of this race" to any Frenchman who would listen. Chevalier, "voyage de notre très-honoré père," 345.

92. Boré, *Correspondance et mémoires*, 294.

93. Boré, "Mémoire adressé aux Conseils centraux," 94.

94. Eugène Boré, Report to the Paris Council of the Œuvre de la Propagation de la Foi, October 24, 1842, E-32, Fonds Lyon, Archives de l'œuvre de la Propagation de la Foi, Lyon (now the Œuvres Pontificales Missionnaires, hereafter OPM). On the influence of the OEuvre de la Propagation de la Foi, see Daughton, *An Empire Divided*, 34–41.

95. See Anonymous [Thomas Dazincourt], *Notice sur M. Joseph Girard*, 43-44, 106; and Jean-Baptiste Etienne to Lyon Council of the Œuvre de la Propagation de la Foi, March 25, 1844, I-23, Fonds Lyon, OPM.

96. Eugène Boré to Council of the Œuvre de la Propagation de la Foi, March 3, 1851, G-8, Fonds Lyon, OPM.

97. Notes from a session of the Council of the Œuvre de la Propagation de la Foi, May 9, 1851, E-32, Fonds Lyon, OPM.

98. Eugène Boré to Council of the Œuvre de la Propagation de la Foi, 3 March 1851.

99. See notes from the session of the Lyon Council of the Œuvre de la Propagation de la Foi, May 9, 1851. The Council voted another allocation for the catechumenate—this one smaller than the first—but once again nothing seems to have come from Boré's hopes to relocate Ottoman converts to Algiers. See Anonymous [Thomas Dazincourt], *Notice sur M. Joseph Girard*; and M. Joseph Girard's numerous letters of 1851, dossier 108a: Alger, Archives de la Congrégation de la Mission (Lazarists) (ACM), Paris.

100. Islam's alleged status as a Christian heresy dates back to medieval Christian apologetics. See Daniel, *Islam and the West*, 184–94.

101. These words are not Boré's but Julia Clancy-Smith's, describing the mission philosophy of Abbé François Bourgade, a French missionary in Tunisia in the 1840s and 1850s who emphasized continuities between Islam and the Gospel, and consequently advocated dialogue with Muslims. I have not been able to verify the source of the brief quotation within her quotation, but it is an apt description of Veuillot's and Boré's approach. Clancy-Smith, *Mediterraneans*, 270.

102. See L. Veuillot, *Les Français en Algérie*, "La controverse," 344 and following.

103. L. Veuillot, *Correspondance de Louis Veuillot*, 101.

104. Boré, "Hérésies chrétiennes," 321–22.

105. Boré, "Hérésies chrétiennes," 322, 325.

106. Boré, "Hérésies chrétiennes," 336.

107. Boré, "Hérésies chrétiennes," 337.

108. Boré, *Correspondance et mémoires*, 295.

109. Boré, *Correspondance et mémoires*, 296.

110. Boré, *Correspondance et mémoires*, 297.

111. See Claire Fredj's narrative of missionary attempts in the early years of colonial Algeria. Fredj, "Une mission impossible?," 163–229.

112. Heyberger and Madinier, "Introduction," 7–8.

113. Said, *Orientalism*, 137–39, 268–72.

114. See "Kreeft-Spencer debate on Islam," November 10, 2010. https://www.catholic-culture.org/news/headlines/index.cfm?storyid=8229 (accessed April 16, 2022)

115. L. Veuillot, *Les Français en Algérie*, 156, 159.

116. L. Veuillot, *Les Français en Algérie*, 156.

117. L. Veuillot, *Les Français en Algérie*, 168.

118. L. Veuillot, *Les Français en Algérie*, 114, 130.

119. Like the Romantic Socialists studied by Naomi Andrews, who expressed "grudging respect for Muslim religious devotion," Veuillot's admiration often seems more about condemning the soullessness and excessive militarism of the colonial project than it was about any genuine concern for Algerian lives and liberty. See Andrews, "Selective Empathy," 15–16.

120. E. Veuillot, *Louis Veuillot*, 246 and ff.

121. I owe this apt description to Chantal Verdeil, email communication, September 11, 2014.

122. E. Veuillot, *Louis Veuillot*, 246 and ff.

123. E. Veuillot, *Louis Veuillot*, 254–60.

124. L. Veuillot, *Les Français en Algérie*, 25.

125. L. Veuillot, *Les Français en Algérie*, 170.

126. Pierrard, *Louis Veuillot* 15.

127. See Luizard, "Introduction," 9–35. I am paraphrasing Luizard here, who calls *civilisation* the imperial *maître mot*, or keyword.

128. Luizard, "Introduction," 12–13.

129. See also Louis Veuillot, "La Croisade en Algérie," *L'Univers*, June 29, 1847.

130. Kselman, *Miracles and Prophecies.*

131. L. Veuillot, *Les odeurs de Paris*, 424.

132. L. Veuillot, *Les odeurs de Paris*, 439–40.

133. Amanat, "Introduction: Apocalyptic Anxieties."

134. On the Biblical parable of the wheat and tares as an affirmation of the "ambivalence" of history, see Maritain, *On the Philosophy of History*, 43–57.

135. Maistre, *The Pope*, 240.

136. M. L. Brown, *Louis Veuillot*, 78–86.

137. L. Veuillot, *Les Français en Algérie*, 69.

138. See also L. Veuillot, "L'islamisme algérien en France."

139. Cf. Warner, "The Question of Faith," 38–39.

140. Keller, *L'encyclique du 8 décembre*, 153.

141. Gautier, *Études et controverses historiques*, 133.

142. Alzon, "La Croix," 4.

143. Prudhomme, *Missions chrétiennes*, 87; and Daughton, *An Empire Divided.*

144. Daughton, *An Empire Divided*, 19. For the modern-day "Clash of Civilizations" narrative, pitting liberalism against "Islam," see Huntington, "The Clash of Civilizations?"

145. Said, *Orientalism*, 137–39; Olender, *The Languages of Paradise*; Renan, *De la part des peuples sémitiques*; Gobineau, *Comte de Gobineau and Orientalism*; Trumbull, *An Empire of Facts*; Reig, "L'orientalisme savant," 632–49; Vaux, *Le Mahométisme.*

Chapter 2

1. "La Supression des Jésuites," 200; also cited in Cubitt, *The Jesuit Myth*, 45.

2. Padberg, *Colleges in Controversy*, 7. This entire paragraph is indebted to Padberg.

3. See Michelet and Quinet, *Des Jésuites*; and Cubitt, *The Jesuit Myth*, 7–8.

4. Lalouette, *La république anticléricale*, 364.

5. M. Lapame, commissaire civil, "Service du culte catholique à Constantine," Cultes Série: F19 6215, Archives Nationales, Paris [hereafter AN].

6. Letter from Minister of War to Governor General of Algeria, 13 April, 1847, Archives Nationales, Centre des Archives d'Outre-Mer, Aix-en-Provence [hereafter ANOM], F80 1628.

7. See, for example, Daughton, *An Empire Divided*, 22; and Prudhomme, *Missions chretiennes*, 88.

8. Cf. Direche-Slimani, *Chrétiens de Kabylie*; and Fredj, "Une mission impossible?," 163–229.

9. Saaïdia, *Algérie coloniale*, 194–95.

10. As parish priests, the Jesuits at Constantine preserved a dual, ambiguous status, reporting both to their own congregational superiors at Lyon and Rome, as well as being subordinated to the "secular" Church hierarchy of the Concordat.

11. See, for example, Michelet and Quinet, *Des Jésuites*; Cubitt, *The Jesuit Myth*; Padberg, *Colleges in Controversy*; and Gibson, *A Social History of French Catholicism*, 104.

Gibson argues that regular clergy such as the Jesuits were subject to much more anticlerical hostility than secular clergy because they violated Enlightenment ideas of "utility" or usefulness.

12. Letter from the Minister of Justice and of Cults to the Minister of War, June 14, 1844; Letter from the Maréchal Bugeaud to the Minister of War, August 8, 1844; and Letter from M. Du Rodan, Procureur Général at Algiers to the Minister of War, August 11, 1844, all in Cultes Série: F19 6223, AN.

13. Prudhomme, *Missions chretiennes*, 87.

14. Surkis, *Sex, Law, and Sovereignty*, 1–2.

15. Qtd. in Oisila Saaïdia, "L'anticléricalisme article d'exportation?," 101.

16. Cf. Comaroff and Comaroff, "Home-Made Hegemony," 38–39.

17. Prudhomme, *Missions chretiennes*, 67–68.

18. Chantal Verdeil, email communication, September 11, 2014.

19. Curtis, "Emilie de Vialar," 261–92; and Curtis, *Civilizing Habits*, 101–73.

20. Qtd. in Riancey, *De la situation religieuse*, 33–34.

21. Chambre des députés, January 17 and 18, 1839. Chambre des députés, *Archives parlementaires de 1787 à 1860*, 428–40.

22. Minister of War to Maréchal Valée, July 17, 1839, F80 1625, ANOM.

23. Minister of War to Maréchal Valée, August 17, 1839, F80 1627, ANOM.

24. Minister of War to Maréchal Valée, August 17, 1839. The Minister insisted that this and his previous note on surveilling religion in Algeria be kept confidential.

25. Anonymous, "Note pour le Directeur," Ministère de la Guerre, Direction des Affaires de l'Algérie, October 1846, F80 1746, ANOM. On female religious congregations in Algeria, cf. Curtis, "Emilie de Vialar"; and Curtis, *Civilizing Habits*.

26. Letter from Minister of War to Duc d'Aumale (Governor General), January 20, 1848, F80 1628, ANOM.

27. Anonymous [but clearly Joseph Girard], "Alger et Kouba: 1843 et annees suivantes," 6bis, dossier 106B (32): Algérie, ACM.

28. As we have seen, Eugene Boré, the orientalist-turned-Lazarist missionary, tried to use Algeria and the Lazarist mission there as a refuge for Ottoman converts. When Boré attempted to reestablish this refuge again in 1851, Père Girard also began surreptitiously catechizing some Algerian Muslim children along with the refugees from Constantinople. But no sooner had the catechumenate begun then Girard was denounced for "kidnapping" these children, since not all had received their parents' permission to be there. See letters from Girard to Étienne [Lazarist Superior General], October 19, 1851 and November 24, 1851, in dossier 108a: Alger; and letter from Etienne to Boré, January 17, 1852, in Fonds de Saint-Benoît de Constantinople, Supérieurs généraux, carton VIII, dossier I, Correspondance de M. Étienne avec M. Boré, 1843–1865, ACM.

29. Anonymous [but clearly Girard], "Alger et Kouba: 1843 et annees suivantes," 8bis, 34bis. For more on Girard and the Lazarists' "precocious" attempts to establish an apostolate among Algeria's Muslims, see Claire Fredj, "Une mission impossible?," 163–229.

30. Cubitt, *The Jesuit Myth*, 105–42.

31. Moulin, "Alger," 146.

32. Moulin, "Alger." This whole paragraph draws heavily from Moulin, especially p. 143.

33. Moulin, "Ben-Aknoun," 595.

34. Moulin, "Ben-Aknoun," 591–602.

35. See Turin, "Enfants trouvés, colonisation et utopie," 329–56.

36. Cf. Francis, "Catholic Missionaries," 690–91.

37. See *Journal des Débats Politiques et Littéraires*, June 13, 1844.

38. Letter from the Minister of Justice and of Cults to the Minister of War, June 14, 1844, Cultes Série: F19 6223, AN.

39. Moulin, "Alger," 145–46.

40. Letter from the Maréchal Bugeaud to the Minister of War, August 8, 1844, Cultes Série: F19 6223, AN.

41. Maréchal Bugeaud to the Minister of War, August, 1844.

42. M. Artaud to the Minister of War, 25 March, 1845, Cultes Série: F19 6223, AN.

43. Anonymous report, "Communautés religieuses en Algérie," August 28, 1848, 16H 114, ANOM.

44. Saaïdia distinguishes between anticlerical debates that were reflections of metropolitan conflicts—such as religious processions, right of religious burial, etc.—and debates specific to the colonial context, such as the question of Muslim conversion. Saaïdia, *Algérie coloniale*, 153–54.

45. Nouschi, "Introduction," 20.

46. Brebner, "The Impact of Thomas-Robert Bugeaud," 6.

47. Kateb, *Européens, "indigènes," et juifs en Algérie*, 71–74.

48. See Cole, *Lethal Provocation*, 15–17.

49. Bernard Pagand, *La médina de Constantine*, 123–30.

50. In 1846, when the European population in Algiers had overtaken that of the "indigènes," Constantine still counted some 15,000 Muslims (and more than 3,000 indigenous "Israelites") against fewer than 2,000 Europeans. And two decades later, in 1866, the Muslim population alone (not counting the previously "indigenous" but soon-to-be naturalized Jews) was still more than twice as large as the European population. *Tableau de la situation des établissements français dans l'Algérie, 1845–46*, 87, 96; and *Tableau de la situation des établissements français dans l'Algérie, 1865–66*, 30.

51. While the eventual effect of this decree was to segregate the population, trapping Muslim Algerians in the oldest and most crowded housing, it did prevent the Europeanization of the original city. Brebner, "The Impact of Thomas-Robert Bugeaud," 6–12; and Cole, *Lethal Provocation*, 22.

52. Nouschi, "Introduction," 20, 22.

53. Pagand, *La médina de Constantine*, 18.

54. Suchet, *Lettres édifiantes et curieuses*, 13.

55. The quoted phrase is in Grangaud, "Un point de vue local, " 97–115; Dournon, "Constantine sous les Turcs," 155–56; and Boudjada, "L'église catholique de Constantine."

56. Pagand, *La médina de Constantine*, 24–26; 30; and Nouschi, "Introduction," 20.

57. Pagand, "De la ville arabe à la ville européenne," 281–94.

58. Tournier, *La conquête religieuse de l'Algérie*, 71–72. I owe this point and this reference to Curtis, *Civilizing Habits*, 124. Whereas the West was dominated by "sharifian aristocracies"—tribal leaders like Abd-el-Kader, who claimed descent from the Prophet and the right to "combine political and religious roles" and resist the colonizers—the East was marked by an organized class of 'ulama and religious scholars, urbanized and centralized at Constantine, who saw themselves as having no overtly political authority, and who were quickly brought under the control of the French. See Christelow, *Muslim Law Courts*, 28–32.

59. Suchet, *Lettres édifiantes et curieuses sur l'Algérie*, 24. As Boudjada points out, Suchet described a scene where the Muslim notables of the city even eagerly offered him a beautiful pulpit for the church. Boudjada, "L'église catholique de Constantine."

60. Suchet, *Lettres édifiantes et curieuses sur l'Algérie*, 24.

61. Suchet, *Lettres édifiantes et curieuses sur l'Algérie*, 24.

62. Suchet, *Lettres édifiantes et curieuses sur l'Algérie*, 26.

63. Suchet, *Lettres édifiantes et curieuses sur l'Algérie*, 30. On his way back to Algiers to take up his post as vicar general, Suchet complained that he was beginning "to breathe the contagious air of the *civilisation* of Algiers... Oh! I loved the pure air of my *sauvage* Constantine better." Suchet, *Lettres édifiantes et curieuses sur l'Algérie*, 94.

64. "Abregé de l'Histoire de la Residence de Constantine," RAl 80, Archives de la Compagnie de Jésus, Province de France, Vanves [hereafter ACJF]. See also Rosette, "Constantine," 1552. Rosette says that Lasserre began his functions in March of 1841.

65. Rosette, "Constantine," 1553.

66. Letter from P. [Pierre] Lasserre, Constantine, to a *Père* of the same society, Lyon, December 3, 1841, RAl 2, ACJF.

67. Letter from P. [Pierre] Lasserre, Constantine, to a *Père* of the same society, Lyon, December 3, 1841.

68. Letter from P. [Pierre] Lasserre, Constantine, to a *Père* of the same society, Lyon, December 3, 1841.

69. "Abregé de l'Histoire de la Residence de Constantine, " p. 2, RAl 80, ACJF; and Maurice de Fenoyl, S.J., "Notes sur la residence S. J. de Constantine" (typed manuscript), March 1990, p. 2, RAl 80, ACJF. De Fenoyl's manuscript is a "hasty survey" and copies references made in the Jesuit Archives at Constantine (diaries, in-house histories, reports of visiting provincial superiors, etc.) to the *mission arabe*. Given that the Jesuit missions in Algeria and Syria both fell under the direction of the Lyon province, Jesuits would sometimes circulate between the two mission fields, perhaps reinforcing an interest in "the Arab world" and language. Verdeil, *La mission jésuite du Mont-Liban*, 79, 81.

70. See de Fenoyl, "Notes sur la residence S. J. de Constantine," p. 3, RAl 80, ACJF.

71. "Abregé de l'Histoire de la Residence de Constantine, " p. 4, RAl 80, ACJF.

72. If such a measure were indeed taken, it would likely not have been to prevent Muslims from learning a little about Catholicism, but rather to prevent intercommunal conflicts from erupting in the Church—conflicts perhaps more likely to be provoked by inhospitable Christians themselves. See Père Girard: "in my beginnings here

I sometimes saw in the church of *N.D. des Victoires* some young Mohammedan people but when the Spanish men and women noticed them they fell on them and with blows and threats quickly forced them out. Now one never sees them in the churches of the province of Algiers." See Anonymous [Joseph Girard], "Alger et Kouba: 1843 et années suivantes," 30 – 30bis, dossier 106B (32): Algérie, ACM.

73. Burnichon, "L'Algérie," 400.

74. See also Letter from Viot to Paris Council of the Œuvre de la Propagation de la Foi, October 14, 1848, in dossier G-8: Alger, Fonds Paris, Archives de l'Œuvre de la Propagation de la Foi, Lyon (now the Œuvres Pontificales Missionnaires [hereafter OPM]); and de Fenoyl, "Notes sur la residence S. J. de Constantine," p. 3, RAl 80, ACJF.

75. Creuzat to Superior General, Constantine, April 22, 1849, Missio Algeriensis, series 1001-VIII, Archivum Romanum Societatis Iesu, Rome [hereafter ARSI].

76. Cf. Županov, *Disputed Mission*, 22–23. On Matteo Ricci, see Wu, *From Christ to Confucius*, 19–20.

77. See Ugo Colonna, "La Compagnie de Jesus en Algérie," 68-78; and also Sievernich, "Jesuit Theologies of Mission," 44–58, esp. 44–45.

78. Letter from March 8, 1847, qtd. in Moulin, "Alger," and found in dossier RAl 2 (large poster gathering quotes about the *mission arabe*), ACJF.

79. Letter from Louis de Baudicour to Paris Council of the Œuvre de la Propagation de la Foi, Blidah, June 28, 1850, dossier G-8: Alger, Fonds Paris, OPM.

80. "Le peu d'action du Christianisme sur le Mahométisme est un mystère," in the original. Notes taken during the Conseil de Lyon's séance of November 23, 1849, dossier I-16: Jésuites, 1835–1867, Fonds Lyon, OPM.

81. Cf. Brumauld to [Superior Provincial?], December 10, 1849, Fonds Prat, vol. 10, ACJF. Letter from Monseigneur Pavy to Council of the Œuvre de la Propagation de la Foi, February 2, 1850; and letter from Plasse to Dartignes, June 14, 1850, dossier G-7: Alger, Fonds Lyon, OPM.

82. Schembri, in particular, refused to help with the little catechumenate because he was discouraged by the government's resistance to his missions around Sétif. Baulard to Provincial Superior, March 2, 1850, and April 24, 1850, both in Fonds Prat, vol. 10[?], ACJF.

83. Baulard to Superior General, Ben Aknoun, November 15, 1851, Missio Algeriensis, series 1001-VII, ARSI.

84. Brumauld to [Propagation of Faith?], February 5, 1851, Fonds Prat, vol. 10, ACJF.

85. Francis, "Catholic Missionaries." See also the statistics in Rogers, *A Frenchwoman's Imperial Story*, 122–23.

86. Meyer to Superior General, Algiers, October 4, 1853, Missio Algeriensis, series 1001-VII, ARSI.

87. Pavy, *Monseigneur Pavy*, 459–60.

88. Pavy, *Monseigneur Pavy*, 460.

89. Letter from Louis-Antoine-Augustin, Évêque d'Alger [Bishop Pavy], to the Minister of War, Aix, September 23, 1850, Cultes Série: F19 6214, AN.

90. Letter from Bishop Pavy to Minister of War, September 23, 1850.

91. Minute of letter from the Minister of War to Monseigneur Pavy, October 5, 1850, in Cultes Série: F19 6214, AN.

92. Cf. Clancy-Smith, *Rebel and Saint*, 35, 117.

93. See J. W. Peterson, "Honor, Excrement, Ethnography."

94. See Lorcin, *Imperial Identities*, 99–117.

95. Abi-Mershed, *Apostles of Modernity*, esp. 8, 90–93.

96. In this they were not unlike the later, interwar "colonial humanists" described by Gary Wilder, who hoped simultaneously "to protect and to transform native society" in West Africa. Wilder, *The French Imperial Nation-State*, 80.

97. Abi-Mershed, *Apostles of Modernity*, 5, 7, 16, 107, 167–68.

98. Urbain, *L'Algérie pour les Algériens*, 29-31. (Both of these citations are also singled out by Levallois in his preface).

99. Conseil Dumesnil to sub-divisional commander at Constantine, November 10, 1850, 1/K/369 (Bureaux arabes Constantine), ANOM.

100. Devoluet to sub-divisional commander at Bône, November 17, 1850, 1/K/369 (Bureaux arabes Constantine), ANOM.

101. Abi-Mershed, *Apostles of Modernity*, 8, 90–93.

102. Commanding officer at subdivision of Constantine to "Mon général," November 19, 1850, 1/K/369 (Bureaux arabes Constantine), ANOM.

103. Devoluet to subdivisional commander at Bône, November 17, 1850, 1/K/369 (Bureaux arabes Constantine), ANOM.

104. Commander of subdivision of Bône to Division of Constantine, November 21, 1850, 1/K/369 (Bureaux arabes Constantine), ANOM.

105. See Schreier, *Arabs of the Jewish Faith*. On shared North African culture, see Katz, *Burdens of Brotherhood*.

106. Schreier, *Arabs of the Jewish Faith*, 2.

107. Schreier, *Arabs of the Jewish Faith*, 10, 2–4.

108. Throughout these paragraphs, I am indebted to Schreier, *Arabs of the Jewish Faith*, especially 143-76. On the later history of this choice to make Algerian Jews French, see Benjamin Stora, *Les trois exils*, 13. Schreier, *Arabs of the Jewish Faith*, quotes Stora, 11. Cf. Katz, *Burdens of Brotherhood*. In the wake of the Algerian War and decolonization in 1962, the majority of Algeria's Jews emigrated to France. Though most had never set foot in France, like other *pieds-noirs*, they were accepted as French citizens, while Algerian Muslims saw their citizenship revoked. Stora, *Les trois exils*, 9–10; and Shepard, *Invention of Decolonization*, 230–42. See also Stein, *Saharan Jews*.

109. Cf. the (to my mind fair) criticism of Charon's leading question in the otherwise polemical Pavy, *Monseigneur Pavy*, 488–89.

110. "We have many reasons to fear that in the cities, our efforts may remain powerless for yet a long time. It would be therefore among the tribes that the missionary should go fix his tent." Letter from [illegible – Creuzat?] to Monseigneur Pavy, February 15, 1850, in Fonds Prat, vol. 10, ACJF. On the ideal of an uncorrupted "hinterland" mission, see Sanneh, *Translating the Message*, 162–63.

111. Cf. Abi-Mershed, *Apostles of Modernity*, 94.

112. Governor General Charon to Minister of War, January 1851, 16H 114, ANOM.

113. I owe this way of thinking about "secularization" to Asad, *Formations of the Secular.*

114. Clancy-Smith, *Rebel and Saint*, 35, 117.

115. Governor General Charon to Minister of War, January 1851, 16H 114, ANOM.

116. Like the interwar French officials studied in Davidson, *Only Muslim.*

117. Pavy, *Monseigneur Pavy*, 489.

118. See references to "civilisation chrétienne" in chapter 1.

119. See Louis de Baudicour, "Correspondance de particulière de *L'Univers*," *L'Univers*, November 1, 1850; Letter from Louis de Baudicour to Paris Council of the Œuvre de la Propagation de la Foi, March 15, 1851, dossier G-8: Alger, Fonds Paris, OPM; and Louis Veuillot, "Une personne digne de confiance . . .," *L'Univers*, November 29, 1850, p. 2. On Baudicour, see Gourinard, *Les royalistes en Algérie*, 154–57. My thanks to Mr. Gourinard for his kind hospitality in allowing me to consult his private collection of Baudicour's correspondence.

120. I was helped in articulating this point by a conversation with Oissila Saaïdia.

121. Quoted in *L'Univers*, November 9, 1851.

122. Qtd. in "Assemblée legislative . . . *Séance du 7 novembre*," *L'Univers*, November 8, 1851.

123. Article by Roux-Lavergne, in *L'Univers*, November 10, 1851.

124. Article by Léon Aubineau, in *L'Univers*, November 13, 1851.

Chapter 3

1. Letter from Henri Ducat to Louis [Khoudja], Fort National, June 21, 1872, pp. 80–81, RAl 105, ACJF,. I do not know if this letter was ever delivered.

2. Henri Ducat, "Croquis ou aperçu d'un Plan de Mission Arabe," March 23, 1861(?), Constantine, Missio Algeriensis, series 1002-XIV, ARSI.

3. "Projet de règlement, prières, cantiques," dossier B-8: Orphelins, Fonds Lavigerie, Archives General of the Missionaries of Africa, Rome (hereafter AGMAfr.).

4. Jordan to Père General, Constantine, October 4, 1851, Missio Algeriensis, series 1001-III, ARSI.

5. One such attempt to open an orphanage at Oued Jacoub outside Constantine failed "because the Arab children preferred the nomadic and free life to the regular and civilized life," but the Jesuits continued to welcome children at their house in Constantine—giving religious instruction to those who came for French courses or to receive some charity—and even offering French lessons in the evenings to "Turcos," members of France's indigenous troops. "Abregé de l'Histoire de la Residence de Constantine," p. 5, RAl 80, ACJF. See also Fenoyl, "Notes sur la residence S. J. de Constantine," p.4–5, RAl 80, ACJF.

6. Cf. conflicts between Pavy and the Jesuits at Constantine, in Letters from Pavy to [Lyon Provincial?], January 15, 1855; November 9, 1855, Fonds Prat, vol. 23, ACJF.

7. Reynaud, "Memorial of the Provincial's Visit," April 22, 1857, RAl 97, ACJF.

8. Reynaud, "Memorial of the Provincial's Visit," April 22, 1857.

9. Reynaud to Superior General, Algiers, January 20, 1857, Missio Algeriensis, series 1002-I, ARSI.

10. Letters from Reynaud to Superior General, March 3 and June 3, 1857, Missio Algeriensis, series 1002-I, ARSI..

11. Ducat, "Faits principaux relatifs à l'Association de prières à N. D. d'Afrique pour la conversion des musulmans, 1857–1869," p. 1, RAl 44, ACJF.

12. Ducat, "Faits principaux relatifs . . .," p. 1.

13. The Jesuit Henri Ramière founded the more general-purpose "Apostolate of Prayer"—complete with a regular publication which recommended topics for prayer—around the same time Ducat was founding his Association de prières à N. D. d'Afrique pour la conversion des musulmans. On the "intransigence" of the "Pères de Lyon" and the Apostolate of Prayer, see Dumons, "Jésuites Lyonnais," 132–33, 135. See also Verdeil, *La mission jésuite*, 79, 97–98.

14. Ducat, "Faits principaux relatifs . . .," p. 2.

15. Articles of the Association de prières à N. D. d'Afrique pour la conversion des musulmans (Association of Prayers to Our Lady of Africa for the Conversion of the Muslims), in Ducat, "Faits principaux relatifs . . .," p. 7–8.

16. Ducat, "Faits principaux relatifs . . .," p. 9.

17. Ducat, "Faits principaux relatifs . . .," p. 14.

18. Pavy, "Discours, prononcé dans la cathédrale d'Alger," 1263–67, 1275.

19. Veuillot, "Notre Dame d'Afrique," *L'Univers*, June 21, 1858. It was none other than Veuillot who authored the article about the chapel's construction, quoting from and inspired by an appeal Pavy had written. It is interesting that Veuillot followed Pavy's very anti-Islamic approach in this case. Perhaps Pavy had won Veuillot over after *l'Univers* published Louis de Baudicour's denunciations of Pavy in 1850-51; or perhaps Veuillot's own trajectory is emblematic of the larger disillusionment with Algerian Muslims experienced by French Catholics in this period.

20. Ducat, "Faits principaux relatifs . . .," p. 7.

21. Ducat, ""Faits principaux relatifs . . .," p. 34, 52. For the boys given names, see the description of their baptism in Henri Ducat, "Histoire de la Constantine, chrétienne, baptêmes . . .," p. 47, RAl 97, ACJF.

22. "Algérie. Constantine. Extrait d'une lettre [from the Père Quenille]," *Lettres de Fourvières, 1859–1869*, vol. SL 48, ACJF.

23"Algérie. Constantine. Extrait d'une lettre [from the Père Quenille]," *Lettres de Fourvières, 1859–1869*, vol. SL 48, ACJF; and "Algérie: Extrait d'une lettre du P. Ducat, Constantine, 23 Mars 1860," *Lettres de Fourvières, 1859–1869*, vol. SL 48, ACJF.

24. "Algérie: Extrait d'une lettre du P. Ducat, Constantine, 23 Mars 1860."

25. Ducat, "Faits principaux relatifs . . .," p. 44.

26. Ducat, "Histoire de la Constantine, chrétienne, baptêmes . . .," p. 47.

27. On Mortara, see Leff, "Jews, Liberals and the Civilizing Mission," 119.

28. Joseph Girard to Superior Etienne, Kouba, November 24, 1851, dossier 108a: Alger, ACM.

29. See "Deux Nouveaux Mortara," *La lanterne: Journal politique quotidien*, February 1, 1881.

30. Cf. Entry from December 10, 1871, "Diaire Mission Arabe Constantine, 1871–1872," RAl 81, ACJF, where some ten years later, now working at the Maison Carrée (Mgr. Lavigerie's seminary and orphanage outside of Algiers), Ducat explained the story of St. Stanislas to the orphans.

31. On these two patron saints, see Van Ortroy, "St. Stanislas Kostka."; and James Martin, S.J. "Who was the real St. Aloysius Gonzaga?" *America: The Jesuit Review*, June 21, 2015, https://www.americamagazine.org/faith/2015/06/21/who-was-real-st-aloysius-gonzaga-218568.

32. Ducat, "Feuilleton: Constantine, Première Partie, Le Pays (Suite)," 10 September 10, 1875(7: 327), 441. And despite the Islamic prohibition to represent the human figure, Ducat was happy to note, the Muslim children had "loved to copy the engravings" of Louis of Gonzaga and Stanislas Kostka—one more evidence that "the French influence was beginning to make itself felt."

33. Ducat, " Feuilleton: Constantine . . .," *Les missions catholiques* 9, no. 406 (March 16, 1877): 130–31. On these corporations, see Chenntouf, "L'évolution du travail," 89. On the brothers' father, and El Hadj's role in their and other baptisms, see Henri Ducat, "Histoire de la Constantine, chrétienne, baptêmes . . .," pp. 47–49, RAl 97, ACJF.

34. Topinard, "Rapport sur la population indigène," 548–55, 550; and "Berbers," 606.

35. Topinard, "Rapport sur la population indigène," 548–55, 549; and Cote, "Biskra," p. 3.

36. On Biskra as a site of anti-French, apocalyptic resistance and rumor throughout this paragraph, see Clancy-Smith, "La révolte de BÛ Ziyân en Algérie" esp. paras. 3, 6–7, 13–17, 30, 33.

37. Ducat, "Constantine, 23 mars 1860," *Lettres de Fourvières, 1859–1869*, vol. SL 48, ACJF.

38. Ducat, "Constantine, 23 mars 1860."

39. "Mustapha Ben El Hadj Otman" would fight in engagements ranging from the Franco-Prussian War to the French occupation of Tunisia, eventually being promoted to *chef de bataillon*. See *Le Gaulois*, March 25, 1890. On Moustafa and his sister Louise, see Ducat, letter to [?], December 31, 1865, Ducat file, Fonds Prat, vol. 21, ACJF.

40. See Rogers, *A Frenchwoman's Imperial Story*, 79–91, 120–36.

41. See Grangaud, "Un point de vue local."

42. F. Colonna, "Le système d'enseignement," 195–220, esp. 198–99.

43. Grangaud, "Un point de vue local."

44. Schreier, *Arabs of the Jewish Faith*, 120.

45. Rogers, *A Frenchwoman's Imperial Story*, 124, 128.

46. Rogers, *A Frenchwoman's Imperial Story*, 120, 128–37. My summary of Rogers here is also influenced by Judith Surkis's argument, in *Sex, Law, and Sovereignty*, 48–54, for example.

47. [Ducat?] "Constantine, 28 février 1862," *Lettres de Fourvières, 1859–1869*, vol. SL 48. ACJF.

48. Entry from May 11, 1861, in "Diaire du Ministre [Constantine]: 1850–1862," RAl 89, ACJF.

49. The day when the Arab King *"est allé adorer N.S.J.C."* according to the Jesuits' diary. Entry from January 6, 1864, in "Diaire du Ministre [Constantine]: 1863–1877,"

RAl 89, ACJF. For other moments of mutual hospitality (including the Christmas Eve mentioned), see entries from June 5 and September 26, 1853, in "Diaire du Ministre [Constantine]: 1850–1862"; July 4, July 7, July 27, December 24 and 25, 1861; February 27, March 26, and April 11, 1862, in "Diaire du Ministre [Constantine]: 1863–1877."

50. "Extrait d'une lettre d'un Père de Constantine à un Scholastique de Fourvieres," October 1862(?), in *Lettres de Fourvières, 1859–1869*, vol. SL 48, ACJF. The young evangelist's family name is somewhat illegible, something like "Louis Codsa." Given the unlikelihood of another young Arab convert in Constantine being given the same Christian name, and possessing such a similar family name, the letter seems to be referring to Louis Khoudja. The misspelling may be the product of different ways of transcribing the Arabic alphabet, possibly compounded by an error in the hand-copying done by the *scholastiques* at Fourvieres. Louis' evangelism involved getting the dying man to admit that Muhammad had been a liar, since he had denied that Jesus was the "Son of God," even though every Arab admits Jesus was the "Word of God," and one's "word" can be seen as one's "son."

51. Entry from October 22, 1862, in "Diaire du Ministre [Constantine]: 1850–1862," RAl 89, ACJF.

52. Entry from January 10, 1863, in "Diaire du Ministre [Constantine]: 1863–1877," RAl 89, ACJF; and Ducat, "Faits principaux relatifs . . .," pp. 52–53.

53. Ducat, "Faits principaux relatifs . . .," pp. 53–53.

54. Ducat, "Faits principaux relatifs . . .," pp. 52.

55. Ducat, "Faits principaux relatifs . . .," p.60.

56. Because colonial Algeria was spiritually a "vast and brush-covered" field, Ducat wrote, whenever any "little flower happens to appear.... one must hurry to transplant it into... some less arid place for fear of seeing it soon stifled by thorns or burnt by the desert wind." Ducat, "Faits principaux relatifs . . .," p. 61.

57. Cf. Pervillé, *Les étudiants algériens*, 45, 240–44, 310.

58. Vernet, *Dom Gréa*, 40–42.

59. Vernet, *Dom Gréa*, 43–44.

60. Vernet, *Dom Gréa*, 54.

61. Ducat, "Faits principaux relatifs . . .," p. 63.

62. Echoing the contrasts between Algiers and Constantine drawn by Suchet back in the 1840s and by Pavy in the 1850s, Ducat complained, "At Algiers, the Association of Prayers for the conversion of the Muslims is hardly known . . . . It seems that we are afraid to injure powerful susceptibilities, in letting it be seen that we desire, that we ask for the conversion of the poor Muslims. Much more even than at Constantine, though [Constantine is] three-quarters Arabic, there is need here for an extreme reserve and a regrettable circumspection." In Ducat, "Faits principaux relatifs . . .," p. 64.

63. Ducat, "Faits principaux relatifs . . .," p. 68–69.

64. Entry from October 1, 1866, "Diaire du Ministre [Constantine]: 1863–1877," RAl 89, ACJF.

65. Ducat, "Faits principaux relatifs . . .," p. 69.

66. Cf. Clancy-Smith, *Rebel and Saint*, 33-35; and "Marabout," 325–26.

67. Dirèche-Slimani, *Chrétiens de Kabylie*, 74, 90.

68. Collot, *Les institutions de l'Algérie durant la période colonial: (1830 – 1962)*, 83–85.

69. Dirèche-Slimani, *Chrétiens de Kabylie*, 83. See also Brock, "New Christians as Evangelists," 151.

70. Entry from 26 February 1867, "Diaire du Ministre [Constantine]: 1863–1877, " RAl 89, ACJF.

71. Section on 1864–1868, "Histoire de la Residence de Constantine," RAl 91, ACJF.

72. Ducat, "Faits principaux relatifs . . .," p. 72. Their cousin Louise—El Hadj's daughter—was less fortunate, from the missionaries' perspective, since she too had been brought home from France, yet El Hadj had refused her wish to return to her *Soeurs* at Besançon. The young girl died shortly after these lines were written, and the family gave her a Muslim funeral, without the aid of a priest. See also entry from May 30, 1867, "Diaire du Ministre [Constantine]: 1863–1877," RAl 89, ACJF.

73. Ducat, entry from April 17, 1872, in "Diaires: 1. Seminaire de Maison Carrée 2. Mission de Kabylie 3. Alger, 1872–1874," pp. 35–36, RAl 105, ACJF.

74. "Abregé de l'Histoire de la Residence de Constantine,"p. 8, RAl 80, ACJF.

75. This paragraph is based on entries from June 19, 25, 27, 1876; July 5, 8, 9, 1876; August 3, 5, 7, 15, 1876; and June 20, 1877, in "Diaire Mission Arabe, 1876–1883," RAl 50, ACJF.

76. Fogarty and Osborne, "Constructions and Functions of Race," 206–7.

77. Stoler, *Carnal Knowledge*, 118. On the use of visible "markers of difference" as evidence of interior religious states in Morisco age Spain, see Agresta, "Culturally Muslim."

78. Section on 1864-1868, "Histoire de la Residence de Constantine," RAl 91, ACJF.

79. Entry from July 9, 1876, in "Diaire Mission Arabe, 1876–1883," RAl 50, ACJF.

80. Entry from April 1, 1877, in "Diaire Mission Arabe, 1876–1883," RAl 50, ACJF.

81. On the ways colonial ethnography separated colonized populations into discrete units, to better administer those populations, see Trumbull, *An Empire of Facts*.

82. The use of the singular definite article—"*the* Arab"—recalls Edward Said's remark that Orientalist discourse is a kind of "radical realism" that considers the object it describes an abstract, "timeless" reality. Said, qtd. in Bhabha, *The Location of Culture*, 101–2.

83. "Constantine," *Les missions catholiques* 9, no. 404 (March 2, 1877): 106, 108–10.

84. "Constantine: Les Habitants," *Les missions catholiques* 9, no. 405 (March 9, 1877): 118, 119, 120.

85. For Khoudja's French citizenship, see naturalization dossier 4765X86 in BB/11/1924/2, Archives Nationales, Pierrefitte-sur-Seine (hereafter AN). Citation information thanks to an email communication with Agnès D'Angio-Barros at the Archives Nationales, December 22, 2021. My thanks to Joëlle Grest for her help in tracking down Louis Khoudja's marriage certificate. Notarial documents of colonial Algeria have been digitized on the website of Archives Nationales, Centre des Archives d'Outre-Mer, Aix-en-Provence ANOM, "État Civil Numerisé," at http://anom.archivesnationales. culture.gouv.fr/caomec2/.

86. Louis's son Joseph—Léonie's brother—succeeded his father as Tunisian consul at Bône, where he functioned as a kind of "double agent," aiding and abetting France's invasion of Tunisia in the early 1880s, for which France rewarded him with a governorship in the new protectorate. See Clancy-Smith, *Mediterraneans*. On the Allegros specifically, see p. 219, and the footnote on p. 393. For an in-depth study of the Allegros and their milieu, see André Martel, *Luis-Arnold et Joseph Allegro*.

87. His new brother-in-law (Gustave Bonnard, married to another of the Allegro daughters) was also a French lawyer at Bône. Martel, *Luis-Arnold et Joseph Allegro*, 81–82.

88. See Ageron, *Les algériens musulmans*, 430–58.

89. "La Commission d'enquête sur l'Algérie," *La Liberté de Bône*, May 30, 1892, 2; see also t Ageron, "Jules Ferry et la question algeriènne," 137.

90. Khoudja, *À la commission du Senat*.

91. Cf. McDougall, *History and the Culture of Nationalism in Algeria*, 65, 74.

92. McDougall, *History and the Culture of Nationalism in Algeria*, 75.

93. Property legislation such as the Senatus Consulte of 1863, promulgated at the height of Napoleon III and the Bureaux Arabes' protectionist "royaume arabe" period had been on the right track, Khoudja believed, since it had recognized that the indigenes were still "minors" with regards to French civilization, were not ready to enter a liberal property market as individual smallholders, and needed to have their collective tribal lands protected from division. Conversely, the settler-inspired legislation of 1873, which overturned the protections of 1863 and carved tribal lands up into individual titles, had led to the Arabs' "ruin," because it ignored the fact that they had not yet "left childhood" and that they were at the mercy of usurers and speculators. Khoudja, *À la commission du Senat*, 49–53.

94. Khoudja, *À la commission du Senat*, 10.

95. Khoudja, *À la commission du Senat*, 8.

96. Khoudja, *À la commission du Senat*, 35, 38.

97. Khoudja, *À la commission du Senat*, 37–38.

98. Gopal, *Insurgent Empire*, 5, 17.

99. Ageron, *Les algériens musulmans*, 450; see also Smati, *Les elites algeriennes*, 190–91; Merdaci, *Auteurs algériens*, 162–63.

100. Pervillé, *Les étudiants algériens*, 45, 240–44, 310.

101. Pervillé, *Les étudiants algériens*, 12.

102. Smati, *Les elites algeriennes*, 212–13. This sense of "double alienation" is a common theme in twentieth-century, postcolonial accounts of colonial education. Cf. Kane, *Ambiguous Adventure*; and Dangarembga, *Nervous Conditions*.

103. Cf. Clancy-Smith, *Mediterraneans*, 250.

104. Khoudja, *À la commission du Senat*, 16. I follow Smati in citing this passage as evidence of the "double alienation" experienced by educated Algerians like Khoudja; yet the deeply personal character of the passage evaded Smati, since he was not aware of Khoudja's own Jesuit education and sojourns in France. Smati, *Les elites algeriennes*, 212–13.

105. Phrase taken from Županov, *Disputed Mission*, 35.

106. Albert Monshan Wu makes a similar point about the "missionary encounter" in *From Christ to Confucius*, 15–17.

107. In highlighting Khoudja's unique educational trajectory, I only mean to highlight how the missionary encounter encourages religious uncertainty and cross-pollination. Of course, I do not mean that Khoudja and other Algerians, like "Caliban," were merely using a "language learned from and deployed against the colonizer" (Gopal, *Insurgent Empire*, 5); or that Algerians somehow needed the French or the Jesuits to bring

them "modernity," or to teach them about the values of self-government, civil rights, and equality. See James McDougall, "A World No Longer Shared," 18–49. On the ways that "modernity" does not belong to the West, see Cooper, *Colonialism in Question*, esp. 114–49.

108. On the Third Republic shift to racial, civilizational rhetoric, cf. Prudhomme, *Missions chrétiennes*, 69–87; and Daughton, *An Empire Divided*.

109. See Beylard, "Joseph Burnichon," 60.

110. Burnichon, "L'Algérie," 400–403.

111. Burnichon, "L'Algérie," 387, 396.

112. Burnichon, "L'Algérie," 414.

113. On settler resistance to education and assimilation for the indigenous Algerians, cf. F. Colonna, "Le système d'enseignement."

114. Burnichon, "L'Algérie," 396–97.

115. Merdaci, *Auteurs algériens*, 206–7.

116. See Jean de B., "Chronique: La Féodalité Arabe," *La Tafna: Journal de l'arrondissement de Tlemcen*, May 3, 1893; and the extracts published from Khoudja's pamphlet in *El Hack*, January 21, 28, 1894; February 11, 1894.

117. See *El Hack*, September 3, 1893; Luizard, "La politique colonial," 89–120; and Charles-Ageron, "Jules Ferry et la question algeriènne."

Chapter 4

1. See Davide Rodogno, *Against Massacre*, 97–98 and ff.; and Makdisi, *The Culture of Sectarianism*, 138. The quoted phrase is from Rodogno, but these opening paragraphs are also heavily indebted to Makdisi throughout.

2. Fawaz, *An Occasion for War*, 25–26, 78–100; Rodogno, *Against Massacre*, 101.

3. Spagnolo, *France and Ottoman Lebanon*, 30; and Rodogno, *Against Massacre*, 101.

4. Makdisi, *The Culture of Sectarianism*, 126; and Verdeil, *La mission jésuite*, 141.

5. Cf. Fortescue, "Eastern Churches."

6. Makdisi, *The Culture of Sectarianism*, 52–57; for more on the Maronites and the history of sectarianization leading up to 1860, see also Fawaz, *An Occasion for War*; and Hakim, *The Origins of the Lebanese National Idea*, 36–98.

7. Makdisi, *The Culture of Sectarianism*, 61.

8. Makdisi, *The Culture of Sectarianism*, 67–80.

9. Makdisi, *The Culture of Sectarianism*, 90–94, 126.

10. Hakim, *The Origins of the Lebanese National Idea*, 49–53, 67–68. Another excellent summary of the background and violence of 1860 is Jens Hanssen and Hicham Safieddine, esp. chap. 1, "The War of 1860: Roots and Ramifications," in Al-Bustani, *The Clarion of Syria*, 13–22.

11. Cf. letters from Père Rousseau, republished in *Bulletin de l'Œuvre des écoles d'Orient*, no. 10, November 1860.

12. On the events of 1860 and the French response, see also Verdeil, *La mission jé-suite*, 138–43.

13. See Trimbur, "Entre politique et religion, " 128.

14. See, for example, J. Landau, *The Politics of Pan-Islam*; and Aydin, *The Idea of the Muslim World*.

15. Cf. Spagnolo, *France and Ottoman Lebanon*, 1-7; and cf. Salibi, *A House of Many Mansions*, 130-50. The men of the Œuvre were the loudest advocates of what Andrew Arsan has termed "affective empire," the discourse of a "family romance" between the French and the Maronites which dated back to the Crusades. See Arsan, "There is, in the Heart of Asia . . .," 76, 80.

16. On Tocqueville's "aristocratic liberalism," cited in the previous paragraph, see Jaume, *Tocqueville*. On how these nineteenth-century liberals viewed religious liberties as hand in hand with political liberties, see Gadille and Mayeur, "Les milieux catholiques," 199. On liberalism as inherently anti-Islamic, see. Massad, *Islam in Liberalism*, 12, 35. Cf. Asad, *Formations of the Secular*, for a more general argument about how Western secularism and liberalism have invented Islam as non-European, nonsecular, and nonindividualistic.

17. Contribution by Eugène Boré in *Bulletin de l'Œuvre des écoles d'Orient*, no. 1, November 1857, 37.

18. Qtd. in Anonymous, *Eugène Boré*, 381–82.

19. Qtd. in Anonymous, *Eugène Boré*, 398. Elsewhere Boré remarked that Armenian Christianity had in some regions been so "degraded by the schism" that "the Muslims unfortunately are right . . . to call [Orthodox Armenians] unbelievers and infidels." Qtd. in Anonymous, *Eugène Boré*, 129.

20. Rodrigue, *French Jews, Turkish Jews*, esp. 4–24.

21. Père Gagarin, *Bulletin de l'Œuvre des écoles d'Orient*, no. 2, April 1858, 11.

22. This Christian-first strategy was a commonplace among missionaries on the ground in the Ottoman Empire, both Catholic and Protestant. Cf. Verdeil, *Les Jésuites en Syrie*, 450–51; and Verdeil, "La classe 'sous le chêne' et le pensionnat," 197–221, esp. 198, 202. On Protestant missionaries' similar strategy, see Kidd, *American Christians and Islam*, 42.

23. Trimbur, "Entre politique et religion,"116–18.

24. Trimbur, "Entre politique et religion," 124.

25. Trimbur, "Entre politique et religion," 120–21. On Charles Lenormant's place in the 1840s culture war over religious education, see F. Lenormant, "Preface," viii–ix.

26. Letters from Jean-Baptiste Etienne to Boré, April 5 and 12, 1856, Correspondance de M. Etienne avec M. Boré, 1843–1865, Fonds de Saint-Benoît de Constantinople, Supérieurs généraux, carton VIII, dossier I, Archives de la Congrégation de la Mission (Lazarists), Paris (hereafter ACM).

27. On Melun and Social Catholicism, see Boudon, "Les catholiques sociaux parisiens"; and Institut catholique de Paris, *Frédéric Ozanam, intellectuel catholique*, 55–73.

28. Cf. the list of officers and council members in Wallon, *Rapport faut au conseil general*, 30–31. For more on Wallon and d'Avril, see "Nécrologie," *Bulletin de l'Œuvre des écoles d'Orient*, no. 23, January 1903–December 1904, 375–80. On Pavet de Courteille, see "Pavet de Courteille," in Vapereau, *Dictionnaire universel des contemporains*, 1416. On Vogüé, see Cagnat, "Notice sur la vie et les travaux," 442–73. For more on the first generation of the Œuvre des écoles d'Orient, see "Lettre de M. le comte Hilaire de Lacombe, à Mgr Charmetant, directeur-général de l'Œuvre," *Bulletin de l'Œuvre des écoles d'Orient*, no. 273, March–April 1906; and no. 274, May–June 1906, 225–31.

29. On the council's diversity, see Trimbur, "Entre politique et religion," 122. For the term "neo-Gallican," see Boudon, "Mgr Lavigerie et l'État, " 110. On the Social Catholicism of this milieu, see Boudon, "Les catholiques sociaux parisiens"; and Lee Shai Weissbach, "Oeuvre Industrielle, Oeuvre Morale," 99–120; and Curtis, "Charitable Ladies," 121–56.

30. Cf. entry of December 9, 1858, Procés verbaux du Conseil de l'Œuvre d'Orient [PVCOO] (cahier 1), p. 17, Archives de l'Œuvre d'Orient, Paris (herafter AOO); and Renault, *Lavigerie*, 7-8, 209–10. See also Lagrange, *Vie de Mgr. Dupanloup*,193–194.

31. Dupanloup, *La convention du 15 septembre*. Marvin R. O'Connell, "Ultramontanism and Dupanloup," 216.

32. "Le centenaire du cardinal Lavigerie et l'oeuvre d'Orient," *Bulletin de l'Œuvre des écoles d'Orient*, no. 366, August 1925, 294. On Cardinal Mathieu, see Goyau, "Besançon (Vesontio)."

33. Boudon, *Paris, capitale religieuse*, 450–45; on Lavigerie's development, see Boudon, "Mgr Lavigerie et l'État." On the other hand, Emma Rothschild, following Lavigerie's biographer Mgr. Baunard, emphasizes that he was already a defender of "papal infallibility" at this early stage. Rothschild, *An Infinite History*, 271.

34. See the call for subscriptions for the *Bulletin de l'Œuvre des écoles d'Orient*, Paris, 25 April, 1856, Cultes Série: F19 6243B, Archives Nationales, Pierrefitte-sur-Seine (hereafter AN).

35. The previous two sentences quote from Spagnolo, *France and Ottoman Lebanon*, 20–21, 28 [Murad quoted on 20]. Cf. Arsan, "There is, in the Heart of Asia," 84–87. On Murad and Azar, see also Hakim, *The Origins of the Lebanese National Idea*, 53–64.

36. Spagnolo, *France and Ottoman Lebanon*, 21–22.

37. See the dossier on Azar in Cultes Série: F19 6243B, AN.

38. Baudicour, *La France au Liban*, 89, 80.

39. Baudicour, *La France au Liban*, 85, 102.

40. On the significance of salons and feminine sociability for liberal Catholics, see Kselman, *Conscience and Conversion*, 136-37, and Priest, *The Gospel according to Renan*, 47.

41. Amelie Ozanam correspondance with Lavigerie, Amiral Mathieu, etc., Fonds Ozanam: 28199, Nouvelles Acquisitions Françaises (NAF), Bibliothèque nationale de France (BNF); and Charles Lavigerie, "Rapport sur l'etat de l'Œuvre des ecoles d'Orient . . . 28 Mai 1858," *Bulletin de l'Œuvre des écoles d'Orient*, no. 3, July 1858, 6.

42. Entry of December 22, 1857, PVCOO (cahier 1), p. 4, AOO.

43. I owe this comparison to a commenter at Johns Hopkins University's Monday History Seminar, in September 2021, and received help formulating this sentence from Heather Stur. Cf. also Curtis, "Charitable Ladies."

44. Ticchi, "Les directeurs de l'Œuvre d'Orient et leurs moyens d'action de 1861 à 1914," 146, 155–56. On a preaching tour of dioceses along the Loire and down to Bordeaux in 1857, for example, Lavigerie met with enthusiastic receptions, establishing diocesan committees—usually of *Dames*, but also occasionally of "hommes honorables"—in Angers, Nantes, Bordeaux, Biarritz, Bayonne, and Pau. See entry of December 22, 1857, PVCOO (cahier 1), pp. 1–4, AOO.

45. Charles Lavigerie, "Rapport sur l'etat de l'Œuvre des ecoles d'Orient . . . 28 Mai 1858," in *Bulletin de l'Œuvre des écoles d'Orient*, no. 3, July 1858, 4; and entries of January 20 and February 24, 1858, PVCOO (cahier 1), pp. 6–9, AOO.

46. Weill, *Histoire du catholicisme libéral*, 1.

47. Weill, "Le catholicisme libéral en France," 100 and ff. Much more recently than Weill, Carol Harrison has focused on the early moments of liberal Catholicism under the July Monarchy and argued that Lamennais and his disciples are better understood as "Romantic" than as "liberal." See Harrison, *Romantic Catholics*, 3–5.

48. For the "apogee," see Weill, "Le catholicisme libéral en France," 102; for their "sensibility" and "socio-cultural *enracinement*," see Gadille et Mayeur, "Les Milieux Catholiques, 186.

49. Weill, "Le catholicisme libéral en France," 108, 104.

50. Harrigan, "French Catholics and Classical Education," 255–78.

51. Falloux, *Le parti catholique*, 8–9.

52. Falloux, *Le parti catholique*, 9; cf. Montalembert, *L'église libre*.

53. Falloux, *Le parti catholique*, 34–43, 54–56.

54. Falloux, *Le parti catholique*, 47, 106–7.

55. Falloux, *Le parti catholique*, 110–12, 149–50.

56. Falloux, *Le parti catholique*, 125–26.

57. Veuillot, *The Liberal Illusion*, 14–17.

58. Falloux, *Le parti catholique*, 147.

59. Falloux, *Le parti catholique*, 154–56.

60. Trimbur, "Entre politique et religion,"136.

61. Trimbur, "Entre politique et religion,"139.

62. These French schools accounted for "10 per cent of those educated" in the Empire, with a majority of the students, predictably, belonging to Christian religious minorities. See Burrows, "'Mission civilisatrice,'" 110; and Jacques Thobie, *Les intérêts culturels français*, xx.

63. Burrows, "'Mission civilisatrice,'" 114.

64. Thobie, *Les intérêts culturels français*, xxviii; Burrows, "'Mission civilisatrice,'" 128. In 1861, for example, some two thirds of the silk produced in the Mountain was exported to France. See Verdeil, *Jésuites en Syrie*, 31.

65. Burrows, "'Mission civilisatrice,'" 110.

66. This approach was also in keeping with the ministry's cultural policies in the Ottoman Empire since at least the 1840s. Burrows, "'Mission civilisatrice,'" 114-115; and

Jean-Baptiste Etienne, Report, *Bulletin de l'Œuvre des écoles d'Orient*, no. 1, November 1857, 1, 10.

67. Minister of Cults to Minister of Foreign Affairs, April 11, 1859, in Cultes Série: F19 6243B, AN.

68. Ticchi, "Les directeurs de l'Œuvre d'Orient et leurs moyens d'action de 1861 à 1914," 146.

69. Etienne to Boré, 12 May 1855, in "Correspondance de M. Etienne avec M. Boré," Papiers Boré, Archives de la Congrégation de la Mission (Lazarists), Paris (hereafter ACM). Or as Matthew Burrows puts it, "the identification of the [Œuvre's] aims with the interests of France was complete." Burrows, "'Mission civilisatrice,'" 120.

70. Verdeil, *La mission jésuite*, 116, 135–36.

71. Verdeil, *La mission jésuite*, 141–44.

72. The tradition of France's right to "protect" Ottoman Christians dated back to the Capitulations granted to France by the Ottoman Porte in the sixteenth and seventeenth centuries. These capitulations, dispensations from Ottoman jurisdiction, technically only applied to French citizens living in the Ottoman Empire. But France increasingly invoked jurisdiction and protection even over Ottoman subjects, for instance, native employees of French embassies. See, for example, Mazower, *Salonica, City of Ghosts*, 119–21. On the capitulations more generally, cf. Verdeil, *Jésuites en Syrie*, 110–12.

73. Rodogno, *Against Massacre*, 22.

74. Cf. Rodogno, *Against Massacre*, 11.

75. Eugène Boré, "Question du Liban," December 10, 1847, doc. 39, Mémoires et Documents (MD) Turquie, vol. 40, Archives de la Ministère des Affaires étrangères, La Courneuve (hereafter AMAE).

76. Louis de Baudicour, "Politique Anglaise au Liban," *Le Correspondant* 23, October 22, 1848, 85–96.

77. Arnaldo Momigliano, qtd. in Peltz and Myrone, "Introduction," 4.

78. Buchanan, "Science and Sensibility," 169–73; Schnapp, "Archéologie et tradition académique," 767.

79. Cf. Peltz and Myrone, "Introduction,"6.

80. On the relationship between professional archeology and wealthy amateurs, see Schnapp, "Archéologie et tradition académique," 768–70.

81. A. von Humboldt, quoted in Schnapp, "Archéologie et tradition académique," 768.

82. For this paragraph's topic sentence and arguments about nationalism throughout, see Díaz-Andreu, *A World History of Nineteenth-Century Archaeology*, 102, 106–8.

83. See Broc, "Les grandes missions scientifiques françaises," 319–58; Greenhalgh, "French Military Reconnaissance," 359–88; and Bercé, "Charles Lenormant," 195–209.

84. For the previous two sentences, Díaz-Andreu, *A World History of Nineteenth-Century Archaeology*, 111–13.

85. Schliemann, qtd. in Díaz-Andreu, *A World History of Nineteenth-Century Archaeology*, 113.

86. See "Académiciens depuis 1663," 462–63.

87. C. Lenormant, *Questions historiques*, 362–63. For an introduction to the history of some of these well-worn anti-Islamic canards, see Tolan, *Faces of Muhammad*.

88. C. Lenormant, *Questions historiques*, 374–75.

89. See Joly, "Les chartistes et la politique"; and Neveu, "L'école des chartes et le catholicisme," 169–81, 182–96.

90. Louis de Mas-Latrie to Vogüé, May 23, 1877, Fonds Vogüé: 567AP 225, AN.

91. Louis de Mas-Latrie, *Histoire de l'île de Chypre*, x–xi.

92. Mas-Latrie, *Histoire de l'île de Chypre*, xiv–xv.

93. Paul Meyer, quoted in "Obsèques de M. le comte de Mas-Latrie," *Bibliothèque de l'école des chartes* 57 (1896), 757.

94. Mas-Latrie, *Traités de paix et de commerce*, 342.

95. And here Mas-Latrie made his Christian sympathies most explicit—how wonderful that France's North African expansion was being aided by the "providential collaboration" of former Œuvre d'Orient director Charles Lavigerie and his missionaries, in the name of "Christian civilization"! Mas-Latrie, *Relations et commerce de l'Afrique*, ii, iv.

96. Cagnat, "Notice sur la vie et les travaux," 442–73, 449.

97. Cagnat, "Notice sur la vie et les travaux," 447, 451–53.

98. Vogüé, *Les églises de la Terre Sainte*, 2, 25–26, 222–23.

99. Vogüé, *Les églises de la Terre Sainte*, 36.

100. Vogüé, *Les églises de la Terre Sainte*, 38.

101. Vogüé, *Les églises de la Terre Sainte*, 40, 175.

102. Vogüé, *Les églises de la Terre Sainte*, 223–25.

103. Vogüé, *Les églises de la Terre Sainte*, 230.

104. Vogüé, *Les églises de la Terre Sainte*, 229, 231.

105. Vogüé, *Les églises de la Terre Sainte*, 405–6.

106. Renan, *Mission de Phénicie*, 1–2, 16.

107. Renan, *Mission de Phénicie*, 12, 14–15; Cagnat, "Notice sur la vie et les travaux," 453–54.

108. The understudied Phoenicians were the main target of Renan's mission, but any interesting inscriptions were fair game: "only Arabic inscriptions, except for very old [ones], have been excluded." Letter from Renan to Vogüé, December 18, 1861, Fonds Vogüé: 567AP /217, AN.

109. Vogüé, "CR" [Compte-Rendu?], in dossier "Voyages en Orient, 1853, 1861–62," Fonds Vogüé: 567AP 217, AN.

110. Acher de Montgascon was posted to embassies in Europe, Saint Petersburg, Constantinople, and Montenegro. See Prevost, "Acher de Montgascon (Ambroise-Justin, Baron d')," 322.

111. Faugère was active enough in the direction of the Œuvre to be involved in the editing of the Abbé Lavigerie's 1861 report on the victims of the massacres of Syria and on the Œuvre's charitable efforts. Letter from Lavigerie to Faugère, April 26–27, 1861, enclosed in Faugère's copy of Lavigerie, *Souscription pour les chrétiens de Syrie*, Fg 1444, Fonds Faugère, Bibliothèque du Ministère des Affaires étrangères.

112. See letter from d'Avril to [Henri?] Delarue, May 20, 1858, in Papiers Delarue: 58PAAP, Archives du Ministère des Affaires Étrangères (hereafter AMAE).

113. While working for the Commission of the Danube, he met and befriended the British delegate, the devout Protestant Charles "Chinese" Gordon, whose later, tragic exploits in the Sudan would inspire d'Avril's own opposition to "Muslim" slavery. Cf. Papiers d'Avril: 7CPAAP, AMAE.

114. Cf. "Lettre de M. le comte Hilaire de Lacombe, à Mgr Charmetant, directeur-général de l'Œuvre," in *Bulletin de l'Œuvre des écoles d'Orient*, no. 273, March–April 1906; and no. 274, May–June 1906, 229.

115. See letter from Vogüé to Duc Decazes, December 21[?], 1873, Correspondance Politique (CP) Turquie, vol. 397, AMAE.

116. Cf. Ferry, "Discours du 28 juillet 1885, " 172 and ff.; esp. 209 and ff.

117. See Conklin, *A Mission to Civilize*, 1–2, 14–23; Daughton, *An Empire Divided*; and Wilder, *French Imperial Nation-State*. For the "civilizing mission" as a secular replacement for the gospel, a tool used by French Jews to "de-Christianize" French foreign policy, see Leff, "Jews, Liberals and the Civilizing Mission," 105–6, 112, 118–19; and Leff, *Sacred Bonds of Solidarity*, 6–11.

118. Todd, "A French Imperial Meridian," esp. 156, 158. See also Dzanic, "France's Informal Empire," 1–22, esp. 2; and Murray-Miller, "A Conflicted Sense of Nationality," 1–38. I am grateful to commenters at Johns Hopkins University's Monday History Seminar, in September 2021, for help in thinking about this "Republican teleology."

119. Dutau, "L'imprimerie catholique de Beyrouth," 387.

120. Dutau, "L'Imprimerie Catholique de Beyrouth," 403.

121. Dutau, "L'Imprimerie Catholique de Beyrouth," 405.

122. Dutau, "L'Imprimerie Catholique de Beyrouth," 413. On French imperialists' almost "magical" confidence in the civilizing capabilities of the printing press, see Asseraf, *Electric News*, 25, 42, 64.

123. Damas, "La science et les missionnaires au Liban," 459.

124. Damas, "La science et les missionnaires au Liban," 462.

125. Damas, "La science et les missionnaires au Liban," 473. The Jesuits were also training a number of orphans—confided to them, as we will see, by the Œuvre d'Orient after the 1860 massacres—in various *métiers*. Damas, "La science et les missionnaires au Liban," 474.

Chapter 5

1. Session of July 16, 1860, PVCOO, cahier 1, AOO.

2. E. Guillaume Rey to Comte de Vogüé, no date, Fonds Vogüé: 567AP/216, AN.

3. Guillaume Rey passed on testimony especially from Jesuit missionaries and the military doctor and amateur archeologist Charles Gaillardot. Guillaume Rey to Vogüé, July 31, 1860, Fonds Vogüé: 567AP/216, AN; and Gran-Aymerich, "Gaillardot, Joseph-Arnaud Charles," 414–15.

4. Guillame Rey to Vogüé, September 28, 1860, Fonds Vogüé: 567AP/216, AN.

5. Session of September 6, 1860, PVCOO, cahier 1, AOO.

6. Gagarin to Vogüé, July 29, 1860, Fonds Vogüé: 567AP/216, AN.

7. Prunières to Guillaume Rey, Beirut, June 12, 1860, Fonds Vogüé: 567AP/216, AN.

8. Fenech to Gagarin, September 21, 1860, in Fonds Vogüé: 567AP/216, AN.

9. Guillaume Rey to Vogüé, July 7, 1860, Fonds Vogüé: 567AP/216, AN.

10. The same Père alleged that the Druze systematically left the English alone. Père Fenech to Père Gagarin, August 14, 1860, Fonds Vogüé: 567AP/216, AN.

11. Verdeil, *La mission jésuite*, 135–36, 139–42.

12. François Lenormant, letter of July 1, 1860, in *Bulletin de l'Œuvre des écoles d'Orient*, no. 10, November 1860, 27.

13. One of *L'Ami de la religion*'s editors, Hilaire de Lacombe, was himself a member of the liberal Catholic "party" and an original member of the Œuvre des écoles d'Orient. For Lacombe's liberal affinities, see his laudatory portraits of Bishop Dupanloup, Montalembert, and Falloux, in the opening pages of Lacombe, *Liberté d'enseignement*.

14. In this, they were completely faithful to the impressions of French missionaries on the ground. Leon Lavedan, "Bulletin Politique," *L'Ami de la religion* July 10, 1860, (Paris: Imprimerie de Soye et Bouchet, 1860 [Tome VI: Nouvelle Série]), 62.

15. Cf. Fawaz, *An Occasion for War*, 78, 100.

16. R. P. Rousseau, letter of June 16, 1860, *L'Ami de la religion*, July 10, 1860, (Paris: Imprimerie de Soye et Bouchet, 1860 [Tome VI: Nouvelle Série]), 68.

17. Abbé Lavigerie, "Appel Aux Catholiques de France en Faveur des Chrétiens de Syrie," *L'Ami de la religion*, July 24, 1860, 188–89.

18. Mandement of the archbishop of Bordeaux, in *L'Ami de la religion*, July 26 1860, 211–12.

19. M. de Vogüé, "Les évènements de Syrie," *L'Ami de la religion*, July 14, 1860, 109–12.

20. Leon Lavedan, "Bulletin Politique," *L'Ami de la religion*, July 10, 1860, 62; and July 14, 1860, 108. In the first case, he is quoting a missionary in Syria.

21. M. de Vogüé, "L'intervention armée en Syrie," *L'Ami de la religion*, July 28, 1860, 224.

22. M. de Vogüé, "La mission de Fuad Pasha," *L'Ami de la religion*, September 1, 1860, 516–18.

23. Throughout this paragraph, M. de Vogüé, "L'intervention armée en Syrie," *L'Ami de la religion*, July 28, 1860, 224–26.

24. François Lenormant, letter from Beirut, July 1, 1860, *L'Ami de la religion*, July 21, 1860, 165–73.

25. Editorial Comments on Lebanon, *Annales de la Propagation de la Foi* 7, no. 37 (July 1834): 207–8.

26. Letters of Mgr Ange de Fazio and Père Riccadonna, *Annales de la Propagation de la Foi* 11, no. 64 (May 1839): xx–xx.

27. François Lenormant, letter from Beirut, July 5, 1860, *L'Ami de la religion*, July 24, 1860, 185.

28. Fawaz, *An Occasion for War*, 100.

29. M. de Vogüé, "Les Massacres de Damas," *L'Ami de la religion*, August 7, 1860, 305–7. The Prophet is traditionally presumed to have been buried at Medina. Nigosian, *Islam*, 13–14. For the longer pre-history of Christian misconceptions about the location of (and ritual practices surrounding) Muhammad's tomb, see Tolan, *Faces of Muhammad*, 25–26, 68–69.

30. M. de Vogüé, "Les Massacres de Damas."

31. Vogüé, *Les événements de Syrie* 8.

32. Vogüé, *Les événements de Syrie*, 21. On French fears of pan-Islamism later in the century (when these fears were more realistic), see Asseraf, *Electric News*, 83–90, 96–97.

33. Vogüé, *Les événements de Syrie*, 22.

34. Vogüé, *Les événements de Syrie*, 22.

35. Vogüé, *Les événements de Syrie*, 22.

36. See Saaïdia, *L'Algérie catholique*, 31–34, 66. On the unpopularity of official *medersas*, see F. Colonna, "Le système d'enseignement"; and Schreier, *Arabs of the Jewish Faith*, 116–20.

37. Saada, *Empire's Children*; and Surkis, *Sex, Law, and Sovereignty*.

38. Saaïdia, *L'Algérie catholique*, 87–149; and Francis, "Catholic Missionaries in Colonial Algeria."

39. Vogüé, *Les événements de Syrie*, 21.

40. Vogüé, *Les événements de Syrie*, 25, 9.

41. Vogüé, *Les événements de Syrie*, 9, 14.

42. Salibi, *A House of Many Mansions*, 130–50.

43. Lavigerie, in Lavigerie, *Notice sur le pèlerinage*, 185–86.

44. Baudicour, *La colonisation de l'Algérie*, 234–51, 245; and Gourinard, *Les Royalistes en Algérie*, 87–105. Cf. Arsan, "'There is, in the Heart of Asia.'" Lavigerie also suggested transplanting indigenous Christian orphans to Algeria. Lavigerie, *Souscription recueillie*, 82.

45. Vogüé's ideological interventions predate the Jesuit Père Henri Lammens' more famous, early-twentieth-century histories which emphasized Lebanese autonomy. Cf. Salibi, *A House of Many Mansions*, 130–50. On the General Beaufort d'Hautpol's similar plan in 1860–61 for a "Greater Lebanon" dominated by Christians, see Hakim, *The Origins of the Lebanese National Idea*, 83–87.

46. Vogüé, *Les événements de Syrie*, 26–27.

47. Vogüé, *Les événements de Syrie*, 27.

48. In Cohen, "Une souscription des Juifs de France, 449.

49. According to historian David Cohen, by initiating this fundraiser on behalf of Christians, the reformist Jews of the Alliance israélite universelle hoped to show their gratitude for the emancipation and citizenship France had granted them in 1789; to prove their Frenchness, above and beyond religious belonging; and perhaps even to symbolically reject, with their support for Christians in Damascus, the anti-Semitic myth that a Jew had committed "ritual murder" in Damascus twenty years before. But the fundraiser was quickly transformed into a political football by the anticlerical press,

which relished the fact that (while ultramontane Catholics were busy taking up collections and volunteering to go fight for the beleaguered Pope) it was the Jews of France who had first thought of this humanitarian campaign. To these taunts, ultramontane Catholics responded with bitterly anti-Semitic tirades or with calls for an armed intervention not to Syria, but to Rome. See Cohen, "Une souscription des Juifs de France"; and Marcel Émerit, "La crise Syrienne," 211–32.

50. For more on these diplomatic and economic considerations, see Émerit, "La crise Syrienne"; and Verdeil, *La mission jésuite*, 141–42.

51. Todd, "A French Imperial Meridian, " esp. 173, 180–81. For the phrase "informal empire" and more on the concept, see Dzanic, "France's Informal Empire." The other quoted phrases are Todd's.

52. Trimbur, "Entre politique et religion," 128.

53. See Burrows, "'Mission civilisatrice,'" 118.

54. Session of September 6, 1860, PVCOO, cahier 1, AOO.

55. See lists of subscribers and note about the Comte de Chambord, *L'Ami de la religion*, July 28, 1860, 226–27.

56. Session of July 20, 1860, PVCOO, cahier 1, AOO.

57. Session of 9 August 9, 1860, PVCOO, cahier 1, AOO. Lavigerie justified this decision to save back the charitable funds as motivated by the desire not to accidentally give any redundant gifts to those already aided by various governments, and the desire to have something to offer during the hard winter to come. Lavigerie, letter of August 16, 1860, in *Bulletin de l'Œuvre des écoles d'Orient*, no. 10, November 1860, 44.

58. Session of September 6, 1860, PVCOO (cahier 1), AOO.

59. Session of September 24, 1860, PVCOO (cahier 1), AOO..

60. The words of the Maronite delegate's accusation are Vogüé's paraphrase. Vogüé to a Lazarist Père [Étienne?], November 22, 1860, dossier 116C: Moyen Orient, généralités Archives de la Congrégation de la Mission (Lazarists), Paris (hereafter ACM).

61. Lavigerie to [Faugère?], December 16, 1860, Mémoires et documents (MD) Turquie, vol. 122, Archives du Ministère des Affaires etrangères, La Courneuve (hereafter AMAE).

62. Minister of Foreign Affairs to Minister of Cults[?], September 25, 1860, Cultes Série: F19 6243B, AN.

63. Lavigerie, *Souscription recueillie*, 18 (this report was also published in the April 1861 (no. 11) volume of the Œuvre's *Bulletin*); and "Faits Divers," *La Presse*, April 16, 1861, 3.

64. Session of February 14, 1861, PVCOO, cahier 1, AOO.

65. Session of November 8 and 29, 1860, PVCOO, cahier 1, AOO.

66. Session of March 22, 1861, PVCOO, cahier 1, AOO.

67. Session of December 6, 1861, PVCOO, cahier 1, AOO.

68. Lavigerie, *Souscription recueillie*, 80–81.

69. Session of January 24, 1861, PVCOO, cahier 1, AOO. At the center of the criticism, it seems, were the orphanages that Lavigerie had established, one for boys run by the Jesuits,

and one for girls by the Lazarist-affiliated Soeurs de la charité. Apparently, some thought Lavigerie should have not accepted orphans at all, some of whose mothers were still alive. Perhaps the criticism was also a continuation of the Maronite delegate's accusation that Lavigerie was not funneling enough funds to the needs of the Maronite community and instead trying to "Latinize" the country. See Lavigerie, *Souscription recueillie*, 55–56.

70. Lavigerie was not the only Œuvre associate to rely on Faugère's article. See Avril, *L'arabie contemporaine*, 218–22.

71. On the later nineteenth-century roots of the "idea of the Muslim world," both as a European invention and as reformist Muslim reality, see Aydin, *The Idea of the Muslim World*.

72. Faugère, *De la propagande musulmane*, 5.

73. A footnote informed readers that the Sublime Porte was in effect the ruler of "hardly a quarter" of the Muslim world, whereas all Muslims were loyal to Mecca. Faugère, *De la propagande musulmane*, 8.

74. Faugère, *De la propagande musulmane*, 10.

75. Faugère, *De la propagande musulmane*, 13.

76. Faugère, *De la propagande musulmane*, 22–23.

77. Faugère, *De la propagande musulmane*, 23–28.

78. Faugère, *De la propagande musulmane*, 47.

79. Faugère, *De la propagande musulmane*, 37–38.

80. Faugère, *De la propagande musulmane*, 36.

81. Lavigerie, *Souscription recueillie*, 89–91.

82. Lavigerie, *Souscription recueillie*, 105.

83. Étienne, "Le rayonnement d'Abd el-Kader," 622–25. For more on Abd el-Kader, and especially on how French and other observers tended to reduce the conquest of Algeria as a whole to the conflict between France and Abd el-Kader, see Brower, "The Amîr 'Abd Al-Qâdir," 169–95.

84. Étienne, "Le rayonnement d'Abd el-Kader," 625. The emir and his Algerians may already have been resented as outsiders by the Muslims of Damascus, and even more so after intervening on behalf of French protegés. Some Algerians in Syria would even go on to opt for French nationality, so they could avoid Ottoman conscription and benefit from French consular protection. See Haddad, "Sur les pas d'Abd el-Kader."

85. Lavigerie, *Souscription revueillie*, 67–68. France's freemasons similarly reached out to Abd el-Kader, believing his actions proved he was no longer a fanatical Muslim but a universalist freemason. The emir responded favorably and even joined a masonic lodge, but he never stopped believing that his protection of Christians had been an "essentially Muslim" act. Cf. Étienne, "Le rayonnement d'Abd el-Kader," 625–28.

86. For the previous two sentences, Hakim, *The Origins of the Lebanese National Idea*, 71–72, 92–98.

87. The summary of the *Règlement* throughout this entire paragraph and the quotation in the penultimate sentence are drawn from Spagnolo, *France and Ottoman*

Lebanon, 36–47. For a more in-depth account of these diplomatic wranglings, see Hakim, *The Origins of the Lebanese National Idea*, 70–80, 92–98.

88. Cf. Hakim, *The Origins of the Lebanese National Idea*, 87–91.

89. On this point, and on Karam's exile and 1866 rebellion more generally, see Spagnolo, *France and Ottoman Lebanon*, 100–110.

90. Draft of letter from Vogüé to Karam, October 26, 1864, Fonds Vogüé: 567AP/216, AN.

91. "The question of Youssef Karam is not [the question] of the Christians of the Orient." Damas to Vogüé, January 16, 1866, and "Note du Pere de Damas à M. le Cte de Vogüé," Fonds Vogüé: 567AP/216, AN.

92. On Carlyle, see Ali, *Lives of Muhammad*, 47–48.

93. See Marquigny, "Les nouveaux panégyristes du mahometisme," 210, 226.

94. Vogüé, "L'islamisme et son fondateur," *Le Correspondant* 30, November 1865, 583–84.

95. Vogüé, "L'islamisme et son fondateur," 594, 600.

96. Lammens, "Mahomet fut-il sincère?"

97. Priest, *The Gospel according to Renan*, 91–108, 108.

98. See Tocqueville, *Writings on Empire and Slavery*.

99. Qtd. in Vogüé, "L'islamisme et son fondateur," 618.

100. Vogüé, "L'islamisme et son fondateur," 587.

101. Vogüé, "L'islamisme et son fondateur," 587.

102. In this, the liberal Catholics of the Œuvre were not unlike twentieth-century Social Catholics who, in their battle against prostitution, used the racialized "bogeyman" of Arab sex trafficking to rally a wider, non-Catholic audience. See Shepard, *Sex, France, and Arab Men*, 132–35, 148–49, 186–88.

103. Cf. Weill, "Le catholicisme liberal en France," 106.

104. Cf. Vogüé to Comte de Rémusat [Minister of Foreign Affairs], May 7, 1873, Correspondance politique (CP) Turquie, vol. 395, AMAE.

105. Vogüé to Comte de Rémusat [Minister of Foreign Affairs], October 16, 1872, CP, vols. 393–94, AMAE; cf. Vogué to Decazes [Minister of Foreign Affairs], March 4, 1874, CP, vol. 398, AMAE. Also see Kartashyan, "Ultramontane Efforts in the Ottoman Empire during the 1860s and 1870s."

106. See, for example, Wilder, *The French Imperial Nation-State*, 119–28, 125.

107. Surkis, *Sex, Law, and Sovereignty in French Algeria*.

108. Al-Bustani, *The Clarion of Syria*, 65, 90, 95–96, 111.

109. Jens Hanssen and Hicham Safieddine, "Butrus al-Bustani: From Protestant Convert to Ottoman Patriot and Arab Reformer," in al-Bustani, *The Clarion of Syria*, 30–31. The quoted phrase is al-Bustani's. See also pp. 108, 120.

110. On the political strategy of interpreting civilizing promises literally, see Wilder, *Freedom Time*, 7.

111. The term "Pan-Islamism" first appeared in European languages in the late 1870s and early 1880s. See Lee, "The Origins of Pan-Islamism," 280.

112. Vogué to de Broglie [Minister of Foreign Affairs], July 22, 1873, CP, vol. 395, AMAE.

113. Report to the Conseil de l'Oeuvre de la Propagation de la Foi, "Écrit à Alger, le 24/1 1888," Fonds Vogüé: 567AP/159, AN.

114. See Goyau, *Un grand missionnaire, le cardinal Lavigerie*; and *Bulletin de la Société antiesclavagiste de France*, 1888–1889, 436.

115. "Lettre de M. le comte Hilaire de Lacombe à Mgr Charmetant, directeur-général de l'Œuvre," *Œuvre des écoles d'Orient: Bulletins périodiques*, no. 273, March–April 1906; and no. 274, May–June 1906," 231.

116. Urbain, *L'Algérie pour les algériens*, 25–28.

117. Ducat, "Faits principaux relatifs . . .," p. 35, RAl 44, ACJF.

118. Ducat, "Faits principaux relatifs . . .," p. 36.

119. Ducat, "Faits principaux relatifs . . .," p. 36 (and cf. pp. 23–24).

120. See the Œuvre d'Orient's donation lists published in *L'Ami de la religion*, September 1, 1860, 530; and September 13, 1860, 631.

Chapter 6

1. Davis, "Colonial Capitalism," 168.

2. This entire paragraph closely follows Bertrand Taithe's account of the famine, in Taithe, "Humanitarianism and Colonialism," 137–42.

3. Cf. Émerit, "Le problème de la conversion des musulmans"; and Clancy-Smith, "Islam and the French Empire," 93–96.

4. Charles Lavigerie to Governor General MacMahon, April 25, 1868, Algérie, Fonds Ministériel: F80/1746, ANOM. Cf. Émerit, "Le problème de la conversion des musulmans."

5. Lavigerie, *Les orphelins arabes d'Alger*, 7–8. See also P Soubiranne, *Œuvre des écoles d'Orient: Bulletins périodique*, May 1870, 78–79; and the lists of baptized and deceased in dossier B8: Orphelins, Fonds Lavigerie, Archives de la Société des Missionnaires d'Afrique (Pères Blancs), Rome (hereafter AGMAfr).

6. This was decades before the more famous use of humanitarian photography to alert the world to the atrocities of the Belgian Congo, for example. See Sliwinksi, "The Childhood of Human Rights," 333–63.

7. See, for example, Borrmans, "Lavigerie et les Musulmans en Afrique du Nord," 39–56; and Cuoq, *Lavigerie, les Pères Blancs, et les musulmans Maghrébins*, 32–49; see also Renault, *Cardinal Lavigerie*, 156. One recent historian, not at all a Lavigerie hagiographer, agrees that the archbishop's method of forbidding baptism was a sign of his "modernity." See Saaïdia, *Algérie catholique*, 178–83.

8. Renault, *Cardinal Lavigerie*, 112.

9. Bertrand Taithe has argued that, while colonists on the ground in Algeria were increasingly susceptible to a new anti-Arab racism, for Lavigerie's missionaries and for French Catholics back home in France, the "religious mode" of discrimination remained more powerful than the "racial mode" in this period. I am more interested in how

Lavigerie served to intertwine more closely the racism of the colony with the metropole. See Bertrand Taithe, "Algerian Orphans," 256–59.

10. See Letters from Pierre Soubiranne to Charles Lavigerie, January 13 and January 29, 1868, dossier A19: Œuvres (306-307), Fonds Lavigerie, AGMAfr.

11. Soubiranne to Lavigerie, January 29, 1868.

12. Cf. Émerit, "Le problème de la conversion des musulmans," 75.

13. Letter reproduced in Lavigerie, *Œuvres choisies*, 164–65.

14. Lavigerie, *Œuvres choisies*, 165–66. Cf. Émerit, "Le Conflit entre MacMahon et Lavigerie," 75.

15. Again, cf. Émerit, "Le Conflit entre MacMahon et Lavigerie." See also Saaïdia, *Algérie coloniale*, 194–95. Saaïdia believes that cooperation between church and state was the norm in the colony, that this conflict was mostly hot air, and that historians have overemphasized its significance.

16. Louis Veuillot, "L'Islamisme Algérien en France," *L'Univers*, May 26, 1868.

17. Cf. Baunard, *Le Cardinal Lavigerie*, 228–64.

18. Typed summary of correspondence, Félix de Las Cases to Lavigerie, May 13, 1868, dossier A16: Algérie (8-11), Fonds Lavigerie, AGMAfr. Las Cases also believed the fundraising campaign was misleading, profiting from an Algeria-wide catastrophe to enrich Lavigerie's personal projects only. P. Soubiranne to Lavigerie, March 18, 1868, dossier A19: Œuvres, Fonds Lavigerie, AGMAfr.

19. Soubiranne reminded Lavigerie that he could call on the liberal bishop Dupanloup to effect a compromise if need be. Soubiranne also suggested that even if Lavigerie decided to forgo a conciliation with the liberals, he should still reconcile himself with the emperor and publish something in the Catholic journals assuring he would not "baptize all the Arabs." Soubiranne to Lavigerie, April 24, 1868, dossier A19: Œuvres, Fonds Lavigerie, AGMAfr.

20. Vogüé—who knew Bishop Lavigerie personally from their days together at the Œuvre—had already felt back in 1867 that he was not a sensible choice for archbishop, that he was too ambitious, "difficult," and "political." Melchior de Vogüé to Robert de Vogüé, July 14, 1867, Fonds Vogüé: 567AP/189, AN.

21. Soubiranne to Robert de Vogüé, Algiers, June 19, 1869, and Melchior de Vogüé to Robert de Vogüé, May 22, 1869, Fonds Vogüé: 567AP/189, AN. M. Vogüé had to play the peacemaker again in 1870, when Lavigerie seems to have vindictively seized some funds sent by the Œuvre de la Propagation de la Foi that were intended for Elizabeth de MacMahon's smaller orphanage. To avoid another intra-Catholic scandal, M. Vogüé urged the board of the missionary association to leave the first gift to Lavigerie and quietly send another identical subvention to the Maréchale. See the letters from Elizabeth de MacMahon to Melchior de Vogüé, and from the Treasurer of the Paris Conseil de la Propagation de la Foi to Melchior de Vogüé, etc. May–July 1870, Fonds Vogüé: 567AP/217, AN.

22. Robert de Vogüé to Melchior de Vogüé, Algiers, 7 April 1870, Fonds Vogüé: 567AP/189, AN.

23. Baunard, *Le Cardinal Lavigerie*, 228–264.

24. Lavigerie, letter of February 20, 1868, printed in a *circulaire* of the Bishop of Arras, March 1, 1868, dossier A16: Algérie, Fonds Lavigerie, AGMAfr.

25. See Davis, "Colonial Capitalism," 163.

26. Carroll, "Imperial Ideologies," esp. 82–83; and Murray-Miller, *The Cult of the Modern*, 95–114. On Ismaÿl Urbain, see my discussion and notes in chapter 2.

27. On these two reforms, see Surkis, *Sex, Law, and Sovereignty*, 71–75, 82–86. See also Blévis, "La citoyenneté française."

28. Throughout this paragraph, I am indebted to Murray-Miller, *The Cult of the Modern*, esp. 209–45; and Carroll, "Imperial Ideologies," 67–100.

29. Murray-Miller, *The Cult of the Modern*, 209–45. Jules Duval is quoted within the quotation, on page 222.

30. Of course, as other historians have observed, in this alliance of convenience, Lavigerie presumably wanted access to the Muslims' hearts, while the settlers wanted their land and labor. Cf. Rey-Goldzeiguer, *Le royaume arabe*, 97. Goldzeiguer's formulation is apt: "The largeholding colonists [*gros colons*] demanded arms, the church demanded souls." See also Taithe, "Evil, Liberalism," 147–71.

31. Quoted in Lavigerie, "Fiches du Cardinal Lavigerie sur l'Algérie et les Bureaux Arabes," dossier A16: Algérie, Fonds Lavigerie, AGMAfr.

32. Gullestad, *Picturing Pity*, xii, 3, 5, 18–19. My analysis throughout this paragraph is heavily indebted to Gullestad.

33. Baunard, *Le Cardinal Lavigerie*, 263–64.

34. Baunard, *Le Cardinal Lavigerie*, 264.

35. Readers were invited to visit Nadar's "atelier photographique" to view the originals, taken by a M. Sarrault. René du Merzer, "La famine en Algérie," *L'Illustration: Journal Universel* 51, no. 1322 (June 27, 1868): 412.

36. Baunard, *Le Cardinal Lavigerie*, 264.

37. Dupanloup to Lavigerie, February 28, 1869, dossier A16: Algérie, Fonds Lavigerie, AGMAfr.

38. Soubiranne to Lavigerie, January 24, 1869, dossier A16: Algérie, Fonds Lavigerie, AGMAfr.

39. "Souscription générale pour les pauvres arabes et les établissements hospitaliers de Mgr. Lavigerie" (Paris: Aux Bureaux de l'Œuvre, n.d.) [brochure and notebook], box "A," AOO; another copy of the notebook, but with a different version of the photograph can be found in dossier A19: Œuvres, Fonds Lavigerie, AGMAfr.

40. The argument that humanitarian photography relies on a sense of superiority and "distance" is in Gullestad, *Picturing Pity*, 27–28; and Twomey, "Framing Atrocity," 55–56. The quoted phrases are Twomey's.

41. Gullestad, *Picturing Pity*, 7.

42. On the "social meaning of gratitude" in missionary and humanitarian fundraising contexts, see Gullestad, *Picturing Pity*, 275 ff.

43. Gullestad, *Picturing Pity*, 273–77.

44. Letter from Lavigerie to Soubiranne, December 28, 1868, in Lavigerie, *Recueil de lettres publiées*, 46–47.

45. Entry of November 8, 1871, in Henri Ducat, "Diaire: Mission Arabe Consantine, 1871–72," RAl 81, ACJF.

46. Letter from Lavigerie to Soubiranne, December 28, 1868, in Lavigerie, *Recueil de lettres publiées*, 47.

47. General de Wimpffen to Lavigerie, January 15, 1868, and April 28, 1869, dossier A16: Algérie, Fonds Lavigerie, AGMAfr.

48. Soubiranne to Lavigerie, April 23, 1869, dossier A19: Œuvres, Fonds Lavigerie, AGMAfr. On Lavigerie's representations of the plight of "the Arab woman," see "Lettre de Mgr Lavigerie" dated July 19, 1871, *Œuvre des écoles d'Orient: Bulletins périodique*, July 1871, 141–43.>

49. Letter from Lavigerie to Soubiranne, December 28, 1868, in Lavigerie, *Recueil de lettres publiées*, 52–54.

50. Letter from Lavigerie to Soubiranne, December 28, 1868, 55.

51. Soubiranne to Lavigerie, January 22, 1869, dossier A19: Œuvres, Fonds Lavigerie, AGMAfr.

52. Lavigerie, *Les orphelins arabes*, 21, and preface [by Soubiranne?]. On fundraising difficulties and conflict with Las Cases, see various letters from Soubiranne in dossier A19: OEuvres, Fonds Lavigerie, AGMAfr.

53. Davis, "Colonial Capitalism," 167–69. For more on the "proletarianization" of Algerians, see Chenntouf, "L'évolution du travail," 85–103.

54. Girard, qtd. in Lavigerie, *Les orphelins arabes*. 9.

55. Soubiranne, "Relation de la Visite Faite aux orphelinats arabes d'Alger," *Œuvre des écoles d'Orient: Bulletins périodique*, January 1870, 4–5.

56. Lavigerie, *Les orphelins arabes d'Alger*, 21–22.

57. Lavigerie, *Les orphelins arabes d'Alger*, 22.

58. On the historically-constructed nature of emotions and affects, see Melani McAlister, "What is your Heart For?: Affect and Internationalism in the Evangelical Public Sphere," *American Literary History*, Vol. 20, No. 4 (Winter 2008), 878–79. The quoted phrase is Sarah Ahmed's, qtd. in McAlister.

59. See Gibson, *A Social History of French Catholicism*, 180–90; and Langlois, *Le catholicisme au féminin*.

60. Cf. Harrison, *Romantic Catholics*, 28–65.

61. On Emilie de Vialar, cf. Curtis, "Emilie de Vialar," 261–92; on the Œuvre de la Propagation de la Foi, see Daughton, *An Empire Divided*; and on Jaricot specifically, see Burton, *Holy Tears, Holy Blood*, xxiii-xxiv. See also Curtis, "Charitable Ladies," 145.

62. Cf. Harrison, *Romantic Catholics*, 259–63. In a bit of a contrast to my emphasis here, Harrison argues persuasively that ultramontane men were as responsible as women for the increased emphasis on expiatory suffering.

63. Burton, *Holy Tears, Holy Blood*, xvi–xxv.

64. Burton, *Holy Tears, Holy Blood*, xviii.

65. Marie Regnault to Lavigerie, May 13, 1873, dossier B8: Orphelins, Fonds Lavigerie, AGMAfr.

66. J. Laffetay to [Lavigerie?], Bayeux, November 20, 1871, dossier B8: Orphelins, Fonds Lavigerie, AGMAfr.

67. Blois Conference of Societé de Saint Vincent de Paul, to [Lavigerie?], March 23, 1872, dossier B8: Orphelins, Fonds Lavigerie, AGMAfr. Blois was far from the only conference of the Society to support Lavigerie's work. Felix Charmetant, in a report to the Society, claimed that—considering the society as a collective as well as donations made by individual members—the men of the Societé de Saint Vincent de Paul had paid for the five-year adoptions of some one hundred orphans, over 100,000 francs. Charmetant, "Rapport d'ensemble sur l'oeuvre des orphelins," (1878?), dossier B9: Orphelins, Fonds Lavigerie, AGMAfr.

68. See Soubiranne to Lavigerie, October 28, 1871, dossier A19: Œuvres, Fonds Lavigerie, AGMAfr. This is also the letter where Soubiranne discusses marketing to the Association of Christian Mothers.

69. Cf. Dirèche, *Chrétiens de Kabylie*; and Lorcin, *Imperial Identities*.

70. See letters from Gueydon to Lavigerie in dossier A16: Algérie, Fonds Lavigerie, AGMAfr; and Dirèche, *Chrétiens de Kabylie*, 30.

71. Baunard, *Le Cardinal Lavigerie*, 346–50; 370–74.

72. "Lettre de Mgr. l'archevêque d'Alger," *Bulletin de l'Œuvre de Sainte Monique* [hereafter *BOSM*], no. 2, February 1872, 20.

73. "Lettre de Mgr. l'archevêque d'Alger," *BOSM*, no. 2, February 1872, 21.

74. "Lettre de Mgr. l'archevêque d'Alger," 21–22.

75. Marie-Cécile Brunet, "Les orphelins de sainte Monique," *BOSM*, no. 3, May 1872, 34–35.

76. Brunet, "Les orphelines de Sainte Monique," 48.

77. Brunet, "Les orphelines de Sainte Monique," 48; and Marie-Cécile Brunet, "La mort d'une orpheline," *BOSM*, no. 4, August 1872, 67.

78. Previous sentences inspired by Surkis, *Sex, Law, and Sovereignty in French Algeria*.

79. Letter from Lavigerie," July 19, 1871, *Œuvre des écoles d'Orient: Bulletins périodique*, July1871, 141–43.

80. Letter from Père Olivier, *Œuvre des écoles d'Orient: Bulletins périodique*, July1871, 70.

81. Letter from Père Olivier, 70–71.

82. Letter from F. Charmetant (19 November 19, 1872), *BOSM*, no. 5, January 1873, 106.

83. F. Charmetant, "Voyage dans le Sahara et le Mzab (Suite)," *BOSM*, no. 5, January 1873, 226.

84. F. Charmetant, "Voyage dans le Sahara et le Mzab (Suite)," 227–29.

85. "Voyage des Orphelins en Kabylie," *BOSM*, no. 5, January 1873, 111–112.

86. Again, I owe these insights about the "social meaning of gratitude" to Gullestad, *Picturing Pity*, 273–77.

87. Cf. Paul Landau's thought-provoking analysis of the individualizing assumptions behind the practice of missionary medicine. P. Landau, "Explaining Surgical Evangelism," 263.

88. Letter from F. Charmetant, *BOSM*, no. 10, April 1874, 276.

89. Letter from F. Charmetant, 283.

90. Letter from F. Charmetant, 282–83.

91. Letter from F. Charmetant, 285–86.

92. Letter from F. Charmetant, 286.

93. Letter from F. Charmetant, 287.

94. Gullestad, *Picturing Pity*, 266.

95. Letter from Père A. Paulmier, *BOSM*, no. 11, July 1874, 305–8.

96. Letter from Père Pascal, *BOSM*, no. 11, July 1874, 321.

97. Père Richard, "Voyage à Tuggurth et à Ouargla," *BOSM*, no. 13, January 1875, 385–87.

98. Bourdieu, *Algeria 1960*, 98–99, 4.

99. Lavigerie underlined these last words not once but three times.

100. Lavigerie to Deguerry, Algiers, July 6, 1873, dossier C2: Deguerry-Lavigerie correspondance (363) [typed copies], Fonds Lavigerie, AGMAfr.

101. Letter from P. Lagrange [to Provincial Superior?], February 11, 1873, Missio Algeriensis, series 1002-VI, ARSI.

102. P. Lagrange to [to Provincial Superior?], Algiers, March 15, 1873, Missio Algeriensis, series 1002-VI, ARSI.

103. Letter from P. Lagrange to [to Provincial Superior?], Algiers, January 20, 1874, Missio Algeriensis, series 1002-VI, ARSI. In Laghouat in 1869, where Jesuits likewise staffed the European parish until Lavigerie's missionaries had enough personnel to take over, they reported that Lavigerie had not permitted them to teach specifically Christian doctrines, only the Pater Noster, the ten commandments, and "natural religion." Letter from Père Gras, Laghouat, October 26, 1869, *Lettres de Fourvière 1859–1869*, vol. SL 48, ACJF.

104. Letter from Charmetant to Lavigerie, March 8, 1874, Ouadhia, dossier C4: Charmetant-Lavigerie correspondance, Fonds Lavigerie, AGMAfr.

105. Letter from Charmetant to Lavigerie, June 20, 1876, typed copy of original from dossier C4, in typed Lavigerie correspondence: "Charmetant au Cardinal, 1871–1877 (+ Notes 1869–1870)," Fonds Lavigerie, AGMAfr.

106. Letter from Gueydon to Minister of Cults, May 12, 1878, dossier A16: Algérie, Fonds Lavigerie, AGMAfr.

107. Entry "1878–79," in "Diaire de Fort National, 1864–1869, 1881" [this diary consists for the most part in detailed entries in Creuzat's hand up until 1869, then much briefer annual summaries in another hand], RA1 102, ACJF.

108. See Duchêne, *Les Pères Blancs*, 51.

109. Marcel Mauss famously called the gift (and the rules and obligations that governed it) a "'total' social phenomenon," one that pervades and implicates every sphere of a society—religious, moral, juridical, and economic. Mauss, *The Gift*, 3, 80.

110. Letters from Creuzat, October 1862, *Lettres de Fourvière, 1859–1869*, vol. SL 48, 16–18, ACJF. Not that Creuzat's every experience with the culture of the gift was fruitful. Once, when a rumor spread among the Kabyles that Creuzat intended to send their children to Algiers for a Christian education, they became suddenly wary of contracting

obligations towards the priest. Four of the poorest children, for whom Creuzat had arranged to provide tunics and red caps, came back and returned the clothes. See Creuzat,
entry of 5 July 1866, in "Diaire de Fort National," RAl 102, ACJF.

111. Letter from P. Vincent, 30 March 1869, *Lettres de Fourvière, 1850–1869*, 8–9, ACJF.

112. Creuzat, entry of 1 Dec. 1865, in "Diaire de Fort National."

113. Letter from P. Vincent, 30 March 1869, *Lettres de Fourvière, 1850–1869*, 6–7, ACJF.

114. Pratt, *Imperial Eyes*, 8–9.

115. Pratt, *Imperial Eyes*, 32, quoted phrase on 56.

116. Cf. Pratt, *Imperial Eyes*, 81.

117. See J. O'Donnell, *Lavigerie in Tunisia*; and Clancy-Smith, "Islam and the
French Empire."

118. O'Donnell, *Lavigerie in Tunisia*, 100-128; cf. Lavigerie to Deguerry, Algiers, 3
May 1881, typed copy of original from dossier C2, in typed Lavigerie correspondence,
vol. 43: "au Père Deguerry: 1871–1881 (I)," Fonds Lavigerie, AGMAfr. For a more general description of Lavigerie's entrepreneurial acumen, see Rothschild, *An Infinite History*, 265–95.

119. Lavigerie, letter of August 21, 1881, *BOSM*, no. 40, October 1881, 413–14.

120. Jean Comaroff and John Comaroff speak of the danger of oversimplifying the
motives of imperialists or missionaries into a "crude calculus of interest and intention."
Comaroff and Comaroff, *Of Revelation and Revolution*, 7. And Julia Clancy-Smith, following Jacques Berque, has reminded of the importance of "believing in the belief of the
believer." Email communication with the author, September 29, 2018.

121. The phrase "agrarian capitalism," again, is from Davis, "Colonial Capitalism," 163.

Chapter 7

1. Baunard, *Lavigerie*, 260, 263, 265–69. For a concise and beautifully written sketch
of Lavigerie's career, see Rothschild, *An Infinite History*, 265–95. And for more on Lavigerie's career and the beginnings of the White Fathers, see the detailed biography by
Renault, *Cardinal Lavigerie*, esp. chaps. 7–8 and 10–13.

2. An eyewitness account of the earliest years of the White Fathers is Félix Charmetant, "Mes notes et mémoires sur les premières années de la Societé des Miss[ionnai]res
d'Afrique," dossier B18: Papiers Charmetant, AOO.

3. Renault, *Cardinal Lavigerie*, 153.

4. Cf. letters from P. Lagrange [to Provincial Superior?], January 19, 1872; and
from Gaillard to [?], May 11, 1872, Missio Algeriensis, series 1002-VI, ARSI; and
Dirèche-Slimani, *Chrétiens de Kabylie*, 25.

5. On these early stages in Lavigerie's mission and on the orphans, see the excellent
articles of Bertrand Taithe cited throughout.

6. Charmetant, "Mes notes et mémoires . . .," 15.

7. Charmetant, "Mes notes et mémoires . . .," 15–17.

8. Charmetant, "Mes notes et mémoires . . .," 18.

9. On children as blank slates, see Curtis, *Educating the Faithful*, 92–95.

10. Citations from Lavigerie's directions to the Frères in the preceding four paragraphs are all from a draft of a letter from Lavigerie to the Frères des Écoles Chrétiennes, [no date], B8: Orphelins (10), Fonds Lavigerie, AGMAfr.

11. Letter from Charmetant to Lavigerie, September 7, 1871, typed copy of original from dossier C4, in typed Lavigerie correspondence: "Charmetant au Cardinal, 1871 – 1877 (+ Notes 1869 – 1870)," Fonds Lavigerie, AGMAfr.

12. Letter from L. Maignan to "Monseigneur," November 20, 1872, dossier B8: Orphelins (31), Fonds Lavigerie, AGMAfr.

13. Charmetant, "Mes notes et mémoires . . .," 8.

14. Charmetant, "Mes notes et mémoires . . .," 10, 19.

15. Letter from P. Vincent to a Père at the College de Mongré (copied in notebook), February 14, 1868, in B19.1: Origines de la Société; Maison mère., Fonds Lavigerie, AGMAfr.

16. Ducat[?], "Projet de Règlements," B8 (11): Orphelins, Fonds Lavigerie, AGMAfr.

17. Charmetant, "Mes notes et mémoires sur les premières années de la Societé des Miss[ionnai]res d'Afrique," 30–34, B18: Papiers Charmetant, AOO.

18. Charmetant, "Mes notes et mémoires . . .," 41–42.

19. Charmetant, "Mes notes et mémoires . . .," 44–46.

20. Charmetant, "Mes notes et mémoires . . .,". 47.

21. Charmetant, "Mes notes et mémoires . . .," 50–51.

22. Charmetant, "Mes notes et mémoires . . .," 56–58.

23. Charmetant, "Mes notes et mémoires . . .," 72.

24. See Williams, "The Necessity of a Native Clergy," 33–52 ["self-supporting" etc. qtd. on p. 49]. See also Wu, *From Christ to Confucius*, 56–57. On reasons for indigenous clergy, see Porter, *Religion versus Empire*, 163–69 (esp. 166); Prudhomme, *Stratégie missionnaire*, esp. 242; Porter, "An Overview, 1700–1914," 53–54; and Brock, "New Christians as Evangelists," 132–52. On the "experiment" of African bishops and their "white successors," see Tishken, "Neither Anglican nor Ethiopian," 85–87.

25. Prudhomme, *Stratégie missionnaire*, 241–50. On this same reluctance among Protestants, see Williams," The Necessity of a Native Clergy."

26. Père Charbonnier, prospectus of the *petit séminaire indigène*, dossier B11: Saint-Eugène (1), Fonds Lavigerie, AGMAfr.

27. Jennings, *Curing the Colonizers*, 12–13.

28. Lucien Duchêne, *Les Pères Blancs, 1868–1893: Depuis l'origine jusqu'à la mort du fondateur*, vol. 1: *La Famine et les orphelins arabes* (Alger: Maison Carrée, 1901), 3–5 [actually, 223–25, according to the pagination of the memoir as a whole. The section on the *petit séminaire indigène* begins on page 221, and then the pagination restarts]. Handwritten memoir from AGMAfr.

29. Also quoted in Duchêne, *Les Pères Blancs*, 1:9.

30. Qtd. in Duchêne, *Les Pères Blancs*, 1:9–10.

31. Cf. Duchêne, *Les Pères Blancs*, 1:31.

32. Duchêne, *Les Pères Blancs*, 1:59–60.

33. Lavigerie to Deguerry, May 20, 1874, typed copy of original from dossier C2, in typed Lavigerie correspondence, vol. 43: "au Père Deguerry: 1871 – 1881 (I)," Fonds Lavigerie, AGMAfr.

34. Duchêne, *Les Pères Blancs*, 1:30–35.

35. Duchêne, *Les Pères Blancs*, 1:35. Also see letters from Lavigerie to Deguerry in August and September 1875, typed copies of originals from dossier C2, in typed Lavigerie correspondence, vol. 43: "au Père Deguerry: 1871 – 1881 (I)," Fonds Lavigerie, AGMAfr.

36. Deguerry to Lavigerie, St. Laurent d'Olt, August 27, 1875, typed copy of original from C2, in "Deguerry au Cardinal: 1872 – 1886," Fonds Lavigerie, AGMAfr.

37. Deguerry to Lavigerie, St. Laurent d'Olt, September 1, 1875, typed copy of original from C2, in "Deguerry au Cardinal: 1872 – 1886," Fonds Lavigerie, AGMAfr.

38. Louail to [Superior General?], December 1876, in B12: Saint-Laurent d'Olt, Fonds Lavigerie, AGMAfr.

39. Duchêne, *Les Pères Blancs, 1868–1893*, 1:41.

40. Duchêne, *Les Pères Blancs, 1868–1893*, 1:48.

41. Duchêne, *Les Pères Blancs, 1868–1893*, 1:48–49.

42. Seminary council of February 14, 1878, in *St. Laurent d'Olt: Cahier des Conseils, 1878–Oct. 1879*, dossier B12: Saint-Laurent d'Olt (7), Fonds Lavigerie, AGMAfr.

43. Seminary council of February 17, 1878, in *St. Laurent d'Olt*.

44. Seminary council of March 4, 1878, in *St. Laurent d'Olt*.

45. Père Le Roy to "Mon révérend Père," August 7, 1880, dossier B12: Saint-Laurent d'Olt, Fonds Lavigerie, AGMAfr.

46. Duchêne, *Les Pères Blancs, 1868–1893*, 1:49. On colonialist anxieties about *déclassés*, see Saada, *Empire's Children*, 52–56; and Wilder, *French Imperial Nation-State*, 119–23.

47. Duchêne, *Les Pères Blancs, 1868–1893*, 1:50.

48. Charmetant, qtd. in Dirèche, *Chrétiens de Kabylie*, 92–93.

49. Duchêne, *Les Pères Blancs, 1868–1893*, 1:51.

50. Père Le Roy [to Superior General?], January 13 and 17, 1881, dossier B12: Saint-Laurent d'Olt, Fonds Lavigerie, AGMAfr.

51. Père Louail [to Superior General?], September 15, 1881, dossier B12: Saint-Laurent d'Olt, Fonds Lavigerie, AGMAfr.

52. Père Le Roy to [Superior General?], January 11, 1882, dossier B12: Saint-Laurent d'Olt, Fonds Lavigerie, AGMAfr.

53. Père Le Roy to [Superior General?], April 4, 1882, dossier B12: Saint-Laurent d'Olt, Fonds Lavigerie, AGMAfr.

54. Duchêne, *Les Pères Blancs, 1868–1893*, 1:52.

55. Louail to [Superior General?], September 15, 1881, dossier B12: Saint-Laurent d'Olt, Fonds Lavigerie, AGMAfr.

56. Louail to [Superior General?], September 29, 1882, dossier B12: Saint-Laurent d'Olt, Fonds Lavigerie, AGMAfr.

57. Duchêne, *Les Pères Blancs, 1868–1893*, 1:53–58.

58. Duchêne, *Les Pères Blancs, 1868–1893*, 1:281.

59. Duchêne, *Les Pères Blancs, 1868–1893*, 1:60–61; 1:80–281.

60. Taithe, "Algerian Orphans, 256–59.

61. Felix Kaddour to "Vénéré Pere" [Lavigerie?], Lille, January 15, dossier B9: Orphelins, Fonds Lavigerie, AGMAfr.

62. Pierre Alexis to [Reverend Pere?], January 15, 1883, dossier B9: Orphelins, Fonds Lavigerie, AGMAfr.

63. Vital Mohamed to [Reverend Pere?], January 19, 1883; and Pierre Alexis to [Reverend Pere?], January 15, 1883, dossier B9: Orphelins, Fonds Lavigerie, AGMAfr.

64. Pierre Alexis to [Reverend Pere?], January 15, 1883, and Vital Mohamed to [Reverend Pere?], January 19, 1883, dossier B9: Orphelins, Fonds Lavigerie, AGMAfr.

65. Pierre Alexis to [Reverend Pere?], January 15, 1883, dossier B9: Orphelins, Fonds Lavigerie, AGMAfr.

66. Felix Kaddour to "Venere Pere," January 15, 1883, dossier B9: Orphelins, Fonds Lavigerie, AGMAfr.

67. Grussenmeyer to [Superior General?], July 10, 1885; and Frederic Mohammed to "Eminence et Bien aimé Père," August 20, 1885, dossier B9: Orphelins, Fonds Lavigerie, AGMAfr.

68. Letter to "Reverend Pere," signed Lin AbdelKader, Felix Kaddour, Vital Mohamed, Lille, February 24, 1886, dossier B9: Orphelins, Fonds Lavigerie, AGMAfr.

69. Felix Kaddour to "Bien Cher Père," Lille, November 11, 1883, dossier B9: Orphelins, Fonds Lavigerie, AGMAfr.

70. "Bebé Jeanne" to Felix Kaddour, April 7, 1884 dossier B9: Orphelins, Fonds Lavigerie, AGMAfr.

71. Michel Hamed to [?], November 11, 1883, dossier B9: Orphelins, Fonds Lavigerie, AGMAfr.

72. Lavigerie to Louail, Carthage, December 6, 1883, typed copy of original from dossier D1, typed Lavigerie correspondence, vol. 54, "à Père Louail: 187.–1892," Fonds Lavigerie, AGMAfr.

73. See also the statement made by Felix Kaddour, April 15, 1884, dossier A11:Sabatier-Kaddour Affair; letter [draft] from Lavigerie to Governor General, April 19, 1884, dossier A11: Sabatier-Kaddour Affair; and various letters from the medical students in dossier B9: Orphelins, all in Fonds Lavigerie, AGMAfr.

74. Letter from Felix Kaddour to "tres reverend père," Tunis, January 7, 1885, dossier B9: Orphelins, Fonds Lavigerie, AGMAfr.

75. Letter from "Bebé Jeanne" to Felix Kaddour, April 7, 1884, dossier B9: Orphelins, Fonds Lavigerie, AGMAfr.

76. Mann, "What was the 'Indigénat'?," 331–53; Saada, *Empire's Children*, 96; Saada, "The Laws of Necessity,"; and Guyot, *Lettres sur la politique coloniale*, 165–72.

77. Guyot, *Lettres sur la politique coloniale*, 166; Mann, "What was the 'Indigènat'?" 333–34.

78. Saada, "The Laws of Necessity," 16–22; Didier Guignard, "L'abus presque ordinaire," in *L'abus de pouvoir dans l'Algérie coloniale*.

79. Saada, *Empire's Children*, 96.

80. Saada, *Empire's Children*; and Saada, "Laws of Necessity," 5, 21–22. "The 'time necessary for the evolution' of the indigenous people," Emmanuelle Saada quips, was "apparently unlimited," 22. On the ways "colonial humanists" practiced "a policy of temporal deferral that racialized and disenfranchised Africans within a republican framework," see Wilder, *French Imperial Nation-State*, 119–21.

81. Prefect to Governor General Tirman, Alger, May 27, 1884, dossier A11: Sabatier-Kaddour Affair, Fonds Lavigerie, AGMAfr.

82. Saada, "The Laws of Necessity," 27. Cf. Lavigerie's notes on the Sabatier-Kaddour Affair in dossier A11, Fonds Lavigerie, AGMAfr; and Sabatier, *La question de la sécurité*.

83. Aug. Bresson to "Reverend Père," Maison Carrée, April 6, 1884, dossier A11: Sabatier-Kaddour Affair, Fonds Lavigerie, AGMAfr. These kinds of politically motivated abuses of the indigénat's discretionary vagueness were not at all uncommon across France's empire. See Mann, "'What was the 'Indigénat'?"

84. Governor General Tirman to Lavigerie, August 1884 [exact date blurry], dossier A11: Sabatier-Kaddour Affair, Fonds Lavigerie, AGMAfr.

85. Throughout this paragraph and the previous one, I am relying on the draft of a statement Kaddour prepared after the fact, with the apparent help of a sympathetic judge at Fort National. Statement of Felix Kaddour, April 15, 1884; supplemented by Sabatier's own record of the interrogation, March 14, 1884. On the "juge d'instruction" who may have helped Kaddour draft this statement, see Kaddour ben Mohamed to "bien cher Père," Tizi Ouzou, March 29, 1884, all in dossier A11: Sabatier-Kaddour Affair, Fonds Lavigerie, AGMAfr.

86. Copy of Sabatier's interrogation of Felix Kaddour, 14 March 1884, dossier A11: Sabatier-Kaddour Affair, Fonds Lavigerie, AGMAfr.

87. Copy of Sabatier's interrogation of Felix Kaddour, March 14, 1884; Kaddour quotations from Kaddour ben Mohamed to "bien cher Père," Tizi Ouzou, March 29, 1884; and (Felix Kaddour?) to Monsieur le Président de la Societé protectrice des indigènes de l'algerie, [no date], dossier A11: Sabatier-Kaddour Affair, Fonds Lavigerie, AGMAfr.

88. Telegraph [draft] from Lavigerie to Gey, April [6?], 1884, dossier A11: Sabatier-Kaddour Affair, Fonds Lavigerie, AGMAfr.

89. Letter [draft] from Lavigerie to Governor General, April 19, 1884, in dossier A11: Sabatier-Kaddour Affair, Fonds Lavigerie, AGMAfr.

90. See Daumalin, "La doctrine coloniale africaine."

91. The phrase is Emmanuelle Saada's, describing the "mixed" children of relationships between the French and their colonial subjects throughout the empire. Saada, *Empire's Children*, 17.

92. Throughout this paragraph, the insights are inspired by Saada, *Empire's Children*, 2, 19. See also the discussion of "cultural" and "biological" racism in my introduction, 9–10, and scholars cited there.

93. The phrase is Saada's, quoted in the subtitle of Mann "What was the 'Indigénat'?"

94. Prefect Report to Governor General Tirman, Alger, May 27, 1884, dossier A11: Sabatier-Kaddour Affair, Fonds Lavigerie, AGMAfr.

95. Governor General Tirman to Lavigerie, August 1884, dossier A11: Sabatier-Kaddour Affair, Fonds Lavigerie, AGMAfr..

96. See Saada, "The Laws of Necessity," 27; see also confidential letter from Lavigerie to Governor General, 1886 [exact date unclear], and Lavigerie's notes summarizing the Kaddour-Sabatier Affair in dossier A11: Sabatier-Kaddour Affair, Fonds Lavigerie, AGMAfr.

97. Draft of letter from Lavigerie to Michel Hamed, October 17, 1889, dossier B9: Orphelins, Fonds Lavigerie, AGMAfr.

98. François Guermonprez to Pere Brinçat, January 3 and 4, 1889, dossier B9: Orphelins, Fonds Lavigerie, AGMAfr.

99. I owe the inspiration for some of this phraseology to Grey Anderson.

100. Gullestad, *Picturing Pity*, 273–77.

101. "Orphelins mariés non etablis aux Attafs," in dossier B8: Orphelins (9), Fonds Lavigerie, AGMAfr.

Epilogue

1. Renault, *Cardinal Lavigerie*, 367ff.

2. Lavigerie, *Lettre de S. Em. le cardinal Lavigerie sur l'esclavage africain*, 1. Lavigerie angrily opposed the Society's lay directors when they suggested that other missionary congregations working in central Africa, such as the Spiritains, should receive a more than perfunctory portion of the society's funds. See Gautherot, *Émile*, 310–11.

3. See Lavigerie, *Lettre de S. Em. le cardinal lavigerie sur l'esclavage africain*: "The Mohammedans cannot, for reasons of debauchery, exhaustion, or laziness, do without slaves, which infuse them with strength and new blood" (4). "For fifty years, and while our eyes were fixed on other countries, Mohammedanism invaded more than the half of Africa, little by little, noiselessly, with an unwearying perseverance" (6). "In order to be in agreement with the Koran, they have devised some truly infernal rules. According to the religious law, the Muslim cannot, of course, be a slave: God gives him the right to command and to remain free; only the infidel must serve. If then the blacks of Sudan all embraced Islamism, the princes could no longer profit from selling them. Consequently, they only force the most vigorous of their subjects to enter into Islamism (force being their only method of conversion). The rest are fattened up for the master" (6–7). "[The leaders of the slave raids] are *les métis*, a horrible race descended from Arabs and coastal blacks, Muslim in name, just [Muslim] enough to profess hatred and contempt for the negro race, which they place below the animals" (11). "One converts pagans. One no longer converts Muslims, and every African pagan who is forced to bow under the yoke of Islam becomes . . . the irreconcilable enemy of Christian Europe" (41), etc. On the anti-Islamic and imperialist complicity of the Antislavery campaign, see Hochschild,

King Leopold's Ghost, 92–95; and Becker, "La Représentation anti-musulmane des swahilis d'Afrique centrale," 611–37. Cf. also Renault, *Cardinal Lavigerie* 372–74.

4. François Renault also makes this point, in *Cardinal Lavigerie*, 368; see also Taithe, "Evil, Liberalism."

5. Qtd. in *Bulletin de la Société antiesclavagiste de France*, no. 1, October 1888, 39; Lavigerie, "Lettre de S. E. le cardinal Lavigerie à M. Keller, président du Conseil d'administration de l'Œuvre antiesclavagiste," Marseille, January 19, 1889, *Bulletin de la Société antiesclavagiste de France*, no. 4, January 1889, 227.

6. Qtd. in *Bulletin de la Société antiesclavagiste de France*, no. 1, October 1888, 31.

7. *Bulletin de la Société antiesclavagiste de France*, no. 1, October 1888, 40–41.

8. *Bulletin de la Société antiesclavagiste de France*, no. 1, October 1888, 63–64.

9. Taithe, "Missionary Militarism," 130, 134.

10. On Jules Simon, see Bertocci, *Jules Simon*.

11. *Bulletin de la Société antiesclavagiste de France*, no. 5, February 1889, 251–56.

12. *Bulletin de la Société antiesclavagiste de France*, no. 5, February 1889, 265.

13. See Lamure, "Les pélerinages catholiques français,".

14. Harris, "The Assumptionists and the Dreyfus Affair," 175–211; and Langlois, "Catholics and Seculars," 127.

15. Alzon, "La Croix," 4.

16. D.M.S., "Sous le Joug Musulman," *La Croix supplément*, January 11, 1896.

17. Diégo, "La Queue de Mahomet," *La Croix supplément*, June 12, 1897. Cf. "La Croisade au XIXe Siècle: Discours du P. Monsabré," *La Croix supplément*, May 21, 1895.

18. See Inayatullah, "Baron Carra de Vaux," 201–7. This open attitude is often depicted as first emerging with Louis Massignon in the interwar period. Waardenburg, "Louis Massignon," 322.

19. Cf. Gobineau, *Les religions et les philosophies*. Gobineau's orientalist writings, which focused primarily on Islamic faith and practice in Persia where he served as a diplomat, were more influential in his day than his now-infamous *Essay on the Inequality of the Human Races*. According to Geoffrey Nash, Gobineau was the originator of the view that Persian Islam was Aryan and therefore basically positive and progressive, in contrast to Semitic Islam. See Geoffrey Nash, "Introduction," in *Comte de Gobineau and Orientalism*, 9–18. Edward Said criticizes Massignon for a similar privileging of Muslim figures who are "Aryan," or unwittingly Christian. See Said, *Orientalism*, 268–72.

20. Carra de Vaux, *Le mahométisme*, 226–27.

21. Carra de Vaux, *Le mahométisme*, 229–30.

22. Here and throughout this paragraph I follow Frank Field's interpretation of Psichari's conversion, in *British and French Writers of the First World War*, 98–99. See also Neau-Dufour, *Ernest Psichari*, 201–2, 216–17.

23. Psichari wrote that instead of the "rarefied air" of France, with its platitudes and constant frivolous debate, Mauritania was filled with the "holy exaltation of the mind, the disdain for earthly goods, [and] the knowledge of the essential." Psichari, *Œuvres complètes*, 19.

24. Psichari, *Œuvres complètes*, 32.

25. Psichari, *Œuvres complètes*, 36. Cf. Edward Said's discussion of the movement from analogy to judgment, in *Orientalism*, 150.

26. Hobsbawm, *The Age of Empire*, 79, 20. Hobsbawm is reflecting on a poem by Hilaire Belloc that makes this sarcastic point about the Maxim gun.

27. Cf. Carnoy-Torabi, "Regards sur l'Islam," 466.

28. Cf. Roy, *Globalized Islam*, esp. 11; and Aydin, *The Idea of the Muslim World*, esp. 227–28.

29. See, for example, Scott, *The Politics of the Veil*; and Gresh, *L'islam, la République, et le monde*.

30. Shepard, *Sex, France, and Arab Men*.

31. Aydin, *The Idea of the Muslim World*, 222, 226, 234; on representations of the Iranian Revolution, see also Shepard, *Sex, France, and Arab Men*, 272–78.

32. Taylor, "Root Causes and Rotten Ideas"; Noah, "Dinesh D'Souza's Mullah Envy"; National Review Symposium, "The Enemy D'Souza Knows."

33. Houellebecq, *Submission*; my interpretation of the novel is influenced by Shatz, "Colombey-les-deux-Mosquées."

34. Houellebecq, *Submission*, 125.

35. "Zemmour."

36. Hoyeau and Raison du Cleuziou, "Quelles sont les six familles de catholiques en France?"

37. Scott, "The Contradictions of French Secularism"; Gresh, "Loi de 1905."

38. Yet the party still tries to retain voters committed to a "traditionalist" Catholic identity and opposed to gay rights. Almeida, "Exclusionary Secularism," 249–63, esp. 259.

39. Gollnisch, "Leur nouveau désordre mondial."

40. The information and political speculations about Macron's relationship with the Œuvre d'Orient drawn from Mélinée Le Priol, "Les reseaux chrétiens, 'bras' de la France au Moyen-Orient," in *La Croix*, February 1, 2022; OLJ/F.N., "Le président Macron remet la Légion d'honneur au directeur général de l'Œuvre d'Orient, Mgr Pascal Gollnisch," in *L'Orient-Le Jour*, February 22, 2022; and Jean-Marie Guénois, "Macron et les chrétiens d'Orient: un hommage intéressé?" in *Le Figaro*, February 2, 2022. My thanks to Rim-Sarah Alouane for bringing Macron's political strategy to my attention.

41. Phrase inspired by Noah, "Dinesh D'Souza's Mullah Envy."

42. Vincent, "Pourquoi des musulmans choisissent l'école catholique pour leurs enfants."

43. Qtd. in Pech, "Ces écoles catholiques plébiscitées par les musulmans."

44. Peiron, "Philippe Delorme"; Peiron, "Les écoles hors contrat catholiques."

45. Cf. Delorme, *L'islam que j'aime, l'islam qui m'inquiète*, esp. 56–57, 146.

46. Cf. Johnston-White and Peterson, "French Secularism, Reinvented."

47. This is a rough paraphrase of Philippe Delorme, qtd. in Peiron, "Philippe Delorme": "Dire . . . qu'une fois franchie la porte de l'école, l'enfant doit oublier les convictions qui s'expriment à la maison est absurde."

48. Asad, *Formations of the Secular*, 180.

BIBLIOGRAPHY

Archival Collections

Archives nationales, Pierrefitte-sur-Seine (AN)
    Cultes Série: F19
    Fonds Vogüé: 567AP
Archives nationales, Centre des archives d'outre-mer, Aix-en-Provence (ANOM)
    Algérie, Fonds Ministériel: F80/1625, F80/1627, F80/1628, F80/1746
    Gouvernement général de l'Algérie, questions religieuses, 16H 114: propagande
        catholique (1850–1944)
    Bureaux Arabes Constantine: 1/K/369
Bibliothèque nationale de France, Département des manuscrits, Paris
    Nouvelles Acquisitions Françaises (NAF)
        Fonds Veuillot: 24223, 24225
        Fonds Ozanam: 28199
Archives de l'Œuvre d'Orient, Paris (AOO)
    Papiers Charmetant (Série B)
    Procès-Verbaux du Conseil de l'Œuvre
Archives de l'Œuvre de la propagation de la Foi, Lyon (now the Œuvres Pontificales
    Missionnaires [OPM])
    Fonds Lyon
        Dossier E-32: Proche Orient, divers
        Dossier G-7: Alger
        Dossier G-8: Alger
        Dossier I-16: Jésuites 1835–1867
        Dossier I-23: Lazaristes
    Fonds Paris
        Dossier G-8: Alger
Archives de la Congrégation de la Mission (Lazarists), Paris (ACM)
    Dossier 106B: Algérie
    Dossier 108A: Alger
    Dossier 116C: Moyen Orient, généralités
    Fonds de Saint-Benoît de Constantinople, Supérieurs généraux
    Papiers Boré

Archives de la Compagnie de Jésus, Province de France, Vanves (ACJF)
   Fonds Prat: vols. 10, 23
   Lettres de Fourvières, 1859–1869: vol. SL 48
   Various diaries and notes from mission posts in Algeria (dossiers): RAl 2, RAl 44,
      RAl 50, RAl 80, RAl 81, RAl 89, RAl 91, RAl 97, RAl 102, RAl 105
Archivum Romanum Societatis Iesu (Archives of the Company of Jesus),
   Rome (ARSI)
   Provincia Lugdunensis, Missio Algeriensis: series 1001, 1002; various dossiers
Archives de la Société des Missionnaires d'Afrique (Pères Blancs), Rome (AGMAfr.)
   Fonds Lavigerie
      A11: Relations avec le saint Siège..., A16: Algérie; A19: Œuvres
      B8–B9: Orphelins; B11: Saint-Eugène; B12: Saint-Laurent d'Olt; B19: Origines de
         la Société; Maison mère.
      C2: Deguerry-Lavigerie correspondence [consulted as typed copies: Lavigerie
         correspondence, vol. 43: "au Père Deguerry: 1871 – 1881 (I)"; and "Deguerry au
         Cardinal: 1872 – 1886"]; C4: Charmetant-Lavigerie correspondence [consulted
         as typed copies: "Charmetant au Cardinal, 1871 – 1877 (+ Notes 1869 – 1870)"]
      D1: Louail-Lavigerie correspondence [consulted as typed copies: Lavigerie corre-
         spondence, vol. 54, "à Père Louail: 187.–1892"]
   Lucien Duchêne, *Les Pères Blancs, 1868–1893: Depuis l'origine jusqu'à la mort du fon-
      dateur*. Vol. 1, *La Famine et les orphelins arabes*. Algiers: Maison Carrée, 1901.
Archives de la Ministère des Affaires étrangères, La Courneuve (AMAE)
   Correspondance politique (CP) Turquie: vols. 393, 394, 395, 397, 398
   Papiers d'Avril: 7CPAAP
   Papiers Delarue: 58PAAP
   Mémoires et documents (MD) Turquie: vols. 40, 122
Bibliothèque du Ministère des Affaires étrangères
   Fonds d'Avril
   Fonds Faugère

Books and Articles

Abi-Mershed, Osama W. *Apostles of Modernity: Saint-Simonians and the Civilizing
   Mission in Algeria*. Stanford: Stanford University Press, 2010.
Abrams, M. H. *Natural Supernaturalism: Tradition and Revolution in Romantic Literature*. New York: Norton, 1971.
"Académiciens depuis 1663." Académie des inscriptions et belles-lettres. Accessed February 24, 2022. https://www.aibl.fr/membres/academiciens-depuis-1663.
Ageron, Charles-Robert. "Jules Ferry et la question algériènne en 1892 (d'après
   quelques inédits)." *Revue d'histoire moderne et contemporaine* 10, no. 2
   (1963): 127–46.

Ageron, Charles-Robert. "Le mouvement 'Jeune-Algérien' de 1900 à 1923." In *Études maghrébines: Mélanges Charles-André Julien*, edited by Pierre Marthelot, Andre Raymond, and Charles Andre Julien, 107–130. Paris: Presses Universitaires de France, 1964.

———. *Les algériens musulmans et la France (1871–1919)*. Vol. 1. Paris: Presses Universitaires de France, 1968.

Agresta, Abigail. "Culturally Muslim in Medieval and Early Modern Spain." Marginalia, August 3, 2018. https://marginalia.lareviewofbooks.org/being-culturally-muslim/.

Al-Bustani, Butrus. *The Clarion of Syria: A Patriot's Call against the Civil War of 1860*. Introduced and translated by Jens Hanssen and Hicham Safieddine. Oakland: University of California Press, 2019.

Ali, Kecia. *Lives of Muhammad*. Cambridge, MA: Harvard University Press, 2014.

Almeida, Dimitri. "Exclusionary Secularism: The Front National and the Reinvention of Laïcité." *Modern and Contemporary France* 25, no. 3 (2017): 249–63.

Alzon, Emmanuel de. "La Croix." *La Croix: Recueil mensuel* (April 1880):1–4.

Amanat, Abbas. "Introduction: Apocalyptic Anxieties and Millenial Hopes in the Salvation Religions of the Middle East." In *Imagining the End: Visions of Apocalypse from the Ancient Middle East to Modern America*, edited by Abbas Amanat and Magnus Bernhardsson. London: I. B. Tauris, 2002.

Andrews, Naomi. "Selective Empathy: Workers, Colonial Subjects, and the Affective Politics of French Romantic Socialism." *French Politics, Culture and Society* 36, no. 1 (Spring 2018): 1–25.

Anonymous. *De la conversion de musulmans au christianisme, considerée comme moyen d'affermir la puissance française en Algérie, par un officier de l'armée d'Afrique*. Paris: Jacques Lecoffre et Cie., 1846.

Anonymous. *Eugène Boré supérieur général des Lazaristes, 1809–1878: L'homme privé, l'homme public, les voyages, les œuvres, par un témoin de sa vie, avec de nombreux souvenirs personnels de Boré*. Lille [ca. 1906].

Anonymous [Thomas Dazincourt]. *Notice sur M. Joseph Girard: Prêtre de la mission, premier supérieur du grand séminaire d'Alger*. Paris: de J. Mersch, 1881.

Armenteros, Carolina. *The French Idea of History: Joseph de Maistre and His Heirs, 1794–1854*. Ithaca, NY: Cornell University Press, 2011.

Arsan, Andrew. "'There is, in the Heart of Asia...an Entirely French Population': France, Mount Lebanon, and the Workings of Affective Empire in the Mediterranean, 1830–1920." In *French Mediterraneans: Transnational and Imperial Histories*, edited by Patricia M. E. Lorcin and Todd Shepard. Lincoln: University of Nebraska Press, 2016.

Asad, Talal. *Formations of the Secular: Christianity, Islam, Modernity*. Stanford, CA: Stanford University Press, 2003.

Asseraf, Arthur. *Electric News in Colonial Algeria*. New York: Oxford University Press, 2019.

Avril, Adolphe de. *L'arabie contemporaine, avec la description du Pèlerinage de la Mec-que*. Paris: E. Maillet, 1868.

———. *Les femmes dans l'épopée iranienne*. Paris: Ernest Leroux, 1888.

Aydin, Cemil. *The Idea of the Muslim World: A Global Intellectual History*. Cambridge, MA: Harvard University Press, 2017.

Ayoun, Richard. "Le décret Crémieux et l'insurrection de 1871 en Algérie." *Revue d'histoire moderne et contemporaine* 35, no. 1 (1988): 61–87. https://www.persee.fr/doc/rhmc_0048-8003_1988_num_35_1_1439.

B., Jean de. "Chronique: La féodalité arabe." *La Tafna: Journal de l'arrondissement de Tlemcen*, May 3 1893.

Bar-Yosef, Eitan. *The Holy Land in English Culture, 1799–1917: Palestine and the Question of Orientalism*. New York: Oxford University Press, 2005.

Baudicour, Louis de. "Correspondance de particulière de *L'Univers*." *L'Univers*, November 1, 1850.

———. *La colonisation de l'Algérie: Ses éléments*. Paris: Challamel Ainé, 1856.

———. *La France au Liban*. Paris: E. Dentu, 1879.

Baunard, Louis. *Le cardinal Lavigerie*. Paris: Librairie Ch. Poussielgue, 1896.

Becker, Quentin de. "La représentation anti-musulmane des swahilis d'Afrique centrale par Godefroid Kurth: Un acteur catholique dans la propagande coloniale (1888–1926)." *Annales Æquatoria* 30 (2009): 611–37.

Benoist, Gustave. *De l'instruction et de l'éducation des indigènes dans la province de Constantine*. Paris: Hachette, 1886.

"Berbers." In *Encyclopédie nouvelle*, vol. 1, edited by P. Leroux and J Reynaud. 1836. Reprint, Geneva: Slatkine Reprints, 1991.

Bercé, Françoise. "Charles Lenormant à la Commission des Monuments historiques (1840–1859). *Bulletin de la Société nationale des antiquaires de France* 2007, no. 1 (2009): 195–209.

Bertocci, Philip A. *Jules Simon: Republican Anticlericalism and Cultural Politics in France, 1848–1886*. Columbia: University of Missouri Press, 1978.

Beylard, Hugues. "Joseph Burnichon." In *Dictionnaire du monde religieux dans la France contemporaine*, vol. 1: *Les jesuites*, edited by Paul Duclos, Jean-Marie Mayeur, and Yves-Marie Hilaire. Paris: Beauchesne, 1985.

Bhabha, Homi. *The Location of Culture*. 1994. Reprint, London: Routledge, 2004.

Blévis, Laure. "La citoyenneté française au miroir de la colonization: Étude des demandes de naturalization des 'sujets français' en Algérie coloniale." *Genèses*, no. 53 (2003): 25–47.

Blumenkranz, Bernhard, et al. "France." In *Encyclopaedia Judaica*, vol. 7, edited by Michael Berenbaum and Fred Skolnik, 146–70. 2nd ed. Detroit: Macmillan Reference, 2007.

Boré, Eugène. *Correspondance et mémoires d'un voyageur en Orient*. Vol. 1. Paris: Olivier-Fulgence, 1840.

————. "Hérésies chrétiennes: Exposition et histoire de la foi musulmane." *Annales de philosophie chrétienne* 12, no. 71 (1836): 321–337.

————. "Lettres sur le Liban." *L'Univers,* August 30, 1848; September, 4, 8, 10, 18, and 25, 1848.

————. "Mémoire adressé aux Conseils centraux de l'Œuvre de la propagation de la Foi, 17 décembre 1843." *Annales de la propagation de la foi: Recueil périodique* 17 (1845): 93–105.

Borrmans, Maurice. "Lavigerie et les musulmans en Afrique du Nord." *Bulletin de littérature ecclésiastique* 95 (1994): 39–56.

Boudjada, Yasmina. "L'église catholique de Constantine de 1839 à 1859: Cas de l'appropriation de la mosquée Souk el Ghzel par les Français." In *Villes rattachées, villes reconfigurées: XVIe–XXe siècles,* edited by Denise Turrel [online]. Tours: Presses universitaires François-Rabelais, 2003. https://books.openedition.org/pufr/3073.

Boudon, Jacques-Olivier. "Les catholiques sociaux parisiens au milieu du XIXe siècle." *Revue d'histoire de l'église de France* 85, no. 214 (1999): 55–73.

————. "Mgr Lavigerie et l'État: De la Seconde République au Ralliement." *Bulletin de littérature ecclesiastique* 95 (1994): 107–134.

————. *Paris, capitale religieuse sous la Second Empire.* Paris: Cerf, 2001.

Bourdieu, Pierre. *Algeria 1960: Essays.* Translated by Richard Nice. Cambridge: Cambridge University Press, 1979.

Brebner, Philip. "The Impact of Thomas-Robert Bugeaud and the Decree of 9 June 1844 on the Development of Constantine, Algeria." *Revue de l'Occident musulman et de la Méditerranée* 38, no. 1 (1984): 5–14. https://doi.org/10.3406/remmm.1984.2041.

Broc, Numa. "Les grandes missions scientifiques françaises au XIXe siècle (Morée, Algérie, Mexique) et leurs travaux géographiques." *Revue d'histoire des sciences* 34, nos. 3–4 (1981): 319–58.

Brock, Peggy. "New Christians as Evangelists." In *Missions and Empire,* edited by Norman Etherington, 132–52. Oxford: Oxford University Press, 2005.

Brower, Benjamin Claude. *A Desert Named Peace: The Violence of France's Empire in the Algerian Sahara, 1844–1902.* New York: Columbia University Press, 2009.

Brower, Benjamin Claude. "The Amîr 'Abd Al-Qâdir and the 'Good War' in Algeria, 1832–1847." *Studia Islamica* 106, no. 2 (2011): 169–95.

Brown, Frederick. *For the Soul of France: Culture Wars in the Age of Dreyfus.* New York: Alfred A. Knopf, 2010.

Brown, Marvin L. *Louis Veuillot: French Ultramontane Catholic Journalist and Layman, 1813–1883.* Durham, NC: Moore Publishing Company, 1977.

Buchanan, Alexandrina. "Science and Sensibility: Architectural Antiquarianism in the Early Nineteenth Century." In *Producing the Past: Aspects of Antiquarian Culture and Practice, 1700–1850,* edited by Lucy Peltz and Martin Myrone, 169–186. Aldershot, UK: Ashgate Publishing, 1999.

Burke, Edmund, III. "The Sociology of Islam: The French Tradition." In Burke and Prochaska, *Genealogies of Orientalism*, 154–173.

Burke, Edmund, III, and David Prochaska. "Introduction: Orientalism from Postcolonial Theory to World History." In *Genealogies of Orientalism: History, Theory, Politics*, edited by Edmund Burke III and David Prochaska. Lincoln: University of Nebraska Press, 2008, 1–71.

Burnichon, Jules. "L'Algérie: Colonisation et assimilation, deuxième partie." *Études*, July 1891.

Burrows, Ma'hew. "'Mission civilisatrice': French Cultural Policy in the Middle East, 1860–1914." *Historical Journal* 29, no. 1 (1986): 109–35.

Burton, Richard D. E. *Holy Tears, Holy Blood: Women, Catholicism, and the Culture of Suffering in Francem 1840–1970*. Ithaca, NY: Cornell University Press, 2004.

Cagnat, René. "Notice sur la vie et les travaux de M. le Marquis de Vogüé." *Comptes-rendus des séanc's de l'Académie des inscriptions et belles-lettres* 62, no. 6 (1918): 442–473.

Carnoy-Torabi, Dominique. "Regards sur l'islam, de l'âge classique aux Lumières." In *Histoire de l'Islam et des musulmans en France: du Moyen Âge à nos jours*, edited by Mohammed Arkoun and Jean Mouttapa, 466–503. Paris: Librairie générale française (La Pochothèque), 2010 (original: Albin Michel, 2006).

Carra de Vaux, Baron. *Le mahométisme: Le génie sémitique et le génie aryen dans l'Islam*. Paris: Honoré Champion, 1897.

Carroll, Christina. "Imperial Ideologies in the Second Empire: The Mexican Expedition and the Royaume Arabe." *French Historical Studies* 42, no. 1 (2019): 67–100.

Chambre des députés. *Archives parlementaires de 1787 à 1860*. Deuxieme serie (1800–1860), vol. 123. Paris: Librairie Administrative Paul Dupont, 1911.

Chenntouf, Tayeb. "L'évolution du travail en Algérie au XIXe siècle." *'Revue de l'Occident musulman et de la Méditerranée*, no. 31 (1981): 85–103.

Chevalier, M. "Voyage de notre très-honoré père, M. Boré, en Algérie." *Annales de la Congrégation de la Mission* 42 (1877): 345. https://via.library.depaul.edu/annales/40/.

Christelow, Allan. *Muslim Law Courts and the French Colonial State in Algeria*. Princeton, NJ: Princeton University Press, 1985.

Clancy-Smith, Julia. "Islam and the French Empire in North Africa." In *Islam and the European Empires*, edited by David Motadel, 90–111(?). Oxford: Oxford University Press, 2014.

———. "La révolte de Bû Ziyân en Algérie, 1849." *Revue des mondes musulmans et de la Méditerranée*, no. 91–94 (2000): 181–208. https://doi.org/10.4000/remmm.255.

———. *Mediterraneans: North Africa and Europe in an Age of Migration, c. 1800–1900*. Berkeley: University of California Press, 2010.

———. *Rebel and Saint: Muslim Notables, Populist Protest, Colonial Encounters (Algeria and Tunisia, 1800–1904)*. Berkeley: University of California Press, 1994.

Clark, Christopher. "The New Catholicism and the European Culture Wars." In *Culture Wars: Secular-Catholic Conflict in Nineteenth-Century Europe*, edited by Christopher Clark and Wolfram Kaiser, 11–46. Cambridge: Cambridge University Press, 2003.

Cohen, David. "Une souscription des Juifs de France en faveur des chrétiens d'Orient en 1860." *Revue d'histoire moderne et contemporaine* 24, no. 3 (1977): 439–454.

Cole, Joshua. *Lethal Provocation: The Constantine Murders and the Politics of French Algeria*. Ithaca, NY: Cornell University Press, 2019.

Coller, Ian. *Arab France: Islam and the Making of Modern Europe, 1798–1831*. Berkeley: University of California Press, 2010.

———. "Islam and the Revolutionary Age." Age of Revolutions, January 27, 2020. https://ageofrevolutions.com/2020/01/27/islam-and-the-revolutionary-age/.

Collin, Thibaud. *Laïcité ou religion nouvelle: L'institution du politique chez Edgar Quinet*. Paris: L'Harmattan, 2007.

Collot, Claude. *Les institutions de l'Algérie durant la période coloniale: (1830 – 1962)*. Paris: Edition du CNRS, 1987.

Colonna, Fanny. "Le système d'enseignement de l'Algérie coloniale." *European Journal of Sociology/Archives européennes de sociologie* 13, no. 2 (1972): 195–220.

Colonna, Ugo. "La compagnie de Jesus en Algérie (1840–1880): L'exemple de la mission de Kabylie (1863–1880)." *Maghreb-Machrek*, no. 135 (1992): 68–78.

Comaroff, Jean, and John L Comaroff. "Home-Made Hegemony: Modernity, Domesticity, and Colonialism in South Africa." In *African Encounters with Domesticity*, edited by Karen Tranberg Hansen, 37–74. New Brunswick, NJ: Rutgers University Press, 1992.

———. *Of Revelation and Revolution*, vol 1: *Christianity, Colonialism, and Consciousness in South Africa*. Chicago: University of Chicago Press, 1991.

Conklin, Alice L. *A Mission to Civilize: The Republican Idea of Empire in France and West Africa*. Stanford: Stanford University Press, 1997.

Cooper, Frederick. *Colonialism in Question: Theory, Knowledge, History*. Berkeley: University of California Press, 2005.

Cote, M. "Biskra." *Encyclopédie berbère*, 10 (1991): 1517–22. https://doi.org/10.4000/encyclopedieberbere.1761.

Crossley, Ceri. *Edgar Quinet (1803–1875): A Study in Romantic Thought*. Lexington, KY: French Forum, 1983.

Crossley, Ceri. "Edgar Quinet and the 'Renaissance orientale.'" *Dalhousie French Studies* 43 (1998): 131–44. https://www.jstor.org/stable/40837239.

Cubitt, Geoffrey. *The Jesuit Myth: Conspiracy Theory and Politics in Nineteenth-Cen tury France*. Oxford: Clarendon Press, 1993.

Cuoq, Joseph. *Lavigerie, les Peres Blancs, et les musulmans maghrébins*. Rome: Société des Missionnaires d'Afrique, 1986.

Curtis, Sarah A. "Charitable Ladies: Gender, Class and Religion in Mid Nineteenth-Century Paris." *Past and Present* 177, no. 1 (2002): 121–56.

———. *Civilizing Habits: Women Missionaries and the Revival of French Empire*. New York: Oxford University Press, 2010.

———. *Educating the Faithful: Religion, Schooling, and Society in Nineteenth-Century France*. DeKalb: Northern Illinois University Press, 2000.

———. "Emilie de Vialar and the Religious Reconquest of Algeria." *French Historical Studies* 29 (2006): 261–92.

Cyrille, [Adolphe d'Avril]. *La France au Monténégro, d'après Vialla de Sommières et Henri Delarue*. Paris: Ernest Leroux, 1876.

Damas, A. de. "La science et les missionaires au Liban." *Études* 4 (1864): 455–477.

Dangarembga, Tsitsi. *Nervous Conditions*. New York: Seal Press, 1989.

Daniel, Norman. *Islam and the West: The Making of an Image*. 1960. Reprint, Edinburgh: The University Press, 1980.

Dansette, Adrien, *Histoire religieuse de la France contemporaine*, 2 vols. Paris: Flammarion, 1948, 1951.

Daughton, J. P. *An Empire Divided: Religion, Republicanism, and the Making of French Colonialism, 1880–1914*. New York: Oxford University Press, 2006.

Daumalin, Xavier. "La doctrine coloniale africaine de Paul Leroy-Beaulieu (1870–1916): Essai d'analyse thématique." In *L'esprit économique impérial (1830–1970): Groupes de pression & réseaux du patronat colonial en France & dans l'empire*, 103–20. Paris: Société française d'histoire d'outre-mer, 2008.

Davidson, Naomi. *Only Muslim: Embodying Islam in Twentieth-Century France*. Ithaca, NY: Cornell University Press, 2012.

Davis, Muriam Haleh. "Colonial Capitalism and Imperial Myth in French North Africa." In *A Critical Political Economy of the Middle East and North Africa*, edited by Joel Beinin, Bassam Haddad, and Sherene Seikaly, 161–178. Stanford, CA: Stanford University Press.

Delorme, Christian. *"L'islam que j'aime, l'Islam qui m'inquiète": Entretien avec Antoine d'Abbundo*. Montrouge: Bayard, 2012.

Demos, John. *The Heathen School: A Story of Hope and Betrayal in the Age of the Early Republic*. New York: Alfred A. Knopf, 2014.

Derré, Jean René, et al., eds. *Civilisation chrétienne: Approche historique d'une idéologie, XVIIIe–XXe siècle*. Paris: Beauchesne, 1975.

Derrida, Jacques. "Faith and Knowledge: The Two Sources of Religion at the Limits of Reason Alone." In *Acts of Religion*, edited by Gil Anidjar, translated by Samuel Weber, 42–101. New York: Routledge, 2002.

Desan, Suzanne. *Reclaiming the Sacred: Lay Religion and Popular Politics in Revolutionary France*. Ithaca, NY: Cornell University Press, 1990.

Díaz-Andreu, Margarita. *A World History of Nineteenth-Century Archaeology: Nationalism, Colonialism, and the Past*. Oxford: Oxford University Press, 2007.

Dirèche-Slimani, Karima. *Chrétiens de Kabylie (1873–1954): Une action missionnaire dans l'Algerie coloniale*. Editions Bouchene, 2004.

Dournon, A. "Constantine sous les Turcs d'après Salah el Antri." In *Recueil des notices et mémoires de la Société archéologique de la province de Constantine*. Constantine: Edition Braham, 1929.

Drevet, Richard. "Frédéric Ozanam et la propagation de la Foi à Lyon: Les raisons d'un échec." In *Frédéric Ozanam: Actes du Colloque des 4 et 5 décembre 1998*, edited by Isabelle Chareire, 112–31. Paris: Bayard, 2001.

Ducat, Henri. "Feuilleton: Constantine . . ." In *Les missions catholiques: Bulletin hebdomadaire illustré de l'Œuvre de la propagation de la Foi*, 1875–1877.

Duffy, Andrea E. *Nomad's Land: Pastoralism and French Environmental Policy in the Nineteenth-Century Mediterranean World*. Lincoln: University of Nebraska Press, 2019.

Dumons, Bruno. "Jésuites lyonnais et catholicisme intransigeant." In *Les jésuites à Lyon, XVIe –XXe siècle*, edited by Étienne Fouilloux and Bernard Hours, 131–143. Lyon: ENS Éditions, 2005.

Dupanloup, Felix. *La convention du 15 septembre et l'encyclique du 8 décembre*. Paris: Charles Douniol, 1865.

Dutau, A. "L'imprimerie catholique de Beyrouth: Lettre du R. P. Dutau à la rédaction des *Études*," *Études religieuses, historiques et littéraires* 3 (1863): 386–413.

Duvernois, Clément. *L'Algérie pittoresque: Description, moeurs, coutumes, commerce, etc., etc.* Paris: J. Rouvier, Libraire-Editeur, 1863.

Dzanic, Dzavid. "France's Informal Empire in the Mediterranean, 1815–1830." *Historical Journal* (2021). 1–22. https://doi.org/10.1017/S0018246X21000340.

Émerit, Marcel. "La crise Syrienne et l'expansion économique Française en 1860." *Revue historique* 207, no. 2 (1952): 211–32.

———. "La lutte entre les généraux et les prêtres au début de l'Algérie française." *Revue africaine* 97 (1953): 66–97.

———. "Le problème de la conversion des musulmans d'Algérie sous le Second Empire: Le Conflit entre MacMahon et Lavigerie." *Revue Historique* 223 (1960): 63–84.

———. "La question algérienne en 1871." *Revue d'histoire moderne et contemporaine* 19, no. 2 (1972): 256–64.

Englund, Steven. *Napoleon: A Political Life*. Cambridge, MA: Harvard University Press, 2005.

Étienne, Bruno. "Le rayonnement d'Abd el-Kader dans les milieux chrétiens et francs-maçons." In *L'histoire de l'Islam et des musulmans en France: du Moyen Âge à nos jours*, edited by Mohammed Arkoun and Jean Mouttapa, 622–628. Paris: Libraire générale française (La Pochothèque), 2010 (original: Albin Michel, 2006).

Falloux, Le Comte de. *Le parti catholique: Ce qu'il a été—ce qu'il est devenu*. Paris: Ambroise Bray, 1856.

Fatih, Zakaria. "Peering into the Mosque: Enlightenment Views of Islam." *French Review* 85, no. 6 (May 2012): 1070–1082.

Faugère, Prosper. *De la propagande musulmane en Afrique et dans les Indes*. Paris: Bureau du Correspondant, 1851.

Fawaz, Leila Tarazi. *An Occasion for War: Civil Conflict in Lebanon and Damascus in 1860*. London: Center for Lebanese Studies and I.B. Tauris.

Ferry, Jules. "Discours du 28 juillet 1885." In *Discours et opinions de Jules Ferry*, vol. 5: *Discours sur la politique extérieure et coloniale, 2ème partie*, edited by Paul Robiquet, 172–220. Paris: Armand Colin & Cie., 1897.

Field, Frank. *British and French Writers of the First World War: Comparative Studies in Cultural History*. Cambridge: Cambridge University Press, 2008.

Fogarty, Richard, and Michael A. Osborne. "Constructions and Functions of Race in French Military Medicine, 1830–1920." In *The Color of Liberty: Histories of Race in France*, edited by Sue Peabody and Tyler Stovall, 206–36. Durham, NC: Duke University Press, 2003.

Fontaine, Darcie. "Treason or Charity? Christian Missions on Trial and the Decolonization of Algeria." Special issue, *International Journal of Middle East Studies* 44, no. 4 (2012): 733–753.

Fortescue, Adrian. "Eastern Churches." In *The Catholic Encyclopedia*, vol. 5. New York: Robert Appleton Company, 1909. http://www.newadvent.org/cathen/05230a.htm.

Foster, Elizabeth. *Faith in Empire: Religion, Politics, and Colonial Rule in French Senegal, 1880–1940*. Stanford, CA: Stanford University Press, 2013.

———. "'Theologies of Colonization': The Catholic Church and the Future of the French Empire in the 1950s." *Journal of Modern History* 87, no. 2 (2015): 281–315.

Francis, Kyle. "Catholic Missionaries in Colonial Algeria: Faith, Foreigners, and France's Other Civilizing Mission, 1848–1883." *French Historical Studies* 39, no. 4 (2016): 685–715.

Fredj, Claire. "Une mission impossible? L'église d'Afrique et la conversion des 'indigènes' (1830–1920)." In *Missions chrétiennes en terre d'islam: Anthologie de textes missionnaires*, edited by Chantal Verdeil, 163–229. Turnhout: Brepols, 2013.

Frémaux, Jacques. *Les bureaux arabes dans l'Algérie de la conquête*. Paris: Editions Denoël, 1993.

Gadille, Jacques, and Jean-Marie Mayeur. "Les milieux catholiques libéraux en France: Continuité et diversité d'une tradition." In *Les catholiques libéraux aux XIXe siècle: Actes du Colloque international d'histoire religieuse de Grenoble des 30 septembre–3 octobre 1971*. Grenoble: Presses Universitaires de Grenoble, 1974. https://archive.org/details/lescatholiqueslioooocoll

Gallois, William. "Dahra and the History of Violence in Early Colonial Algeria." In *The French Colonial Mind*, vol. 2: *Violence, Military Encounters, and Colonialism*, edited by Martin Thomas, 3–25. Lincoln, Nebraska: University of Nebraska Press, 2011.

Gautherot, Gustave. *Émile Keller (1828–1909): Un demi-siecle de défense nationale et religieuse*. Paris: Plon, 1922.

Gautier, Léon. *Études et controverses historiques*. Paris: Hervé 1866.

Gay, Peter. *Schnitzler's Century: The Making of Middle-Class Culture, 1815–1914*. New York: Norton, 2002.

Gibson, Ralph. *A Social History of French Catholicism, 1789–1914*. London: Routledge, 1989.

Gildea, Robert. *Children of the Revolution: The French, 1799–1914*. Cambridge, MA: Harvard University Press, 2008.

Gobineau, Arthur de. *Les religions et les philosophies dans l'Asie centrale*. Paris: Didier, 1866.

Gopal, Priyamvada. *Insurgent Empire: Anticolonial Resistance and British Dissent.* London: Verso, 2019.

Gough, Austin. *Paris and Rome: The Gallican Church and the Ultramontane Campaign, 1848–1853.* Oxford: Oxford University Press, 1986.

Gourinard, Pierre. *Les royalistes en Algérie de 1830 à 1962: De la colonisation au drame.* Anet: Atelier Fol'fer: 2012.

Goyau, Georges. "Besançon (Vesontio)." In *The Catholic Encyclop*edia, vol. 2. New York: Robert Appleton Company, 1907. http://www.newadvent.org/cathen/02525b.htm.

Goyau, Georges. *Un grand missionnaire, le cardinal Lavigerie: Avec deux portraits.* Paris: Plon-Nourrit, 1925.

Gran-Aymerich, Ève. "Gaillardot, Joseph-Arnaud Charles." In *Dictionnaire des orientalists de langue française*, edited by François Pouillon, 414–415. Paris: Karthala, 2008.

Grangaud, Isabelle. "Un point de vue local sur le milieu du XIXe siècle: À propos d'historiens de la conquête." In *Insaniyat: Revue algérienne d'anthropologie et de sciences sociales* 19–20 (2003): 97–115. https://journals.openedition.org/insaniyat/5828 (accessed June 24, 2022).

Greenberg, Udi. "Protestants, Decolonization, and European Integration, 1885–1961." *Journal of Modern History* 89, no. 2 (2017): 314–354.

Greenhalgh, Michael. "French Military Reconnaissance in the Ottoman Empire during the Eighteenth and Nineteenth Centuries as a Source for Our Knowledge of Ancient Monuments." *Journal of Military History* 66, no. 2 (2002): 359–88.

Gresh, Alain. *L'islam, la République, et le monde.* Paris: Fayard: 2004.

———. "Loi de 1905: Dévoyer la laïcité pour guerroyer contre Islam." *OrientXXI*, December 8, 2020. https://orientxxi.info/magazine/loi-de-1905-devoyer-la-laicite-pour-guerroyer-contre-l-islam,4343.

Grubb, Alan. *The Politics of Pessimism: Albert de Broglie and Conservative Politics in the Early Third Republic.* Newark: University of Delaware Press, 1996.

Guénois, Jean-Marie. "Macron et les chrétiens d'Orient: un hommage intéressé?" in *Le Figaro*, February 2, 2022.

Guignard, Didier. *L'abus de pouvoir dans l'Algérie coloniale (1880–1914): Visibilité et singularité.* Nanterre: Presses universitaires de Paris Nanterre, 2010. http://books.openedition.org/pupo/3121.

Gullestad, Marianne. *Picturing Pity: Pitfalls and Pleasures in Cross-Cultural Communication. Image and Word in a North Cameroon Mission.* New York: Bergahn Books, 2007.

Guyot, Yves. *Lettres sur la politique coloniale.* Paris: C. Reinwald, 1885.

Haddad, Mouloud. "Sur les pas d'Abd el-Kader: la hijra des algériens en Syrie au XIXe siècle." In *Abd el-Kader, un spirituel dans la modernité*, edited by Ahmed Bouyerdene, Eric Geoffroy, and Setty G. Simon-Khedis, 51–68. Damas: Presses de l'Ifpo, 2012. https://books.openedition.org/ifpo/1772.

Hakim, Carol. *The Origins of the Lebanese National Idea, 1840–1920.* Berkeley: University of California Press, 2013.

Harrigan, Patrick J. "French Catholics and Classical Education after the Falloux Law." *French Historical Studies* 8, no. 2 (1973): 255–78.

Harris, Ruth. *Lourdes: Body and Spirit in the Secular Age*. London: Penguin Books, 1999.

———. "The Assumptionists and the Dreyfus Affair." *Past and Present*, no. 194 (2007): 175–211.

Harrison, Carol. *Romantic Catholics: France's Postrevolutionary Generation in Search of a Modern Faith*. Ithaca, NY: Cornell University Press, 2014.

Hastings, Adrian. "Ultramontanism." In *The Oxford Companion to Christian Thought*, edited by eds. Hastings, Alistair Mason, and Hugh Pyper, 730. Oxford: Oxford University Press, 2000.

Healy, George R. "The French Jesuits and the Idea of the Noble Savage." *William and Mary Quarterly* 15 (1958): 143–67.

Heyberger, Bernard, and Rémy Madinier. "Introduction." In *L'Islam des marges: Mission chrétienne et espaces péripheriques du monde musulman, XVIe–XXe siecles*, edited by Bernard Heyberger and Remy Madinier, xxx–xx. Paris: Karthala, 2011.

Hobsbawm, Eric John. *The Age of Empire: 1875–1914*. New York: Sphere, 1989.

Hochschild, Adam. *King Leopold's Ghost: A Story of Greed, Terror, and Heroism in Colonial Africa*. Boston: Houghton Mifflin Company, 1998.

Houellebecq, Michel. *Submission: A Novel*. Translated by Lorin Stein. New York: Picador, 2016.

Hoyeau, Céline, and Yann Raison du Cleuziou. "Quelles sont les six familles de catholiques en France?" *La Croix*, January 11, 2017. http://www.la-croix.com/Religion/France/Les-profils-catholiques-engages-2017-01-11-1200816415.

Hübsch, Bruno. "Frédéric Ozanam et la Propagation de la foi: Etude suivie de trois lettres inedites d'Ozanam à André Terret." *Mémoire spiritaine* 6 (1997): 143–64.

Huntington, Samuel P. "The Clash of Civilizations?" *Foreign Affairs* (Summer 1993).

Inayatullah, Shaikh. "Baron Carra de Vaux: His Life and Works (1867–1953)." *Islamic Studies* 10, no. 3 (September 1971): 201–207.

Israel, Jonathan. *A Revolution of the Mind: Radical Enlightenment and the Intellectual Origins of Modern Democracy*. Princeton, NJ: Princeton University Press, 2009.

Jaume, Lucien. *Tocqueville: The Aristocratic Sources of Liberty*. Translated by Arthur Goldhammer. Princeton, NJ: Princeton University Press, 2013.

Jennings, Eric T. *Curing the Colonizers: Hydrotherapy, Climatology, and French Colonial Spas*. Durham, NC: Duke University Press, 2006.

Johnston-White, Rachel, and Joseph Peterson. "French Secularism, Reinvented." Los Angeles Review of Books, February 11, 2021. https://www.lareviewofbooks.org/article/french-secularism-reinvented/.

Joly, Bertrand. "Les chartistes et la politique." In *L'école nationale des chartes: Histoire de l'école depuis 1821*, edited by Jean-Pierre Babelon, Yves-Marie Bercé, and Olivier Guyotjeannin, 169–81. Thionville: Gérard Klopp, 1997.

Kane, Cheikh Hamidou. *Ambitious Adventure*. Translated by Katherine Woods. Brooklyn, NY: Melville House, 2012.

Kartashyan, Mariam. "Ultramontane Efforts in the Ottoman Empire during the 1860s and 1870s." Studies in Church History 54 (2018) 345–358. doi: 10.1017/stc.2017.13.

Kateb, Kamel. *Européens, "indigènes," et juifs en Algérie (1830–1962): Représentations et réalités des populations*. Algiers: Éditions el Maarifa, 2010.

Katz, Ethan. *Burdens of Brotherhood: Jews and Muslims from North Africa to France*. Cambridge, MA: Harvard University Press, 2015.

Kaufman, Suzanne K. *Consuming Visions: Mass Culture and the Lourdes Shrine*. Ithaca, NY: Cornell University Press, 2005.

Keith, Charles. *Catholic Vietnam: A Church from Empire to Nation*. Berkeley: University of California Press, 2012.

Keller, Émile. *L'encyclique du 8 décembre et les principes de 1789*. Paris: Poussielgue et Fils, 1865.

Khoudja, Louis. *La question indigène: À la Commission du Senat, par un Français d'adoption*. Vienne: Imprimerie L. Girard, 1891.

Kidd, Thomas S. *American Christians and Islam: Evangelical Culture and Muslims from the Colonial Period to the Age of Terrorism*. Princeton, NJ: Princeton University Press, 2009.

"Kreeft-Spencer debate on Islam," *Catholic Culture*, November 10, 2010. https://www.catholicculture.org/news/headlines/index.cfm?storyid=8229 (accessed April 16, 2022).

Kselman, Thomas. *Conscience and Conversion: Religious Liberty in Post-Revolutionary France*. New Haven, CT: Yale University Press, 2018.

———. *Miracles and Prophecies in Nineteenth-Century France*. New Brunswick, NJ: Rutgers University Press, 1983.

Lacombe, Hilaire de. *Liberté d'enseignement: Les débats de la Commission de 1849*. Paris: Bureaux du Correspondant, 1879.

Lagrange, Mgr. F. *Vie de Mgr. Dupanloup, evêque d'Orléans, membre de l'académie française* (Vol. 1). Paris: Libraire Ch. Poussielgue, 1895.

Lagrée, Michel. *Religion et cultures en Bretagne (1850–1950)*. Paris: Fayard, 1992.

Lalouette, Jacqueline. *La république anticléricale: XIXe–XXe siècles*. Paris: Seuil, 2003.

Lambert, Edmond. *L'Algérie: I, Deux mois dans la province d'Oran*. Paris: Curot, 1877.

Lammens, Henri. "Mahomet fut-il sincère?" *Recherches de science religieuse*. 1911.

Lamure, Bertrand. "Les pèlerinages catholiques français en terre sainte au XIXe siècle." PhD diss., Université Lumière Lyon, 2006.

Landau, Jacob M. *The Politics of Pan-Islam: Ideology and Organization*. Oxford: Clarendon Press, 1990.

Landau, Paul. "Explaining Surgical Evangelism in Colonial Southern Africa: Teeth, Pain and Faith." *Journal of African History* 37, no. 2 (1996): 261–281.

Langlois, Claude. "Catholics and Seculars." In *Realms of Memory: Rethinking the French Past*, vol. 1: *Conflicts and Divisions*, edited by Pierre Nora, translated by Arthur Goldhammer, 109–143. New York: Columbia University Press, 1996.

———. *Le catholicisme au féminin: Les congrégations françaises à supérieure générale au XIXe siècle*. Paris: Cerf, 1984.

"La Supression des Jésuites: Arrest de la Cour du 6 AoÛt 1761." In *Documents relatifs aux rapports du clergé avec la royauté de 1705 à 1789*, edited by ed. Louis Menton, 155–219. Paris: Alphonse Picard, 1903.

Laurens, Henry. "La projection chrétienne de l'Europe industrielle sur les provinces arabes de l'Empire ottoman." In *Le choc colonial et l'Islam: Les politiques religieuses des puissances coloniales en terres d'islam*, edited by Pierre-Jean Luizard, 39–55. Paris: La Découverte, 2006.

———. "L'islam dans la pensée française, des Lumières à la IIIe République." In *L'histoire de l'Islam et des musulmans en France: Du Moyen Âge à nos jours*, edited by Mohammed Arkoun and Jean Mouttapa, 515-531. Paris: Libraire générale française (La Pochothèque), 2010 (original: Albin Michel, 2006).

Lavigerie, Charles. *Les orphelins arabes d'Alger: Leur passé, leur avenir, leur adoption en France et en Belgique*. Paris: Œuvre des Ecoles d'Orient, 1870.

———. *Lettre de Monseigneur l'Archevêque d'Alger a M. Warnier, Député de l'Algérie . . . .* Paris: Jules Le Clerc et Cie, 1874.

———. *Lettre de S. Em. le cardinal Lavigerie sur l'esclavage africain à Messieurs les directeurs de l'Œuvre de la propagation de la foi*. Lyon, 1888. https://gallica.bnf.fr/ark:/12148/bpt6k103602m.texteImage.

———. *Notice sur le pèlerinage de Notre-Dame d'Afrique à Alger*. 1885. Algiers: E. Gaudet, 1924.

———. *Œuvres choisies de S. É. le cardinal Lavigerie*. Paris: Poussielgue frères, 1884.

———. *Recueil de lettres publiées par Mgr. l'archevêque d'Alger . . . sur les oeuvres et missions Africaines*. Paris: Henri Plon, 1869.

———. *Souscripion recueillie en faveur des chrétiens de Syrie: Voyage en Orient; Exposé de l'état actuel des chrétiens du Liban*. Paris: Œuvre d'Orient and E. Belin, 1861.

Le Priol, Mélinée. "Les reseaux chrétiens, 'bras' de la France au Moyen-Orient," in *La Croix*, February 1, 2022.

Lee, Dwight E. "The Origins of Pan-Islamism." *American Historical Review* 47, no. 2 (1942): 278–287.

Leff, Lisa Moses. "Jews, Liberals and the Civilizing Mission in Nineteenth-Century France." *Historical Reflections/Réflexions Historiques* 32, no. 1 (2006): 105–28.

———. *Sacred Bonds of Solidarity: The Rise of Jewish Internationalism in Nineteenth-Century France*. Stanford, CA: Stanford University Press, 2006.

Lenormant, Charles. *Questions historiques (Ve–IXe Siècles): Cours d'histoire moderne, 1844–1845*. Paris: V.-A. Waille, 1845.

Lenormant, François. "Preface," In *De la divinité du christianisme dans ses rapports avec l'histoire: Leçons professées à la Sorbonne par Charles Lenormant, publiées par son fils*, by Charles Lenormant, i–xv. Paris: A. Lévy, 1869.

Lesourd, P. "Le réveil des missions: Grégoire XVI (1831–1846)." *Histoire des missions catholiques: Les missions contemporaines (1800–1957)*, edited by Simon Delacroix, 52–71. Paris: Grund, 1957.

"Leur nouveau désordre mondial." Bruno Gollnisch, February 26, 2015. https://gollnisch.com/2015/02/26/leur-nouveau-desordre-mondial.

Lorcin, Patricia M. E. *Imperial Identities: Stereotyping, Prejudice and Race in Colonial Algeria*. London: I. B. Tauris, 1995.

———. "Rome and France in Africa: Recovering Colonial Algeria's Latin Past." *French Historical Studies* 25, no. 2 (2002): 295–29.

Lowe, Lisa. *Critical Terrains: French and British Orientalisms*. Ithaca, NY: Cornell University Press, 1991.

Luizard, Pierre-Jean. "Introduction." In *Le choc colonial et l'Islam: Les politiques religieuses des puissances coloniales en terres d'Islam*, edited by Pierre-Jean Luizard, 9–35. Paris: Le Découverte, 2006.

———. "La politique colonial de Jules Ferry en Algérie et en Tunisie." In *Le choc colonial et l'Islam: Les politiques religieuses des puissances coloniales en terres d'Islam*, edited by Pierre-Jean Luizard, 89–120. Paris: La Découverte, 2006).

Maistre, Joseph de. *Les soirées de Saint-Petersbourg*. Vol. 4 of *Œuvres completes*. Lyon: Vitte et Perrussel, 1884.

———. *The Pope: Considered in His Relations with the Church, Temporal Sovereignties, Separated Churches, and the Cause of Civilization*. Translated byAeneas McD. Dawson. London: C. Dolman, 1850. Reprint, New York, 1975.

Makdisi, Ussama. *The Culture of Sectarianism: Community, History, and Violence in Nineteenth-Century Ottoman Lebanon*. Berkeley: University of California Press, 2000.

Mann, Gregory. "What was the 'Indigénat'? The 'Empire of Law' in French West Africa." *Journal of African History* 50, no. 3 (2009): 331–53.

"Marabout." In *Concise Encyclopedia of Islam*, edited by H. A. R. Gibb and J.H. Kramers, 325–326. 1953. Boston, Leiden: Brill, 2001.

Maritain, Jacques. *On the Philosophy of History*. New York: Charles Scribner's Sons, 1957.

Marquigny, E. "Les nouveaux panégyristes du mahometisme." *Études* 8 (1865): 210–226; 446–466.

Martel, André. *Luis-Arnold et Joseph Allegro: Consuls du Bey de Tunis à Bône*. Paris: Presses Universitaires de France, 1967.

Mas-Latrie, Louis de. *Histoire de l'Ile de Chypre sous le règne des princes de la maison de Lusignan*. Paris: L'Imprimerie Impériale, 1861.

———. *Relations et commerce de l'Afrique septentrionale ou Mághreb avec les nations chrétiennes au moyen âge*. Paris: Firmin-Didot, 1886.

———. *Traités de paix et de commerce et documents divers concernant les relations des chrétiens avec les Arabes de l'Afrique septentrionale au Moyen-Âge*. Paris: Plon, 1866.

Massad, Joseph A. *Islam in Liberalism*. Chicago: University of Chicago Press.

Mauss, Marcel. *The Gift: The Form and Reason for Exchange in Archaic Societies*, trans. W.D. Halls. 1950. New York: W.W. Norton, 1990.

Mazower, Mark. *Salonica, City of Ghosts: Christians, Muslims, and Jews, 1430–1950*. New York: Vintage Books, 2006.

McAlister, Melani. "What Is Your Heart For?: Affect and Internationalism in the Evangelical Public Sphere." *American Literary History* 20, no. 4 (2008): 870–895.

McCance, Dawne. *Derrida on Religion: Thinker of Differance*. London: Equinox, 2009.

McDougall, James. *A History of Algeria*. Cambridge: Cambridge University Press, 2017.

———. "A World No Longer Shared: Losing the Droit De Cité in Nineteenth Century Algiers." *Journal of the Economic and Social History of the Orient* 60, nos. 1–2 (2017): 18–49.

———. *History and the Culture of Nationalism in Algeria*. Cambridge: Cambridge University Press, 2006.

McMillan, James F. "Louis Veuillot, L'Univers and the Ultramontane network in nineteenth-century France." In *Liens personnels, réseaux, solidarités en France et dans les îles Britanniques (XIe–XXe siècle)*, edited by David Bates and Véronique Gazeau, 221–35. Paris: Éditions de la Sorbonne, 2006. https://books.openedition.org/psorbonne/74839

McPhee, Peter. *Social History of France, 1789–1914*. Basingstoke: Palgrave Macmillan, 2004.

Mehta, Uday S. "Liberal Strategies of Exclusion." In *Tensions of Empire: Colonial Cultures in a Bourgeois World*, edited by Frederick Cooper and Laura Ann Stoler, 59–86. Berkeley: University of California Press, 1997.

Mercier, Ernest. *Histoire de Constantine*. Constantine: J. Marle et F. Biron, 1903.

Merdaci, Abdellali. *Auteurs algériens de langue française de la période coloniale: Dictionnaire biographique*. Alger: Chihab éditions, 2010.

Merzer, René du. "La Famine en Algérie." *L'illustration: Journal universel* 51, no. 1322 (June 1868).

Michelet, Jules, and Edgar Quinet. *Des Jésuites*. Paris: Comptoir des imprimeurs-unis, 1843.

Milbach, Sylvain. "Les catholiques libéraux et la presse entre 1831 et 1855." *Le mouvement social*, no. 215 (2006): 9–34.

Montalembert, Charles de. *L'église libre dans l'État libre: Discours prononcé au Congrès Catholique de Malines*. Paris: Ch. Douniol, 1863.

Moody, Joseph N. "The French Catholic Press in the Education Conflict of the 1840s." *French Historical Studies* 7, no. 3 (1972): 394–415.

Mosher, Michael A. "The Judgmental Gaze of European Women: Gender, Sexuality, and the Critique of Republican Rule." *Political Theory* 22, no. 1 (1994): 25–44.

Moulin, Dominique. "Alger." In *Les établissements des Jésuites en France depuis quatre siècles*, vol. 1: *Abbeville. –Cyriacum*, edited by Pierre Delattre. Enghien, Belgium: Institut Supérieur de Théologie, 1949.

———. "Ben-Aknoun." In *Les établissements des Jésuites en France depuis quatre siècles*, vol. 1: *Abbeville –Cyriacum*, edited by Pierre Delattre. Enghien, Belgium: Institut Supérieur de Théologie, 1949.

Murray-Miller, Gavin. "A Conflicted Sense of Nationality: Napoleon III's Arab Kingdom and the Paradoxes of French Multiculturalism." *French Colonial History* 15 (2014): 1–38.

———. *The Cult of the Modern: Trans-Mediterranean France and the Construction of French Modernity*. Lincoln: University of Nebraska Press, 2017.

Muthu, Sankar. *Enlightenment against Empire*. Princeton, NJ: Princeton University Press, 2003.

Nash, Geoffrey, ed. *Comte de Gobineau and Orientalism: Selected Eastern Writings*. Translated by Daniel O'Donoghue. London: Routledge, 2009.

National Review Symposium. "The Enemy D'Souza Knows." *National Review*, March 16, 2007. https://www.nationalreview.com/2007/03/enemy-dsouza-knows-nro-symposium/.

Neau-Dufour, Frédérique. *Ernest Psichari: L'ordre et l'errance*. Paris. Éditions du CERF, 2001.

Neveu, Bruno. "L'école des chartes et le catholicisme." In *L'École nationale des chartes: Histoire de l'école depuis 1821*, edited by Yves-Marie Bercé, 182–96. Thionville: Gérard Klopp, 1997.

Nigosian, S. A. *Islam: Its History, Teaching, and Practices*. Bloomington: Indiana University Press, 2004.

Noah, Timothy. "Dinesh D'Souza's Mullah Envy." *Slate*, January 10, 2007. https://slate.com/news-and-politics/2007/01/dinesh-d-souza-s-mullah-envy.html.

Nouschi, André. "Introduction." In *Correspondance du docteur A. Vital avec I. Urbain (1845–1874): L'opinion et la vie publique constantinoises sous le Second Empire et les débuts de la Troisième République*, edited by André Nouschi. Alger: Imprimerie E. Imbert, 1958.

O'Connell, Marvin R. "Ultramontanism and Dupanloup: The Compromise of 1865." *Church History* 53, No. 2 (June 1984): 200–217.

O'Donnell, Jr. J. Dean. *Lavigerie in Tunisia: The Interplay of Imperialist and Missionary*. Athens: University of Georgia Press, 1979.

Olender, Maurice. *The Languages of Paradise: Race, Religion, and Philology in the Nineteenth Century*. Translated by Arthur Goldhammer. Cambridge, MA: Harvard University Press, 1992.

OLJ/F.N. "Le président Macron remet la Légion d'honneur au directeur général de l'Œuvre d'Orient, Mgr Pascal Gollnisch," in *L'Orient-Le Jour*, February 22, 2022.

Padberg, John W. *Colleges in Controversy: The Jesuit Schools in France from Revival to Supression, 1815–1880*. Cambridge, MA: Harvard University Press, 1969.

Pagand, Bernard. "De la ville arabe à la ville européenne: Architecture et formation urbaine à Constantine au XIXe siècle." *Revue du monde musulman et de la Mediterranée* 73, no. 1 (1994): 281–294.

Pagand, Bernard. *La médina de Constantine (Algérie): De la ville traditionnelle au centre de l'agglomération contemporaine*. Poitiers: Centre Interuniversitaire d'Études Méditerranéennes, 1989.

Pavy, L.-C. *Monseigneur Pavy: Sa vie et ses œuvres*, 2 vols. Paris: Lecoffre fils et cie., 1870.

272 *Bibliography*

Pavy, Louis. "Discours, prononcé dans la cathédrale d'Alger, sur le mahométisme." In *Collection intégrale et universelle des orateurs sacrés du premier et du second ordre . . .*, edited by Jacques-Paul Migne. Paris: Chez l'editeur, à l'Imprimerie Catholique du Petit-Montrouge, 1856.

Pech, Marie-Estelle. "'Ces écoles catholiques plébiscitées par les musulmans' (*Le Figaro*, 7 av 14)." *Comité Laïcité République*, May 2, 2020. https://www.laicite-republique. org/ces-ecoles-catholiques-plebiscitees-par-les-musulmans-le-figaro-7-av-14.html.

Peiron, Denis. "Les écoles hors contrat catholiques concernées par la loi contre le 'séparatisme.'" *La Croix*, December 7, 2020. https://www.la-croix. com/Famille/ecoles-hors-contrat-catholiques-concernees-loi-contre-separati sme-2020-12-07-1201128647.

———. "Philippe Delorme: 'La loi "séparatisme" aboutit à une privation de liberté.'" *La Croix*, December 29, 2020. https://www.la-croix.com/Famille/ Philippe-Delorme-loi-separatisme-aboutit-privation-liberte-2020-12-29-1201132339.

Peltz, Lucy, and Martin Myrone. "Introduction." In *Producing the Past: Aspects of Antiquarian Culture and Practice, 1700–1850*, edited by Lucy Peltz and Martin Myrone, 1–14(?). Aldershot, England: Ashgate Publishing, 1999.

Pervillé, Guy. *Les étudiants algériens de l'université française, 1880–1962: Populisme et nationalisme chez les etudiants et intellectuels algeriens de formation française*. Paris: Éditions du Centre National de la Recherche Scientifique, 1984.

Peterson, Derek R. "Morality Plays: Marriage, Church Courts, and Colonial Agency in Central Tanganyika, ca. 1876–1928." *American Historical Review* 111, no. 4 (2006): xxx–xx.

Peterson, Joseph W. "Honor, Excrement, Ethnography: Colonial Knowledge between Missionary and *Militaire* in French Algeria." *Journal of Modern History* 93, no. 1 (March 2021): 34–67.

Pierrard, Pierre, *Louis Veuillot*. Paris: Beauchesne, 1998.

Porter, Andrew. "An Overview, 1700–1914." In *Missions and Empire*, edited by Norman Etherington, 40–63. Oxford: Oxford University Press, 2005.

———. *Religion versus Empire? British Protestant missionaries and overseas expansion, 1700–1914*. Manchester: Manchester University Press, 2004.

Pratt, Mary Louise. *Imperial Eyes: Travel Writing and Transculturation*. 1992. London: Routledge, 2008.

Prevost, M. "Acher de Montgascon (Ambroise-Justin, Baron d')." In *Dictionnaire de biographie française*, vol. 1, edited by J. Baltau, M. Barroux, and M. Prevost, 322. Paris: Letouzey et Ané, 1933.

Priest, Robert. *The Gospel according to Renan: Reading, Writing, and Religion in Nineteenth-Century France*. Oxford: Oxford University Press, 2015.

Prochaska, David. *Making Algeria French: Colonialism in Bône, 1870–1920*. Cambridge: Cambridge University Press, 1990.

Prudhomme, Claude. *Missions chrétiennes et colonisation, XVIe–XXe siècle*. Paris: Cerf, 2004.

———. *Stratégie missionnaire du Saint-Siège sous Léon XIII (1878–1903): Centralisation romaine et défis culturels*. Rome: École Française de Rome, 1994.

Psichari, Ernest. *Œuvres complètes de Ernest Psichari: Le Voyage du centurion et Les Voix qui crient dans le désert*. Paris: Éditions d'Aujourd'hui, 1984.

Quinet, Edgar. *Le christianisme et la révolution française*. Paris: Comptoir des Imprimeurs-Unis, 1845.

Reig, Daniel. "L'orientalisme savant: de l'humanisme au politique." In *Histoire de l'Islam et des musulmans en France: du Moyen Âge à nos jours*, edited by Mohammed Arkoun and Jean Mouttapa, 632–49. Paris: Librairie générale française (La Pochothèque), 2010 (original: Albin Michel, 2006).

Renan, Ernest. *De la part des peuples sémitiques dans l'histoire de la civilisation: discours d'ouverture du cours de langues hébraïque, chaldaïque et syriaque, au Collège de France*. Paris: Michel Lévy, 1862.

———. *Mission de Phénicie*. Paris: Imprimerie Impériale, 1864.

Renault, François. *Cardinal Lavigerie: Churchman, Prophet and Missionary*. Translated by John O'Donohue. London: Athlone Press, 1994.

Rey-Goldzeiguer, Annie. *Le royaume arabe: La politique algérienne de Napoleon III, 1861–1870*. Alger: Société Nationale d'Édition et de Diffusion, 1977.

Riancey, Charles de. *De la situation religieuse de l'Algérie*. Paris: Jacques Lecoffre, 1846.

Ribeill, Georges. "Gestion et organisation du travail dans les compagnies de chemins de fer, des origines à 1860." *Annales: Histoire, Sciences Sociales* 42, no. 5 (1987): 999–1029.

Rigny, M. H. *Allocution prononcée au service funèbre fait en l'église de Saint-Pierre, pour le R. P. Henri Ducat de la Compagnie de Jésus, missionnaire en Algérie*. Besançon: Paul Jacquin, 1885.

Rodinson, Maxime. *Europe and the Mystique of Islam*. Translated by Roger Veinus. London: I. B. Tauris, 1988.

Rodogno, Davide. *Against Massacre: Humanitarian Interventions in the Ottoman Empire, 1815–1914*. Princeton, NJ: Princeton University Press, 2012.

Rodrigue, Aron. *French Jews, Turkish Jews: The Alliance Israélite Universelle and the Politics of Jewish Schooling in Turkey, 1860–1925*. Bloomington: Indiana University Press, 1990.

Rogers, Rebecca. *A Frenchwoman's Imperial Story: Madam Luce in Nineteenth-Century Algeria*. Stanford, CA: Stanford University Press, 2013.

———. "Teaching Morality and Religion in Nineteenth-Century Colonial Algeria: Gender and the Civilising Mission." *History of Education* 40, no. 6 (November 2011): 741–759.

Romilly, Jean-Edme. "Tolerance." In *The Encyclopedia of Diderot & d'Alembert Collaborative Translation Project*, translated by Leslie Tuttle. Ann Arbor: Michigan Publishing, University of Michigan Library, 2010. Originally published as "Tolérance," in *Encyclopédie ou Dictionnaire raisonné des sciences, des arts et des métiers*, 16:390. Paris, 1765.

Rosenblatt, Helena. *Liberal Values: Benjamin Constant and the Politics of Religion*. Cambridge: Cambridge University Press, 2008.

Rosette, Louis. "Constantine." In *Les établissements des jésuites en France depuis quatre siècles*, vol. 1: *Abbeville – Cyriacum*, edited by Pierre Delattre. Enghien, Belgium: Institut Supérieur de Théologie, 1949.

Rothschild, Emma. *An Infinite History: The Story of a Family in France over Three Centuries*. Princeton, NJ: Princeton University Press, 2021.

Rousseau, Jean-Jacques. *The Social Contract*, translated by Gerard Hopkins. In *Social Contract: Essays by Locke, Hume and Rousseau*, edited by Ernest Barker. London: Oxford University Press, 1970.

Roy, Olivier. *Globalized Islam: The Search for a New Ummah*. New York: Columbia University Press, 2004.

Ruedy, John. "Chérif Benhabylès and Ferhat Abbas: Case Studies in the Contradictions of the 'Mission civilisatrice.'" Special issue, *Historical Reflections / Réflexions Historiques* 28, no. 2 (2002): 185–201.

Saada, Emmanuelle. *Empire's Children: Race, Filiation, and Citizenship in the French Empire*. Translated by Arthur Goldhammer, Chicago: University of Chicago Press, 2012.

———. "The Laws of Necessity: From the 'Native Code' in Colonial Algeria to the State of Emergency in Contemporary France." Paper prepared for the Comparative Research Workshop, Yale University, April 19, 2016.

Saaïdia, Oissila. *Algérie coloniale: Musulmans et chrétiens; Le contrôle de l'État (1830–1914)*. Paris: CNRS Éditions, 2015.

———. "De l'histoire de l'Orient à l'histoire d'un Occident (Al-Maghrîb): Essai sur une historiographie du Maghreb colonial." In *La construction du discours colonial: L'empire français aux XIXe et XXe siècles*, edited by Oissila Saaïdia and Laurick Zerbini. Paris: Karthala, 2009.

———. *L'Algérie catholique: Une histoire de l'église catholique en Algérie, XIXe–XXIe siècles*. Paris: CNRS Éditions, 2018.

———. "L'anticléricalisme article d'exportation? Le cas de l'Algérie avant la première guerre mondiale." *Vingtième siècle: Revue d'histoire* 87 (2005): 101–12.

Sabatier, Camille. *La question de la sécurité, insurrections, criminalité: Les difficultés algériennes*. Alger: Adolphe Jourdan, 1882.

Said, Edward W. *Orientalism*. New York: Vintage, 1979.

Salibi, Kamal. *A House of Many Mansions: The History of Lebanon Reconsidered*. London: I. B. Tauris, 1988.

Sanneh, Lamin. *Translating the Message: The Missionary Impact on Culture*. Rev. ed. Maryknoll, NY: Orbis, 2009.

Schmitt, Carl. "A Pan-European Interpretation of Donoso Cortés." translated by Mark Grzeskowiak. *Telos* 125 (2002):100–115.

Schnapp, Alain. "Archéologie et tradition académique en Europe aux XVIIIe et XIXe siècles." *Annales: Histoire, Sciences Sociales* 37, nos. 5–6 (1982):760–77.

Schreier, Joshua. *Arabs of the Jewish Faith: The Civilizing Mission in Colonial Algeria*. New Brunswick, NJ: Rutgers University Press, 2010.

Schwab, Raymond. *The Oriental Renaissance: Europe's Rediscovery of India and the East, 1680–1880*. Translated by Gene Patterson-Black and Victor Reinking. New York: Columbia University Press, 1984.

Scott, Joan Wallach. "The Contradictions of French Secularism." *New Statesman*, November 18, 2020. https://www.newstatesman.com/world/europe/2020/11/contradictions-french-secularism.

——. *The Politics of the Veil*. Princeton, NJ: Princeton University Press, 2007.

Sessions, Jennifer E. *By Sword and Plow: France and the Conquest of Algeria*. Ithaca, NY: Cornell University Press, 2011.

Shatz, Adam. "Colombey-les-deux-Mosquées." *London Review of Books* 37, no. 7 (April 9, 2015). https://www.lrb.co.uk/the-paper/v37/no7/adam-shatz/colombey-les-deux-mosquees.

Shepard, Todd. *Invention of Decolonization: The Algerian War and the Remaking of France*. Ithaca, NY: Cornell University Press, 2006.

——. *Sex, France, and Arab Men, 1962–1979*. Chicago: University of Chicago Press, 2017.

Sievernich, Michael. "Jesuit Theologies of Mission." *The Way* 42, no. 1 (January 2003): 44–58.

Sliwinksi, Sharon. "The Childhood of Human Rights: The Kodak on the Congo." *Journal of Visual Culture* 5, no.3 (2006): 333–63.

Smati, Mahfoud. *Les elites algériennes sous la colonisation*. Vol. 1. Alger: Dahlab, Maisonneuve et Larose, 1998.

Smith, Andrea. "Citizenship in the Colony: Naturalization Law and Legal Assimilation in 19th Century Algeria." *PoLAR* 19, no. 1 (1996): 33–49.

Spagnolo, John P. *France and Ottoman Lebanon, 1861–1914*. London: Ithaca Press, 1977.

Stein, Sarah Abrevaya. *Saharan Jews and the Fate of French Algeria*. Chicago: University of Chicago Press, 2014.

Stoler, Ann Laura. *Carnal Knowledge and Imperial Power: Race and the Intimate in Colonial Rule*. Berkeley: University of California Press, 2010.

Stora, Benjamin. *Les trois exils: Juifs d'Algérie*. Paris: Éditions Stock, 2006.

Suchet, L'Abbé Jacques. *Lettres édifiantes et curieuses sur l'Algérie*. Tours: A. Mame, 1840.

Surkis, Judith. *Sex, Law, and Sovereignty in French Algeria, 1830–1930*. Ithaca, NY: Cornell University Press, 2019.

Tableau de la situation des établissements français dans l'Algérie, 1845–46. Paris: Imprimerie Impériale, 1847.

Tableau de la situation des établissements français dans l'Algérie, 1865–66. Paris: Imprimerie Impériale, 1868.

Tackett, Timothy. *Religion, Revolution, and Regional Culture in Eighteenth-Century France: The Ecclesiastical Oath of 1791*. Princeton: Princeton University Press, 1986.

Taithe, Bertrand. "Algerian Orphans and Colonial Christianity in Algeria, 1866–1939." *French History* 20, no. 3 (2006): 240–59.

———. "Evil, Liberalism, and the Imperial Designs of the Catholic Church." In *Evil, Barbarism, and Empire, c. 1830–2000*, edited by Tom Crook, Rebecca Gill, and Bertrand Taithe, 141–71. Palgrave Macmillan, 2011.

———. "Humanitarianism and Colonialism: Religious Responses to the Drought and Famine of 1866–1870." In *Natural Disasters, Cultural Responses: Case Studies toward a Global Environmental History*, edited by Christof Mauch and Christian Pfister, 137–163. Lanham, MD: Rowman and Littlefield, 2009.

———. "Missionary Militarism: The Armed Brothers of the Sahara and Léopold Joubert in the Congo." In *In God's Empire: French Missionaries and the Modern World*, edited by Owen White and J. P. Daughton, 129–150. New York: Oxford University Press, 2012.

Taylor, Charles. "Root Causes and Rotten Ideas." *Dissent* 54, no. 3 (2007): 102–6.

Thobie, Jacques. *Les intérêts culturels français dans l'empire ottoman finissant: L'enseignement laïque et en partenariat*. Leuven: Peeters, 2008.

Thomson, Ann. *Barbary and Enlightenment: European Attitudes towards the Maghreb in the 18th Century*. Leiden: E. J. Brill, 1987.

Ticchi, Jean-Marc. "Les directeurs de l'Œuvre d'Orient et leurs moyens d'action de 1861 à 1914." In *L'Œuvre d'Orient: Solidarités anciennes et nouveaux defis*, edited by Hervé Lerand and Giuseppe Maria Croce, 143–171. Paris: Cerf, 2010.

Tishken, Joel E. "Neither Anglican nor Ethiopian: Schism, Race, and Ecclesiastical Politics in the Nineteenth-Century Liberian Episcopal Church." *Journal of Africana Religions* 2, no. 1 (2014): 67–94.

Tocqueville, Alexis de. *Writings on Empire and Slavery*. Edited and translated by Jennifer Pitts. Baltimore, MD: Johns Hopkins University Press, 2001.

Todd, David. "A French Imperial Meridian, 1814–1870." *Past and Present* 210, no. 1 (2011): 155–86.

Tolan, John V. *Faces of Muhammad: Western Perceptions of the Prophet of Islam from the Middle Ages to Today*. Princeton, NJ: Princeton University Press, 2019.

Topinard, Paul. "Rapport sur la population indigène de l'oasis de Biskra par M. Seriziat." *Bulletins de la Société d'anthropologie de Paris* 5, no. 1 (1870): 548–55.

Tournier, Jules. *La conquête religieuse de l'Algérie, 1830–1845*. Paris: Librairie Plon, 1930.

Trimbur, Dominique. "Entre politique et religion: Les origines et les premières années de l'œuvre des écoles d'Orient." In *L'Œuvre d'Orient: Solidarités anciennes et nouveaux defis*, edited by Hervé Lerand and Giuseppe Maria Croce, 115–141. Paris: Cerf, 2010.

Trumbull, George R., IV. *An Empire of Facts: Colonial Power, Cultural Knowledge, and Islam in Algeria, 1870–1914*. Cambridge: Cambridge University Press, 2009.

Turin, Y. "Enfants trouvés, colonisation et utopie: Etude d'un comportement social au XIXe siècle." *Revue historique* 244, no. 2 (496) (1970): 329–56.

Twomey, Christina. "Framing Atrocity: Photography and Humanitarianism." In *Humanitarian Photography: A History*, edited by Heide Fehrenbach and Davide Rodogno, 47–63. Cambridge: Cambridge University Press, 2015.

Urbain, Ismaÿl. *L'Algérie pour les algériens*. Preface by Michel Levallois. Paris: Séguier, 2000.

Van Ortroy, Francis. "St. Stanislas Kostka." *The Catholic Encyclopedia*, vol. 14. New York: Robert Appleton Company, 1912. http://www.newadvent.org/cathen/14245b.htm.

Vapereau, G. *Dictionnaire universel des contemporains*. Paris: Librairie Hachette, 1880.

Verdeil, Chantal. "La classe 'sous le chêne' et le pensionnat: Les écoles missionnaires en Syrie (1860–1914) entre impérialisme et désir d'éducation." *Outre-mers: Revue d'histoire* 94, no. 354–55 (2007): 197–221.

———. *La mission jésuite du Mont-Liban et de Syrie (1830–1864)*. Paris: Les Indes Savantes, 2011.

———. *Les Jésuites en Syrie (1830–1864)*. Paris: Les Indes Savantes. [Author's thesis, shared as PDF via email of September 11, 2014. Appeared in 2011 as *La mission jésuite...*]

Vernet, Felix. *Dom Gréa, 1828–1917*. Paris: Labergerie, 1937.

Veuillot, Eugène. *Louis Veuillot (1813–1845)*. Vol. 1. Paris: Victor Retaux, [1899?].

Veuillot, Louis. *Correspondance de Louis Veuillot*. Vol. 1, *Lettres à son frère, à sa famille, à divers*. Paris: Victor Palmé, 1884.

———. *Les français en Algérie: Souvenirs d'un voyage fait en 1841*. Tours: A. Mame, 1846.

———. *Les odeurs de Paris*. Paris: Palmé, 1867.

———. *The Liberal Illusion*. Translated by George Barry O'Toole. Washington, D.C., 1939. http://strobertbellarmine.net/books/Veuillot--Liberal_Illusion_V02.pdf.

Vincent, Faustine. "Pourquoi des musulmans choisissent l'école catholique pour leurs enfants." *20minutes*, 14 April 2014. http://www.20minutes.fr/societe/1351609-20140414-pourquoi-musulmans-choisissent-ecole-catholique-enfants.

Vogüé, Melchior de. *Les églises de la Terre Sainte: Fragments d'un voyage en Orient*. Paris: Victor Didron, 1859.

———. *Les événements de Syrie*. Paris: Charles Douniol, 1860.

Waardenburg, Jacques. "Louis Massignon (1883–1962) as a Student of Islam." *Die Welt des Islams* 45, no. 3 (2005): 312–342.

Walker-Said, Charlotte. "Wealth, Law, and Moral Authority: Marriage and Christian Mobilization in Interwar Cameroon." Special issue, *International Journal of African Historical Studies* 48, no. 3 (2015): 393–424.

Wallon, M. H. *Rapport faut au conseil general de l'œuvre des écoles de L'Orient. . . .* Paris: Aug. Vaton, 1857.

Warner, Malcolm. "The Question of Faith: Orientalism, Christianity, and Islam." In *The Orientalists: Delacroix to Matisse: the Allure of North Africa and the Near East*, edited by Mary Anne Stevens, 32–39. New York: Thames and Hudson and the National Gallery of Art, 1984.

Weill, Georges. *Histoire du catholicisme libéral en France, 1828–1908*. Paris: Felix Alcan, 1909.

———. "Le catholicisme libéral en France." *Revue d'histoire moderne et contemporaine (1899–1914)* 12, no. 2 (1909): 100–111.

Weiss, Gillian. *Captives and Corsairs: France and Slavery in the Early Modern Mediterranean*. Stanford, CA: Stanford University Press, 2011.

Weissbach, Lee Shai. "Oeuvre Industrielle, Oeuvre Morale: The Sociétés de Patronage of Nineteenth-Century France." *French Historical Studies* 15, no. 1 (1987): 99–120.

White, Owen, and J. P. Daughton. *In God's Empire: French Missionaries and the Modern World*. New York: Oxford University Press, 2012.

Wilder, Gary. *Freedom Time: Negritude, Decolonization, and the Future of the World*. Durham: Duke University Press, 2015.

———. *The French Imperial Nation-State: Negritude and Colonial Humanism Between the Two World Wars*. Chicago: University of Chicago Press, 2005.

Williams, C. Peter. "The Necessity of a Native Clergy: The Failure of Victorian Missions to Develop Indigenous Leadership (The Laing Lecture for 1990)." *Vox Evangelica* 21 (1991): 33–52. Accessed at: https://biblicalstudies.org.uk/pdf/vox/vol21/clergy_williams.pdf ("Prepared for the Web in May 2009 by Robert I. Bradshaw").

Wu, Albert Monshan. *From Christ to Confucius: German Missionaries, Chinese Christians, and the Globalization of Christianity, 1860–1950*. New Haven, CT: Yale University Press, 2016.

"Zemmour: 'Entre la France et l'Islam, les musulmans doivent choisir.'" *Causeur*, January 17, 2017. https://www.causeur.fr/eric-zemmour-islam-immigration-quinquennat-140443.

Županov, Ines. *Disputed Mission: Jesuit Experiments and Brahmanical Knowledge in Seventeenth-Century India*. Oxford: Oxford University Press, 1999.

INDEX

Page numbers in *italics* refer to illustrations.